W9-CAY-511

Singing Whales and Flying Squid

The Discovery of Marine Life

Also by Richard Ellis

The Book of Sharks

The Book of Whales

Dolphins and Porpoises

Men and Whales

Great White Shark (with John McCosker)

Monsters of the Sea

Deep Atlantic: Life, Death, and Exploration in the Abyss

Imagining Atlantis

The Search for the Giant Squid

Encyclopedia of the Sea

Aquagenesis: The Origin and Evolution of Life in the Sea

Sea Dragons: Predators of the Prehistoric Oceans

No Turning Back: The Life and Death of Animal Species

The Empty Ocean

Tiger Bone and Rhino Horn

Singing Whales and Flying Squid

The Discovery of Marine Life

Written and Illustrated by
Richard Ellis

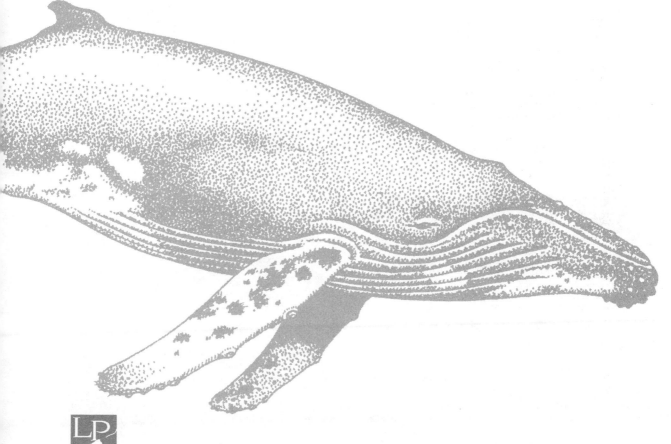

THE LYONS PRESS
Guilford, Connecticut
An imprint of The Globe Pequot Press

To buy books in quantity for corporate use
or incentives, call **(800) 962–0973, ext. 4551,**
or e-mail **premiums@GlobePequot.com.**

Copyright © 2005 by Richard Ellis

ALL RIGHTS RESERVED. No part of this book may be reproduced or transmitted in any form by any means, electronic or mechanical, including photocopying and recording, or by any information storage and retrieval system, except as may be expressly permitted in writing from the publisher. Requests for permission should be addressed to The Lyons Press, Attn: Rights and Permissions Department, P.O. Box 480, Guilford, CT 06437.

The Lyons Press is an imprint of The Globe Pequot Press.

10 9 8 7 6 5 4 3 2 1

Printed in the United States of America

All illustrations copyright © Richard Ellis

Designed by Sheryl P. Kober

Library of Congress Cataloging-in-Publication Data

Ellis, Richard, 1938–
    Singing whales and flying squid : the discovery of marine life / Richard Ellis.
        p. cm.
    Includes bibliographical references and index.
    ISBN 1-59228-842-1
    1. Marine biology—History. 2. Marine organisms. I. Title.
QH91.25.E45 2005
578.77'9—dc22

2005027602

Contents

Preface   vii

Introduction   ix

News Flash   xvii

I. The History of the Discovery of Marine Life

From the Mediterranean to a New World   3

Enter the Russians and Americans   11

Ichthyology Takes a Name   17

Organization Assists Discovery   23

Creationism and Evolution   29

"Monsters" of Inner Space   37

Dark but Still Filled with Life   47

Picture Mountains and Jets in the Floor   51

Names and Barcodes for Positive Identification   59

II. The Acceleration of Discovery

Monsters, Real or Imagined   65

Fossils Brought to Life   69

Accident Reveals a Big Mouth   77

A Whole New Inner World   81

The Novelty of Swimming Cucumbers   99

Discovery Followed by Near-Destruction   105

The Orange Roughy and the Convict   111

Finding the Body to Fit the Skull   115

Why Carry a Sword?   121

Most Marine Life Is Too Small to See   131

A Legend Authenticated: The Giant Squid   141

Mysterious Squid and Octopuses Appear   153

Do Whales Sing in Inner Space?   159

III. Putting Discovery to Work

Getting the Numbers Right   167

Dolphins, Whales, and Whaling   177

The "Right" Whales   189

Squid "Fishing"   193

Overfishing Fishes, Too   203

IV. Conclusion

Where Do We Go From Here?   215

Guide to Further Reading   223

References   225

Index of Subjects   255

Index of People   263

Preface

This book is supposed to be about what lives in the ocean, how we found out what lives in the ocean, and what is to become of what lives in the ocean. That, indeed, is the mission of the Census of Marine Life, hereafter, CoML. The breadth and depth of CoML rivals the oceans themselves. In the 2003 *Baseline Report,*

J. Frederick Grassle, chairman of the CoML International Steering Committee, wrote, "Overall, the strategy of CoML is to clarify and make much more accessible what we know, to identify what we do not know and why we do not know it, to learn much more of what is knowable, and also to identify what we may never know or at least not learn for a very long time. . . . A census requires dividing the whole of the oceans into parts. The oceans do not divide into easily defined, separate compartments. Waters and animals move. . . . The baseline offers facts, for example, about numbers of known and unknown species and the quantity of marine life and how it is broadly distributed. However the baseline is not a great wet database reporting estimates of the number of tonnage of animals in every species." Ron O'Dor, primary author of the 2003 *Baseline Report,* wrote, "The Census of Marine Life is dedicated to learning what once lived in the oceans and projecting what will live there, divided by a third watershed task of what lives in the oceans today."

In pursuit of my subject matter, I've traveled from one end of the earth to the other, from the North Pole to South Georgia, from Nantucket to Japan, but in fact, most of my research has been

conducted in libraries, my own and others. I have managed to amass a considerable collection of marine biology books and papers, but my library is minuscule compared with the vast holdings of the American Museum of Natural History, where I am a research associate, and have access to their collections. Access to the AMNH database is a special privilege, but access to the Internet is not. Indeed, the component of the Census of Marine Life known as OBIS (Ocean Biographic Information System) is an Internet tool for professionals, but it can be used by anyone with an interest in marine life.

My first thought in writing this book was to incorporate everything into an imaginary submarine ride around the world, something like the voyage of Captain Nemo's *Nautilus* in *Twenty Thousand Leagues Under the Sea.* This, I thought, would enable me (and the reader) to career around the world underwater, looking at everything from giant squid to coral reefs, from icebergs to swordfish. The idea intrigued me until I realized that it would be difficult—all right, impossible—to get Georges Cuvier, Captain Cook, or Charles Darwin aboard the submarine so that we could take advantage of their expertise. (I thought of having their published works aboard, but this turned out to be more than a little awkward.) So I dropped the submarine idea, and decided to concentrate on the known, the unknown, and the unknowable aspects of marine biology.

To date, I have written books about sharks, whales, dolphins, whaling history, sea monsters, deep-sea creatures, the giant squid, Atlantis, prehistoric marine reptiles (ichthyosaurs, mosasaurs, and plesiosaurs), the evolution of life in the sea, and the depletion of the world's marine resources. I came out of the water to write a book in 2005 about the destruction of rhinos, tigers, and bears for traditional Chinese medicine, but for the most part, I have spent the better part of the last thirty years writing about (and illustrating) marine life of the past and present. I'm ready to go back into the water one more time. Join me on an underwater adventure like no other you've ever taken or heard of: a voyage to discover the mysteries and reveal the wonders of marine life—more unusual and more astonishing than you—or anyone else—ever imagined.

There were many people who helped on this voyage. Bob Pitman of NOAA's Southwest Fisheries Lab in La Jolla read my discourse on "new" whales (one of which he helped discover); Dick Rosenblatt of Scripps read my essay on William Beebe's cryptozoological fishes (and agreed with my somewhat ungenerous conclusions); Peter Rona of Rutgers helped me with the mysterious *Paleodictyon*, and even arranged for me to get a DVD so I could see it for myself; Sara Hickox of the University of Rhode Island read an early draft of this manuscript and made many helpful suggestions. Brad Matsen, who wrote a terrific book about William Beebe and Otis Barton (upon which I consulted), gave me all his swordfish

files when I told him I wanted to write about the aggressive propensities of *Xiphias gladius*. Because squid fisheries are so important in a study of the future of marine life, I asked many people for help in my attempt to understand how the interaction of cephalopods, finfish, and people might play out, including Ron O'Dor, Uwe Piatkowski, Bill Gilly, Peter Boyle, George Jackson, Paul Rodhouse, Steve O'Shea, and my old buddy, Clyde Roper. In its early stages, the manuscript was read by Paul Waggoner, Alasdair McIntyre, Meryl Williams, and Jesse Ausubel. All made constructive criticisms, and I (sometimes) modified the text accordingly. I didn't always agree with their recommendations, and sometimes I stubbornly stuck to my own versions. Where there are errors, they are mine, despite the efforts to correct them.

It was Jesse Ausubel of the Sloan Foundation who got me into this project, and Jay Cassell of Lyons/Globe Pequot Press who came to our rescue by agreeing to publish a book three months after the delivery of the manuscript. Jesse's first call came in November of 2004, and if you're reading these words in an early edition of this book, it might be November 2005, but if we didn't make the deadline, you're probably reading this sometime in (or after) 2006. After Jay Cassell left Lyons Press, the project was placed in the capable hands of Lisa Purcell, who saw it through to the final product—the book you hold in your hands.

Because this is essentially a book about predicting the future of life in the oceans, I would like to dedicate it to three people who will be there to see if we got any of it right: my grandchildren, Lochlan, Stella, and Felix. ⌘

Introduction

Two-thirds of this planet is covered by water inhabited by an incredible variety of living organisms, ranging in size from microbe to whale, and in abundance from scarce to uncountable. Whales and dolphins must surface to breathe, and some fishes occupy surface waters and can easily be seen from boats or shore, but most of the marine bio-profusion is hidden from human eyes, often under thousands of feet and millions of tons of water, which is usually cold, dark, and utterly inhospitable to humans. The vast majority of marine creatures breathe water, but like all other mammals, marine biologists and oceanographers are required to breathe the substance in which they live, so access to the subterranean world of marine life has been restricted by our inability to respire in that environment. By definition, the study of marine life has been quantitatively and qualitatively different from the study of terrestrial life—it is, if you will, a different kettle of fish. What do we know today, how have we learned it, and what remains unknown and unknowable about inner space? Today, the exponential expansion of the known during the twentieth century merits reporting. It sets the stage for the exploration in the twenty-first century that will be accelerated by new technology and international cooperation.

The ocean's size is so daunting—the volume of the Pacific, for example, has been estimated at 173 million cubic miles—that we can only hope to catch occasional specimens or fleeting glimpses of its inhabitants. Most oceanic life can be found in the uppermost six hundred feet, where sunlight penetrates with sufficient intensity to enable plants to grow and to photosynthesize food. Some greatly diminished light may reach as deep as one thousand feet, but without sunlight to energize photosynthesis, there will be no plants. Everything that lives below a thousand feet is an animal. Animal life of one sort or another has populated virtually every available habitat on earth, from the peaks of the highest mountains to the polar ice caps; from the hot, vacant Sahara to the dank, polluted alleys of urban centers. But there is no habitat on earth that equals the deep oceans' cold, black density for sheer inhospitality. A mile below the surface, the pressure is more than a ton per square inch; beyond two miles of depth, the temperature remains only a couple of degrees above the freezing point of seawater. In 1851, Edward Forbes wrote, "as we descend deeper and deeper . . . the inhabitants [of the sea] become more and more modified, and fewer and fewer, indicating our approach towards an abyss where life is extinguished." This is inner space.

It was not until the surprisingly successful deepwater trawls of the research vessel *Challenger* in 1872 that the presence of life in the abyss was universally acknowledged. All food available in the depths of the ocean is animal matter, and the food chain depends upon the constant rain of minuscule particles ("undersea snow") from the surface layers, usually the remains of animals that have died. "When I think of the floor of the deep sea," wrote Rachel Carson, "the single overwhelming fact that possesses my imagination is the accumulation of sediments. I always see the steady, unremitting, downward drift of materials from above, flake upon flake, layer upon layer—a drift that has continued for hundreds of millions of years, that will go on as long as there are seas and continents." Life in the depths depends upon death in the shallows.

Because there have been so few human visitors to the uninviting world of the deep sea, scientists have had to rely on trawled specimens, photographs taken by robotic cameras, or occasionally, observations from deep-diving submersibles, to get even the vaguest idea of the nature of life in the abyss. So far, even our most elaborate efforts to penetrate the blackness have produced only minimal results. It is as if someone lowered a collecting basket from a balloon high above the tropical rain forest floor, and tried to analyze the nature of life in the jungle from a couple of random hauls. The deep sea, the largest environment on earth, is still the least known.

Life in the ocean is conducted by a completely different set of rules than on *terra firma*. Because water is eight hundred times more buoyant than air, marine creatures are less affected by gravity than their terrestrial cousins. Consider the jellyfishes, or siphonophores—gelatinous, floating creatures with no visible means of internal support. Strong skeletons and muscles are not required for support, which means that many marine creatures have developed weird and wonderful shapes that would be totally impractical in air. It is not an accident that the sea is the home of the largest animal that has ever lived; the hundred-ton bulk of the blue whale needs the support of water.

Despite its mountains and valleys, the surface of the land can be mapped as a two-dimensional environment, but the inner world of the sea is very much three-dimensional. Terrestrial animals, such as ourselves, can occasionally operate in three dimensions—when we ride in an elevator, fly in an airplane, or scuba dive, for example—but compared with the three-dimensionality of the oceans, our movements are largely restricted to forward and back, north and south, east and west. In the sea, movement is also forward and back, but "up and down" play much more important roles. (Birds, insects, and flying mammals live in a more three-dimensional world than we do.) The average depth of the ocean is 2.4 miles, or 12,566 feet. By and large, the salinity and oxygen content of the vast deep sea are homogeneous, and the temperature varies only five degrees Celsius, making pressure—the accumulated weight of all that water—the most important variable.

Unlike the waters of the surface, where wind, weather, tides, and other influences create variations that can range from glassy calm to force-12 gales, the "weather" under the sea is comparatively tranquil. The temperature of the deep sea varies from +4 degrees to –1 degree Celsius. Currents that circulate deep within the ocean affect the shape of the bottom and, more important, transport deeper, colder water from the poles around the world. On the sea bottom, "benthic storms" can last anywhere from a few days to several weeks, can alter the temperature balance of the abyss, and stir up bottom sediments. Volcanic action, where the seafloor is opening up, can also affect the weather on the bottom. In some areas, this activity takes the form of hydrothermal vents, where superheated water (and occasionally lava) spews from cracks in the seafloor. In this sunless world, miniature monsters chase and are chased by diminutive dragons; fishes flash, sea cucumbers light up, and giant squid, with eyes as big as volleyballs, lurk at the fringes of our consciousness.

The inner space of the deep offers the last frontier on the planet. Even now, we know more about the back side of the moon than we do about the bottom of the ocean, but then the surface of the moon is not hidden under miles of impenetrable water.

Living in this inaccessible medium are some of the most fascinating creatures on earth, adapted for life in an environment that is as foreign to our understanding as another universe. Consider *Prochlorococcus*, the bacterium that E. O. Wilson (2002) called "arguably the most abundant organisms on the planet and responsible for a large part in the organic production of the ocean—yet unknown to science until 1988:" He continued:

> *Prochlorococcus* cells float passively in open water at 70,000 to 200,000 per milliliter, multiplying with energy captured from sunlight. Their extremely small size is what makes them so elusive. They belong to a special

group called picoplankton, forms even smaller than conventional bacteria and barely visible even at the highest optical magnification.

Scientists' belief in an endless frontier means that the state of our knowledge is incomplete; new discoveries, or new ways of interpreting older data, will increase or restructure our knowledge. Nowhere has this belief been more rewarded than in the study of life in the sea: new life-forms like *Prochlorococcus* are being discovered with gratifying regularity; the habits of some of the familiar forms are being investigated and our understanding of their behavior revised; the study of populations has showed us how little we knew about the numbers of fish in the sea—or what was happening to them. We have learned much about marine life, but perhaps the most important lesson is that we are a part of every ecosystem, whether snow-capped mountains, steaming rain forests, or the forbidding world of "black smokers"—underwater volcanoes where nobody had expected to find volcanoes. While the discovery of plate tectonics completely revised our understanding of seafloor geology, the discovery of the hydrothermal vents introduced us to a completely unexpected biosystem, where all the rules were discarded—including the one that said that all life on earth is dependent upon sunlight.

Beginning with Aristotle, when scientists began the investigation of life in the ocean, it was usually because they wanted to know more about the various creatures that were being taken for food. By the fifteenth century, the first ichthyologists, whose interests superseded those of their predecessors, appeared and fishes became a prime subject for scientific investigation. Voyages of exploration, such as those of Vitus Bering and Captain Cook, awakened the world to the exotica of distant waters, and their discoveries made a lasting impact on the study of biological oceanography. Few people associate Darwin with marine life, but *Origin of Species* concerned all life, and the theory of evolution applies as much to fishes and squid as it does to pigeons and monkeys. (Darwin was also an eminent marine biologist, and contributed the theory of how coral atolls were formed, wrote extensively on fishes, and undertook a major revision of the classification of barnacles.) There were many nineteenth-century oceanographic expeditions dedicated to collecting and investigating cephalopods, fishes, whales, and deep-sea animals, and these also became the subjects studied at marine laboratories around the world. Although David Bushnell of Yale University invented the egg-shaped submersible vessel *Turtle* in 1775, it was a failure, and another century would pass before the development of (relatively) safe underwater boats. Submarines, in use since the early twentieth century, have no windows, so those who would investigate underwater life developed submersible vehicles with portholes, and from William Beebe's bathysphere of 1930 to the manned and remotely operated camera vehicles of today, science has been able to see into the depths of the ocean for the first time. Often what they saw was astonishing. In 1943, Jacques Cousteau and Emile Gagnan invented the Aqua-Lung, which enabled men and women to swim (sort of) like fishes and remain underwater for longer than they could while holding their

breath. While most scuba divers today are recreational, many scientists and underwater photographers made use of scuba to further their studies. Although two thousand years have transpired since the idea of studying the ocean's inhabitants arose, the sea still has the power to astonish us with its solved and unsolved mysteries.

There is nothing on earth that comes close to the discovery of hydrothermal vents for sheer excitement and for the electrifying—and literal—refutation of the old maxim that there is nothing new under the sun. Before 1977 it was universally accepted that all life, terrestrial and aquatic, relied upon light from the sun. Even creatures that lived in darkness—cave fishes, bioluminescent fishes and cephalopods, echinoderms, and other creatures of the benthos—depend on the photosynthetic cycle for life. But when scientists in the submersible *Alvin*, investigating the geology of the Galápagos Rift Zone, came across a smoking vent site populated by life-forms that had never before been seen by human eyes, it was as if they had come across an ecosystem from another galaxy. Illuminated by *Alvin*'s lights, where no lights had ever shone before, were eight-foot-long tube worms with blood-red plumes; ghostly white crabs and clams the size of footballs; eyeless shrimp in vast colonies amidst towering mineral spires; and superheated water bubbling as dense black "smoke" from volcanic cracks in the seafloor. The worms, clams, crabs and shrimp were sustained by hydrogen sulfide and had no connection whatever with oxygen or light from the sun. At the hydrothermal vent sites, now known to exist in all oceans, photosynthesis had been replaced by chemosynthesis. Since their 1977 discovery, the hydrothermal vents have been investigated by geologists, biologists, paleontologists, microbiologists, and filmmakers, all of whom were awestruck by the presence of totally unexpected life-forms in a phantasmagorical setting that had to be seen to be believed. The discovery of these deep-sea formations, hidden until technology made vent tourism a possibility, is surely the most dramatic example of a previously unknown (and completely unsuspected) undersea phenomenon coming online into the scientific and popular awareness.

From the earliest days, the sea provided a surface to travel on and a plenitude of creatures for people to eat. For the most part, it was research on those "edible" creatures that was the primary focus of what is generally known as "marine biology," but now that we recognize the interaction of all marine creatures, we must perforce address the complexities of marine biodiversity. An early "holy grail" of marine biology was the determination of population size as a necessary, albeit imprecise, mechanism to help commercial fishermen understand when they had taken too many as they hauled in large numbers of a particular species of edible fish. For the most part, the only usable numbers for fish populations were the number of fish (or pounds, or tons) caught, but this was not particularly helpful in estimating the number *not* caught. Fishing provided the most primitive data, but science soon provided more and better ways of estimating marine populations.

We eat fish, crabs, clams, scallops, mussels, oysters, shrimp, lobsters, squid, octopuses, cuttlefish, and, in some parts of the world, whales and dolphins. Sixteenth- and seventeenth-century European whalers hunted the Greenland whale (now known as the bowhead) for its long baleen plates, which were used in the manufacture of skirt hoops, corset stays, and buggy whips. Around 1715, Nantucket whalers killed a sperm whale and inspired a hunt for these huge, square-headed whales around the world. The sperm whale's head contains a clear, amber oil that hardens to a waxy consistency upon exposure to air. The entire Yankee whale fishery was dedicated to collecting this oil; after the oil was collected, the rest of the whale was left to the sharks. In 1867, the Norwegian whaler Svend Foyn invented the grenade harpoon, which made it possible to kill the gigantic blue and fin whales that could not be taken with a hand-thrown harpoon. (As a result of his invention, Foyn became the richest man in Norway.) Until it was replaced by petroleum in the middle of the nineteenth century, whale oil was used for nearly all of the lighting requirements in the world's cities. The rorquals of the Antarctic were discovered around 1904 and harvested by whalers in diesel catcher boats, who towed the carcasses to huge factory ships, where the oil was boiled out of their blubber and bones. The oil was used for lighting and lubrication and in the manufacture of margarine, lipstick, shoe polish, nitroglycerin, and pet food, but nobody ate whale meat—except the Japanese.

Plastics replaced baleen and petroleum took the place of whale oil, so it appeared that the 1983 moratorium on commercial whaling would save the whales from further depredations. Alas, it was not to be. Since the moratorium, the Japanese have been harvesting whales under a "scientific permit," but after the research has been completed, the meat somehow ends up in the marketplace. (There are also parts of Japan where schools of dolphins, suspected of robbing fishermen's nets, are driven into shallow water and stabbed to death, after which the meat is eaten.) As of 2005, the Japanese are again threatening to ignore the 1983 moratorium on commercial whaling and begin hunting whales off the coast of Australia.

There are literally billions of living things in the ocean that have nothing to do with humans, except perhaps as elements in the complex web of marine life, which affects humans in many ways, some of which we are only beginning to understand. When we choose to interact with the oceans' living inhabitants, it is not necessarily because they were put there for us to eat; we make use of many inedible creatures too. Corals are harvested for jewelry; after the meat has been removed, abalone shells provide "mother of pearl"; and while nobody eats the original owner, the graceful, striped shells of the chambered nautilus can be found in souvenir shops around the world. The pearl industry exploits an oyster's irritation by sand, and "sea shells," so popular with collectors, are actually manufactured by the gastropods that live in them, and with the exception of those found on the beach, the animals have to be killed in order for the shells to find their way into collectors' cabinets. Until they were replaced by synthetics in Western countries, sponges were harvested for cleaning purposes.

Tropical coral reefs around the world—somewhat easier to count and observe than, say, pelagic dolphins—are in terrible shape as a result of runoff from terrestrial farming, deforestation, pollution, overfishing, and dynamiting. As Jeremy Jackson wrote in 1997, "Coral reefs are the most structurally complex and taxonomically diverse marine ecosystems, providing habitat for tens of thousands of associated fishes and invertebrates. Recently, coral reefs have experienced dramatic phase shifts in dominant species due to intensified human disturbance beginning centuries ago. The effects are most pronounced in the Caribbean, but are also apparent on the Great Barrier Reef in Australia, despite extensive protection over the past three decades." With so many of our marine resources in seeming decline (I discuss the depletion of marine resources at some length in my book *The Empty Ocean*), it is becoming more and more critical to census marine life, providing a foundation firmer than anecdote for focusing management efforts.

When fish populations began to drop, some people believed that we could supplement this shortfall by catching large quantities of squid. For many marine predators, squid are their primary food item, so if dolphins, whales, and fishes could catch and eat squid, why not *Homo sapiens*? Squid fisheries have been carried on in China and Japan for centuries, so when the fish started to run out, some Western fishers changed to squid fishing, and calamari began appearing in restaurants in Europe and America. (Squid, octopus, and cuttlefish have been appearing on Mediterranean menus as long as there have been menus.) We had even less of an idea about the size of various squid populations than we did about fish populations, but ignorance has never slowed down fishermen, and they began hauling in heretofore unimaginably large numbers of squid. Records of the UN Food and Agriculture Organization show a world total cephalopod catch of 3,354,004 tons in 2001, the most recent year published. China leads the world in squid catches with 678,408 tons, followed by Japan with 566,371, and South Korea with 412,513; Argentina, 229,874; Thailand, 170,945; Morocco, 140,829; Vietnam, 130,000; and the United States, 105,125. It would help both the squid and their human consumers if we had an idea of how many cephalopods were out there and how many it was safe to catch.

Everybody knows about the food chain—the big fish eat the little fish, and so on ad infinitum—but it is actually much more complicated than that. Big fish are more likely to eat little fish than vice versa, but there are elements in the chain where little fish—think of piranhas—can eat creatures much larger than themselves; a whale carcass on the sea bottom will be eaten by scavengers that range in size from twenty-foot-long sharks and foot-long hagfish to crabs and bacteria. There are no creatures in the sea that are always predators or always prey: in their early stages, juvenile sharks, swordfish, or tuna can be eaten by fishes they would prey on if and when they made it to maturity.

Humans sometimes think of themselves as outside such arcane biological constructs as the food chain, largely because they can control or modify the links in the chain, and in some cases, such as aquaculture, rearrange the entire process. Because so many people around the world depend on food from the sea, we are an inescapable part of the chain. We want to think of killer whales or great white sharks as the sea's "apex predators," but a glimpse of the uncontested apex predator of the ocean can be obtained simply by looking in a mirror. It has been human predation—which in this case we call "fishing"—that has reduced some whale populations to relics; that has harvested so many codfish that there aren't enough left to sustain a fishery; that has eaten the Patagonian toothfish and the orange roughy almost out of existence; and that threatens bluefin tuna and swordfish with extinction. (Tuna and swordfish are "big-game fishes" and are therefore occasionally caught for sport, but sport fishermen have had a minimal effect on populations compared with the hundreds of thousands of tons that are taken on commercial longlines every year.)

An understanding of the interrelationships between various creatures—including the one predator that has the power to distort, damage, or even eliminate populations of marine animals—is necessary if we are to survive in harmony with these populations. Although new technologies have given us tools to better census the whales, dolphins, and fishes, and to see heretofore unexpected life and geological forms deep under the sea, we are a long way from comprehending the nature and importance of marine biodiversity. What follows is an attempt to put the search for knowledge into perspective— to try to find out how we got here, and where, with the help of curiosity, science, and technology, we might be headed.

With this as our Baedeker, we will voyage through time and space, tracing the history of the discovery of marine biology, from the moment that the first scientists—although for the most part, "science" had barely been invented— tried to figure out what sorts of creatures lived in the Mediterranean, the sea right off their shores. (No doubt Chinese, Japanese, Indian, Indonesian, or African fishermen were also curious about marine life, but the ancient Greeks and Romans were the first to attempt a systematic analysis.) Marine biology blossomed in the Renaissance, and by the eighteenth century, it was ready to assume an honored and respected place in the pantheon of investigative disciplines. As with virtually every other field of science, the available technology greatly accelerated the learning curve of marine studies. First came counting and identifying fishes in nets; then scooping up almost unimaginable creatures from the depths; then sending humans down to see what was there; and today, remotely-operated camera and work vehicles that can see and sample marine life where no human beings could ever venture. Throughout its remarkable history, marine biology has proven to be one of the most exciting and rewarding of modern sciences. (How many kids nowadays think that "marine biologist" is a cool thing to aspire to?)

The new understanding of marine life, as exemplified by the ongoing Census of Marine Life, opens doors that were previously locked—or not even known to exist. The Census is not a list of various marine species, but rather a massive, coordinated effort to investigate the ecology of that vast, heretofore unfathomable environment we call the ocean. There is life in the nearshore zones, along the continental shelves, in the light-bathed surface layers and the lightless depths; in the icy polar waters and the warm tropical seas. The world's oceans are all interconnected and all life, on land or in the sea, is related. ✎

News Flash

In September, 2004, a giant squid attacked a bait deployed at 900 meters (2,952 feet) off the Ogasawara (Bonin) Islands, south of Japan, a known haunt of sperm whales. The "attack" was filmed by a robot camera, and in the process of trying to remove the bait, one of the squid's feeding tentacles was torn off. The

tentacle was hauled in with the camera, and an examination revealed that the squid was unquestionably *Architeuthis*: over 8 meters (25 feet) long from tail tip to tentacle tip. (The torn-off tentacle was 5.5 meters long.) The 2005 report by Tsunemi Kubodera and Kyoichi Mori included several digital images and the DNA sequence extracted from the tentacle, confirming the identification of the animal as a giant squid.

After a thousand years of fear, fantasy, and several expeditions failed to reveal the lifestyle of the giant squid, Japanese scientists, using the most advanced robot camera technology, have recorded the first-ever observations of a live giant squid in the wild. Further analysis of the film will show behavior and physical characteristics of the giant squid that up to now have been speculative. "Our images," wrote the authors, "suggest that giant squids are much more active predators than previously suggested and appear to attack their prey from a horizontal orientation. The long tentacles are clearly not weak fishing lines dangled below the body. . . . It appears that the tentacles coil into an irregular ball in much the same way that pythons rapidly envelop their prey within coils of their body immediately after striking."

Although I managed barely to get the news item into this book, the main text was written before these photos of *Architeuthis* were published. Therefore, there are references within to our ignorance of the behavior of the giant squid, and to the fact that nobody has ever seen or filmed a live one. It was too late to change the text, but I am delighted to be able to include this story as an example of technology and science being used to shatter old myths and solve long-standing mysteries. What else will we learn about the creatures that were hidden for so long in the depths and darkness of the abyss?

Part One
The History of the Discovery of Marine Life

From the Mediterranean to a New World

From the sunshine-flecked, wave-enhanced surface, downward through diminishing light to the abyssal levels never reached by sunlight, and to the silty bottom of the deepest trenches, the expansion of our knowledge of marine life is accelerating. Aristotle, Aelian, Pliny, Oppian, and other ancient chroniclers of marine life began a process that would continue until the present moment—and will continue into the future, abetted by radical transformations in technology that enable us to learn more and more about life in the oceans. At first, we learned about fishes that were caught from shore or from the first vessels dedicated to fishing. In *Fishing From the Earliest Times*, William Radcliffe asks, "How did the earliest fisherman secure his prey? Was it by means of the Spear, under which term I include harpoons and barbed fishing spears of any kind, the Net or the Line?" He cannot, of course, answer his own question, because the answer is deeply shrouded in the mists of history, but suffice it to say that even as the first anglers (or spearers or netters) hauled in their prey, they wanted to learn—indeed, they *had* to learn—as much as possible about the lives of the creatures they would prepare for the pot or throw on the fire.

In the excavations of the Minoan structures at Akrotiri on the Aegean island of Santorini (also known as Thera), several dramatic wall paintings were discovered. The settlement at Akrotiri was buried in volcanic ash when most of the island exploded around 1600 B.C., so we can date the paintings from at least that date, if not earlier. (Fishing probably predates farming, and there is evidence of farming ten thousand years ago.) In the building known as Xesté 3, there are two paintings that show "fishermen," among the earliest depictions of this activity. Two naked youths with shaven heads are shown holding bunches of fish, drawn so realistically that the species are easily identifiable. One fisherman holds seven dolphin fish (*Coryphaena hippurus*, also known as dorado or mahi-mahi) in his right hand, and five more in his left. The other boy holds a bunch of three mackerel. Both of these species are fast swimmers and would not be—even today, with sophisticated spearguns—easily catchable by divers. Why then are these two naked boys shown with strings of fish? In her 1985 discussion of *Art and Religion in Thera*, Nanno Marinatos writes that "their blue heads, which denote partial shaving, and their nudity indicate that they are "performing a special function as youthful adorants," and suggests that they are making an offering to their deity. The Minoan god of fish and fishing?

The first marine biologists were fishermen—and women. (Many of the earliest fishers were probably women collecting shellfish on the shore.) To net, hook, or spear their prey, ancient mariners and shoreside fishers must have had some basic knowledge of the species they hunted, otherwise their nets would come up unoccupied and their hooks empty. From their wall paintings, we know that the Minoans of 1500 B.C. built ships and sailed them in the Mediterranean, once populated by innumerable fishes, dolphins, and whales. Before the year 1100 B.C., the Phoenicians, from their outpost at Carthage on the North African coast, had in all probability explored the shores of the Atlantic outside the protection of the Pillars of Hercules, that is, the Straits of Gibraltar. From archeological evidence, it has been ascertained that the Carthaginians had established a trading post at Essaouria (modern Mogador), about six hundred miles south of Gibraltar on the Atlantic coast of Morocco, some twenty-five hundred years ago. The Greek poet Homer, who wrote about the "wine-dark sea" several hundred years after the mysterious demise of the Minoans, knew nothing about what could be found below the surface of the sea except for the fish that his fellow Greeks caught.

There are few records of ancient fishermen, although reports of whale sightings are not uncommon. While water-breathing fishes usually remain submerged, whales surface to breathe, and this made it easier to see them. Of course, most whales are much larger than most fishes and are therefore that much more visible from ships. Aristotle, who lived from 384 to 322 B.C., was selected by King Philip of Macedonia as tutor for his son Alexander, later to be known as Alexander the Great, so Alexander was trained by one of the greatest scientists in history. When his plan for world conquest took Alexander's army into the Indian Ocean, the Greek historian Arrian recorded the following description of the behavior of whales:

In this foreign sea there lived great whales and other large fish, much bigger than ours in the Mediterranean. . . . The whales, which could be seen just in front of the ships, dived terrified into the depths. Not long after that, they surfaced behind the fleet, blowing water into the air as before. Now and again a few of these whales come ashore, having been stranded on the flat beaches by the ebb tide.

It would be millennia before observers realized that it was not water that whales "blew" into the air, but condensed, heated air that vaporized upon exhalation. The reasons for whale strandings are as unknown now as they were twenty-three centuries ago, when Aristotle wrote, "It is not known for what reason they run themselves aground on dry land; at all events, it is said that they do so at times and for no obvious reason." Aristotle also realized that whales were mammals and not fish, for in his *Historia Animalium* he wrote, "The dolphin, the whale, and the rest of the cetacea . . . are provided with a blow-hole instead of gills [and] are viviparous . . . just as in the case of mankind and the viviparous quadrupeds." Aristotle, who had no predecessor—and no equal—in recording the nature of animal life, on land as well as in the sea, codified much of what was known about other marine creatures, including crustaceans, worms, mollusks, and 116 species of fishes, all found in the Aegean, and can thus be called the father (and founder) of marine biology.

In his *Historia Animalium*, Aristotle described more than a hundred fish species, including the tuna, one of the most important food fishes of the Mediterranean:

Tunny fish also burst asunder by reason of their fat. They live for two years; and the fishermen infer this age from the circumstance that once when there was a failure of the young tunny fish for a year there was a failure of the full-grown tunny the next summer. . . . The growth of the young tunny is rapid. After the females have spawned in the Euxine, there comes from the egg what some call scordylae, but what the Byzantines nickname the "auxids" or "growers," from their growing to a considerable size in a few days; these fish go out of the Pontus [the northeastern section of the Mediterranean] in autumn along with the young tunnies, and enter Pontus in the spring as pelamyds. Fishes as a rule take on growth with rapidity, but this is peculiarly the case with all species of fish found in the Pontus; the growth, for instance, of the amia-tunny is quite visible from day to day.

Five centuries later, Oppian, the second-century Greek poet and naturalist, wrote a poem on fishing called *Halieutica*, in which he described the method of fishing for tuna:

Dropped in the water are nets arranged like a city. There are rooms and gates and deep tunnels and atria and courtyards. The tuna arrive in great haste, drawn together like a phalanx of men who march in rank: there are the young, the old, the adults. And they swim, innumerable, inside the nets and the movement is stopped only when there is no more room for new arrivals; then the net is pulled up and a rich haul of excellent tuna is made.

This method of net-fishing for tuna in the Mediterranean, called *mattanza* ("the killing") in Italian, is still practiced today by Sicilian fishermen, but it is on the wane because the tuna populations have fallen precipitously. The canneries in Sicily are closed; almost all of the tuna caught in Favignana is shipped to Japan, and like everyone else, the Japanese fish-buyers await the annual *mattanza*. There is a rumor in Favignana that the gaffing will be eliminated and the fishermen would simply wait for the tuna to die in the nets, because the gaffs make too many holes in the flesh. "Once," wrote Teresa Maggio in her 2000 book *Mattanza*, "the tuna snares thrived in Algeria, Corsica, Tunisia, Malta, Dalmatia, and Turkey. In Portugal they were called *armaçoes*; in Spain, *almandrabas*; in France, *madragues*. The cause of abandon: insufficient fish to make a profit. Once there were tonnaras all over Sicily . . . Gone, all gone."

Fishes appear early in the Bible; in Genesis 1:26, God gives man "dominion over the fish of the sea, and over the fowl of the air, and over the cattle, and over all the earth, and over every creeping thing that creepeth upon the earth." (In Genesis 2:19, Adam was also designated as the first taxonomist: "whatsoever Adam called every living creature, that was the name thereof.") Later on, when Noah is commanded to build an ark and bring aboard two of every living thing, the fishes are not included. Maybe they just paired up and swam along in the wake of the ark with the whales and dolphins. But what happened to the fishes and whales when the waters receded is not recorded, for "the waters were dried up from off the earth; and Noah removed the covering of the ark, and looked and behold,

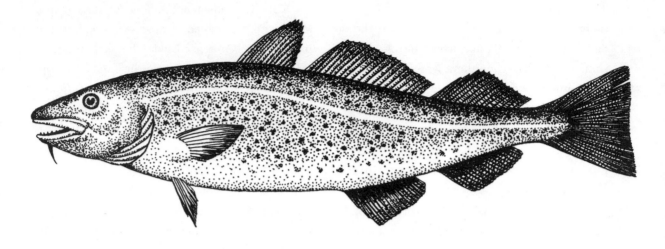

Codfish (*Gadus morhua*)

the face of the ground was dry." Generally speaking, the Old Testament was not sympathetic to ichthyology, but in Luke 9:17, Jesus does something with five loaves and two fishes that feeds five thousand people.

Sometime between the second and the fourth centuries, the *Physiologus*, a book of animal legends, was produced in Alexandria and subsequently translated into Syrian, Arabic, Armenian, Ethiopian, Latin, German, French, Provençal, Icelandic, Italian, and Anglo-Saxon. It was not, however, a single work in serial translations but rather an ongoing work-in-progress with no single author, with material being added and modified as the work wandered through time and geography. The *Physiologus* eventually metamorphosed into the medieval bestiary. Whales appear in the *Physiologus*, but so do dragons, griffins, and unicorns, with appropriate descriptions. In *The Book of Beasts*, T. H. White's 1954 translation of a twelfth-century bestiary, we read this about fishes:

Fish, like cattle, get their name because they browse in flocks. Moreover, they are known as reptiles because they have the same shape and natural disposition for swimming about. However deeply they can plunge into the abyss, yet in swimming itself they are slow movers. This is why David says, "In the sea great and spacious in power there are reptiles of which there is no number."

Because the North Atlantic is the home and breeding ground of the codfish (*Gadus morhua*), historically one of the most important marine food fishes in the world, the exploitation of this resource was one of the most significant factors in the economic development of countries that border the Atlantic. Among those countries that can attribute a portion of their history to the fortuitous occurrence of shoals of cod are Iceland, Norway, Britain, France, Spain, Portugal, Canada, and the United States. The first landfall of English settlers (as opposed to adventurers like John Cabot) in America was the narrow spit of land that Bartholomew Gosnold christened "Cape Cod" in 1602, because the eponymous fish were so plentiful.

The eating of fish had positive religious connotations for medieval Christians: *ichthus*, the Greek word for fish, is made up of the initial letters of *Ieosus Christos Theou Uios Soter*, "Jesus Christ, Son of God, Saviour." Moreover, fish became an integral part of the European diet because of the intricate and variable schedule of fast days, where people were forbidden to eat meat. (In Christianity's early years, "fast days" were literally that; the faithful were not supposed to eat anything at all, but later, these days of abstinence were modified so that only certain foods were eschewed.) The most strictly observed of the fast days was Friday, in honor of the Crucifixion, but on occasion, Wednesday was added, because that was the day Judas accepted money for his promise to betray Jesus, and also Saturday, the day consecrated to Mary in celebration of her virginity.

Even more important than the fast days, however, were the enduring fasts of Lent and Advent, which ushered in, respectively, the festive seasons of Easter and Christmas. Lent, which lasted for six weeks, was the major fast of the year, and while its observance included cutting down on meals and the amount of food consumed, the major modification in the dietary habits of the populace was the change from meat to fish. As Bridget Henisch wrote in *Fast and Feast*, a study of food in medieval society:

Fish, providentially, had escaped God's curse on earth by living in the water. Water itself was an element of special sanctity,

washing away the sins of the world in Noah's Flood, and the sins of the individual in baptism. Its creatures might be said to share something of its virtues. Once the choice had been justified, the rest was easy. Fish was plentiful, fish was cheap, and in the season of Lent, fish was king.

Herring was not only eaten during Lent, of course; it was a staple in the diet of Europeans throughout the year. It was only after the discovery of the codfish stocks of the Grand Banks—and the still unexplained disappearance of the Atlantic herring in the early fifteenth century—that *Gadus morhua* displaced *Clupea harengus* as the predominant fish on European tables. No amount of fancy preparation could make the herring or the cod—or, for that matter, the hake, sole, plaice, whiting, or turbot—tasty or desirable to the medieval palate. They were primarily regarded as Lenten fare and, as such, foods to be suffered, rather than enjoyed. Here is the "recipe" for the preparation of cod from a fourteenth-century daybook:

When it is taken in the far seas and it is desired to keep it for ten or twelve years, it is gutted and the head removed and it is dried in the air and sun and in no wise by a fire, or smoked; and when this is done it is called stockfish. And when it hath been kept a long time and it is desired to eat it, it behooves to beat it with a wooden hammer for a full hour, and then set it to soak in warm water for a full two hours or more, then cook and scour it very well like beef; then eat it with mustard or soaked in butter.

Twelve years old, hammered or buttered, codfish was a major part of the medieval European diet. Nobody except the fishermen worried about where they came from or how many there were—it almost seemed that their astronomical abundance was a gift from God—but because of their dietary restrictions, faithful Christians were forced to think about fish more than anybody had ever done before. "Science" was still centuries away, but as the light of the Renaissance began to illuminate the Dark Ages, a revival of interest in the long-dormant terrestrial and marine sciences had begun. "In the fourteen hundred years which elapsed between the writing of Pliny's *Natural History* and the Renaissance, knowledge in the maritime sciences scarcely advanced at all," wrote Margaret Deacon in her 1971 *Scientists and the Sea, 1650–1900*—but change was coming.

In 1553, Pierre Belon (1517–64), a French naturalist whose discussion of dolphin embryos and systematic comparisons of the skeletons of birds and humans mark the beginning of comparative anatomy, wrote *De aquatilibus libri duo*, in which he discussed about a hundred fish species, categorizing them according to size, shape, scales, and skeletons. He referred to the cetaceans as the "larger fishes." Guillaume Rondelet published *De Piscibis Marinum* in 1566, in which—among other ichthyological observations—he noted the voracious appetite of the *Lamia* (great white shark), whose diet included tuna and even the occasional human, and suggested that it was the *Lamia* (rather than a whale), that swallowed Jonah in the biblical fable.

The son of a blacksmith, John Ray was born on November 29, 1627, in the English village of Black Notley in Essex. Unlike most other Cambridge students who were the sons of rich gentlemen, Ray was poor and unable to pay the necessary fees. As with Isaac Newton, Ray was exempted from fees by acting as a servant for the staff of Trinity College. He obtained his master's degree in 1651 and then stayed on at Trinity as a lecturer. Francis Willughby (1635–72), a wealthy former student of Ray's, suggested that they should undertake scientific research together at Willughby's expense. For ten years, Ray and Willughby traveled around the British Isles and the rest of Europe, making observations and collecting specimens. While Willughby focused on animals, Ray focused on plants, intending to document living organisms and classify them according to structure. Although Willughby died in 1672, Ray was able to continue their project with funds generously provided for this purpose in Willughby's will. Their *Historia Piscium*, published in Oxford in 1686, has Willughby's name on the title page but was edited by John Ray. It contained 420 species, including 178 new species, but as Albert Günther (1880) wrote, "Ray seems to have been afraid of so great an innovation as the separation of whales from fishes, and therefore invented a definition of fish which comprises both."

The great maritime explorers of the late fifteenth and early sixteenth centuries—Bartolomeu Dias, Vasco da Gama, Christopher Columbus, Ferdinand Magellan, and others—driven by their hunger (or that of their sovereigns) for power, glory, or treasure, set out in small, unhandy ships in pursuit of the unknown. Their oceanographic interests lay primarily in winds, tides, and currents, not in marine life, but sailing far from land or entering uncharted anchorages, they could not help but notice the unusual birds or marine mammals the likes of which they had never seen before. During his first voyage, Columbus kept a daily account of his adventures, which he presented to Queen Isabella upon his return to Spain in 1493. The log, translated in 1987 by Robert Fuson, contains many references to the birds they saw, and the fish, turtles, and porpoises they caught for food. On his second voyage in 1494, when he arrived at the island of Alta Vela, south of Haiti, Columbus saw a group of eight "sea wolves" on the beach. A shore party killed them all, and, as Peter Knudtson wrote, "thus ended, in a prophetically bloody manner, the first recorded encounter between Europeans and the sea mammal now known as the Caribbean monk seal, *Monachus tropicalis.*" Their placid and unaggressive nature made them easy to kill, and there was already a fishery for these animals in 1675 when William Dampier visited the Bay of Campeachy on the western Yucatán:

> . . . there being such plenty of Fowls and Seals (especially of the latter) that the Spaniards do often come hither to make Oyl of their fat; upon which account it has been visited by English-men of Jamaica, particularly by Capt. Long; who, having command of a small Bark, came hither purposely to make Seal-Oyl, and anchored on the North side of one of the sandy Islands, the most convenient Place for his design.

William Dampier, born in 1652, achieved fame as a pirate, explorer, and naturalist. Apprenticed to a ship's captain at age eighteen, he made a voyage to the Newfoundland fisheries, and when his apprenticeship was duly served, he joined an East Indiaman and sailed to Java. From 1678 to 1691, he was engaged in piracy along the west coast of South America and in the South Seas, a voyage that would maroon him on the Nicobar Islands but ultimately take him around the world. His journal was published in 1697 as *A New Voyage Around the World,* complete with maps and drawings of the exotic wildlife he had seen. Dampier's fame as a buccaneer tends to overshadow his incisive descriptions of the marine life he encountered during his long career at sea. Here, for example, is his description of the manatee he saw in the Bay of Campeche, which is as accurate today as it was when he wrote it in 1681:

> This Creature is about the Bigness of a Horse, and 10 or 12 Foot long. The Mouth of it is much like the Mouth of a Cow, having great thick Lips. The Eyes are no bigger than a small Pea; the Ears are only two small holes on each side of the Head. The Neck is short and thick, bigger than the Head. The biggest part of this Creature is at the Shoulders, where it has two large Fins, one on each side of its Belly. Under each of these Fins the Female hath a small Dug to suckle her young. From the Shoulders towards the Tail it retains its bigness for about a Foot, then groweth smaller and smaller to the very Tail, which is flat, and about 14 Inches broad and 20 Inches long, and in the Middle 4 or 5 Inches thick. From the Head to the Tail it is round and smooth without any Fin but those two before-mentioned.

On his journey to western Australia in 1699, Dampier saw many species of birds that had never been described before, and because he had Francis Willughby's *Historia Piscium*, he was able to identify some of the common fishes he saw and describe and illustrate many new ones. Along with remoras, triggerfish, dolphinfish, gars, flying fish, and mackerel, he also spotted tiger sharks, humpback whales, bottlenose dolphins, and assorted sea snakes. Dampier's books—*A New Voyage Around the World*, published in 1697, and *A Supplement to the Voyage Around the World* (including *Voyages to Campeachey* and *Discourse on the Trade Winds*) in 1699—became best-sellers, and contributed substantially to the seventeenth-century English-man's knowledge of the world's oceans, winds, and wildlife. Dampier was an instinctive, intuitive naturalist. He pioneered what is today known as descriptive botany and zoology, later developed by Joseph Banks, the naturalist who sailed with Captain James Cook. Dampier was the first naturalist to visit all five continents and was therefore able to compare and contrast animals, birds, reptiles, and plants across the globe. He wrote the first descriptions of migration patterns. His observations of turtles in the Galápagos and the Caribbean led him to identify location-dependent differences within species, prefiguring Charles Darwin. Dampier was also the first to introduce "sub-species" both as a word and as a concept. 🐟

Enter the Russians and Americans

⬡ In 1740, leading a massive overland expedition, Commander Vitus Bering left Moscow under instructions from Tsar Peter the Great to discover if Asia was separate from America. Bering died of scurvy on a lonely, uninhabited island in the sea that was later named for him, but his journey stands as one of the most dramatic and productive "scientific" explorations of all time.

Bering headed east from Moscow with three thousand men, and what they believed to be instructions for reprovisioning along the way. No such instructions had reached the remote way stations, so when Bering and his men tried to obtain food and supplies to continue their journey, no one had anything to spare, and they reached the ocean, frozen and starving, at Okhotsk, the first Russian settlement in the Far East, established less than a century before. They built two ships, the *St. Peter* and the *St. Paul*, in a village on the eastern shore of Russia, which they named Petropavlovsk for the ships that they built there. On May 29, 1741, the ships set sail for the unknown reaches of the "Sea of Tartary" in search of mysterious (and nonexistent) islands that were shown on their maps as "Gama Land." The two ships became separated in a storm and were never reunited. Under Alexei Chirikov, the *St. Paul* encountered the Alaskan mainland—thus becoming the first European ship to land in Alaska—but a longboat sent ashore never returned, and Chirikov feared (probably correctly) that the men had been killed by natives. He returned via the Aleutians,

the first European to see and report on these volcanic and hostile islands.

Having lost Chirikov, and also having failed to find Gama Land, Bering sailed around in circles until he became convinced that he could relocate the strait that he had found fifteen years earlier, and took the *St. Peter* eastward. He, too, reached Alaska, but on his return voyage, he and his men were struck by scurvy, and because neither the reason nor the cure for this deadly disease were known in 1741, the men began to weaken and die. (It was not until 1753 that James Lind, a Scottish physician, recognized that scurvy could be prevented by the ingestion of the juices of fruits, particularly oranges, lemons, and limes.) The *St. Peter* was hit by a succession of terrible storms—the winter weather in the Bering Sea is generally considered the worst in the world—and with the men too few and too weak to man her, she eventually ran aground on an island that was not shown on any map. Bering, age sixty, was dying of scurvy and other afflictions, so command of the expedition fell to Lieutenant Sven Waxell and Georg Wilhelm Steller, the German naturalist and mineralogist who had signed on in Petropavlovsk after taking himself across Siberia to join Bering. Steller's

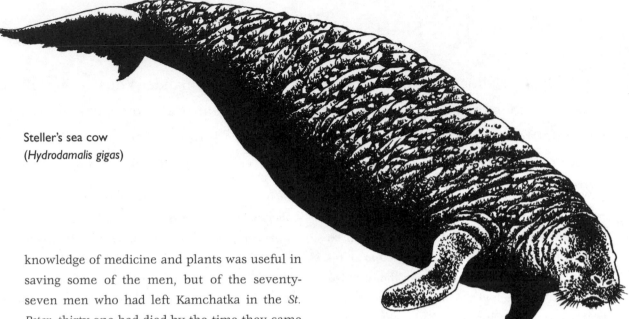

Steller's sea cow
(*Hydrodamalis gigas*)

knowledge of medicine and plants was useful in saving some of the men, but of the seventy-seven men who had left Kamchatka in the *St. Peter*, thirty-one had died by the time they came ashore on this uninhabited island. The survivors dug holes in the sandbanks and lived for eight months through a horrendous Siberian winter, ate sea otters, an occasional bird, and a dead whale that they found washed up on the beach. The following spring, they managed to kill some of the gigantic, manatee-like animals they saw swimming in the shallows, and the fat and meat sustained them until they could build a small boat out of the wreckage of the *St. Peter* and sail back to Kamchatka.

Steller is immortalized in the names of various mammals and birds that he was the first to describe. He lived to write up his observations of the voyage (published posthumously), including the first scientific descriptions of the sea otter, the fur seal, the northern jay, the sea lion, and the sea cow—the last three of which were named for him. Steller's eider, a seagoing duck, was also named for him. Steller's descriptions of the fur seals and sea otters encouraged a rush of Russian

fur hunters (*promyshlenniki*) to the Aleutians, and it was on Bering Island that the hunters managed to kill off the last of the northern sea cows.

Now known as Steller's sea cow, *Hydrodamalis gigas* was one of the most unusual mammals that ever lived. Although it is extinct, there was enough information recorded about its appearance and habits for us to get an idea of what it looked like and how it lived. The animal the Russians called *morskaya korova* was an overstuffed sausage of a beast, with a small head, piggy eyes, and skin that was likened to the bark of a tree. It probably reached a length of thirty feet and may have weighed as much as four tons. It had a forked, horizontal tail like its relative the dugong (the manatee has a rounded, paddlelike tail), and its forelegs were unique in the mammalian kingdom: they had no finger bones, and they ended at the elbow. The great sea cow could not dive below the surface and pulled itself along the

Sea otter (*Enhydra lutris*)

bottom on its stumps as it browsed on kelp. Its mouth had no teeth; instead, there were horny plates that it rubbed together to grind plant matter into a pulp.

Upon Steller's return to Kamchatka on the Russian mainland, the existence of the sea otters, the sea cow, and the islands themselves was made known. The pelt of the sea otter is one of the most luxurious furs in the world, and it was not long before Russian trappers arrived on the islands. It is said that they killed more than eleven thousand foxes and two thousand otters. Russian sealers began to visit Bering and Copper Islands for the sea lions that bear Steller's name and also for meat and oil for their voyages. They killed the slow moving sea cows in such numbers that there were none left by 1768. (We have no way of knowing how many sea cows were on the islands when Bering landed, but Leonhard Stejneger, Steller's biographer, has estimated that there were some fifteen hundred.) It had taken only twenty-seven years for the Russian adventurers to eliminate the hapless sea cow from the face of the earth, but the sealers had no way of knowing that this was the last of them; they

probably assumed that there were similar undiscovered islands with more sea cows. There weren't, but there were still plenty of undiscovered islands, in oceans that had never been seen by Europeans.

On his three epic voyages of exploration (1769–79) Captain James Cook brought along artists, naturalists, and Joseph Banks, the botanist who in 1778 was to become *Sir* Joseph Banks, president of the Royal Society, Britain's most prestigious scientific organization. Other naturalists aboard Cook's three voyages included biologist Daniel Solander, draftsman Heinrich Spöring, and Sydney Parkinson, a natural history illustrator. It fell to these men to collect, catalog, and describe the nearly one thousand plant specimens, five hundred birds, five hundred fish, and hundreds of insects, shells, corals, and other invertebrates that they encountered. Most of the fishes collected on Cook's expeditions were previously unknown, and as Adrienne Kaeppler wrote in 1978,

Northern fur seal (*Callorhinus ursinus*)

"the 270 known paintings and drawings of fish from Cook's voyages were used by scientists of the 19th century as the basis for description of 50 new species." James Cook, whose life ended tragically when he was killed by Hawaiians at Kealakekua Bay on February 14, 1779, was one of the greatest explorers in history. He sailed farther south than any man before him, explored and charted the coasts of New Zealand, landed in Botany Bay (it was Banks who would later suggest to the British government that the place would be ideal for a colony of transported convicts), explored the Great Barrier Reef, and attempted the Northwest Passage. Circumnavigating the globe three times, Cook could not help but make major contributions to oceanography, navigation, cartography, and biology.

One of the first "official" U.S. government scientific expeditions was the Great United States Exploring Expedition of 1838–42. Under the command of forty-year-old Lieutenant Charles Wilkes, the six-ship squadron was originally commissioned to search for the hollow center of the earth, which a man named John Cleves Symmes had determined could be reached through an entrance under the South Pole. However crackbrained this "holes in the poles" idea sounds now—we must remember that Jules Verne's *Voyage to the Center of the Earth* was published in France in 1864—on its face, it was enough to get President John Quincy Adams to encourage Congress to support the venture. (A more realistic, commercial objective was the search for new sealing and whaling grounds in the South Pacific, but Symmes's goofy plan was the nominal impetus for the expedition.) Symmes died in 1829, one year after Congress

had authorized funds for the expedition (and nine years before the expedition actually set sail), and the job fell to Jeremiah N. Reynolds, who quickly recognized that the "holes in the poles" theory could be abandoned in favor of a more rational, scientific approach.

The expedition, consisting of the flagship *Vincennes*, the *Porpoise*, *Peacock*, *Relief*, *Flying Fish*, and *Sea Gull*, departed from Hampton Roads, Virginia, on August 18, 1838. Most of their "exploring" would take them to the South Pacific and the Antarctic, but they had a complement of scientists aboard—known as "the scientifics"—which gave the expedition an oceanographic importance far beyond its stated or subliminal warrants. The European nations had begun the tradition of scientific exploration, led by the redoubtable Captain Cook and by James Fitzroy of the *Beagle*, who had as his naturalist Charles Darwin. The French had sponsored Dumont d'Urville, Louis-Antoine de Bougainville, and Jean-François la Perouse, so asserting themselves in the quest for scientific stature and legitimacy was a significant factor in the U.S. expedition. On board were mineralogist James Dwight Dana, philologist Horatio Hale, naturalists Titian R. Peale and Charles Pickering, botanists William Brackenridge and William Rich, conchologist Joseph Couthouy, and artists Alfred Agate and Joseph Drayton.

On the outward leg of the voyage, the squadron put into Madeira for provisions, passed the bulge of Africa and stopped briefly at the Cape Verdes en route to Rio de Janeiro, where the botanists collected some fifty thousand specimens. Wilkes maintained the scientific nature of the voyage by seeing to it that hydrographic and meteorological data were collected regularly, and they traced the course of the Gulf Stream by taking the temperature of the water.* From Rio, they sailed south to round Cape Horn, passed Tierra del Fuego, and entered the South Pacific. In the 1985 book *Magnificent Voyagers* (a catalog of a major Smithsonian Institution exhibit), the details of the vertebrate and invertebrate collections of the expedition are given. Much of the vertebrate collecting was devoted to previously unknown species of birds, but artist-naturalist Titian Peale, son of the famed portraitist Charles Willson Peale, discovered a completely new species of dolphin. In the 1858 folio "Mammals and Ornithology," the species was identified as *Delphinus obscurus*, captured off Patagonia. Peale's dolphin (now known as *Lagenorhynchus australis*) is one of the enduring legacies of this remarkable expedition. Lieutenant Wilkes persuaded Louis Agassiz of the Harvard Museum of Comparative Zoology to curate and publish the fish collection, but through a succession of mishaps, the publication never appeared, and most of the actual specimens deteriorated or were lost. The rest of the collection—2,000 birds, 150 mammals, 1,000 shells and corals, and thousands of drawings of assorted other material—was donated to the U.S. government and became the basis for the establishment of the U.S. National Museum. ✍

---

* In 1497, when John and Sebastian Cabot sailed up the eastern coast of North America in search of the Northwest Passage, they noted that the unaccountable warmth below-decks fermented the beer in the hold and turned it sour. They thus became the first explorers to record their observations of what would later be known as the Gulf Stream.

Ichthyology Takes a Name

Peter Artedi was the first true ichthyologist. Born in Anundsjö, Sweden, in 1705, he devoted his entire professional life to the study of fishes, producing the massive, five-part *Ichthyologica,* issued in one volume in 1738. The first part is the *Bibliotheca ichthyologica,* a critical review of the literature of fishes, with special emphasis on the work of Ray and Willughby. Then came the *Philosophia ichthyologica,* which contained descriptions of the internal and external parts of fishes, and the *Species piscium,* which included descriptions of seventy-two species. In this third section, he laid down his extremely strict views on the generic and specific names that could be used for fishes, to avoid the confusion that had existed when one name was in use for two or more different animals. Artedi advanced a classification of fishes with single-word generic names and detailed generic descriptions, followed by a list of the species known in each genus. The final part was the *Synonymia piscium,* in which all previous authors were arranged for every species, much in the same manner that synonymies are arranged today in systematic works. Artedi drowned before his studies were published, but his notes and manuscripts were purchased by Carolus Linnaeus, who edited the material and issued it in 1738. Linnaeus based many of his descriptions on those of Artedi and added the binomials that changed taxonomy, the science of classification. Linnaeus finally separated the whales from the fishes in the tenth edition of his *Systema naturae* in 1758.

During the eighteenth century, two church doctrines provided sweeping biblical explanations for most questions about biological diversity: one was "Separate Creation," the idea that all creatures have been created independently of one another by God and organized into a hierarchy—the "chain of being"—with man occupying the most elevated rank beneath God; the other was a six-thousand-year limit on the age of the planet. It is not the average person who questions two thousand years of dogma, but that is what Georges-Louis Leclerc, Comte de Buffon (1707–88) did. A hundred years before Darwin, Buffon produced the *Histoire Naturelle,* a forty-four-volume encyclopedia describing everything known about the natural world. Although Buffon believed in organic change, he did not provide a coherent mechanism for such changes. He thought that the environment acted directly on organisms through what he called "organic particles." In 1788 Buffon also published *Les Epoques de la Nature,* in which he openly suggested that the planet was much older than the six thousand years proclaimed by the church, and discussed concepts very similar to Charles Lyell's "uniformitarianism" which were formulated forty years later.

Bernard Germain Étienne de la Ville, Comte de Lacépède (1756–1826) built his ichthyological reputation on the sturdy framework erected by his predecessors. In 1788 he published *Histoire des quadrupèdes, ovipares et des serpents*, and *Histoire naturelle des reptiles* the following year. When the Jardin du Roi was reorganized as the Jardin des Plantes, Lacépède was appointed to the chair allocated to the study of reptiles and fishes. In 1798 he published the first volume of *Histoire naturelle des poissons*, the fifth volume appearing in 1803, and in 1804 his *Histoire des cétacés* appeared. Because he was often separated from his reference materials, he had to work largely from memory and notes, therefore *Histoire naturelle des Poissons* is filled with what Günther calls "those errors to which a compiler is subject . . . the same species not only appears under two and more distinct specific names . . . but sometimes the description is referred to one genus and the accompanying figure to another."

Georges Cuvier (1769–1832) was one of the most influential figures in science during the early nineteenth century. In 1795 Geoffroy Saint-Hilaire invited Cuvier to come to Paris, where he was appointed an assistant and later a professor of animal anatomy at the post–French Revolution Musée National d'Histoire Naturelle. His work is considered the foundation of vertebrate paleontology. Cuvier expanded Linnaean taxonomy by grouping classes into phyla. Although the study of fishes was not his highest priority, his *Regne animal distribué d'après son organisation* of 1817–30 was a key step forward for fish classification. With his pupil Achille Valenciennes, he produced the twenty-two-volume *Histoire Naturelle des Poissons* during the decade from 1830 to 1839, and while never completed, the work described 4,514 species of fishes. But, wrote Albert Günther, "Cuvier himself, at a late period of his life, seems to have grown in-

different as to the exact definition of his species: a failing commonly observed among Zoologists when attention to descriptive details becomes to them a tedious task."

No such criticism could be leveled against the man who wrote those words in 1880; between 1859 and 1870 Albert G. L. C. Günther would go on to write the eight-volume *Catalogue of the Fishes of the British Museum*, describing over sixty-eight hundred species and mentioning another seventeen hundred. In 1857 Günther, born in Germany in 1830, was appointed Keeper of the Zoological Department of the British Museum of Natural History, where his responsibilities included recording the multitude of specimens in the museum's collection. In 1880 he would write *Introduction to the Study of Fishes*, which included the history of ichthyology, chapters on the anatomy, distribution, and paleontology of fishes, and four hundred pages on the known families.

Born in Cropton, Yorkshire, in 1789, William Scoresby was the son of a whaler, also named William Scoresby. He went to sea on Scoresby senior's *Resolution* in 1799, at the age of ten. Before his next voyage to the Arctic, he went back to school, and in 1806 he entered the University of Edinburgh, where he studied chemistry, natural philosophy, and anatomy. Unlike most of his contemporaries in the whaling business, he was remarkably proficient in languages, being able to read and translate Latin, French, German, and even Anglo-Saxon in his researches on the early history of whaling. In 1820 he completed *An Account of the Arctic Regions, with a History and Description of the Northern Whale Fishery*, which, as its title suggests, contained a detailed history of the whale fishery. But the *Account of the Arctic*

Bowhead whale
(*Balaena mysticetus*)

Regions also incorporates an astonishingly accurate account of the natural history of Arctic fishes, birds, polar bears, and of course, the specific object of his northern voyages, the whale we know as the bowhead, which he and his contemporaries called "The Whale," "The Greenland Whale," or "The Mysticetus." His monumental work also contains descriptions of the fin whale, blue whale, humpback, narwhal, pilot whale, beluga, walrus, and seals, as well as birds such as the guillemot, fulmar, tern, and gull. The following example is from his description of the narwhal, demonstrating his familiarity with earlier authorities, and also his first-hand observations:

La Cèpede notices three species of narwhal; I have seen but one; and perhaps the others are only imaginary, for the animal varies in appearance. This animal, when full grown, is from 13 to 16 feet in length, exclusive of the tusk, and in circumference (two feet behind the fins, where it is thickest) 8 to 9 feet. . . . A long prominent tusk, with which some narwhals are furnished, is considered as a horn by the whale-fishers; and as such, has given occasion for the name of Unicorn being applied to this animal. The tusk occurs on the left side of the head, and is sometimes found of a length of 9 or 10 feet, according to Egede, 14 or 15. . . . It is spirally striated from right to left; is nearly straight, and tapers to a round blunt point; it is yellowish-white in color and consists of a compact kind of ivory.

It is safe to assume that the only people who had ever seen a living narwhal were the Eskimos and the Arctic whalers. It is an even safer assumption that few people realized that the "spirally striated" ivory shaft came from a whale and not from the legendary unicorn. Scorseby's *Account of the Whale Fishery* was a natural history for its time and played a significant role in the exposition of marine science in the early decades of the nineteenth century. Scoresby himself appears in the

"Cetology" chapter of *Moby-Dick*, often pseudony-mously cast as "Charley Coffin." Melville sees Scorseby's veneration of the bowhead as compet-ing with his own paean to the sperm whale, and says, "Scoresby knew nothing and says nothing about the sperm whale, compared with which the Greenland whale is almost unworthy mention-ing." But Melville recognizes Scoresby's expertise and writes that he was "a real professional har-pooner and whaleman. . . . On the separate sub-ject of the Greenland or right-whale, he is the best existing authority."

"It was in the early nineteenth century," wrote Margaret Deacon in her compilation of im-portant studies in marine science, "that marine biology began its great period of expansion. Per-haps it was the work of Linnaeus, Buffon, and Cuvier, together with the growing interest in bi-ology that caused biologists to turn with increas-ing enthusiasm to the sea." Considered by many to be the first oceanographer, Edward Forbes was born in 1815 on the Isle of Man. While studying medicine at Edinburgh, he developed a passion-ate interest in mollusks, starfishes, and other an-imals of the littoral zone. He worked mostly with dredges in water less than 100 fathoms (600 feet) deep, but in 1841, while sailing aboard the naval vessel *Beacon* in the Mediterranean, he winched in a haul from 230 fathoms (then the record depth for a bottom haul), which inspired him to develop a theory of the eight bands of depth that could each be characterized by the presence of certain animals. He believed that the lower limit for living creatures was about 300 fathoms, and wrote, "As we descend deeper and deeper . . . the inhabitants [of the sea] become more and more modified, and fewer and fewer, indicating our

approach to an abyss where life is extinguished or exhibits but a few sparks of its lingering pres-ence." Forbes was a dedicated student of the shallower-water species he did recognize, and until his untimely death at the age of thirty-nine in 1854, did much to popularize the investigation of the marine environment.

While Forbes did not believe that life could exist at great depths, others were refuting this idea almost as it was being proposed. In his 1818 voy-age to Baffin Bay in search of the Northwest Pas-sage, Sir John Ross's crew brought up a starfish along with several pounds of greenish mud and worms from a depth of 1,050 fathoms, and Sir John's nephew, James Clark Ross, successfully dredged living organisms from 300 fathoms during the 1839–43 Antarctic voyages of *Erebus* and *Ter-ror*. Either they did not know of Ross's discoveries or they chose to ignore them, but most scientists continued to argue that no life-forms could exist in the dark, cold waters below a thousand feet, where, they believed, the enormous weight of the water would crush any living thing. There were even popularly accepted ideas that water itself was compressed at great depths, causing sunken ships and other aquatic detritus to remain suspended above the floor of the ocean. François Peron be-lieved (and published) the theory that the bottom of the ocean was a frozen mass of ice, and since nothing could live in solid ice, the question of life in the depths was answered. Others were con-vinced that the deep ocean basins contained water that never moved. Without movement, there could be no renewal of food sources, and without food sources, there could be no life. Still others supposed that life in the abyss was quite different from that of the shallower regions and that the deep sea harbored extinct creatures—"living fossils." Such luminaries as Louis Agassiz thought that the depths of the ocean preserved environments that had expired on the land, and others suggested that the deeper seas were inhabited by the oldest animals, much the way the oldest rocks harbored the earliest fossils.

While aboard the *Beagle* from 1831 to 1836, Darwin collected "fifteen kinds of sea-fish which are . . . all new species; they belong to twelve genera, all widely distributed. . . ." And in *Origin of Species* (1859), he speculated on the mystery of the eyes of the flatfish, which start out on either side of the head, but then "migrate" until both are on the same side. The father of evolutionary theory entered the contentious world of ichthyological determinism when he wrote:

The Pleuronectidae, or Flat-fish, are remarkable for their asymmetrical bodies. They rest on one side—in the greater number of species on the left, but in some on the right side; and occasionally reversed adult specimens occur. . . . But the eyes offer the most remarkable peculiarity, for they are both placed on the upper side of the head. During early youth, however, they stand opposite to each other, and the whole body is then symmetrical, with both sides equally coloured. Soon the eye proper to the lower side begins to glide slowly round the head to the upper side; but does not pass right through the skull, as was formerly thought to be the case. It is obvious that unless the lower eye did thus travel round, it could not be used by the fish whilst lying in its habitual position on one side. The lower eye would, also, have

been liable to be abraded by the sandy bottom. That the Pleuronectidae are admirably adapted by their flattened and asymmetrical structure for their habits of life, is manifest from several species, such as soles, flounders, &c., being extremely common.

Following Darwin, zoology was primarily directed toward discovering whether living organisms were the descendants of common ancestors, and phylogeny was the chief preoccupation of the period. It was in 1866 that Ernst Haeckel put forth his "Biogenetic Law" that "ontogeny recapitulates phylogeny," in which he said that during the human embryonic development, the embryo "recapitulates" (repeats) its evolutionary stages, from fish to chicken, thence from dog to man. Included in his claims were what Haeckel said were gill slits (from our fish ancestors), a yolk sac (from our bird ancestors), and a lizard's tail (from when we were reptiles). Unfortunately, Haeckel manipulated the images that he used to illustrate his theory, and in fact, ontogeny does *not* recapitulate phylogeny; every creature does *not* pass through stages that represent its evolutionary heritage. Despite this unfortunate miscalculation, Haeckel's contributions to marine biology included studies of *Siphonophora* (1869), *Monera* (1870), *Calcareous Sponges* (1872), and several of the *Challenger* reports, including *Deep-Sea Medusae* (1881), *Siphonophora* (1888), and *Radiolaria* (1887), the last accompanied by 140 plates and enumerating over four thousand new species.

Until the middle of the nineteenth century, marine biological research was carried on by individuals, often associated with universities or museums. Then, organization accelerated research.

The first marine laboratory was created in 1843 at Ostend, Belgium, by Pierre-Joseph van Beneden, a zoologist and parasitologist, and the father of the better-known Edouard, the discover of meiosis. Educated as a doctor, van Benden was appointed curator of the natural history museum at the University of Louvain in 1831. Five years later he became professor of zoology and comparative anatomy in the Catholic University at Louvain. Early in his career he directed his attention to marine invertebrates, but he also studied fossil whalebones, and in collaboration with Paul Gervais, published the multivolume *Ostéographie des cétacés vivants et fossiles* between 1868 and 1880. Marine biology laboratories also played an important role in France as a new generation of biologists and physiologists became a part of the scientific establishment for the first time. The first French laboratory on the sea edge was founded in the 1850s at Concarneau, on the southern coast of Bretagne, by J.-J. Coste, a professor at the Collège de France. Although they commissioned no expeditions specifically intended for oceanographic research, the French of the nineteenth century were as curious as any other Europeans about *la vie marine*.

In 1857 the British steam frigate HMS *Cyclops* returned to England with bottom samples collected in the North Atlantic. Nine years later (and well after the 1859 publication of Darwin's *Origin of Species*), these muds were examined by Thomas Henry Huxley, who decided that the gluey sediment containing tiny, chalky granules was the protoplasm of the earliest life-form, and he named it *Bathybius haeckeli*, in honor of Ernst Haeckel, the German biologist. In 1868 Haeckel had devised the *Protista*, a third kingdom that he believed bridged the gap between the simplest protozoans and the smallest plants. The simplest members of this kingdom were the *Monera*, which Haeckel believed to be the lowest form of life, lacking both a nucleus and an external cell membrane. So when Huxley published his description of *Bathybius*, which he believed was a creeping form of ooze that provided food for the "higher organisms," Haeckel concluded that this primordial slime (which he translated into German as *Urschleim*), was one of the taproots of the evolutionary tree; the form of life from which all others had evolved. Upon examination of this precipitated mud, Charles Wyville Thomson, who would later become the leader of the *Challenger* expedition (and spend a lot of time searching for this nonexistent material), wrote, "The mud was actually alive; it stuck together in lumps, as if there were white of egg mixed with it; and the glairy mass proved, under the microscope, to be a living sarcode. Prof. Huxley . . . calls it *Bathybius*." William Carpenter, another organizer of the *Challenger* expedition, wrote, "It seems to be clearly indicated that there is a vast sheet of the lowest type of animal life, which probably extends over the whole of the warmer regions of the sea." But J. Y. Buchanan, the chemist aboard the *Challenger*, realized that the primordial ooze that Huxley examined was actually bottom mud that had been sitting in alcohol for several years, and was simply a colloidal precipitate of calcium sulfate with radiolarian skeletons embedded in it; it was a chemical reaction, not a primordial life-form. *Bathybius* disappeared forever into the abyssal oblivion reserved for "hopeful monsters"—those scientific discoveries that their introducers are so anxious to find that they overlook the facts that might disprove the existence of their inventions. ✧

Organization Assists Discovery

Men have always been curious about life in the sea—often for reasons no more noble than that they wanted to remove potential food items, often in large quantities. However, the concentrated effort to learn about the numbers and nature of marine life probably began with the *Challenger* expedition. The two-hundred-foot-long British auxiliary steam corvette *Challenger* was built in 1858 and sailed around the world from 1873 to 1876 on an international oceanographic cruise, the first major expedition dedicated to the exploration of the floor of the ocean. Under Captain George Nares, the 2,306-ton steam corvette sailed from Portsmouth on December 21, 1872, manned by a crew of 240 able-bodied seamen and six civilians. The scientific staff was led by Charles Wyville Thomson, Edward Forbes's successor as professor of natural history at the University of Edinburgh, and consisted of five other civilians: naturalists John Murray, H. N. Moseley, and Rudolf von Willemöes-Suhm, chemist John Buchanan, and the expedition's artist, J. J. Wild.

Originally commissioned as a warship, the *Challenger* was fitted out as a floating laboratory, with instruments for taking bottom samples and water temperatures; 144 miles of sounding rope (they had planned to use piano wire for the dredges, but on the first haul, the wire tangled so badly that one-inch hemp was substituted, and rope was used for the remainder of the voyage). All of this materiel, according to Wyville Thomson, was to be used to investigate "the conditions of the Deep Sea throughout all the Great Oceanic Basins." On the hauls, an astonishing plenitude of living things was brought aboard the research ship, including sea anemones, urchins, jellyfishes, snails, sea slugs, squid, worms, barnacles, isopods, amphipods, and broken hunks of coral, proving conclusively that there was life at the ocean's greatest depths. (Because of the open nature of the nets, midwater and even surface fishes were also trapped as the hauls were pulled up. It would be only after the *Challenger's* epochal voyage that a device for closing the nets was introduced to ensure that the contents of a trawl came only from the bottom.) It was demonstrated that the seafloor was far from "azoic"; in fact, there proved to be a far greater density—and diversity—of living animals on and in the bottom than in the water column above it.

"From the days of the *Challenger* expedition," wrote Gage and Tyler (1991), "biological oceanographers had relied on intuition that the extreme physical conditions and the impoverished nutritional input could be tolerated only by a small number of specialized forms of life." But in 1967, after dragging the bottom with a fine-meshed "epibenthic" sled, Robert Hessler and Howard Sanders found that "the most striking aspect of the fauna obtained by the sled is the very large number of species represented in each sample. Station 73 from 1400m depth on the continental slope [off Massachusetts] contained the largest number of species, 365. Even the poorest sample in the series . . . yielded a surprisingly diverse fauna, 196 species." (In 1968, Sanders would publish a comprehensive study of marine benthic biodiversity from sites around the world, which would verify the earlier findings, although not explain "why some environments harbor many kinds of organisms while others support a very limited number.") Danish zoologist Torben Wolff (1977) attributed the remarkably high species diversity to long-term environmental stability, where "each species may have evolved a high food specialization, avoiding competitive overlap with other species of the community."

In 1978, J. Fred Grassle, one of the foremost observers of the phenomena of deep-sea biodiversity (and subsequently one of the organizers of CoML), wrote, "Although disturbance is infrequent, when it does occur, a few species slowly colonize. . . . The very slow rates of colonization in the deep sea mean that an environmental mosaic is created. Each small patch differs, depending upon the length of time following the disturbance and the particular species that happen to settle there." In 1992 (with Ron Etter), Grassle wrote that "many hypotheses have been proposed concerning the forces that shape patterns of species diversity in the deep sea, but so far, it has not been possible to relate these patterns to potential causes in a direct quantitative way." Some deep-sea sites, however, such as those influenced by abyssal storms (Thistle 1981), or hydrothermal vents, show a comparatively low diversity.*

The *Challenger* expedition traversed 68,890 nautical miles, visiting the North and South Atlantic, the North and South Pacific, the Arctic and the Antarctic, taking 362 "samples" at specific locations, recording the exact depth, a sample of the bottom, the temperature at the bottom, and a collection of the bottom fauna. The expedition returned to England with over 13,000 plants and animals, 1,441 water samples, and hundreds of containers of seafloor samples. Under the editorship of John Murray, the official fifty-volume *Report of the Scientific Results of the Voyage of the H.M.S. Challenger* was published between 1885 and 1895, and among other important observations, identified 4,417 new species and 715 new genera.

During her thousand-day voyage, the *Challenger* crisscrossed the North Atlantic twice, rounded the Cape of Good Hope, sailed among—and crashed into—Antarctic icebergs (she was the first steam-powered ship to cross the Antarctic Circle), visited Australia, New Zealand, New Guinea, Fiji, the Philippines, Japan, Tahiti, Hawaii, and Tierra del Fuego. On their passage to Tahiti, the *Challenger* expedition discovered that the Pacific seabed was covered with manganese nodules—round balls of manganese ranging in

---

* At the conclusion of another article (in 1991) on deep-sea benthic biodiversity, Grassle warned: "Almost nothing is known about the tolerances of deep-sea organisms to the gradual build-up of anthropogenic chemicals, and there is a potential for changes to be widespread if they do occur. Measurement of pollutants, descriptions of deep-sea communities from many parts of the ocean, and in situ toxicity studies are urgently needed. The establishment of long-term stations to better understand the interactions of deep sea organisms with their natural environment and to monitor the potential effects of pollution are necessary to provide the information required for wise management of ocean resources." Of course *Challenger* sailed long before people realized how much of an effect they could have on the environment, marine or terrestrial.

size from hen's egg to cannonball, the origin of which is still unknown. It would be another nineteen years before the results of the expedition were published, during which time Wyville Thomson died and John Murray was named head of the *Challenger* Commission.

In her 2005 study of the exploration and discovery of the deep sea, Helen Rozwadowski observed, "Ocean scientists gravitated to the traditional genre of explorers partly to bring their work to an interested public who could experience the sea through their narratives. By rhetorically placing themselves in the role of great explorers and discoverers who charted and named the far corners of the world, scientists transformed the sea into the next frontier." Because so many people depended upon fish for sustenance or livelihood, the study of marine life—particularly ichthyology—ascended to the forefront of the investigative biological sciences.

In 1850 American ichthyology was still very much an individual activity, pursued without much institutional support. Those institutions that did exist were largely associations of enthusiastic amateurs with little more than their own personal resources to call on. Small natural history collections were maintained by the Boston Society of Natural History, the Academy of Natural Sciences of Philadelphia, and a few others. Louis Agassiz, the well-known Swiss scientist, had recently arrived in the United States and was beginning to assemble a collection at Harvard University. The U.S. government itself maintained a collection, under somewhat chaotic conditions, in the Patent Office building in Washington, D.C. None of these, however, could compare with the great museums of Europe. The

only ichthyologist in America who could compete in stature with the leading figures in Europe was Louis Agassiz, and he was a European transplant. Agassiz achieved fame in Europe for his publications on fossil mollusks and fishes (and also the glaciers of Switzerland), and came to the United States in 1846 to lecture at the Lowell Institute in Boston. The following year, he accepted a professorship of zoology at Harvard, and developed the collections that were to become the Museum of Comparative Zoology (MCZ) in 1858. When Charles Darwin published his *Origin of Species* in 1859, Agassiz objected violently to Darwin's theory of evolution, claiming that the world had been created by God and that species were immutable thoughts in the mind of the Supreme Intelligence. In 1873 Agassiz built a "gem of a laboratory" at Newport, Rhode Island, and spent the summer of 1874 building a marine biological teaching laboratory on Penikese Island (invariably misspelled "Pekinese") in Buzzard's Bay. A year later the laboratories were moved to Woods Hole, to become the core of the marine biology and oceanography complex there. Louis Agassiz, who was responsible for the Woods Hole motto "Study nature, not books," led expeditions to Brazil in 1865, to Cuba in 1869, and around Cape Horn to California in 1871. He died in 1873.

The son of the eminent Louis, Alexander Emmanuel Rodolphe Agassiz was born in Neuchâtel, Switzerland, in 1835. He came to the United States in 1849, and after earning an engineering degree from Harvard in 1855, he managed the Museum of Comparative Zoology for a year and then headed west to become a mine superintendent in Calumet, Michigan. By 1869 he had turned the Calumet and Hecla mines into the most profitable copper mines in the world—and himself into a millionaire. When he returned to Massachusetts, he made large donations to the MCZ, where he served as curator from 1874 to 1885. He conducted important voyages in the steamer *Blake* in the Caribbean and the Gulf of Mexico, and later he would sail aboard the U.S. Fish Commission steamer *Albatross*, dredging and collecting deep-sea specimens on expeditions to South America, the Gulf Stream, the West Indies, Hawaii, the Bahamas, Bermuda, and the Great Barrier Reef. Alexander Agassiz was the first to use wire rope for dredging, which was stronger and less cumbersome than the fiber rope used before, but despite mounting evidence to the contrary, he clung to Forbes's azoic theory and claimed that life would be found only in the top few hundred fathoms. He had also taken strong exception to Charles Darwin's theory of how coral atolls were formed and spent the last twenty years of his life gathering data to refute Darwin's idea that corals accumulated around sinking volcanoes until an atoll was formed.

Elkhorn coral (*Acropora palmata*)

Corals, the building blocks of reef formations, are small, sedentary marine organisms that are characterized by an external skeleton of a stone-like, horny, or leathery consistency. They are classified as Cnidarians, with the jellyfishes, hydroids, sea fans, and sea anemones. There are true or stony corals (scleractinians), which are the most familiar forms, occurring in various shapes such as brain coral, mushroom coral, star coral, staghorn and elkhorn coral, black and thorny corals (antipatharia), horny corals or gorgonians (gorgonacea), and blue corals (coenothecalia). The body of a coral animal consists of a polyp, a hollow, soft cylinder, with a mouth surrounded by tentacles, attached at its base to some surface. The tentacles are equipped with stinging cells (nematocysts) that paralyze their prey. At night they withdraw into the external skeleton, a cylindrical container known as a corallite or theca. Reproduction can be accomplished by releasing eggs and sperm into the water, or asexually by budding, where a fingerlike extension matures into a new polyp.

Creationism and Evolution

Coral reefs are limestone formations composed of the skeletons of dead corals that are bound together by their own limestone. Over thousands of years, coral growth and death builds a structure on which the living corals continue to live, but contributors to the reefs also include plants such as coralline algae, and also

protozoans, mollusks, and tube-building worms. Most reefs occur within a band thirty degrees north or south of the equator, but deep-water corals do not conform to the usual restrictions, having been found at depths of more than a thousand feet off Alaska, Atlantic Canada, Ireland, Norway, Sweden, Australia, New Zealand, and even the Antarctic. These corals of darkness have no symbiotic zooxanthellae (there is no light available for photosynthesis at those depths), and are therefore known as "azooxanthellate" corals. They also subsist on the minute plankton and on the "rain" of minute marine detritus that is constantly falling through the sea, and while the polyps of shallow-water corals emerge at night to feed, the deep-water corals know only darkness, and feed day and night.

While on the 1831–36 voyage of the *Beagle*, Charles Darwin became intrigued by coral reefs and identified three different kinds: fringing reefs that grew alongside the sloping shores of many islands and continents, forming broad, shallow platforms that can extend as much as a mile offshore and are exposed at low tide; and barrier reefs separated from shore by a lagoon or channel, such as the Great Barrier Reef, which runs parallel to the east coast of Australian continent

for twelve hundred miles. Then there were the atolls, irregularly shaped or oval reefs enclosing a lagoon that has no central island, with through passages to the sea. In *The Voyage of the Beagle* in 1839, and in more detail in *Structure and Distribution of Coral Reefs* in 1842, Darwin published his original ideas about how such structures could be formed. He believed that coral atolls arose on the flanks of sinking volcanic islands; as the island slowly sank beneath the sea, coral polyps built up and reached toward the surface. By the time the volcanic island has disappeared entirely, the circular ring of coral—the atoll—is the only remaining surface structure in the sea. In 1880—two years before Darwin died—Scottish oceanographer John Murray of the *Challenger* expedition read his paper "On the Structure of Coral Reefs and Islands" before the Royal Society, in which he maintained that Darwin was wrong. Murray did not believe that corals built up as volcanoes sank, but rather, that detritus raining down on already-submerged mountains built up until it was close enough to the surface for coral larvae to colonize the accumulated sediments and thus produce an atoll. The "Coral Reef Problem" engaged the scientific community for years, and in 1888, Alexander Agassiz entered the fray on Murray's side, arguing that Darwin's theory was wrong and that mountains didn't sink to form atolls. The younger Agassiz, who had followed his father as director of Harvard's Museum of Comparative Zoology, thus found himself an opponent of Darwin, just as his father had been. The elder Agassiz, who died in 1873, was one of the most fervent opponents of Darwin's theory of evolution. A year after Darwin's book appeared, Louis Agassiz wrote a rebuttal that appeared in *The American Journal of Science*. In "On the Origin of Species," he wrote:

> Individuals alone have a material existence, [while] species, genera, families, orders, classes and branches of the animal kingdom exist only as categories of thought in the Supreme Intelligence, but as such have as truly an independent existence and are as unvarying as thought itself after it has once been expressed.

This "creationist" position toppled Louis Agassiz from his pinnacle as America's foremost naturalist, a fall from which his reputation never recovered. Perhaps to restore his father's standing, Alexander, who had accumulated a fortune from his mining career, spent the next twenty years collecting data to prove that Darwin was wrong about the origin of coral reefs and that "other agencies"—specifically planktonic organisms falling to the bottom—had been responsible for the formation of atolls. For all the data he collected, however, Agassiz never published his alternative theory.

In an attempt to resolve the dispute, the Royal Society in 1897 sent a drilling expedition to the South Pacific atoll Funafuti, where they drilled 1,150 feet into the atoll but brought up nothing but coral. The question was finally resolved in 1950, when the U.S. Navy, preparing to test nuclear weapons on the island of Enewetak in the Marshall Islands, did some deep core drilling in an environmental survey of the island they were about to blow up. The first cores brought up reef rock and coral limestone. "So it went as the drills cut deeper," wrote David Dobbs in his 2005 book on the coral reef question:

> . . . 500 feet, 1,000, 2,000, 3,000, 4,000. Finally, at 4,200 feet, the drills hit what was unequivocally basement, a greenish basalt, the volcanic mountain on which the reef had originated. Dating of the tiny fossils in the bottommost layer of coral showed that the reef had gotten its start in the Eocene. For more than thirty million years this reef had been growing—an inch every millennium—on a sinking volcano, thickening as the lava beneath it subsided.

Although their Museum of Comparative Zoology at Harvard is still one of the premier institutions of its kind, it appears that Agassiz *pere et fils* both paid a heavy price for publicly disputing a theory of Charles Darwin's. As with evolution, Darwin has been proven correct about the formation of atolls.

A useful summary of the contentious interactions of Louis and Alexander Agassiz, Charles Darwin, and others involved in the Coral Reef Problem, can be found in Dobbs's *Reef Madness: Charles Darwin, Alexander Agassiz, and the Meaning of Coral*. In a review that appeared in *Nature* in May 2005, Rachel Ward of Cambridge

University wrote that the book is "a beautiful illustration of how theories can, or must, be built slowly and painfully, brick by brick, by a dynamic combination of both imaginative leaps and factual observation."

Born rich and with a passion for oceanographic explorations, Prince Albert I of Monaco financed his own expeditions at the turn of the nineteenth century, first aboard his 200-foot yacht *Hirondelle* and then aboard the even larger *Princesse Alice II*. He investigated the surface currents of the Atlantic and the Mediterranean by releasing thousands of floats, marked with instructions in nine languages to return them to Monaco, but he is remembered for developing a unique method of studying those fast-moving creatures that could not easily be caught in nets or trawls. He collected those animals that might themselves have captured midwater speedsters such as squid, and upon opening their stomachs, *voila*! the elusive cephalopods. While sailing *Princesse Alice II* through the Azores in 1895, Albert approached some Azorean whalers who had harpooned a forty-foot sperm whale and observed that the dying whale was vomiting up large pieces of squid. His crew collected the "precious regurgitations" and upon analysis recognized that they had the tentacles of a giant squid. This technique so intrigued the prince that he promptly went into the whaling business and commissioned two boats to collect various cetaceans and report to him with the stomach contents. In one instance, the crew collected two large cephalopods that were previously unknown to science. One of them (according to an 1896 article in *Nature* by J. Y. Buchanan) was "covered with large, solid, rhomboidal scales, arranged spirally like those of a pine cone." A squid with scales was highly unusual, but later examinations revealed that these were actually nipple-like projections called papillae, which only looked like scales. The species was named *Lepidoteuthis grimaldii*; *lepidos* is Greek for "scale," *teuthis* is "squid," and Grimaldi is the family name of the reigning house of Monaco.* Prince Albert I founded the Oceanographic Institute at the Sorbonne in Paris in 1906, and four years later, the Oceanographic Museum in Monaco, which was under the directorship of Jacques Cousteau from 1957 to 1988.

In 1907 the first research vessel commissioned by the Marine Biological Laboratory at La Jolla, California (later to become the Scripps Institution of Oceanography), was christened *Alexander Agassiz*. The investigations that led to the founding of Scripps Institution of Oceanography (SIO) began as summer marine biological studies conducted by University of California Professor William E. Ritter beginning in 1892. In 1903, with a group from San Diego, Ritter, who studied with Alexander Agassiz at the MCZ, established SIO, whose charter includes biological research as well as physical, chemical, geological, and geophysical studies of the oceans, earth, and atmosphere.

---

* While it doesn't have scales, *Lepidoteuthis grimaldii* is equipped with something almost as unusual: "grossly enlarged saber-like hooks" on two of the arms of the males, which, wrote Jackson and O'Shea (2003) "are more likely to be involved in reproduction than predation." The hook itself, a bladelike projection from the sucker ring, is almost an inch and a half long. The specimen they examined, a male with a mantle (body) length of 442 millimeters (17 inches), was caught about three thousand feet down, close to the bottom, by a commercial trawler off Tasmania. Since its original discovery off the Azores, *Lepidoteuthis* has been found in the deep waters of the Atlantic, in the southern Indian Ocean, and in the Pacific, from eastern Australia and Japan to Hawaii.

Marine life consists of more than fishes, and there were numerous expeditions directed toward the collection and study of other marine creatures, ranging from the smallest phytoplankton to the largest whales. German biologist Victor Hensen (1835–1924) dedicated his professional life to the study of plankton, and organized several expeditions with the goal of analyzing the minute oceanic plants and animals. (He coined the term "plankton" to refer to floating organisms that are carried passively by currents; Ernst Haeckel introduced "nekton" for those organisms that can swim against the current.) In 1889 the German ship National sailed from Kiel in what later became known as the Plankton Expedition, covering fifteen thousand miles and collecting samples from Greenland to Brazil. The expedition demonstrated, as Susan Schlee (1973) wrote, "that cold and temperate seas of the North Atlantic supported a much greater mass of planktonic life than did warm, tropical waters. Previously, it had been assumed that the reverse was true and that the sea, like the land, produced its most luxuriant growth in the tropics."

After visiting Anton Dohrn's Stazione Zoologica in Naples, E. Ray Lankester, a professor of zoology at University College, London, with Albert Günther of the British Museum, founded the Marine Biological Association (MBA) in 1886, with headquarters and laboratory at Plymouth. Largely because of anti-German sentiments that persisted long after the end of World War I, the "Kiel School" of oceanography had lost much of its influence, so biological oceanographers working at the Plymouth laboratory took the lead in oceanographic biological studies, especially of plankton. As Eric Mills (1989) wrote, they "identified the nutrient salts in seawater, extended and made more sophisticated and causal analysis of the plankton cycle that had originated at Kiel, and demonstrated the role of biological as well as chemical ones in controlling the cycle."

Until 1958 the MBA was the world leader in the study of plankton dynamics, but then the scene shifted to the United States, where G. Evelyn Hutchinson, a limnologist at Yale University, had begun a rigorous mathematical analysis of the plankton cycle. With Gordon Riley and Alfred E. Parr, Hutchinson produced one of the earliest regression analyses of factors at work in the environment—and eventually postulated what he called "the paradox of the plankton" in 1961, in which he wondered "how it is possible for a number of species to coexist in a relatively unstructured environment all competing for the same sorts of materials." It is almost axiomatic that as a result of interspecific competition, no similar species can occupy the same niche at the same time; the "competitive exclusion principle"—sometimes known as Gause's Law—suggests that in homogeneous, well-mixed environments, species that compete for the same resources cannot coexist. Hutchinson observed that plankton communities might not be in equilibrium but might be modified regularly by weather driven fluctuations. Then, in 1990, Marten Scheffer, Sergio Rinaldi, Jef Huisman, and Franz Weissing published "Why plankton communities have no equilibrium: solutions to the paradox," in which they opined that many species can indeed coexist, because fluctuations, vortices, and predation insure that no single species ever settles into equilibrium, and the "interactions between multiple species may give rise to oscillation and chaos, with continuous wax and wane of species within the community." Evidently, Hutchinson's paradox has been resolved.

Oxford-educated Alister Hardy (1896–1985) was an acknowledged authority on plankton and marine ecosystems. He was chief zoologist on the *Discovery* voyage to the Antarctic in 1925–27 (in 1967, he described his adventures and accomplishments in *Great Waters*), and in 1931 he developed the Continuous Plankton Recorder, a revolutionary collecting device that was fitted to merchant vessels, enabling them to collect samples while on their usual trading routes. His own studies of phytoplankton—summarized in his 1956 *The Open Sea: The World of Plankton*—led him to the dubious "animal exclusion hypothesis," where he postulated that toxic plant products would repel copepods. "Is it possible," he asked, "that the plants in the upper layers are giving off some substances which are injurious to the animals—having some antibiotic effect as we should say today? If so, then the animals might find it advantageous to come up in darkness to escape from their enemies?" No, said Gordon Riley and Dean Bumpus (1946), who saw that Hardy's mechanism could not be valid on Georges Bank a hundred miles off Massachusetts—and probably not elsewhere—because the mixing was so great that the zooplankton could not avoid the plant cells.

Hardy founded (and directed till 1976) the Religious Experience Research Unit at Manchester College, Oxford, which is still in existence. As time went on, he became increasingly interested in spiritual phenomena and compiled a database of religious experiences, eventually founding the Alister Hardy Trust Fund, which still investigates and tracks religious experiences. In 1949 he suggested in his presidential address to the British Association for the Advancement of Science that telepathy was relevant to biological studies. In the 1960s he published two articles in *New Scientist* in which he noted that humans, unlike all other land mammals, had subcutaneous fat, rather like the blubber of marine mammals, which led to the suggestion that humans might have gone through an aquatic period in their development. This hypothesis was elaborated and refined by Elaine Morgan in her several books and articles about the "Aquatic Ape Theory."

From Denmark in 1928–30, the Carlsberg Foundation sponsored the research vessel *Dana* as she sailed around the world collecting specimens from the surface to the depths, and publishing the results in the series known as the *Dana Reports*. Under the leadership of Johannes Schmidt, who had already solved the mystery of the spawning ground of Atlantic eels, the *Dana* sailed around the world in search of specimens and data. While the *Dana* expeditions were dedicated to the quest for information on some of the oceans' smaller inhabitants, the British *Discovery* expeditions were designed to learn about the largest creatures on earth: the whales of the Southern Ocean.

The *Discovery* first sailed to the south in 1901, with Robert Falcon Scott as expedition leader on his unsuccessful quest to be the first to reach the South Pole. Scott's expedition reached the pole on January 17, 1912, only to learn that Roald Amundsen had beaten them by about a month, and upon their return attempt, Scott's men all froze to death before they could reach the food and fuel that had been left for them at a supply depot. Refitted as a research vessel in 1925, *Discovery* sailed for the Antarctic again, with a cadre of scientists aboard (led by Alister Hardy) who would study the blue, fin, humpback, sperm, and sei whales of Antarctic waters. In 1929 the British "Discovery Committee" sent the 174-foot-long steamer *Discovery* south, and the next generation of marine scientists, cetologists, and oceanographers visited Antarctic waters and also the British whaling stations on South Georgia, where they documented, measured, photographed, and analyzed whale carcasses. The information was published in a series of *Discovery Reports*, which represented the first significant body of data about the great whales that had been gathered by anyone but whalers.[†]

Emphasizing deep waters, the Norwegian research steamer *Michael Sars* in 1900 began a series of cruises in the Norwegian Sea (between Norway and Greenland) to study salinity, temperature, movements of the water layers, floating organisms of various sizes and kinds, and the bottom fauna, especially bottom fishes. The final voyage embarked in April 1910 with various scientists aboard and an assignment that included

the publication of the results of the voyage "as soon as possible after the return of the expedition." Accordingly, in 1912 Sir John Murray, of the *Challenger* Expedition, and Johan Hjort, director of Norwegian Fisheries, compiled *The Depths of the Ocean*, which was 821 pages long and included chapters on physical oceanography, pelagic plant life, fishes from the sea bottom, invertebrate bottom fauna, pelagic animal life, and general biology. The observations were limited to the Norwegian Sea, but many of the creatures are found in other—if not all—oceans, so *The Depths of the Ocean* became the first comprehensive study of oceanography and deep-sea marine life.

David Starr Jordan (1851–1931) was probably the most influential of all American ichthyologists. He and his students dominated the field in the late nineteenth and early twentieth centuries. It has been said that all ichthyologists today can trace their professional ancestry back to Jordan. Most of his scientific career was spent on the faculty of Indiana University (1879–91) and at Stanford University (1891–1931), where he was instrumental in the founding of the Hopkins Marine Station in 1892. He served as president of Stanford until 1913 and as chancellor until 1916, whereupon he retired as chancellor emeritus. His earliest important work, *A Manual of the Vertebrate Animals of Northern United States* (1876), went through many editions. He also wrote the four-volume *The Fishes of North and Middle America* (1896–1900), *A Guide to the Study of Fishes* (1905), and with Barton W. Evermann, *The Fishes of North and Middle America: A Descriptive Catalogue of the Species of Fish-like Vertebrates Found in the Waters of North America, North of the*

[†] Whalers had previously contributed substantially to our knowledge of whales. In 1820, Captain William Scoresby wrote *An Account of the Arctic Regions with a History and Description of the Northern Whale Fishery*, which included information on the bowhead, the object of his hunt, and also on other species of whales, walruses, polar bears, and sea birds. Herman Melville was only briefly a whaler—he served for eighteen months on the whaleship *Acushnet* out of New Bedford in 1841–42—but for those who read it, *Moby-Dick* (published in 1850) contained an enormous amount of accurate information on whales and whaling. Charles Melville Scammon (no relative of Herman) was a whaling captain who wrote *The Marine Mammals of the Northwestern Coast of North America; Together with an Account of the American Whale Fishery* in 1874, which was not only a discourse on the California gray whale but a plea for the preservation of the by then overhunted whales and pinnipeds.

Isthmus of Panama (1896), and *American Food and Game Fishes* (1923.)

There were two different types of marine laboratories: the Stazione Zoologica di Napoli and the laboratories in Trieste and Sebastopole, which were exclusively devoted to research and advanced training; and the French and American institutions that were mainly aimed at teaching. Anton Dohrn, founder and first director of the Stazione Zoologica in Naples, was born in Poland in 1840 into a wealthy bourgeois family. He studied zoology and medicine at various German universities without much enthusiasm, but his life was changed in 1862 when Ernst Haeckel introduced him to Darwin's work and theories. The foundations of the Stazione Zoologica were laid in March 1872, and by September 1873, the building was finished. The core building contained laboratories, pumps, machines, storerooms, and a public aquarium in the basement. The aquarium was opened on January 26, 1874. It has changed little since its creation; it is the oldest nineteenth-century aquarium still functioning, as well as the only one exclusively dedicated to Mediterranean fauna. Many marine biology institutions now have attached aquariums—the New York Zoological Society (opened in 1896), Scripps (1905), Monaco (1910), the California Academy of Sciences (1929), Woods Hole (1930)—but the Stazione Zoologica was the first.

Henry Bigelow (1879–1967) was a pioneering ocean researcher whose extensive investigations in the early part of the twentieth century were later recognized as the foundation of modern oceanography. Bigelow's work stressed the interdependence of biology, chemistry, and physical science in studying the ocean. His 1929 report to the U.S. National Academy of Sciences led to establishment of the Woods Hole Oceanographic Institution in 1930, of which he was the founding director. After joining the staff of Harvard's Museum of Comparative Zoology in 1905, Bigelow published papers on various biological subjects. He joined the teaching faculty of Harvard in 1921 and became an internationally known expert on the coelenterates and on fishes, especially sharks and rays. With William C. Schroeder, Bigelow authored volumes I and II of the multivolume *Fishes of the Western North Atlantic* (sharks and rays), and later, *Fishes of the Gulf of Maine* (1953). The Sears Foundation for Marine Research at Yale University has now published nine volumes of *Fishes of the Western North Atlantic*, which are considered the definitive works on the subject.

After graduating from Yale in 1910, industrialist Harry Payne Bingham (1887–1955) became interested in marine biology and began collecting fishes as a hobby. In his yachts *Pawnee I* and *Pawnee II*, Bingham explored the waters of the Caribbean and the Gulf of California, collecting fish and other marine organisms. When he had collected enough specimens to populate a private museum, he hired ichthyologists as curators and in 1927 began publication of the *Bulletin of the Bingham Oceanographic Collection*. (The Bingham Lab was originally housed in a former residential mansion on Hillhouse Avenue in New Haven, where the library was in the grand ballroom lit by a crystal chandelier, and the fish collection was stored in the wine cellar.) Bingham's collection was donated to Yale in 1930, and the Bingham Oceanographic Foundation was established, with Alfred E. Parr as its first director. The

Bingham Oceanographic Laboratory financed Parr's research expeditions to the Gulf of Mexico, and Gordon Riley's plankton studies in Long Island Sound and Georges Bank. In 1959 the Bingham Oceanographic Collection was integrated into the Yale Peabody Museum's ichthyology collection.

Bingham's endeavors exemplified the early years of "marine biology," which consisted of collecting as many specimens as possible of species of fishes, sharks, squids, octopuses, shrimps, oysters, clams, crabs, sponges, sea cucumbers, worms, starfishes, jellyfishes, and other macrofauna, as well as the radiolarians, foraminifera, fish larvae, and other minuscule creatures. In addition to its inhabitants, the water itself was studied, its temperature taken, its depths plumbed, its quality sampled, and the shape and structure of its basins analyzed. Sounding lines and collecting trawls were lowered into the depths, but for the most part, marine scientists on the decks of ships collected their material, brought it up, and analyzed it in the laboratory. Although Jules Verne—the father of "science fiction"—predicted it in his 1870 *Twenty Thousand Leagues Under the Sea*, the actual exploration of the depths by people who descended in some sort of a self-contained underwater vessel did not begin until the 1930s.

Most people know the exploits of Verne's *Nautilus*, either through the book *Twenty Thousand Leagues Under the Sea* or through the 1954 Disney film, starring Kirk Douglas as Ned Land, the Canadian harpooner, Paul Lukas as Professor Arronax of the Paris Museum, Peter Lorre as his servant Conseil, and James Mason as Captain Nemo. The submarine sails around the world several times; encounters all sorts of fishes, whales, sharks, manatees, and corals; battles a giant squid; sails through a subterranean tunnel that connects the Red Sea with the Mediterranean; explores the sunken city of Atlantis; sails to the South Pole and thence to the Amazon; and finally, off the coast of Norway, the *Nautilus* is lost in the dreaded Maelstrom. (Nemo goes down with his ship, but Arronax, Conseil, and Ned Land are cast ashore on one of the Lofoten Islands, there to await the next steamboat to France.)

Twenty Thousand Leagues Under the Sea is a marvelous tale and demonstrates what Walter Miller describes as "typical of Verne's approach that he would choose a scientific subject at this stage in its development. Thus his immediate readers would live to see some of his prophecies borne out, while later generations would still be waiting for others to be realized." In some cases, they would have to wait a long time. Verne applies a scientific veneer to his work, and while some of his observations are based on the state of scientific knowledge of his times, others are pure fantasy, like the submarine itself. His descriptions of sharks, whales, giant squid, manatees, and dugongs, not to mention Atlantis and the tunnel from the Red Sea into the Mediterranean, are literary devices designed to move his story along, and bear no recognizable relationship to zoology, geology, or history as we now understand these subjects. *Twenty Thousand Leagues Under the Sea* was enormously popular and has gone through countless printings, not to mention several movie versions, so what many people knew (or know) of marine biology, they learned from Jules Verne. ✍

"Monsters" of Inner Space

The oceanographers and marine biologists who followed the redoubtable Captain Nemo believed that one of the best ways to learn about marine life was to observe it first-hand, and this required a way to descend below the surface and remain there long enough to see what was going on. A way to breathe while underwater was also necessary. Alexander the Great, who died in 323 B.C., is—among his other accomplishments—considered the father of submersible diving, primarily because of legends that tell of his descent in a glass "barrel." No further explanation of the Macedonian king's craft or exploits exists—the story first appeared in a thirteenth-century French manuscript—but salvage divers of sixteenth-century Italy are known to have descended in bells containing air reservoirs to explore sunken barges, and Leonardo da Vinci (1452–1519) toyed with the idea of a device for underwater exploration.* In 1578 an Englishman named William Bourne described a primitive submarine in his *Inventions and Devises* (subtitled "Very Necessary for Generalles, Captaines or Leaders of Men"), a vessel with a rigid wooden outer hull and a flexible inner hull that was made of leather. The double hull, of course, is still used in submarine design, as is his concept of submerging or surfacing the vessel by varying the amount of water it displaced. As far as we know, Bourne's invention was never implemented, but in 1620, Dutch physician Cornelis van Drebbel moved to London as tutor to the children of King James I. He delighted Londoners—the King among them—with his "submarine displays," which evidently consisted of rowers powering a greased leather boat downward until it was awash in the Thames. Van Drebbel, who dabbled in magic and perpetual motion, claimed to have discovered a "liquor" that could purify the air in his submarine, but he was so secretive about his inventions that the nature of his air purifier was never revealed.

Since Alexander the Great saw a creature that took three days to pass his submerged barrel, the idea of descending into the depths has fascinated mankind. Some of the problems—breathing, locomotion, stability—had been tentatively resolved during the development of the submarine, but except in fiction, no one had yet equipped a submersible vessel with the necessary equipment that would enable its passengers to submerge for any length of time and observe what could be

---

* Leonardo's device, known only from his sketchbooks, appeared to consist of a breathing tube that was kept at the surface by a float. A diver using such an arrangement only four feet below the surface would be unable to expand his lungs to overcome the external water pressure and, therefore, could not draw air into the tube. Unlike water, air is compressible, and as water pressure increases around it, it occupies a progressively smaller space, whether or not the water is actually in contact with the air-holding vessel, be it a submarine or human lungs. In a submersible vessel, on the other hand, the air pressures in the submersible and in the lungs of the occupants remains equal, and as long as enough fresh air is provided, the occupants of a submersible can continue expanding their chests to breathe.

seen around them. Jules Verne took us twenty thousand leagues around the world underwater in 1870, and shortly before the turn of the century, the man who was responsible for *The Time Machine* and *War of the Worlds* wrote a story that presaged the first descent in a bathysphere. Herbert George Wells (1866–1946), a former schoolmaster with a vivid and wonderful imagination, published a story he called "In the Abyss."

From shipboard in an unspecified location, a man called Elstead prepares to descend in a nine-foot-diameter steel sphere equipped with "a couple of windows of enormously thick glass." With a complement of lead weights, the device is to be lowered overboard to sink five miles to the bottom, where Elstead proposes "to stay for half an hour, with the electric light on, looking about. . . ." At the conclusion of his visit to the bottom, the sinkers will be cast off as a complicated clockwork mechanism releases a spring knife that cuts the rope so the sphere will shoot to the surface "like a soda-water bubble." (Elstead has calculated that at a rate of two feet per second, it would take three-quarters of a minute to reach the bottom, and the same amount of time to ascend.) Even in his wild imaginings, Wells could not make this Rube Goldberg contraption work, and instead of rocketing to the surface in a couple of minutes, the sphere does not reappear until dawn of the following day, when it is found bobbing at the surface with Elstead still alive.

Elstead tells a story that would embarrass Jules Verne. Upon reaching bottom, he was surrounded by "a heavy blackness—as black as black velvet," but soon saw "small, large-eyed or blind things, [some] having a curious resemblance to woodlice, some to lobsters." No one, especially Elstead, was prepared for what appeared next:

It was a strange vertebrated animal. Its dark purple head was dimly suggestive of a chameleon, but it had such a high forehead and such a braincase as no reptile had ever displayed before; the vertical pitch of its face gave it a most extraordinary resemblance to a human being. Two large and protruding eyes projected from sockets in chameleon fashion, and it had a broad reptilian mouth with horny lips beneath its little nostrils. In the position of the ears were two huge gill-covers, and out of these floated a branching tree of coraline filaments, almost like the tree-like gills that very young sharks and rays possess.

We do not know if William Beebe (1877–1962) ever read H. G. Wells's story, but within thirty years of its publication, Beebe was being lowered toward the abyss in a steel sphere with thick windows. (We can safely assume that he was not looking for Wells's "unsuspected cities.") Designed and operated in 1930 by Beebe and Otis Barton for the New York Zoological Society, the bathysphere was the first purely investigative submersible. It was made of cast steel an inch and a quarter thick. Three inches less than five feet in diameter, it weighed two and a quarter tons, and had three "windows" made of three-inch-thick quartz, because, according to Beebe, "it is the strongest transparent substance known and it transmits all wavelengths of light." The bathysphere's passengers—there was only room for two—climbed in and out through a fourteen-inch door, which had to be lifted on and off with a block and tackle and bolted shut with ten heavy bolts. The sphere was suspended from a braided steel cable that was seven-eighths of an inch in diameter and thirty-five hundred feet long. There was an additional electrical cable that carried the lights and telephone wires, and the air came from oxygen tanks fitted to the interior, with trays of "powdered chemicals" to absorb the moisture and carbon dioxide. The air in the capsule was kept circulating by hand-held, woven palm-frond fans.

Charles William Beebe was recognized as one of the foremost scientists—and popularizers of science—of his or any other time. He wrote more than eight hundred scientific and popular articles in magazines and journals ranging from the *Bulletin of the New York Zoological Society* and *National Geographic* to *Harper's* and *Ladies Home Journal*. He studied a wide range of subjects, including pheasants (on which he wrote a definitive monograph in 1922) and also what was probably his consuming passion, the exploration of the sea. In *The Arcturus Adventure* (1926) he discussed his expeditions to the Sargasso Sea, the Galápagos, and Hudson Gorge (off New York City); in *Nonsuch: Land of Water*, he visited Nonsuch Island off Bermuda, and two years later, he published what he and many others considered his most enduring work: *Half Mile Down*. Brad Matsen's 2005 book about Beebe's adventures in the bathysphere is called *Descent: The Heroic Discovery of the Abyss*.

Off Nonsuch Island in Bermuda, theirs was a simple descent; they climbed into the cramped, cold sphere, the hatch was bolted shut, and then the ball was lifted up by a crane and lowered into the ocean. As they descended, Beebe and his fellow aquanaut Barton[†] watched the light change, and carefully recorded each creature that passed before the quartz portholes. They saw many species of fishes and invertebrates that they expected to see and many that they believed had

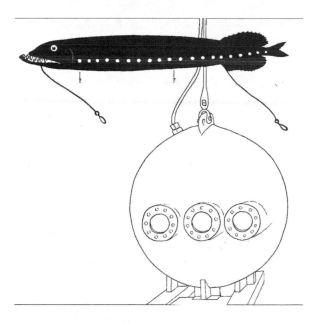

William Beebe's bathysphere with the "untouchable bathysphere fish," *Bathysphaera intacta*. (From the *Bulletin of the New York Zoological Society*, 1932. Vol. 35, No. 5: p. 175.)

never before been seen by the eyes of man. At a depth of twenty-one hundred feet, Beebe saw a pair of fishes that passed within eight feet of the windows. His description first appears in a two-page note (plus drawing) in 1932 in the New York Zoological Society's *Bulletin*; and then, along with the same illustration, in his book *Half Mile Down*.

---

† Both Beebe and Barton wrote books on the subject of diving in the bathysphere. Beebe's is *Half Mile Down* (1934), and Barton's is *The World Beneath the Sea* (1953), but their bathysphere unexpectedly appears in Thomas Mann's *Dr. Faustus*, written in 1948. In Mann's story, composer Adrian Leverkühn enters into a pact with the devil, where he offers to exchange his soul for twenty-eight years of musical success. Because he was seeking every sort of heightened experience, Leverkühn descends in "a bullet-shaped diving bell . . . equipped somewhat like a stratosphere balloon, and dropped from a crane into the sea." It is lowered to 2,509 feet (765 meters), and they observe "predatory mouths opening and shutting; obscene jaws, telescope eyes; the paper nautilus; silver- and gold-fish with goggling eyes on top of their heads; heteropods and pteropods up to two or three yards long."

The "untouchable bathysphere fish" (*Bathysphaera intacta*) was "at least six feet in length . . . there was a single row of strong, pale blue lights along the side. . . . There were two ventral tentacles, each tipped with a pair of separate, luminous bodies, the superior reddish, the lower one blue . . . the position of the fish must be somewhere near the Melanostomiatidae, but the single line of large, lateral photophores and the two ventral tentacles set it apart from any known species or genus." In *Fishes of the Western North Atlantic,* where it is listed as *incertae cedis*—"relationships uncertain," Morrow and Gibbs (1964) wrote, "As Beebe noted, the systematic position of this fish is most uncertain. However, it is probably as near to the Melanostomiatidae as to any other group, and it is included here on the off chance that some day a specimen may be found."

In the ensuing years, no specimen of "*Bathysphaera*" has been found. Although we cannot say with certainty that it will not be, it seems somewhat unlikely that a six-foot-long stomiatid will appear when all the known varieties are less than two feet in length and the majority much smaller than that. In his review of Beebe's *Half Mile Down*, Carl Hubbs (1935) wrote that *Bathysphaera* was "twice as long as any known fish with this general type of illumination," and Beebe and Crane (1939)—in the same article in which *Bathysphaera* was described as "still uncertain"—wrote that "the largest known melanostomiatid is the unique specimen of *Opostomias*, measuring 380 mm [15 inches] in length." The red and blue lights on the "tentacles" are another anomaly, but then, the only person ever to claim to have seen this creature in its natural habitat—or anywhere

else—was William Beebe. Why didn't Barton see *Bathysphaera*?

In a paper entitled "Three New Deep-sea Fish Seen from the Bathysphere," Beebe described the "pallid sailfin" (*Bathyembryx istiophasma*), which he saw twice; once at fifteen hundred feet, and again at twenty-five hundred feet on August 11, 1934, six and a half miles south by east of Nonsuch Island. It was a cigar-shaped fish, about two feet long, with sail-like, triangular fins and a tiny

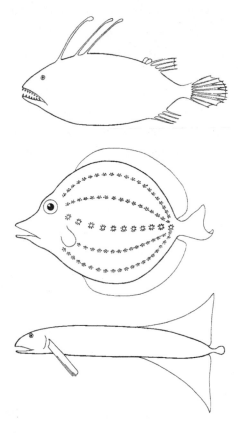

Three species seen from Beebe's bathysphere and never seen again: the "Three-starred Anglerfish," the "Five-lined Constellationfish," and the "Pallid Sailfin." (From the *Bulletin of the New York Zoological Society,* 1934. Vol. 37, No. 6: pp. 190–193.)

tail. "The color," wrote Beebe, "was peculiar, an unpleasant, pale, olive drab, like water-soaked flesh, an unhealthy-looking buff." Unfortunately, the appearance of a second specimen seems to have so unnerved Beebe that he missed the opportunity to photograph the pallid sailfin. He wrote, "as I was getting ready to hold Mr. Barton's camera for a possible exposure, I had a distinct if brief glimpse of a fish which came down the light, head on. When it turned quickly, I saw that it was the same, or another individual *Bathyembryx*."

From the bathysphere at a depth of 2,470 feet in Bermuda waters, Beebe recorded the second mystery fish; a six-inch-long anglerfish with "three tall illicia [lures], slender, apparently stiff, each about one-third the length of the fish . . . each had a slightly enlarged tip [that] gave out a strong, pale yellow light, powerful enough to illuminate the adjacent dorsal skin when the fish was not in the path of my beam." He named it *Bathyceratias trilychnus*, the "three-starred angler-fish."

The last of the three "new" fishes was probably the most unusual of all. While it might be possible for something like the "pallid sailfin" or the "three-starred anglerfish" to inhabit the black depths, the appearance of a butterfly fish or a surgeonfish at three hundred fathoms (1,800 feet) in the open ocean would be surprising indeed. And yet, there it was, outside the bathysphere, "one of the most unexpected and gorgeous deep-sea inhabitants I have ever seen." It was round and flattened, rather like a surgeonfish, "with long, moderately high, continuous, vertical fins and a deeply concave tail, exactly like the fins of *Acanthurus*." But unlike the fishes of the reefs that it resembled in shape, the five-lined constellation-fish *(Bathysidus pentagrammus)*

was bedecked with five rows of photophores, all consisting of a pale yellow central component, surrounded by rows of tiny, brilliant purple lights. "I can assign this fish to no known family," wrote Beebe, "but the Five-lined Constellation-fish assuredly deserves a name, pending the time when, with improved trawling nets, we will be able to bring one to the surface." The "constellation fish" outraged ichthyologist Carl Hubbs, and in the journal *Copeia* (1933), he said that it was "so utterly at variance with any system of fish photophores that I am forced to suggest that whatever the author saw might have been a phosphorescent coelenterate whose lights were beautified by halation in passing through a misty film breathed onto the quartz window by Mr. Beebe's eagerly appressed face."

Another sight vouchsafed to Beebe and no one else was the "rainbow gars," which he spotted in a group of four, swimming vertically, head-up, off Bermuda, at a depth of twenty-five hundred feet. Following his historic dive in the bathysphere, Beebe issued a stream of publications, many of which appeared in the scientific as well as the popular canon. The description of the "rainbow gars" (with an illustration by Else Bostelmann), appeared in the *National Geographic* in 1934, and also in his book *Half Mile Down*, published in the same year. In many instances, he bestowed a scientific name on these hitherto undescribed species, but for the "rainbow gars," he restricted himself to a common name. Here is his account from *Half Mile Down*:

At 11:17 o'clock I turned the light on suddenly, and saw a strange quartet of fish, to which I have not been able to fit a genus or family. Shape, size, and one fin I saw clearly, but Abyssal Rainbow Gars is as far as I dare go, and they may be anything but gars. About four inches over all, they were slender and stiff with long, sharply pointed jaws. . . . There they stood, for they were almost upright, and I could see only a slight fanning with the dorsal fin . . . the amazing thing about them was their unexpected pattern and color. The jaws and head were brilliant scarlet, which, back of the gills, changed abruptly into a light but strong blue and this merged insensibly into a clear yellow on the posterior body and tail.

No one has ever seen or captured anything that remotely resembles Beebe's "rainbow gars," and the "unexpected pattern and color" have not been observed in any fish, at any depth, on the surface or even among the usually brightly colored inhabitants of coral reefs.

In various articles and then again in *Half Mile Down*, Beebe described another creature that nobody saw but him:

At 2450 [feet] a very large, dim, but not indistinct outline came into view for a fraction of a second, and at 2500 a delicately illumined ctenophore jelly throbbed past. Without warning, the large fish returned and this time I saw its complete, shadow-like contour as it passed through the farthest end of the beam. Twenty feet is the least possible estimate I can give to its full length, and it was deep in proportion. The whole fish was monochrome, and I could not see even an eye or a fin. For the majority of the "size-conscious" human race this MARINE MONSTER would, I suppose, be the supreme sight of the expedition. In shape it was a deep oval, it swam without evident effort, and it did not return. That is all I can contribute, and while its unusual size so excited me that for several hundred feet I kept keenly on the lookout for hints of the same or other large fish, I soon forgot it in the (very literal) light of smaller, but more distinct and interesting organisms.

What this great creature was I cannot say. A first, and most reasonable guess would be a small whale or blackfish. We know that whales have a special chemical adjustment of the blood which makes it possible for them to dive a mile or more, and come up without getting the "bends." So this paltry depth of 2450 feet would be nothing for any similarly equipped cetacean. Or, less likely, it may have been a whale shark, which is known to reach a length of forty feet. Whatever it was, it appeared and vanished so unexpectedly and showed so dimly that it was quite unidentifiable except as a large, living creature.

In his 2001 book *Creatures of the Deep*, science writer Erich Hoyt had this to say about Beebe's mystery monster:

Many animals were only barely seen or were too strange for Beebe to name, much less attempt to draw. One of these—the big one that got away on his record dive—involved a massive, colorless 20-foot-long (6m) fish at 2,450 feet (750m). Beebe missed the face as well as the fins of the behemoth as it glided into and then immediately out of view. He called for Barton to check it out, but by the time Barton looked though his porthole, the creature was gone.

It would not be until 1975 that John Isaacs and Richard Schwartzlose would publish a photograph of a sixgill shark (*Hexanchus griseus*) taken at a depth of 2,460 feet in the eastern Mediterranean, establishing the species as one of the largest of the known deep-sea vertebrates. (Some of the cetaceans that Beebe refers to—particularly the sperm whale—can dive even deeper, but they are not full-time inhabitants of the depths.) *Hexanchus griseus* is known to reach a length of eighteen feet, but there are even larger deep-sea sharks, such as the Greenland shark (*Somniosus microcephalus*), whose range includes Bermuda waters, so if Beebe actually saw this MARINE MONSTER (the caps are his), it is very likely to have been a species of large deep-sea shark.

It is possible that Beebe was the only person ever to see these mysterious creatures. It is also possible that he made them up, but although he wrote cleverly and well, there is very little in his published work to indicate that he was a practical joker. In Otis Barton's 1953 book *The World Beneath the Sea*, he describes an incident where they were both looking out of a porthole of the bathysphere, when Barton saw some lights that he thought "must be a string of invertebrates," but Beebe "suggested that it was the lights at the base of the teeth of a giant toadfish." Was this an attempt at humor? Perhaps the temptation to put one over on the academic community was too great for Beebe, who had neither a graduate nor an undergraduate degree. (His only degree was an honorary Sc.D. awarded to him by Tufts University in 1928, and according to Berra (1977), "the statement in

Current Biography that Beebe received a Bachelor of Science degree from Columbia is incorrect.")‡

Beebe had to know that even if future investigators lowered a submersible in the same location, to the same depth, even at the same time of year, there was no guarantee that they would see the same things that he had seen. His *incertae cedis* reports could enter the literature—as they have done—with virtually no possibility of being discounted. It is, after all, one of the basic tenets of cryptozoology that negative evidence cannot be disproved. The fact that no one has ever seen a Sasquatch does not prove that it does not exist. Except for Beebe's descriptions, the "untouchable bathysphere fish," the "pallid sailfin," and the "five-lined constellation fish" are still unknown. No further sightings or specimens have appeared.

It is impossible to say with certainty that these fishes do not exist; it may require another thousand dives or ten thousand trawls to collect them. But the very fact that they have not been seen since Beebe originally described them casts their existence into doubt. We will never know if he really saw the "abyssal rainbow gars" or the

---

‡ Incredibly, there is a precedent for falsifying fishes and publishing the descriptions in scientific journals. As told by Australian ichthyologist Gilbert Whitley in a 1933 article, "In the Proceedings of the Linnaean Society of New South Wales . . .," Count F. de Castelnau wrote a short paper, "On a New Ganoid Fish from Queensland," in which he described "*Ompax spatuloides*," found in a single waterhole in the Burnett River. No size was recorded, but it was described (and illustrated) as "a ganoid fish with a very elongate and very depressed spatuli-form snout . . . having much the form of the beak of the Platypus. . . . the body is covered with large ganoid scales . . . nothing is said of the dentition." It was later revealed that "*Ompax spatuloides*" was a prank played on Carl T. Staiger, director of the Brisbane Museum, but by the time Whitley published his story in *The American Midland Naturalist* in 1933, and again in his 1940 Fishes of Australia, the damage had been done, and *Ompax* appears occasionally in the legitimate ichthyological literature

"three-starred anglerfish"; all we know is that nobody else has ever seen them. To cement his reputation as a proper scientist, Beebe wrote dozens of descriptions of new species, usually accompanied by their newly minted scientific names. (He also liked to give them popular names, such as "beacon-finned dragonfish" or "saber-toothed viperfish," which speaks to his celebrity as a popular author.) The existence of the great majority of deep-sea fishes described by Beebe is confirmed by specimens that reside in jars in the collections of various museums and laboratories, available for examination by interested scientists. (A new species is erected when comparison with similar specimens shows that the new one is sufficiently different from the others to warrant its designation as a new species.)

In *Creatures of the Deep*, Erich Hoyt wrote that most of Beebe's descriptions "fit creatures that we know today inhabit the middle layers, just where he saw them. . . . Beebe's 'untouchable bathysphere fish' turned out to be a new species of dragonfish." But Beebe's picture of *Bathysphera intacta* belies such a statement: there is no known species of dragonfish that is six feet long; none with a chin and a fin barbel; and none with two different-colored lights on each "tentacle." Despite their official-sounding names, there are no specimens of *Bathysphera intacta*, *Bathyceratias trilychnus*, *Bathysidus pentagrammus*, or *Bathyembryx istiophasma* for scientists to examine; there are only Beebe's descriptions. Three-quarters of a century after his observations were published, not a single specimen of any of Beebe's mystery fishes has appeared in a net, in a trawl, or on a video screen. Assuming that we will not find evidence of their existence, we must perforce assign them to what is certainly the most esoteric category in all of biology: the unknowable.

Although he later traveled all over the world, exploring, diving, collecting, and filming, Otis Barton's true love was the bathysphere. He wrote: "Since coming home from the war, I had been living in a world bereft of meaning. . . . Only in the machine shop where parts of hydraulic presses moved about overhead, did I feel that I was touching reality." He designed and had built the "benthoscope," another fifty-four-inch diameter steel sphere with walls that were a half inch thicker than those of the bathysphere. With this extra thickness, he wrote, "the benthoscope could dive to ten thousand feet whereas the bathysphere could in theory dive to only forty-five hundred feet before the water flattened it out." Where the bathysphere had cost Barton a total of twelve thousand dollars (he financed most of the expedition out of an inheritance), the 1948 version cost him sixteen thousand dollars. After several aborted tries in the Bahamas, Barton took the benthoscope to California, where he was lowered to a then-record forty-five hundred feet in the Santa Cruz Canyon. This 1948 dive stood as the record for manned submersibles until 1960, when *Trieste* broke all the records.

Earlier oceanographers, such as Edward Forbes, had dismissed the possibilities of life at great depths, referring to the regions below three hundred fathoms as the "azoic," or lifeless, zone. But the collecting expeditions of Wyville Thomson's *Porcupine* and the *Challenger* in the latter half of the nineteenth century demonstrated that this was far from correct. The seabed was alive with invertebrate animals, such as sponges, hydroids, anemones, gorgonians, worms, starfish, and so on, which were brought up for examination, first by using various nets and dredges, and later by "grabs," that consisted of a pair of metal jaws that could take great bites of the bottom and its fauna. On their 1950–52 expedition, *Galathea*'s crew used a "Petersen Grab" to make twenty-eight samplings from two thousand meters, seven of which were from trenches deeper than six thousand meters. In an article entitled "The Density of Animals on the Ocean Floor," Ragnar Spärck of the *Galathea* wrote:

> The result of our investigations in this field, therefore, is that on the ocean floor there are about 10 animals per square metre with a total weight of about one gram. This is an astonishingly large figure considering that at a depth of a few hundred metres in Northern European and Mediterranean waters there are only a few grams of animals per square metre. This surprising density right down to between 5,000 and 8,000 metres suggests that food conditions in the abyss are not so poor as we have been inclined to think, and this in turn leads us to suppose that abyssal water currents may be stronger than formerly believed.

At ten animals per square meter, with a total weight of about one gram, the "density" of invertebrates on the seabed seems rather sparse, but it is orders of magnitude greater than the lifeless emptiness imagined by Edward Forbes. In *The Face of the Deep*, a 1971 collection of more than six hundred seafloor photographs, renowned oceanographers Bruce Heezen and Charles Hollister wrote:

The animals living on the abyssal floor are rarely as large as a robin, and only a few are as large as a mouse. In fact, most deep sea creatures are smaller than honeybees, and thus are far too small to be seen in normal photographs. For example, clams, worms, and crustaceans are extremely common forms brought up in trawls with meshes finer than one-quarter millimeter, but only a few of these are large enough to be seen in photographs. . . . Only the sponges, fans, pens, fans, anemones, corals, mosses, lilies, starfish, brittle stars, urchins, cucumbers, squid and octopuses, crabs, spiders, acorn worms, eels, squirts, and fish include a number of large identifiable forms.

It was not enough just to haul mud and little animals up from the bottom; people had to see for themselves what the seafloor looked like. (Beebe's bathysphere never approached the floor of the ocean; the technology available at that time was barely adequate to lower the bathysphere "a half mile down," and let it hang there until it was time to winch it up.) Auguste Piccard's first attempt to send an unattached submersible vessel into the depths—and most important, bring it back—occurred in 1948 off Dakar in West Africa. Based on the principle he had used to ascend into the atmosphere in a balloon filled with lighter-than-air hydrogen gas, Piccard designed a submarine that carried as its buoyancy device a huge quantity of gasoline, which is lighter than water, and more important, is compressible with increased depth. The flotation tank was open to the sea, which meant that the gasoline always sat on top of the entering water, to provide buoyancy. In addition to the gasoline-filled "blimp," *FNRS-2* consisted of a ten-ton steel sphere that served as the cockpit, two air tanks, and ballast hoppers filled with tons of magnetized iron pellets that would be demagnetized and dropped should there be a power failure, thus causing the vessel to "fall up" toward the surface. On November 3, 1948, from the Belgian cargo vessel *Scaldis*, the fifteen-ton, robot-operated *FNRS-2* was lowered over the side, and its tether slipped. The unmanned submersible had descended to 4,554 feet and returned when an automatic timing device had unballasted it. The cabin withstood the pressure successfully, but the float was severely damaged upon surfacing in heavy swells, and more solid structures were designed for surface towing.

Encouraged by their experiments with *FNRS-2*, Auguste Piccard and his son Jacques ranged the European capitals for funds, and finally amassed enough money to build *Trieste*, named for the Adriatic seaport where she was built. The fifty-foot-long flotation hull was designed to hold twenty-eight thousand gallons of gasoline, and suspended below it was the passenger compartment, a ten-ton, forged-steel chamber with an inside diameter of seven feet. The portholes were six-inch-thick truncated cones made of a newly developed, shatterproof plastic called Plexiglas. The bathyscaph descended by taking on water ballast into the forward and aft tanks and by valving off small quantities of gasoline. She could be moved forward or backward by the use of propellers located on top of the hull, but only in a limited way. In August 1953, off Castellammare in southern Italy, with Piccard *pere et fils* aboard, *Trieste* made her first successful manned descent—twenty-six feet down to the bottom of the harbor. There followed a succession of deeper dives in the Mediterranean from 1953 to 1956: 3,540 feet in the Bay of Naples; 10,300 feet in the Tyrrhenian Sea. ❧

Dark but Still Filled with Life

In 1958 Piccard sold the *Trieste* to the U.S. Office of Naval Research (ONR), but stayed on as a consultant. (Jacques was the primary pilot.) Previously, she had been based in Castellammare in Italy, but Piccard could not afford the upkeep and expenses on his own and needed government support. Robert Dietz, a geological

oceanographer, was working for ONR at this time, and with Piccard realized the potential of the submersible for on-site observations of the deep ocean. In 1959 ONR transported *Trieste* to Guam for "Project Nekton," which Dietz named for the free-swimming animals of the sea, as contrasted with the plankton, which moves at the mercy of currents. They were going to send the submersible down 35,800 feet, to the bottom of the Challenger Deep* in the Marianas Trench—the *dive to la plus grande profondeur*, the deepest possible dive in the world.

The sphere that had been forged in Italy was not considered strong enough for such a dive, so a new one was manufactured by the Krupp steel works in Germany. New instrumentation was designed and built in Switzerland, and the revised electronics were supplied by the U.S. Navy. Record after record fell as the bathyscaph made practice dives: 18,150 feet; 24,000 feet; and finally, on January 23, 1960, with Lieutenant Don Walsh

---

* Although the greatest depth in the ocean probably ought to have been named for the greatest oceanographic expedition of all time, it was in fact named for a successor to the original *Challenger*, the British research vessel *Challenger II*. In 1949 at the southern end of the Marianas Trench, oceanographers recorded an echo that corresponded to a depth of 5,900 fathoms, almost a thousand feet deeper than the previously known greatest depth in the Philippine Trench.

as copilot, Jacques Piccard and the *Trieste* landed on the bottom at 5,966 fathoms (35,800 feet). As Piccard described it:

> The bottom appeared light and clear, a waste of snuff-colored ooze. We were landing on a nice, flat bottom of firm diatomaceous ooze. Indifferent to the nearly 200,000 tons of pressure clamped on her metal sphere, the *Trieste* balanced herself delicately on the few pounds of guide rope that lay on the bottom, making token claim, in the name of science and humanity, to the ultimate depths in all our oceans—the Challenger Deep.
>
> Immediately, Edward Forbes' smug declaration, that no life could exist in the depths, was resoundingly refuted once for all, as a foot-long flatfish moved out of the way of the descending steel monster. At the very bottom of creation, in water that was seven miles deep, there was a fish, and even more startling, a fish with eyes.

It is unfortunate that *Trieste* was not equipped with an external camera. Shortly after *Trieste*'s historic dive, Torben Wolff of the Zoological Museum of Copenhagen published a note in *Nature* in which he disputed the identification of the fish. Despite the "eyes," he suggested that it was not a fish at all, but probably a holothurian, or sea cucumber, "perhaps related to the bathypelagic, cushion-shaped *Galatheathuria aspera*, which is almost a foot long and oval in outline." Even though he knew that "negative records are naturally of less value," he wrote that "no flatfish was collected in or close to any of the [other] trenches investigated" and that *Chascanopsetta lugubris* [the fish tentatively identified by Piccard] "was previously recorded only between depths of 220 and 977 m." (720 and 3,204 feet). In a *Newsweek* article published in July 1993 (on the subject of submersibles), writer Tony Emerson quoted ichthyologist Richard Rosenblatt of Scripps as saying, "Everyone agrees it was a sea cucumber."

Fish or sea cucumber, the presence of a living creature at the oceans' greatest depth was a further stimulus for bathypelagic exploration. Around 1966 J. Louis Reynolds of Reynolds Metals (later Reynolds Aluminum) commissioned *Aluminaut*. Built by Electric Boat of Groton, Connecticut, the fifty-one-foot reinforced aluminum cylinder weighed seventy-three tons in air. Positive buoyancy was provided by the rigid, lightweight hull (the aluminum is less compressible than seawater, so the deeper *Aluminaut* went, the more buoyant she became), and negative buoyancy—the ability to descend—was provided by shot ballast. With a crew of three operators and three observers as well as a substantial array of equipment, she could perform many different chores, often simultaneously. Her great size and weight, however, meant that *Aluminaut* could not be lifted aboard conventional oceanographic vessels, and she had to be towed—often infuriat-

ingly slowly—to her destinations. Originally designed to reach depths of 22,000 feet, she tested successfully only to 15,000, and in fact, the maximum depth she achieved was 6,250 feet. When *Aluminaut* proved incapable of diving to great depths, Woods Hole Oceanographic Institution let out bids for a more efficient deep-diving submersible. The competition was won by General Mills—the cereal manufacturer—but before construction was completed, Litton Industries purchased the General Mills electronics and manipulator division and in 1964, delivered *Alvin*.

Named for its designer, Allyn Vine (1915–1994), an engineer at Woods Hole (but also named for "The Chipmunk Song" that was popular during the design phase), *Alvin* was built for about a million dollars. Although the twenty-five-foot sub is more mobile than its predecessors, the people-capsule is essentially the same as the bathysphere; a metal sphere that encloses and protects the passengers and can be separated from the frame in case of trouble. Like the submersibles that preceded her, *Alvin* depends on ballast—in this case, 200-pound blocks of steel—that can be jettisoned to allow the submersible to rise. There is one porthole in front for the pilot, two on the sides for the observers, and one that looks straight down. Passengers breathe oxygen from tanks, and canisters of lithium hydroxide absorb carbon dioxide, a system that provides two days' worth of livable atmosphere, even though most dives are supposed to last no more than eight hours. The original aluminum frame has been replaced by titanium, and her depth range has been increased from 6,000 to 14,764 feet.

"The study of the deep-sea benthos," wrote Frederick Grassle and colleagues in 1975, "has added greatly to our understanding. . . . Yet such investigations suffer because of the remoteness of the study area. Unlike our shallow-water colleagues, we do not have a framework based on the sort of common sense gained only through direct observation." Between 1967 and 1972, *Alvin* was used by biologists in a series of dives designed to investigate the megafuana ("operationally defined as organisms readily visible in photographs") of the Atlantic at depths between 1,600 feet (500 meters) and 5,900 feet (1,800 meters). Photographs were taken with a pair of cameras (one color and one black and white), mounted on the front of the vehicle. Since the angle of the camera was a constant, they overlaid all photographs with a "Canadian grid," originally designed to delineate a study area in aerial photography. In their observations they were able to record that the predominant animals in the fauna were brittle stars, anemones, and urchins, but they also photographed various holothurians and fishes.

In 1971, only a couple of years after *Alvin* was launched, and long before the advent of remote-controlled video cameras, Bruce Heezen and Charles Hollister published *The Face of the Deep*, which contains an astonishing collection of photographs of the seafloor and its inhabitants, revealing that hidden world to the public for the first time. In the introduction, they wrote:

There is at the present time a great acceleration in oceanic exploration. Bathy-scaphes, until recently, have been used largely by adventure-seeking "submarine mountain climbers" for the purpose of breaking depth records. Now that the greatest depth of the ocean has been reached by man, these submersibles are being equipped as useful research tools. More and more scientists will have the opportunity to view the deep-sea floor through the portholes of bathyscaphes and other deep submersibles. Many of the things which will be seen from future deep submersibles will be new to the world, yet perhaps the majority will have been previously recorded by automatic deep-sea cameras. Since the vast majority of existing deep-sea photographs remains unpublished, it seems now a particularly opportune time to present a summary of the knowledge so far gained through remote deep-sea photography.

They were right, of course; but they did not forsee the development of ROVs that could photograph and collect specimens, arrays of sound-sensing and video equipment that could track living creatures through the blackness of the abyss, or electron microscopy that would enable researchers to see creatures so small that nobody had ever suspected their existence. ❧

Picture Mountains and Jets in the Floor

Since 1974 oceanographic research vessels had been investigating the Mid-Atlantic Ridge to learn what they could about the phenomenon known as seafloor spreading. This movement of the crust of the ocean floor, which has resulted in the movement of the continents, is known as "continental drift" but also as "seafloor expansion," "continental displacement," or "plate tectonics." The mechanism that moves the continents is not clearly understood, but it is accompanied by molten rock welling upward through the ever-widening rift valley of the world-spanning mid-ocean ridge. When *Alvin* descended to 8,860 feet (2,700 meters) on the Mid-Atlantic Ridge (the Atlantic segment of the mid-ocean ridge) in February, 1977, scientists aboard were treated to sights no human being had ever seen.

Of course, they did not simply lower the submersible and hope; the original bathymetric groundwork had been done by the research

vessel *Knorr*, using narrow-beam echo-sounding to map the ocean's floor and locate the valley; then the remotely operated camera sled ANGUS (acoustically navigated geophysical underwater survey) photographed some mighty unusual creatures, and only when the location of these mysterious animals was corroborated did the scientists go down in *Alvin* to have a look. Illuminated by *Alvin*'s lights were large white clams and white crabs that were living in water that was saturated with hydrogen sulfide. At another site (dubbed "The Garden of Eden"), they saw the crabs and clams, a strange animal that looked like a dandelion gone to seed, and ten-foot-long worms with bright red plumes emerging from their elongated, tubelike white shells. All these creatures appeared to be thriving in an environment that was totally devoid of light—and therefore unable to employ a photosynthetic basis—and at a much higher temperature than the surrounding seawater. The heat vents spewed plumes of superheated water at temperatures of 350 degrees Celsius (650 degrees Fahrenheit) but the animals lived alongside these vents, not in them.

Deepwater crab (*Lithodes agassizii*)

The towed camera sled ANGUS was useful in early seafloor exploration but quite primitive in contemporary terms. Controlled from a surface ship, the two-ton sled was first used for Project FAMOUS in 1974 and subsequently involved in the discovery of hydrothermal vent animals in 1977. Onboard still cameras recorded images at predetermined intervals as the vehicle was towed blindly over regions of suspected interest. In the Galápagos Rift, ANGUS's cameras took a picture every ten seconds for fourteen hours, mostly of barren seafloor. When the film ran out, the vehicle was winched aboard and the pictures developed as the crew waited anxiously to see if anything of interest had been photographed, or if the camera had malfunctioned.

In *Water Baby*, her celebratory history of *Alvin*, Victoria Kaharl quotes various scientists on the romance and importance of submersible exploration. Whether exploring inner or outer space, one must choose either the adventure of going there and collecting a specimen in person or watching pictures and receiving a specimen from a mechanical claw. As Tanya Atwater, a geophysicist from California, told Kaharl, "There's a profound thing that happens to every single person who gets in that sphere even if they don't get samples—they come back a changed scientist. Some jobs cannot be done except with *Alvin*: to explore in fine detail and get your eyeball and your gut calibrated." And Bill Ryan, a Lamont-Doherty geologist, said, "We found as much variability in one dive in FAMOUS as we got in dredging the whole Atlantic." *Alvin* found the H-bomb off Spain; she led the flotilla of submersibles on Project FAMOUS; through her portholes scientists marveled at the first rift animals

and black smokers; and she enabled human beings to see the *Titanic* for the first time in seventy-three years. Without what Kaharl called "that pregnant guppy, that washing machine, that chewed off cigar with a helmet," we might still be dredging samples from the sea bottom and taking photographs of tube worms and vent clams. "How could anyone have known," asked Kaharl, "that it would so profoundly change the way we look at the world?" Indeed, *Alvin* has changed the way we look at the world, because it has changed the way we *can* look at the world.

The Woods Hole Oceanographic Institute (WHOI) now operates *Alvin* as a national oceanographic facility. A typical eight-hour dive takes two scientists and a pilot as deep as 14,800 feet (4,500 meters). When working at maximum depth, it takes about two hours for the submersible to reach the seafloor and another two to return to the surface. The four hours of working time on the bottom are crammed with carefully planned photography, sampling, and experiments conducted by the scientists using three twelve-inch view ports. *Alvin* can hover, maneuver in rugged topography, or rest on the bottom. Typically, four video cameras are mounted on *Alvin*'s exterior with zoom and focus controls. Because there is no light in the deep sea, the submersible carries quartz iodide and metal halide lights to illuminate the bottom. Two hydraulic, robotic arms may be used to manipulate sampling and experimental gear. A sample basket mounted on the front of the submersible can carry a variety of instruments. Scientists can load up to a thousand pounds of their own gear that may include sediment corers, temperature probes, water samplers, and biological sample pumps.

Alvin is still functioning as the workhorse of the deep-diving vessels, approaching her 3,700th dive. No other manned submersible is even close to this figure. Newer submersibles are now active in the depths, and robotically controlled cameras enable scientists to probe the ocean floor and even examine the deep flora and fauna with minimal risk. During 1988 salvage operations for the SS *Central America* about three hundred miles off Cape Hatteras, the unmanned submersible *Nemo* filmed a large shark at a depth of 7,436 feet (2,200 meters). It was a Greenland shark (*Somniosus microcephalus*), estimated to be nearly twenty feet in length, and the depth is a record for any shark other than the Portuguese shark (*Centroscymnus coelolepis*).

A man who may have spent more time on the deep-ocean floor than anyone alive is oceanographer Robert Ballard. He has descended in *Alvin* to explore the mid-ocean ridge, to examine hydrothermal rift animals, and even to look for the *Titanic*. But after many scientifically important voyages, he decided that the future of underwater exploration lay not in submersibles, but rather in ROVs—remotely operated vehicles. In 1984, from his base at Woods Hole, Ballard gave an interview to the *Cape Cod Times* in which he was quoted as saying, "You'll never see much in *Alvin*; manned submersibles are doomed."

Born in Kansas in 1942, and raised in Southern California, Robert Ballard has been the acknowledged leader in undersea exploration since his days in the U.S. Navy during the Vietnam War in 1967. He earned a Ph.D. in marine geology and geophysics at the University of Rhode Island while working at Woods Hole and participated in Project FAMOUS, the mapping of the

Mid-Atlantic Ridge. Ballard developed the ANGUS camera system, which could remain underwater for twelve to fourteen hours, and take up to sixteen thousand photographs on a single lowering. He was aboard *Alvin* when the first hydrothermal vents were explored in 1977, and his name became even better known when he located the final resting place of the *Titanic* in 1985. He made many observations of the sunken liner and campaigned forcefully to protect the wreck from salvage and souvenir hunters. (He lost the battle, and *Titanic* had been stripped of many valuable artifacts.) He also located the wrecks of the liner *Lusitania* and the World War II German battleship *Bismarck*. When he left Woods Hole after thirty years, he relocated to Mystic, Connecticut, where he founded the Institute for Exploration at the Mystic Aquarium and this affiliation continues. In 2002, Ballard was appointed professor of oceanography at the Graduate School of Oceanography at the University of Rhode Island, where he created the Inner Space Center and launched a graduate degree program in archaeological oceanography.

At Woods Hole the group of engineers who developed ANGUS, the towed camera sled that was used in 1974 for Project FAMOUS, and later, Ballard's "Deep Submergence Laboratory" (DSL), also worked on the *Argo/Jason* complex, so named because Jason and the Argonauts searched for the Golden Fleece aboard the *Argo*. *Argo/Jason* was a remotely controlled, deep-towed vehicle system that carried both sonar and television, combined with a tethered, self-propelled swimming robot that could be used for closer survey work. By 1982 *Argo* had been built by the U.S. Navy for use in undersea search programs, and *Jason Jr.* was constructed in 1986 and tested from *Alvin*—"the very vehicle it will someday replace," wrote Ballard. (In his 1987 book on the discovery of the *Titanic*, Ballard wrote, "I could now imagine the day when we would replace *Alvin* altogether with remote-controlled eyes of the deep.") Video cameras aboard *Argo* picked up the first signs of the *Titanic* in 1985; a view of one of the boilers resting on the bottom at thirteen thousand feet showed the topside viewers that they had found the final resting place of the great liner. After Ballard and his crew had photographed the wreck from the *Alvin*, they sent *Jason Jr.* down the *Titanic's* Grand Staircase for a view that would have been far too risky for a manned submersible. For his 1994 expedition to the *Lusitania*, torpedoed in 1915 off the coast of Ireland and now resting on the bottom in 295 feet of water, Ballard employed no submersibles whatsoever; his entire investigation was conducted with robot television cameras.

In 1985 the French submersible *Nautile* joined the ranks of deep-diving submarines; others rated at over twenty thousand feet include the U.S. Navy's *Sea Cliff*, which was given a titanium hull in 1984; the Finnish-built, Russian-operated *Mir-1* and *Mir-2* (launched in 1987); the Japanese *Shinkai-6500*, which in 1989 dived in the Japan Trench to the record-depth of 21,320 feet.* *Shinkai-6500*—which is "about the size of a small camper and looks something like a whale with a serious overbite"—in 1994 was participating in

the exploration and mapping of the TAG (Trans-Atlantic Geo-traverse) field, part of the Mid-Atlantic Ridge, first described by Peter Rona in 1985 and discussed in detail in *Nature* (1986) by Rona, Klinkhammer, Nelsen, Trefry, and Elderfield. Located roughly midway between Florida and West Africa at thirty-six degrees north latitude, TAG is the first hydrothermal field to be found on an oceanic ridge. Rona suggested that "other such ridges may exist along slow spreading oceanic ridges in the Atlantic Ocean," and indeed, this turned out to be true. In 1993 *Alvin* made six dives on the "Lucky Strike" vent field (37.28 degrees north latitude) and encountered black smokers, along with a previously undescribed species of yellow mussels, shrimp, brachyuran crabs, and for the first time at a vent site, sea urchins.

Dubbed "The Mother of All Vent Fields," the TAG Field has been known since 1972, when the National Oceanic and Atmospheric Administration (NOAA) research vessel *Discoverer* hauled up a black, crumbly, hundred-pound slab of almost pure manganese oxide. Peter Rona realized that such a slab had to have come from a mineral-rich vent, and with geochemist Geoff Thompson, he has been studying this extraordinary site for more than twenty years. From repeated dives in submersibles, they have surveyed a fifteen-square-mile zone that proved to be the largest, most varied vent site in the world. Ten sloping volcanic domes may mark the magma chambers that supply TAG's heat, and cracks and fissures spew forth plumes of black and white smoke. There are inactive zones named for *Alvin* and the Russian submersible *Mir*, and a sloping mound of strangely shaped chimneys known as "The Kremlin" for its resem-

---

* Although the record depth for a submersible descent is *Trieste's* 1960 dive of 35,800 feet to the floor of the Marianas Trench, *Trieste* was tethered to a surface ship and lowered to the bottom. *Shinkai's* record of 6,500 meters (21,320 feet) is for an *untethered* submersible; a vessel not attached in any way to a mother ship.

blance to Moscow's onion-shaped domes. New crust spreads out from the axial valley at about two centimeters per year—the speed at which fingernails grow—which may account for TAG's abundance of features.

The bottom of the ocean is a goal in itself, whether or not there is anything to find there. Most scientists now believe that the future lies in "telepresence" as opposed to manned submersibles, but a Japanese quasi-governmental consortium of industrial corporations (Mitsui, Mitsubishi, and Kawasaki), and American inventor Graham Hawkes are competing to become the first to take a manned submersible to the oceans' greatest depth. (In a 1993 *Newsweek* article, Ballard is quoted as calling the race "a stunt; there's nothing there but mud.") The Japanese Marine Science and Technology Center (JAMSTEC) has launched the two-part unmanned submersible known as *Kaiko* (Japanese for "trench"), that is said to have cost 5.4 billion yen, or almost fifty million dollars. Tethered to the support vessel *Yokosuka* by seven miles of cable, the five-ton, seventeen-foot "launcher" is equipped with side-scan sonar, a sub-bottom profiler that can do geological research as deeply as thirty meters below the seafloor, and various other sophisticated sensors. Attached by another cable to the launcher are the eyes of *Kaiko*, a ten-foot "roving vehicle" with color and monochrome television cameras, still cameras, depth sensors, and manipulator arms. In March 1994 a test dive took *Kaiko* to 35,797 feet (10,911 meters) in the Marianas Trench, only three feet short of the depth reached by the manned submersible *Trieste* in 1960. An "equipment failure" caused the Japanese to abort the mission, just feet short of the bottom,

but before the failure of the video cable, pictures of the deepest part of the ocean were transmitted to the mother ship. (*Kaiko* and *Shinkai-6500* are both owned and operated by JAMSTEC.) From 1989 onward, *Shinkai-6500* dived at various locations in the Pacific, and using what is probably the most advanced equipment ever designed for this work, photographed (video and still) an astonishing array of creatures, many of whose images had never been seen before. On March 24, 1995, *Kaiko* descended to a measured depth of 35,798 feet at the bottom of the Challenger Deep, and, like a fifteenth-century discoverer or an astronaut on the moon, planted a little sign to prove that she had been there.

Unlike the peak of Mount Everest, at 29,028 feet the earth's greatest terrestrial altitude, the deepest level of the ocean—the Challenger Deep in the Marianas Trench—is something of a variable. When the bathyscaph *Trieste* touched down in 1960, the depth gauge read 6,300 fathoms (37,800 feet), but according to a note in Piccard's *Seven Miles Down*, the gauge had originally been calibrated for freshwater, and corrections for "salinity, compressibility, temperature, and gravity" produced the new reading of 35,800 feet. This is not a particularly precise way to establish a record, so it is possible that *Kaiko* did break the record. Also, the configuration of the bottom of the trench varies enough to produce different depth readings at different locations.

In a 1994 article in *Currents*, the newsletter of the Woods Hole Oceanographic Institution, Robert Ballard discussed the video technology that made it possible to obtain high-quality, color television images from the floor of the ocean, and then wrote:

One of the major programs we're trying to work with now is the challenge of exploration in the Black Sea, the only major body of water in the world that does not have oxygen on the bottom. It's anaerobic, which means wood-boring organisms are not there. The potential of finding bronze-age ships or even older ships preserved is ideal in the Black Sea.

In *Oceanus* in 1991, Dana Yoerger introduced the Autonomous Benthic Explorer (ABE), then the latest development in deep-sea exploration. Developed by engineers at WHOI, ABE is untethered, that is, able to move without the restrictions of a cable. It is designed to spend months underwater, taking pictures, sampling water, and performing other chores as directed by its internal computer system. "ABE is designed for a wide variety of missions," wrote Bradley, Yoerger, and Walden in 1995, "but foremost is monitoring geological and biological changes in hydrothermal vent regions." Albert Bradley, one of ABE's designers, is quoted as saying, "Submarines only go forward; ABE can move up, down, left, right, back, forth and sideways." The three-bodied robot is about the size of a small car and will be able to descend to depths of several thousand meters. It will also be able to "go to sleep" for months at a time to conserve battery power when not in use. In *Currents*, Yoerger (the designer of ABE's control-system software), said, "You can't go back to the seafloor with *Jason* or *Alvin* every month to get data. There's only one *Alvin* and only one *Jason*. They can't be all over the world and back at the same experimental site every month." But there can certainly be more

than one ABE; by becoming a part of the environment we wish to investigate, rather than an awkward, alien presence, we may be looking at a new age of undersea exploration.

In 2005 the U.S. National Science Foundation announced funding for a new Human Operated Vehicle (HOV) through a cooperative agreement with the Woods Hole Oceanographic Institution that will be launched in 2008. According to a 2005 WHOI press release, "The replacement vehicle will be capable of reaching more than 99 percent of the seafloor to depths of 6,500 meters (21,320 feet) and conducting a broader range of research projects around the world. When completed in 2008, it will be the most capable deep-sea research vehicle in the world. In addition to diving 40 percent deeper than *Alvin* can, major upgrades in the new vehicle include: A faster descent speed, and faster submerged forward speed; better visibility and lighting for the pilot and two observers, with five view ports instead of the three on the current submersible; a variable ballast system that will enable the vehicle to hover to conduct mid-water research at multiple depths anywhere in the water column on a single dive; more space in the 2.1-meter (7-foot) diameter personnel sphere for the pilot and two scientists; the ability to carry heavier science payloads, and more storage space for samples; improved sensors, tools and data collection systems; improved maneuverability and manipulation, and upgraded navigation systems; and higher speed data communication with the surface ship, and via satellite to shore."

In his 2004 book, *Mystery of the Ancient Seafarers*, Ballard describes "the new era of discovery," in which explorations will be carried out by video cameras controlled not only from ships but from land-based laboratories as well. First came the JASON Project, which was designed to create a "telepresence" in hundreds of classrooms simultaneously, as students could watch real-time broadcasts of ocean explorers practicing their profession. "The students," wrote Ballard in *Explorations*, "would see and hear exactly what we did. . . . I believed strongly that once students experienced this direct connection between their theoretical classroom work and the practical reality of an exploration cruise, many of them would be channeled toward careers in science and technology." With JASON, Ballard was enhancing the study of marine oceanography by exponentially expanding the base. The next phase of JASON incorporates Internet2, a consortium of research universities designed to deploy an Internet network that operates at ten gigabits per second, where any number of viewers can share in real-time observations with colleagues around the world.

Designed primarily for underwater archaeology, but being used for oceanographic science as well, the ROV (remotely operated vehicle) *Hercules* is the latest of Ballard's inventions, designed to enable explorers and scientists to visit and work in the depths—while remaining safely on land. It is equipped with high-definition fiber-optic camera systems that can transmit images to the operator and also, like JASON, to viewers around the world. But while the JASON system transmits images and enables viewers to talk directly to the scientists, *Hercules* is a working vehicle, with a bottom-profiling system and mechanical arms that can pick up and collect objects—animal, vegetable, or mineral—and bring them back for study and to prove their sighting was no fantasy. While manned submersibles like *Alvin* also have mechanical arms and bio-bottles that can be used to collect specimens, *Hercules*, with no humans aboard, can stay down almost indefinitely, and neither its launch nor its deployment is affected by surface weather. The manufacture of *Hercules*-like ROVs is now a big business; companies around the world are turning out these vehicles for use in underwater archaeology, oil exploration, biological and geological sampling, exploratory mining operations, and even the study of deep-sea vent communities. ⟨⟩

Names and Barcodes for Positive Identification

Over the centuries, what began as a basic and necessary study of sea life for food has been transformed. The cumulative research on, in, and under the ocean has produced a picture of marine life that is beautiful, varied, and astoundingly complex. Mostly because of the microscopic creatures that dominate the marine

biota, the living resources of the oceans are literally uncountable. Our inability to count individual diatoms, however, does not diminish their importance; the very profusion of creatures that make up the base of the food pyramid may be the definition of their importance. Even though we might think it is us, on an evolutionary scale, no one creature—or species, or genus, or family—is any more "important" than any other. (There are few other creatures that can *intentionally* alter the balance of nature, so in this negative regard, it might be said that we are more "important" than, say, hummingbirds or wombats.) To understand the relationships of living things, the U.S. National Science Foundation is funding the Tree of Life initiative, where biologists across the United States are identifying the holes in the knowledge of how various organisms are related to one another, and doing the necessary research to close these holes. Of course, the Tree of Life is not restricted to American researchers; it is practically worldwide in scope. The ethic of science, especially when taxpayers pay, obliges the Tree of Life to share their results with other scientists, but also with teachers, amateur naturalists, and anyone with an inquiring mind. To promote collaboration, train

new researchers, and educate the public about evolution and systematics, or systematic biology, these data must be not only made available for scientists to check and build on, but also visualized effectively. Just as satellite views have illuminated the spawning of hurricanes off Africa into the Caribbean, visualizing inner space will illuminate oceanography.

Taxonomy, the science of naming living things (from the Greek *taxis* = "arrangement"), has long been the keystone of biological study; a *taxon* (plural: *taxa*) is a unit in the classification of plants and animals. In the eighteenth century, Carolus Linnaeus developed the system of binomial nomenclature that is still in use today, but the system is showing its age. When relatively few plants and animals were recognized, it was useful to know that wherever it might be found, and however its common name was rendered, the scientific name of the horse was *Equus caballus*, the crow was *Corvus brachyrhynchos*, and the codfish was *Gadus morhua*. The profusion of species, terrestrial and marine, however, has put a great strain on the system, as taxonomists attempt to name species and subspecies with only the most minor differences. Moreover, the introduction of a new system of classification, known as cladistics, and based not so much on the appearance of a particular creature but on its relationship to others in terms of shared characteristics, now threatens the once-sturdy foundations of traditional Linnaean taxonomy. Systematics now uses recently developed techniques such as chromosomal studies, electron microscopy, or molecular biology to answer questions about relationships and thus define various taxa. New species are continually being discovered, and we need to name them in order to classify them, but the science of naming and classifying is becoming less and less important in the grand scheme of biology. It is not so much that taxonomy is dying, but rather that few scientists are prepared to devote themselves to this arcane field of study, recognizing that the future of biology does not lie in counting the fin spines of the stickleback or the intensity of the eye-ring in the vireo.

With Alina Cywinska, Shelley Hall, and Jeremy deWaard, population geneticist Paul Hebert of the University of Guelph in Ontario proposed a system of biological identification that he called "barcodes." The term is derived from the familiar eleven-digit code, expressed as a small white label with series of closely-spaced vertical lines and numbers that can be read by a scanner in a supermarket to ascertain a price, or by a scanner in a library when books are checked in or out. In their 2003 introduction of the system, Hebert and his colleagues wrote, "The limitations inherent in morphology-based identification systems and the dwindling pool of taxonomists signals the need for a new approach to taxon recognition." Under their system, every living creature will have a certain DNA sequence (the mitochondrial gene cyctochrome c oxidase [CO1])

used as an identifying "marker" for the organism. The barcode system, which proved to be accurate in a test of more than two hundred closely related butterfly species, reduces the possibility of the misinterpretation of physical characteristics, eliminates the confusion caused by the often significant differences of taxa at different life stages, and removes the requirement that the taxonomist have an exceptionally high level of expertise. (How many non-ichthyologists can differentiate a blue marlin from a black marlin?)

When Hebert et al. (2004) sequenced the DNA of the Costa Rican butterfly *Astrapes fulgerator*, they found that what was long believed to be a single species, was, in fact, ten different species occupying overlapping territories. They wrote, "Our results add to the evidence that cryptic species are prevalent in tropical regions, a critical issue in efforts to document global species richness. They also illustrate the value of DNA barcoding, especially when coupled with traditional taxonomic tools, in disclosing hidden diversity."

The genetic markers of every species are identifiable in every cell. In their 2003 introduction, Hebert et al. wrote, "We believe that a CO1 database can be developed within twenty years for the five million to ten million animal species on the planet for about a billion dollars, far less than that directed to other major science initiatives such as the Human Genome Project or the International Space Station." Indeed, DNA barcoding probably does not require an elaborate laboratory or expensive gene-sequencing equipment. A handheld DNA-barcoding device, similar to those used in stores, could provide a quick and cheap way for field researchers to identify animal species. The Consortium for the Barcode of Life (CBoL) was established in 2004 with its secretariat hosted by the Smithsonian Institution in Washington, D.C. The fist two major barcoding initiatives are the All Birds Barcoding Initiative (ABBI), organized by Rockefeller University, the University of Guelph, and the Smithsonian, which has set the goal of determining the barcodes of ten thousand avian species by 2010, and the All Fishes Initiative (AFI), organized by Paul Hebert and Robert Ward of CSIRO (Commonwealth Scientific and Industrial Research Organisation) of Australia, which has targeted twelve thousand marine fish species by 2010. For fishes—and for all other life-forms—the reference database known appropriately as BoLD (Barcode of Life Database) is critical to research, regulation, and enforcement of laws that pertain to the sustainability of marine fisheries.

Current marine biology is no longer directed towards the discovery of new and exotic species, although they continue to show up. Rather, with exotic new technologies—many of which involve computers, unknown for the first two millennia of marine studies—we can look to a greater understanding of marine life; how much of it there is, where it lives, what affects it, and what we can do to preserve it. Technology has bestowed upon us the ability to count and track populations of fishes, whales, and other denizens of the seas, but the results of these surveys are not always encouraging. What we suspected was happening to codfish, tuna, swordfish, and certain whale species, has unfortunately been confirmed. Their numbers have fallen dramatically, and for the first time, we can drop the dreaded word "extinction" into our discussions of some of these beleaguered marine animals.

The study of the underwater realm has revealed a multitude of wonders, some well-known, some previously unknown, some astonishing. Some marine creatures exhibit unusual behaviors (swimming sea cucumbers); there are some whose activities defy understanding (swordfish that attack whales and sailing ships); others so completely unexpected that prior to their discovery, every scientist would—and did—emphatically insist that all life on earth depended upon the sun and that a chemosynthetic lifestyle was more than a little unlikely. Then there are the unexceptional species, such as the Patagonian toothfish and the orange roughy, whose celebrity lies in their recent discovery and precipitous decline; "monstrous" fishes and cephalopods that objective analysis showed to be familiar forms; and recent discoveries—squid with "elbows"; a previously unknown shark discovered because it swallowed a parachute; a living specimen of a six-foot-long, steely-scaled fish that was thought to have gone extinct with the dinosaurs 65 million years ago. Surprises come in all sizes: hydrothermal vents circle the globe under all the oceans for 40,000 miles; some newly discovered photosynthesizing bacteria are so tiny that they evaded detection until a decade ago.

In the chapters that follow we will encounter some of the more sensational aspects of marine biology over the past century. Hardly any of these discoveries was intentional—researchers were not fishing for a shark with a parachute, after all—which points up the often serendipitous nature of marine discovery. Rumors of sea monsters encouraged the occasional expedition (think of the search for Loch Ness Monster or the giant squid), and cetologists were seeking more information on *Indopacetus*, the least-known whale in the world. It is the ocean that binds these discoveries together, and they are presented in more or less chronological order. The discovery of the giant leptocephalus occurred in 1930, and the first coelacanth was seen by Marjorie Courtney-Latimer in 1938. Curiosity does not end with the initial discovery—it escalates. Since 1938, coelacanth studies have continued apace, and have produced a detailed analysis of the physiology of *Latimeria chalumnae*, underwater films of this fabulous fish, and even the discovery of another population of coelacanths, far from African waters. Nobody expected to find a new system of life on the sea floor until *Alvin* stumbled (if a submersible can "stumble") upon the hydrothermal vents of the Galápagos Rift Zone. The 1977 discovery of the vents and their associated fauna has engendered an entirely new discipline and spawned a generation of biologists and geologists dedicated to unraveling the myriad mysteries of the vents.

There is no connection between the discovery of the coelacanth and the discovery of megamouth, except that they are both unexpected, very large, finny inhabitants of the ocean. Likewise, the swordfish and the sea cucumber are about as distant from one another as two marine creatures can be, but however well we thought we knew them (people have been eating both for centuries) they were both found to exhibit weird and wonderful behavior. Although the terms apply—often spectacularly—the oceans' inhabitants should not be defined only by weird and wonderful; a great many sea creatures earn a living in a pedestrian manner, and are notable for their ordinariness. (The sea cucumbers that are related to those that swim are pedestrian almost by definition: they crawl across the bottom on little tube feet, hoovering up detritus from the sediments.) Even in this ordinariness lies wonder: what could be more wonderful than thousands of species of deep-sea fishes that glow in the dark? In keeping with the strategy and spirit of CoML, I offer a selection of some of the more spectacular discoveries of recent years, connected by time, their marine origins, and their often sensational un-ordinariness. ❧

Part Two
The Acceleration of Discovery

Monsters, Real or Imagined

Ardently pursued, purportedly photographed, and universally publicized for nearly a century, the ultimate aquatic mystery of the Loch Ness Monster fuels the arguments of those who would convince us of the persistence of sea monsters of every size, shape, and habitat. After all goes the argument, if there can be a

"monster" in a Scottish lake, why not sea serpents, giant sharks, mermaids, or gigantic octopuses? Well, as it turns out, the "monster" was a hoax, perpetrated in 1933 by Marmaduke Arundel Wetherell, who staged the famous photograph using a toy submarine with the head of a "dinosaur" affixed to it, and then sent it to the newspapers. In a deathbed confession, Wetherell's nephew, Christian Spurling, explained how he and his uncle made the model. Wetherell and Spurling coerced R. Kenneth Wilson, a respected London surgeon, into claiming that he took the picture—which became famous as the "surgeon's

photograph." Although the *London Sunday Telegraph* on March 13, 1994, and then *Newsweek* and *People* magazines published the nephew's confession, people still head to the Scottish loch, hoping to catch a glimpse of the fabled monster.

So the existence of "Nessie" cannot be used to argue for the existence of other sea (or lake) monsters, but even without the support of Nessie, we have more than enough marine mysteries to go around. They may not have the romantic cachet of the Loch Ness Monster, but they have something that Nessie never had: a specimen proving their existence beyond any

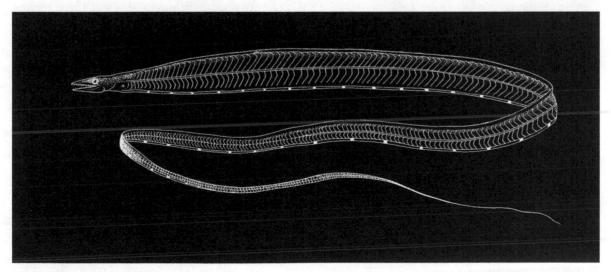

Giant leptocephalus (*Species unknown*)

doubt. Some, like the giant leptocephalus, are so rare that if a single specimen had not been caught in a net, nobody would have known of its existence. The term *leptocephalus*, from the Greek *leptos* for "slender" and *cephalos* for "head," was originally applied to a group of small, laterally flattened, semitransparent fishes, often with disproportionately small heads. Unlike lantern fish or krill, which exist in countless profusion, this six-foot-long, translucent ribbon of living matter appeared only once, but its discovery caused so much confusion and controversy within the ichthyological fraternity that you would have thought they'd captured a baby Loch Ness Monster. Some people actually thought they had.

From 1904 to 1922 Danish ichthyologist Johannes Schmidt (1877–1933) studied the life cycle of the freshwater eel, whose mysteries had puzzled biologists for centuries. In 1904, when Schmidt found the first eel larva ever seen outside the Mediterranean in deep water west of the Faeroes, he began to study the unresolved question of eel migrations. From 1905 to 1920 he scoured the Atlantic studying the eels that he captured, and finally, on an expedition aboard the *Dana* in 1922, he established that eels migrate to the Sargasso Sea, where they breed and die. The young eels (known as "elvers") then return to either side of the North Atlantic, where they ascend the same freshwater streams and rivers where they were born and begin the process anew. From 1924 to 1930 Schmidt led a series of expeditions aboard the *Dana*, making detailed observations of marine life, many of which were published in the *Dana Reports*, issued by the Zoological Museum of the University of Copenhagen. Of the major oceanographic expeditions of the twentieth century, two were Danish: the *Dana*'s round-the-world voyage in 1928, and the *Galathea* expedition of 1950–52. Even the early expeditions, however, encountered mysteries that they could not immediately (or easily) solve.

Until the middle of the nineteenth century, leptocephali were classified as a distinct group, usually, but not always, in the genus *Leptocephalus*. Then, after the midpoint of the nineteenth century, the idea began to take hold that leptocephali were the larval form of something else. In 1864 Theodore Gill suggested that they were larval eels, and he specifically suggested that *Leptocephalus morrisii* was the young of *Conger conger*, the conger eel. Other leptocephali raised in an aquarium metamorphosed into eels; *Leptocephalus brevirostris* became *Anguilla anguilla*, the freshwater eel.

The six-foot-long leptocephalus brought up from one thousand feet in 1930 off South Africa hinted at a monster. Before it metamorphoses into an elver, the leptocephalus of the common eel only reaches a length of about three inches. Extrapolating from the known twelvefold growth ratio of this leptocephalus to its adult size of about three feet—and even more dramatically, the thirtyfold growth of the conger eel from its four-inch leptocephalus—believers in sea serpents concluded that the *Dana*'s leptocephalus would have matured to a monstrous one hundred feet. In *The Wake of the Sea-Serpents*, Bernard Heuvelmans wrote, "there is no doubt that giant eels are responsible for *some* sightings of sea serpents" and Léon Bertin, one of the world's foremost authorities on eels, discussed this creature in a 1954 article he called "*Les Larves Leptocephaliennes Géantes et le Probleme du 'Serpent de Mer'*." Bertin pointed out that there are many other species of eels where the ratio of leptocephalus to adult is much more than 12 or 30 to 1, and in fact, he wrote, "If the two giant leptocephali . . . belong to the *Nemichthys* group [snipe-eels] it is therefore very likely that the adult is no more than 16 to 20 feet long and not 100 feet as has been suggested." Twenty feet is still twice as long as the longest known conger eel, and monsterologists were not willing to let the subject of the giant leptocephalus drop so easily. In 1957 zoologist Maurice Burton incorporated these data into a book called *Animal Legends*, and proposed that the Loch Ness Monster was "a giant eel, one of greater proportions than any known to science."

Because the odds of finding even a twenty-foot-long eel, let alone a hundred-footer, are about the same as finding the Loch Ness Monster, the giant leptocephalus is probably the larval form of an unspecified notacanth. Notacanths, also known as "spiny eels," are deepwater fishes characterized by a row of isolated spines along the back that are not connected by a dorsal fin; as with the bonefishes, ladyfishes, and tarpon, they develop from leptocephali. In collections around the world, there reside other elongated, unidentified leptocephali, some of which were collected in the early twentieth century, and one may have been described by Rafinesque in 1810. When leptocephali were believed to be distinct species and not the larval forms of other fishes, there was nothing particularly unusual about these specimens (except that they were considerably longer than any similar species), and they remained in their jars, specifically unidentified. In 1911 the French ichthyologist Roule called them "*larves Tiluriennes*," and they were variously named

Tilurus, Tiluropsis, and *Tilurella.* (According to Smith's 1970 discussion, "*Tilurella* was later identified as a post-larval *Nemichthys* . . . and clearly does not belong with the others.") In 1959 a thirty-four inch specimen was collected off New Zealand, and officially named *Leptocephalus giganteus.*

The popular press will more likely spread sensational revelations of "monsters" than the arcane theorizing of ichthyologists, and it has been much easier—and a lot more fun—to write about hundred-foot-long monster eels than the speculations of Monsieur Roule. The real but complicated story is fascinating and includes not only several unidentified large leptocephali but also several papers that suggested possibilities other than monsters. In 1970, David G. Smith published an article in *Copeia* ("Notacanthiform Leptocephali in the Western North Atlantic"), in which he proposed that the very large larvae were notacanths or halosaurs, but although "*Tiluropsis* was probably a halosaurid, *L. giganteus* cannot be identified to family." Also in 1970, Danish scientists Jørgen Nielsen and Verner Larsen published their "Remarks on the Identity of the Giant *Dana* Eel Larva," in which they discounted Bertin's 1954 suggestion that it might be a twenty-foot-long *Nemichthys* (to date, the longest *Nemichthys* known measured fifty-seven inches) and supported Smith's contention that the *Dana's* larva was indeed *L. giganteus.* In his 1932 discussion of the *Dana's* collections, Taning did not give the giant leptocephalus a name; it was not officially christened until 1970, when Smith affiliated it with the New Zealand specimen.

Finally (or more accurately, "most recently"), in the 1989 leptocephalus volume of *Fishes of the Western North Atlantic,* Smith lists *Tilurus* and *L.*

giganteus as notacanthiform leptocephali, but he modified his conclusion by writing *"Leptocephalus giganteus* may represent a species group within the Notacanthidae or Halosauridae, or it may represent a group yet unknown as adults." As for the six-foot larva maturing into a hundred-foot-long eel, Smith wrote, "In reality, the relationship between the size of the leptocephalus and the size of the adult varies widely among elopomorph fishes, and there is no way to predict it beforehand. Indeed, the evidence suggests that halosaurids, at least, undergo a drastic reduction in length at metamorphosis." In other words, the giant leptocephalus was more likely to shrink into a *smaller* adult than expand into a larger monster.

We may never see a one-hundred-foot eel, but just about every evolutionary biologist and ichthyologist (and anybody else who wanted to see the "zoological find of the century") has seen *Latimeria chalumnae*, the coelacanth ("*see*-la-canth"). A five-foot-long fish with bluish, metallic-looking scales and fins that seem to be on stalks, the coelacanth rose from the murky depths of the Cretaceous to arrive in the present, creating a furor not unlike that which would have accompanied the arrival of a fresh *T. rex* carcass, with the flesh, bones, and teeth intact. ∾

Fossils Brought to Life

On December 23, 1938, fishermen from the South African city of East London hauled in a five-foot-long fish that was steely blue in color, with large bony scales and fins that appeared to be on leglike stalks. It was first examined by Marjorie Courtney-Latimer, and when she could not identify it, she contacted J. L. B. Smith,

an amateur ichthyologist and professor of chemistry at Rhodes University at Grahamstown. Smith correctly verified it as a relative of a lobe-finned fish known as *Macropoma,* extinct for about seventy million years. He realized it was a coelacanth, and named it *Latimeria chalumnae* after Miss Latimer and the Chalumna River, near which it was found. Another coelacanth was not seen until 1952, but since then, many more have been caught, usually in the vicinity of the Comoro Islands between Mozambique and the island of Madagascar. The name *coelacanth*—which means "hollow spines" and refers to the first dorsal fin—was originally used in 1836 to describe the fossil species. Local fishermen unintentionally catch them—usually while fishing for the oilfish (*Ruvettus pretiosus*). What was once believed to be a stable population of about 650 animals is now thought to number no more than 300, and this rare and zoologically significant creature is probably on the brink of extinction. Female coelacanths give birth to live young and did so long before the arrival of mammals. They spend the day in lava caves and descend to around two thousand feet to forage at night.

The discovery of a living coelacanth has given us an opportunity to peer into the distant geological past and see a living creature that was previously available only as a fossil. As Keith Thomson wrote in *Living Fossil: The Story of the Coelacanth*:

We cannot take a perch or a cod as a model for understanding its early Devonian ancestors. But *Latimeria* looks very much like the Devonian *Diplocercides* or *Nesides.* Therefore, by studying *Latimeria* in detail, alongside the three lungfishes and in conjunction with the fossils and physical evidence that the rocks themselves provide about the ancient environments in which they lived, we might be able to reconstruct a lot about the biology of these long-distant Devonian forms. And not just the evolution of the skeleton, but the blood, the liver, how they breathed, how they reproduced, how they fed and swam; their whole biology.

Instead of the stiffening vertebrae that developed in most bony fishes, the coelacanth, like other lobe-finned fishes, has a vertebral column that consists of bony rings around a stiff, hollow, fluid-filled chord, a primitive feature that the coelacanths shared. Many other anatomical differences distinguish the lobe-finned fishes. The

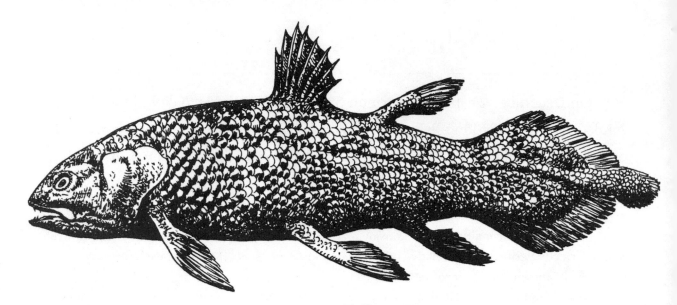

Coelacanth (*Latimeria chalumnae*)

heart is merely an S-shaped tube, simpler than that of any other living fish, and the brain is also tiny, occupying only 1.5 percent of the cranial cavity, which is otherwise filled with fats and oils. Coelacanths have paired nasal sacs, each of which contains papillae that increase the surface area, and a "rostral organ" that is separate from and above the nasal sacs. Through three paired tubes, the rostral organ is open to the surrounding water and is filled with a gelatinous substance. It is believed that the organ is part of the fish's sensory system and may be used to detect weak electrical fields, like the ampullae of Lorenzini in sharks. As with sharks, the coelacanth's skeleton is made of cartilage, but the skull is bone with an unusual hinge running across the top, allowing a wider gape. Powerful jaw muscles indicate that this slow-swimming predator uses its short, sharp teeth for catching smaller fishes and squid. Although the coelacanth

lacks lungs, it does have a fat-filled swim bladder that contributes to its buoyancy. A pregnant female caught in 1972 showed that the coelacanth is ovoviviparous, which means that its huge eggs— approximately the size of an orange, and the largest eggs of any living fish—hatch inside the body, and the young are born alive.

In addition to examining collected specimens, biologists have also entered the realm of the living coelacanth and filmed it in action, providing a heretofore unavailable view of the life of a Devonian fish. Hans Fricke, a physiologist from the Max Planck Institute in Germany, descended in a submersible off the Comoros and on January 17, 1987, became the first human being to film a coelacanth swimming in its natural habitat. Although they are probably capable of short bursts of speed, coelacanths seem to spend most of their time hovering near the bottom with their fins flared. According to Fricke, the extra fin at the tip of the tail is flicked back and forth "like a metronome," and acts as a sort of trim tab. The lobed fins had encouraged biologists to believe that *Latimeria* might spend some time on the bottom, either "walking" or propping itself up on its fins, but Fricke's films showed only that it swam by moving its pectoral and pelvic fins alternately, rather like the walking motions of a tetrapod, such as a dog or a horse. But since alternating movement is a consequence of the way fishes normally move by bending their bodies, it does not show that *Latimeria* lent this movement to four-legged animals. Even though much of the popular literature places the coelacanth on the list of mammalian ancestors, it is only a distant cousin. Adult coelacanths are roughly the size of an adult human being—nearly six feet long and weighing up to 175 pounds—and while this fact has absolutely nothing to do with its recent or fossil history, it has been noted in the popular press. J. L. B. Smith did little to discourage the idea of a walking coelacanth—and hence an ancestor of four-legged animals—when he titled his 1956 book *Old Fourlegs*.

Comoran fishermen catch coelacanths on a hand line, usually in water around two thousand feet deep. The fishes have been caught at depths of a thousand feet or less, always at night. From his submersible, Fricke has now filmed more than one hundred adult individuals (he has never seen a juvenile), and they have been seen at depths ranging from 385 to 650 feet. They spend the day in lava caves and descend to around two thousand feet to forage at night. They are seen to be passive drift feeders, opportunistically capturing fishes, squid, and octopuses,

much in the manner of a large grouper. Fricke also observed a peculiar "head-down" behavior, where the fish spent several minutes at a time in a vertical position with its snout close to the bottom. The reason for this behavior is unknown but it might have something to do with an organ at the end of the snout, the function of which has not been determined but may be electrically sensitive.

With the exception of the first one, which was caught off East London, all the coelacanths until 1992 had been caught in the vicinity of the Comoros. But in that year, a pregnant female was caught at a depth of about 150 feet off the coast of Mozambique, some eight hundred miles west of the Comoros, and in 1995 another one was caught off the southeast coast of Madagascar. In 1997 the story changed dramatically. In July, while on their honeymoon, zoologist Mark Erdmann and his new wife, Arnaz Mehta, spotted a coelacanth in a fish market on the tiny island of Manado Tua off the northern tip of the Indonesian island of Sulawesi. Assuming the coelacanth was already known from the western Pacific, the Erdmanns were unaware of the importance of the fish the Indonesians called *raja laut* ("king of the sea"). When they returned to America, however, and reported what they had seen, they learned of the significance of their sighting, and with funding from the National Geographic Society, came back to Sulawesi the following year, determined to rectify their mistake. For ten months, they scoured the fish markets of northern Sulawesi and hit pay dirt on July 30, 1998, when they were brought a specimen that was alive, but only barely. (Coincidentally, the Sulawesi coelacanths are caught by fishermen whose target is the same oilfish sought by the Comoran fishermen.) Before they released it, they swam with it and photographed it, hoping it would return to the depths, but it died. Some six thousand miles from East Africa, it appears that there is another, completely unexpected, population of coelacanths. Where the Comoran coelacanths have all been dark blue, the Indonesian ones were brown, suggesting a separate species or subspecies. Are there other undiscovered populations?

When Erdmann donated the carcass of the coelacanth to the Indonesian authorities, he expected to be able to publish the description himself. Erdmann's account of the finding of the coelacanth—which he suggested was *Latimeria chalumnae*, the same species as all the other coelacanths—was published in *Nature* in 1998, but Laurent Pouyaud of the French Scientific Institute and Indonesian coauthors published a description in the April 1999 *Comptes Rendus de L'Academie des Sciences*, claiming that "the Comorean and Indonesian coelacanths belong to distinct populations," and they named the new species *Latimeria menadoensis*, after the village off which it was found.

The story took a surprising turn in July 2000, when the French team (Séret, Pouyard, and Serre) submitted an article to *Nature*, claiming that they actually found a coelacanth in Indonesia three years before Erdmann saw one in the fish market of Manado Tua. George Serre said that a specimen had been caught in 1995 at the Bay of Pangandaran, in southwest Java, about twelve hundred miles from Manado, suggesting *another* undiscovered population of coelacanths. When the editors of *Nature* noticed that the fish

in the photograph submitted by Serre was virtually identical to Erdmann's photograph of the Manado specimen, they concluded that Serre's photograph was nothing but a doctored version of Erdmann's, and refused to publish the article. (The story, entitled "Tangled tale of a lost, stolen, and disputed coelacanth," was written by Heather McCabe and Janet Wright, and appeared in *Nature* July 13, 2000.) The last word came from Erdmann (and Roy Caldwell, one of the authors of the original paper on the Sulawesi coelacanth), who documented the shameful hoax in a later issue of *Nature* (July 27, 2000), in a letter entitled, "How new technology put a coelacanth among the heirs of Piltdown Man.") He wrote, "the Séret, Pouyard and Serre image . . . is clearly an altered copy of a photograph taken by M. V. E. in 1998 off Manado Tua and printed in *Nature* soon afterwards," and they concluded, "The Indonesians and Comorans are rightfully proud of efforts in their two countries to preserve these rare and very special fish. What pride can we in the western scientific community take in this affair?"

In 1999 researchers returned to Manado Tua to look for more Indonesian coelacanths. Although seven dives in the research submersible *JAGO* produced no results, some two hundred miles to the southwest, in the region of Kuandang, they found two specimens living in deep caves at a depth of five hundred feet. Whereas the Comoran coelacanths inhabit lava caves on young volcanic slopes, those off Sulawesi live near much older, less steep, and more eroded formations, with very few caves. Moreover, the waters of north Sulawesi are subject to much stronger currents (estimated peak velocity of three or four knots) than the regions where the

Comoran coelacanths have been observed, suggesting a different lifestyle for the two species. "The biogeography of the new coelacanth population remains enigmatic," wrote Fricke and colleagues (one of whom was Mark Erdmann), "although perhaps this is for the best. An undiscovered home is probably the best possible protection for these endangered fish."

At first, the physical similarities of the two populations of coelacanths led researchers to presume that they were the same species, descended from a common ancestor and separated by thousands of miles of Indian Ocean. In a 1999 study, however, Mark Erdmann and several colleagues assumed that *Latimeria menadoensis* was not a valid species, but that "ongoing genetic analysis should reveal the depth of divergence between the two known populations of living coelacanths and help to determine if the specimen is conspecific with its Comoran counterparts." Victor Springer, a Smithsonian Institution ichthyologist, opined that the two populations would prove to be a single species, separated for millions of years by the movement of tectonic plates after the docking of India with Eurasia. (Springer and Williams (1990) had earlier identified several species of fishes with separated populations—"sister groups"—in the Indian and Pacific Oceans.) But when Holder, Erdmann, Wilcox, Caldwell, and Hillis (1999) actually analyzed the mitochondrial DNA sequences of *Latimeria menadoensis* and *Latimeria chalumnae*, they found enough differences to conclude that "the Comoran and Indonesian populations represent distinct evolutionary lineages of *Latimeria*." Morphological similarities are no longer sufficient to lump two species together; advances in

molecular biology have provided much more accurate techniques for the identification of the lineage and relationships of animals.

Has a third species of coelacanth been discovered far from either the Comoros or Indonesia? Off the South African town of St. Lucia in Kwa-Zulu-Natal, is Sodwana Bay, part of the Greater St. Lucia Wetland Park, where two submarine canyons indent the continental shelf near Sodwana Bay to a depth of about three thousand feet. Pleasure divers Pieter Venter, Peter Timm, and Etienne leRoux made a dive to 320 feet using a mixture of diving gases. Beneath an overhang, Venter saw a fish, approximately six feet long, and realized that it was a coelacanth. He signaled Timm, and they spotted two more. Unfortunately, they had no cameras. "It was," said Venter, "like seeing a UFO without taking a photograph." Calling themselves SA Coelacanth Expedition 2000, the group, with several additional members (and cameras), returned in late November. On November 27, 2000, Pieter Venter, Gilbert Gunn, and cameramen Christo Serfontein and Dennis Harding, assisted by a five-member team, went down again to a depth of 350 feet using four different mixes of gas for a dive lasting 134 minutes, which only permitted fifteen minutes on the bottom. Twelve minutes into the dive they found three coelacanths, from three and a half feet (one meter) to six and a half feet (two meters) long. The fish swam head-down and appeared to be feeding off ledges. The cameramen shot video footage and still photos of the three. Then disaster struck. Assisting Serfontein, who had passed out under water, thirty-four-year-old Dennis Harding rose to the surface with him in an uncontrolled ascent. After Harding complained of neck pains, fellow divers tried to resuscitate him, but he died in the boat, apparently, from a cerebral embolism from "the bends." Serfontein recovered after being taken underwater for decompression.

The coelacanths of Sodwana Bay are far enough from East London (where the first specimen was found in 1938) and also from the Comoros to suggest that they represent another heretofore unknown population. Unlikely to be strays from the Comoros, they may be more widespread than previously thought. In the spring of 2005, for the first time, an ROV (remotely operated vehicle) was used to film coelacanths. In Sodwana Bay, where the coelacanths had been spotted five years earlier, a total of eight individual coelacanths were filmed from the ROV, demonstrating the practicality and cost effectiveness—not to mention the safety factor—of remote cameras for undersea exploration.

By now, the reader will expect to encounter more "living fossils" and startling behavior, especially in the oceans' depths. What the *Galathea* Expedition found in the depths during 1950–52 meets this expectation and then some. According to expedition leader Anton Bruun (1956b), "the primary purpose of the *Galathea* Expedition was to explore the ocean trenches in order to find out whether life occurred under the extreme conditions prevailing there—and if so, to what extent." *Galathea*, a 266-foot-long converted naval vessel equipped with the latest in trawling gear, set sail from Copenhagen on October 15, 1950. Countless fishes, cephalopods, and other invertebrates were trawled up from the abyssal depths, many seen for the first time. The expedition rounded Africa into the Indian Ocean and then visited the

deep waters of India, Southeast Asia, Australia, New Zealand, and various Pacific islands, passed through the Panama Canal in May 1952, and arrived back in Copenhagen in June of that year. The *Galathea* covered 63,700 miles, the equivalent of three times around the earth at the equator.

On May 6, 1952, in a *Galathea* trawl pulled up from 11,878 feet in the Mexican Pacific, Danish malacologist Henning Lemche found ten specimens of a segmented, limpetlike mollusk with gills—a combination that had been recorded only from fossils of the Cambrian Period, 350 million years ago. A true living fossil—of equal zoological importance but less showy than the discovery of the living coelacanth in 1938— *Neopilina galatheae* has a single spoon-shaped shell about an inch and a half long, and an animal with five pairs of gills, a radula, and, around the mouth, fleshy structures that are thought to

Neopilina

assist in bringing in food. Neither a clam nor a snail, *Neopilina* is one of two living members of the Monoplacophora ("one plate-bearers"); a similar species was hauled up from almost twenty thousand feet off the coast of Peru in 1958.

The discovery of living fossils permits the study of almost extinct groups of organisms in ways that would be impossible from the preserved hard parts of the fossils alone. As the coelacanth is a link to its Devonian ancestors, so other living fossils link the present back to groups that are now generally extinct. In the fossil Monoplacophora, a unique serial repetition of paired muscle scars occurred on the inner surface of the shell. Interestingly, although originally a main characteristic of the group when all specimens were fossils, these muscle scars do not occur in the single living representative of the group. *Neopilina* does, however, have eight pairs of serially arranged muscles to retract its foot. Not only are the muscles serially arranged, but there is also a serial repetition of paired nerve connectives, nephridia (kidneys), gills, and to a lesser extent, perhaps gonads and auricles.

Before *Neopilina* was discovered, similar fossil shells were known, but they were classified either as chitons (class Polyplacophora) or as limpets (class Gastropoda, which includes snails, slugs, etc.). Eventually, however, a unique characteristic of the shell justified a new molluscan class for these fossils. On the inner surface of the shell, several pairs of serially arranged muscle scars occur. Other than *Neopilina*, plants and animals commonly referred to as living fossils are the horsetails or scouring rushes, the gingko or maidenhair tree, the coelacanth, the horseshoe crab, the chambered nautilus, and the brachiopod *Lingula*. Sharks, which have been around for three hundred million years, are sometimes characterized as living fossils, but early sharks bore hardly any similarity to today's species, and many sharks evolved to their present form relatively recently.

On the other hand, a new kind of shark appeared in 1976, and because it resembled no other shark, taxonomists originally had a problem classifying it. It was surely a shark because it had dermal denticles in place of scales; five gill slits on each side of its massive head; and an arrangement of fins—including a tail fin with a much longer upper lobe than lower—that is found in no other fishes. Eventually, it was found to have a cartilaginous skeleton, which is the primary characteristic that separates the sharks (and rays) from the bony fishes. It was hauled aboard a U.S. Navy vessel because it had swallowed a parachute. ☜

Accident Reveals a Big Mouth

In deep water off the northern coast of the Hawaiian island of Oahu on November 15, 1976, the naval reasearch vessel *AFB-14* had deployed two orange-and-white parachutes as sea anchors, and when they were hauled in, the crew discovered that one of the parachutes had been swallowed by a very large shark. Parachute-eating

sharks are remarkable enough, but this creature was more than a little unusual: it was of a type totally unrecognizable to the crew. Dubbed "megamouth," the huge-mouthed creature was over fourteen feet long, and weighed three-quarters of a ton. It had thousands of tiny teeth, and its rubbery lips made it look like a seagoing hippopotamus. The sea anchor had been deployed at about five hundred feet, suggesting that this shark was a deepwater plankton-feeder, and therefore unlikely to have ever taken a baited hook. Were it not for the pure coincidence of the ship and the shark being in the same place at the same time—and the bizarre inclination of the shark to swallow the chute—this monster might never have been discovered.

The discovery of a brand-new species of shark fourteen feet long, weighing 1,650 pounds, with blubbery lips and tiny teeth, made big news—at least in zoological circles. Shortly after it was hauled aboard the naval vessel, the carcass was delivered to the Waikiki Aquarium, and dropped, as it were, on the doorstep of the aquarium's director, Leighton Taylor. (As they were hauling it aboard, the tail broke off under the shark's great weight, so it was actually delivered in two pieces, the body and the tail.) It was the find of a lifetime, a chance for Taylor to publish, and therefore be permanently associated with, one of the great zoological discoveries of the twentieth century. Only the coelacanth,

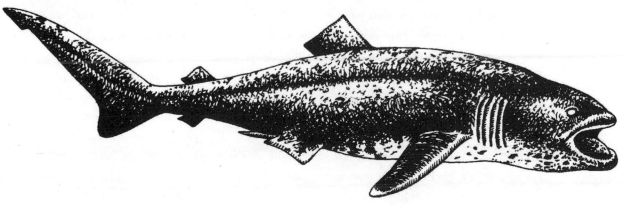

Megamouth (*Megachasma pelagios*)

which was found in South African waters in 1938, was a comparable discovery, but we knew that coelacanths had existed—seventy-five million years ago, to be sure—but until that moment in 1976, when Ensign Linda Hubble aboard the *AFB-14* recognized—or rather *didn't* recognize—the strange large shark with the blubbery lips, nobody had even suspected its existence.

More megamouths soon appeared. In 1984 a second specimen, also a male, was caught off southern California. A third male washed ashore near Perth in Western Australia in 1988, and a fourth, a badly decomposed male, washed ashore in Japan in January 1989, and another six months later, also in Japan. The first living megamouth was not seen until October 21, 1990, when a commercial fisherman snagged one in his gill net, seven miles off Dana Point in southern California. He brought the fifteen-foot male into the harbor, where ichthyologists marveled at it and television crews filmed it for science, for posterity, and for the whole world to see. Since no aquarium had the facilities to exhibit this massive creature, the authorities wisely and sensitively decided to release it. On October 23, the shark dubbed "Mega" by the media (and *Megachasma pelagios*—"deepwater bigmouth"—by science) was returned to the Pacific. A radio transmitter attached to its hide allowed scientists to track it for several days.

In November 1994, at Hakata Bay, Fukuoka, Japan, the first female megamouth washed ashore. A team of Japanese ichthyologists examined her—and ultimately produced an entire book about the biology of megamouth. In one chapter, Americans Eugenie Clark and José Castro (1995) examined her reproductive system,

and wrote, "'Megamama' is a virgin: dissection of the first female specimen of *Megachasma pelagios*." She was 4.8 meters (15.75 feet) in length—larger than the first one, but not as large as the Perth megamouth—but, as the authors pointed out, she was immature. Male sharks achieve sexual penetration by means of dual intromittent organs known as "claspers," and both of the twin hymens of the Fukuoka female were intact. The researchers were disappointed that the Fukuoka female was immature, because they could have learned much more from embryos or from a mature but not pregnant female.

In May 1995 an immature male, only six feet long, was found on the beach in Senegal, and six months later, the first *Atlantic* megamouth was found in Brazil. Numbers 10 and 11 were found in Japan and the Philippines respectively; and number 12, also found in Japan, was the only known mature female; the right ovary held many whitish-yellow eggs. Number 13 was not collected at all, but observed offshore north of Manado on the Indonesian Island of Sulawesi (where the second population of coelacanths was discovered), being harassed by sperm whales. A large female (5.18 meters) was caught in a drift net off San Diego, California, in October 1999, photographed and released, and two years later, a large male (5.5 meters) was entrapped in a drift gill net, hauled on deck and photographed, and then thrown overboard. Megamouth number 16 was an immature male caught in a tuna purse seine in the east Indian Ocean in January 2002, and in April of that year, the first South African megamouth, which became number 17, stranded at Natures Valley in the Western Cape Province. Number 18 came from the Philippines; number 19 was sighted at sea off California; and number 20 was caught on July 4, 2003, off Taiwan.

The megamouth count accelerates. The first from the eastern South Pacific was found off Peru in March 2004, and number 23 was found in Tokyo Bay, in April, 2004. From November 2004 to May 2005, three more specimens washed ashore in the Philippines, and on May 4, 2005, a large female was caught in a net off Hualien, eastern Taiwan. It was alive when it was brought in, then put on ice so it could be examined by scientists. Within ten days, four more megamouths were recorded from Hualien, bringing the total (as of June 2005), to thirty-three. Most came from the Pacific—one from Hawaii, four from the Philippines, five from California, five from Taiwan, and nine from Japan. The remaining eight came from various disparate locations, such as Brazil, Sulawesi, and South Africa. From this wide and sporadic record, it is almost impossible to make any sort of a statement of megamouth's distribution except that it is cosmopolitan in temperate or tropical waters.

Leonard Compagno, a Californian transplanted to South Africa, was one of the original authors of the 1983 megamouth paper and is the principal author of the 1984 *Species Catalogue: An Annotated and Illustrated Catalogue of Shark Species Known to Date*, published by the United Nations Food and Agriculture Organization (FAO). When Compagno was preparing the "Megamouth" entry for his encyclopedic 1984 catalog, only one specimen had been found, so he wrote, "Known only from the type locality, but likely to be wide-ranging, like other gigantic, plankton-feeding sharks." (He also wrote, "This recently described shark, a giant pelagic filter-feeder, is perhaps the most spectacular discovery of a new shark in the Twentieth Century.") In Compagno's 2005 field guide, *Sharks of the World*, however, the range map for megamouth covers most of the tropical and temperate waters of the world, except for the North Atlantic.

Like the two other large filter-feeding sharks—the whale shark and the basking shark—megamouth is wide-ranging, but it is considered to be less active and a poorer swimmer than the basking or whale sharks. Of all living sharks, only the whale shark, basking shark, Greenland shark, and great white are known to exceed megamouth's known maximum length of eighteen feet. (Such a small sample, however, cannot show its maximum length.) Megamouth has a gigantic, bulbous head, like a giant tadpole, and the enormous mouth that has inspired its nickname. It can protrude its great jaws beyond the rubbery lips. The body tapers to a narrow tail-stock, and the upper lobe of the caudal (tail) fin is much longer than the lower. All the other fins are relatively small, and all are narrowly edged in white. All the megamouth specimens have been dark brown to black above, with whitish underparts.

Megamouth's thousands of tiny teeth indicate that it feeds on plankton. Indeed, when the stomach contents of stranded specimens were examined, nothing larger than copepods and shrimps were found. To follow megamouth's foraging, biologists under the leadership of Don Nelson outfitted megamouth number 6, trapped alive in the gill net off California in 1990, with an acoustic transmitter. For two days, the shark spent the daytime hours between 400 and 550 feet and migrated toward the surface at night, coming as close as 40 feet. (Remember, the first megamouth, caught during the day, swallowed the parachute at 500 feet.) The shark probably coordinates its vertical migrations with the "deep-scattering layer" (DSL), a horizontal, mobile zone of living organisms occurring below the surface in many oceans, and so called because it is so dense that it scatters or reflects sound waves. This phantom layer was not recognized until 1942, when Navy scientists, experimenting with underwater sound for locating submarines, detected an echo from 900 feet where no bottom existed. The DSL was later observed to move toward the surface in the evening and sink again at dawn, a most unlikely activity for the seafloor. Trawls pulled through the DSL have not resolved the mystery of its composition, but it is believed to consist of countless small organisms—lantern fish or bristlemouths, considered the most numerous fish in the ocean; small squids, siphonophores, planktonic organisms, or a mixed or layered aggregation of all of them.

In their 1983 description, Taylor, Compagno, and Struhsaker wrote, "Inspection of the mouth of megamouth 24 hr after capture revealed a bright silvery lining punctuated by small circular porelike structures. At the time it was speculated that these might be bioluminescent organs, but we have no evidence of this." To date, there is still no evidence of bioluminescent mouth parts that might serve to attract microorganisms into the mouth of *Megachasma*, but when the upper jaw is protruded, a startling white band is exposed, about which Nakaya et al. (1997) wrote:

We suggest that the white band on the snout has some behavioral significance, because the bright white band is so sharply demarcated by the dark or black coloration of the snout and upper jaw, and because this band becomes remarkably more prominent when the upper jaw is protruded, and almost invisible when the upper jaw is retracted. Under low-light conditions, such as twilight and at night, and/or when they are ranging near the limit of visibility, only this white line may be visible. Because the white band is facing interiorly on the snout just above the upper jaw, this band might be related to megamouth's feeding behavior, or with the recognition of other individuals of the same species.

Perhaps even more than the coelacanth, megamouth buoys the spirits of monster watchers. After all, here is a very large fish whose existence was completely unsuspected. If such a creature exists, who can truly say that there aren't monsters in Loch Ness or two-hundred-foot-long giant squid? Throughout Hawaiian history—from the early days of the Polynesian sailing canoes, through the Pacific explorers of the eighteenth and nineteenth centuries, and past World War II in the Pacific (when there was considerable naval action off Hawaii)—no hint of the existence of this fish had ever appeared. And no record of a stranded megamouth was found in Japan until 1989. Much is weird and peculiar about the megamouth shark, but it is incredible that the species went undiscovered until 1976, and since then, thirty-two additional specimens have washed ashore or been captured by fishermen around the world. Where were they and what were they doing before 1976? ⤫

A Whole New Inner World

Before 1977 every popular or technical book about the fauna and flora of the deep sea was written with the assumption that even if all of its subject matter was not yet known, they were either animals or plants, and all were fueled by sunlight. While the lifestyle of creatures that lived in the deep sea varied from one phylum

to another—some were sedentary, some swam or floated around, some burrowed in the bottom layer—the basic mechanics were the same. In one way or another, all life as we knew it was dependent on sunlight; photosynthesis fueled everything in the food chain, from the tiniest bacteria to the largest whale.

Then in 1977 the submersible *Alvin*, diving off the Galápagos Islands, changed all that. What was seen from her windows shook the foundations of conventional knowledge and set the stage for learning how fast communities of life could adapt, grow, and migrate. (It is a happy coincidence that this discovery occurred in the same area where Darwin had gained many of his insights on evolution.) *Alvin* came upon fissures from which spewed hot water of partial volcanic origin. The mid-ocean ridges are volcanically active, and the molten rock heats seawater in cracks, often several hundred degrees in the pressure of the deep. The underwater landscape often consisted of a series of "smoking chimneys" emanating hot water loaded with high concentrations of various metals and dissolved sulfide.

From the submersible's viewing ports, scientists observed biological wonders that matched the geological. They saw what was probably the most unusual collection of living creatures ever beheld by the eyes of man. John Corliss, Tjeerd van Andel, John Edmund, and Robert Ballard were the first humans to see what appeared to be gigantic tube worms with vivid red gills emerging from thick, ghostly white tubes that were as much as ten feet long. They also saw blind white crabs, pink fishes that resembled no known species, and clams that were as big as footballs.

First identified along the Galápagos Rift, what became known as "hydrothermal vent animals" were subsequently discovered scattered along the Pacific coast of North and South America, from Vancouver Island to the coast of northern Chile, and most recently, in the Atlantic, first in the Gulf of Mexico and then along the Atlantic mid-ocean ridge. These vent systems are always associated with hot springs. A far cry from warm, groundwater emanations that the word first brings to mind, these hot springs are caused by cold seawater seeping into cracks in the seafloor, where molten material, bubbling through the earth's mantle, heats the water to unexpected temperatures.

"Sea-floor spreading" splits the seafloors, creating cracks or rifts in the crust of the earth. This activity usually (but not always) takes place along the mid-ocean ridge, a forty-thousand-mile-long undersea mountain range that is the largest single feature on the earth's surface. The rifts mark the edges of the lithospheric plates that bear the continents in their inexorable movement on the top 100 to 250 kilometers of the surface of the planet. Much like seaborne giant icebergs, the lithospheric plates such as those of North America and Africa, drift over the flowing, denser layer known as the asthenosphere, the movement of which is also activated by convection currents.

The plates grow at the mid-ocean ridge and sink at "subduction trenches," where one plate slides under the lip of another. Where plates interact, earthquakes occur, volcanoes erupt, and mountains are pushed up. (All three were manifest in November 1963, as the Icelandic island of Surtsey was born in a spectacular cataclysm of fire, lava, and steam.) The rifts caused by the separation of the plates fill up with lava that wells up from within the earth, flowing outward from the center, and moving across the ocean floor. As described by J. R. Heirtzler and W. B. Bryan in 1975, "Bizarre as the idea seemed at first, it was becoming evident that the mid-ocean-ridge system was nothing less than a vast unhealed volcanic wound."

The mid-ocean ridge is far too large to be seen as anything but isolated geological formations, but when lit by the lights of a submersible or camera, it reveals recently erupted volcanoes with hardened lava tubes, basaltic rocks stained orange or yellow by mineral emissions, and the characteristic feature of the hydrothermal vents, the "black smoker chimneys." As seen by the crew of *Alvin*, and subsequently by other scientists in other submersibles, the landscape of the thermal vents is one of the most amazing sights on earth. Although only a handful of people have ever seen the pillow-lava, black and white smoking chimneys, and the hot, shimmering water of the vents directly, photography has revealed some aspects of this mysterious world to millions of people. Photographs published in *National Geographic* magazine showed the Galápagos hydrothermal vents to tens of millions of people. Then the National Geographic Society—a partial sponsor of some of the earliest dives—produced a television film called *Dive to the Edge of Creation*, first aired in January 1980, that contained some of *Alvin*'s spectacular images of tube worms, black smokers, and vent fauna. Since the first dives, images of the vents have been featured in every magazine and on virtually every television station, whether educational or commercial.

The chimneys are formed by the minerals spewing hot water from the cracks in the earth's crust; some of this metal-rich water has been measured at 350 degrees Celsius (662 degrees Fahrenheit), which is near the melting point of lead. The particulate matter from the fissure forms a tube that is composed of fine-grained sulfides and oxides, which can build to a height of twenty feet. Because each vent differs in its mineral content, temperature, geologic setting, and size, the chimneys—which eventually collapse from their own weight—form deposits on the valley floor. For the first time, we can see the actual formation of mineral deposits. At about eight thousand feet, the landscape looks like—

"Black smoker" with grenadier
(*Coelorhynchus coelorhynchus*)

because it is—the side of a recently erupted volcano. Some of the lava surfaces are wrinkled like the hide of an elephant; others are glass-smooth because they have not yet been covered by the constant rain of sediment. On the seafloor, metals erupting from the sea formed mounds of black manganese and yellow iron oxides from deep in the earth.

Throughout the vent fields, organisms are scattered around, completing the other-worldly aspect of this unsuspected landscape—a landscape that was lit before only by the glow of underwater sizzling lava before *Alvin*'s lamps emblazoned it. Before the arrival of the submersible, this world, and everything in it, had never been subjected to the one thing that surface creatures (like ourselves) take so much for granted: light. And even more astonishing, the absence of light, rather than being a handicap, is the *modus vivendi* of many of the hydrothermal vent creatures. Most of the "vent animals" discovered in 1977, such as crabs, clams, mussels, and shrimps, are related to known species, and to the untrained eye, they resemble the more familiar forms. But there are some, like the vestimentifaran worms, that presented a major taxonomic problem to the scientists: they are different from any other creatures above or below the surface of the sea. Their discovery, according to Ann Bucklin of the Scripps Institution of Oceanography, "added an entirely new and unexpected element to deep-sea biology."

As first seen in the *Alvin*'s lights, these worms were four to six feet long, white tubes with blood-red, feathery plumes emerging from the top. At first they were believed to be related to the thread-sized pogonophores, worms that also live in self-secreted tubes, but further examination indicated that they ought to be placed in a new and distinct phylum, the vestimentifera. (The name comes from the *vestimentum*, a unique, collarlike arrangement at the head of the tube.) Like the pogonophores, the vestimentiferan worms have no gut and no mouth, structures their discoverer, Meredith Jones, calls "of more than passing import . . . in other animals." They were named *Riftia* (for the rift) *pachyptila* (from the Greek *pachys*, which means "thick," and *ptilon*, which means "feather," referring to the plumes.) These worms are found densely packed together, always associated with mussels, and less frequently with clams, affixed to crevices.

The pogonophores themselves are only a recent discovery. Although the first specimens were dredged up in Indonesian waters in 1900, it took another fourteen years before a description was published, and it was not until 1937 that a Swedish zoologist named Johansson designated them as a new class and gave them the name pogonophores, which means "beard-bearers." After further study, mostly by Soviet scientists, it became apparent that they were not only a new class of animals but a new phylum. Like the vestimentifera, they live in tubes; they have no digestive tract, mouth, anus, or intestine, and digestion takes place through small structures in the tentacles. In *Living Invertebrates of the World*, Buschbaum and Milne described them as "among the most astonishing discoveries made with deep-sea dredges in the twentieth century," and in *Abyss*, C. P. Idyll quoted Libby Hyman of the American Museum of Natural History: "The finding of an entirely new phylum of animals in the twentieth century is certainly astounding, and ranks in zoological importance with the finding of the coelacanth fish and the archaic gastropod [*Neopilina*], both belonging to groups believed to be extinct for hundreds of millions of years." If the discovery of the pogonophores was "astonishing" and "astounding," imagine the shock attendant upon the discovery of ten-foot-long worms with bright red plumes, densely clustered around the vents.

When specimens were brought up for examination, it was revealed that they were more than a little unusual. *Riftia pachyptila* lived at great depths—not in the superheated water of the smoking vents, but alongside—in water that is never visited by light. Virtually all the photosynthesis in the ocean occurs in the upper one hundred to two hundred meters of the water column, by one-celled plants that fix oxygen. To be available to these bottom-dwelling creatures, sufficient foodstuffs would have to fall through twenty-five hundred meters (about eight thousand feet) of water, an unlikely proposition. But if photosynthesis was not the main source of energy for life in these deep-sea oases of smoking chimneys, what was?

The waters flowing from the vents are rich in hydrogen sulfide, a substance highly toxic to most living things, but the vestimentiferan worms were not only not adversely affected by this toxic substance, they also existed on it. Not directly, of course, but because they were packed with bacteria that could "eat" the inorganic chemicals like hydrogen sulfide, fix the carbon dioxide, and synthesize reduced carbon compounds (e.g., sugars) and thus provide nourishment for the host organisms. Sulfide-dependent bacteria also are found in "bacterial snow" that

has been observed in the water column coming from vent waters. This material is also a source of nutrition, but many (and perhaps most) vent animals do not seem to feed directly from the external medium.

In 1996 Cindy Lee Van Dover, the first woman pilot of *Alvin*, published *The Octopus's Garden: Hydrothermal Vents and Other Mysteries of the Deep Sea*, a book about her early adventures and the discovery of the vent animals. She said:

What still seems remarkable to me is that less than twenty years ago we could not even imagine the existence of the hydrothermal vent communities, and we know next to nothing about the biota that wander the abyssal plains. We landed a man on the moon nearly a decade before we even saw the heat of our own ocean's crust exhaled through black smokers.

Van Dover did her graduate work at Woods Hole, and in 1989 wrote her Ph.D. dissertation on chemosynthetic communities in the deep sea. She is also the author (and coauthor) of numerous scientific papers, and she wrote the textbook on *The Ecology of Deep-Sea Hydrothermal Vents* (2000), considered the definitive study of this fascinating subject. She wrote that her book was not a "comprehensive bestiary, since this already exists as a stunning collection of photographs, illustrations and text in a volume by Daniel Desbruyères and Michel Segonzac, the *Handbook of Deep-Sea Hydrothermal Vent Fauna*."

Some deep-sea animals—if indeed they really are animals—have defied all efforts to identify them. Peter Rona of Rutgers University, who was involved in the discovery and analysis of the TAG [Trans-Atlantic Geotraverse] Hydrothermal Field deep in the North Atlantic, was confounded by photographs taken there that showed "a distinctive pattern of black dots . . . evenly spaced and arranged in crisscrossing rows, forming a perfect six-sided feature that resembled the center of a board of Chinese checkers." Rona circulated the photographs among various experts, and was told that the pictures did not show any known form of coral, nor did they fit in any other known invertebrate category. But when invertebrate paleontologist Adolf Seilacher saw the photographs, he suggested that they closely resembled the traces left by *Paleodictyon nodosum*, believed to have gone extinct fifty million years ago. Except that it was also arranged in hexagonal tiles, *Paleodictyon* was as mysterious as Rona's holes-in-a-checkerboard; nobody knew what *Paleodictyon* was either. Seilacher accompanied Rona on an *Alvin* dive in 2003, and as they "landed knee-deep in hexagon country," they had a "eureka moment" and realized that Rona's "secret survivor" (the title of his 2004 article in *Natural History* magazine) was indeed *Paleodictyon nodosum*. But recognizing the pattern as resembling that made by something fifty million years ago brought them no closer to figuring out what it was.* Nevertheless, said Rona, "The deep

---

* In his *Natural History* article, Rona mentioned that he was planning to write an article for a scientific publication that would include a photograph of the "invertebrate of uncertain identity." When I asked him about the publication, he said it wasn't ready, but I could see *Paleodictyon* in the IMAX film *Volcanoes of the Deep Sea*. I watched the DVD and realized in addition to the technology that enabled Rona and Seilacher to see the hexagons in situ, the technology was also available for me—and many other people—to see the "invertebrate" and listen to Rona and Seilacher talking about it.

---

ocean had served as a sanctuary, a place where *Paleodictyon* had lived on for an unimaginably long time, protected even from the global environmental changes that caused the extinction of many of the animals living in shallow water and on land. . . . After more than thirty years, to my surprise, the mystery of *Paleodictyon* still seems as deep as the waters where it lives."

And now bacteria have been found deep below the ocean floor. From the examination of samples brought up from the earth's crust under the Pacific Ocean, investigators discovered colonies of microbes that live in a completely anaerobic (oxygen-free) environment, at temperatures that may reach 167 degrees Celsius, feeding on methane and other hydrocarbons. The proposed name for these unexpected bacteria is *Bacillus infernus* (bacillus from hell). In the *Proceedings of the National Academy of Sciences* (1992), Thomas Gold (1920–2004) of Cornell University wrote that there were "strong indications that microbial life is widespread at depth in the crust of the earth." Gold was a controversial astronomer and geoscientist best known for developing, along with Hermann Bondi and the late Fred Hoyle, the steady-state theory of the universe. It assumes that we live in a world that has no beginning or end, in which matter is constantly being created. Although the big-bang theory currently holds sway, much of the steady-state theory has stood the test of time. In his 1999 book, *The Deep Hot Biosphere*, Gold presented his most recent far-out idea, which was that oil and coal are not remnants of ancient surface life that became buried and subjected to high temperatures and pressures, but rather deposits produced from primordial hydrocarbons dating back to when Earth was formed. He claimed that volatile gases then migrate toward the surface through cracks in the crust and either leak into the atmosphere as methane, become trapped in subsurface gas fields, or lose their hydrogen to become oil, tar or coal. In other words, the petroleum and gas reserves are refilling far faster than the gas and petroleum industry estimates.

In a 1996 *Scientific American* article, James Frederickson and Tullis Onstott said that "deep-living microbes pervade both oceanic and continental crust and are especially abundant in sedimentary formations." Then, in a 1997 article in *Annual Review of Earth and Planetary Sciences*, Kenneth Nealson asked about sediment bacteria: "Who's there, what are they doing, and what's new?" His answer:

The prokaryotes (bacteria) comprise the bulk of the biomass and chemical activity in sediments. They are well suited to their role as sediment chemists, as they are the right size and have the required metabolic versatility to oxidize the organic carbon in a variety of different ways. The characteristic vertical nutrient (electron donor and electron acceptor) profiles seen in sediments are produced as a result of microbial activities, with each nutrient a product or reactant of one or more metabolic groups. Thus, understanding the mechanisms by which the chemical environment of a sediment is generated and stabilized requires a knowledge of resident populations, something that has been very difficult to obtain, given the techniques available to microbiologists. However, the new approaches of molecular biology, which have added insights into the phylogenetic relationships of the prokaryotes, have also provided tools whereby sedimentary populations can be examined without the need for culturing the organisms. These techniques, in concert with new methods of microscopy, isolation of new metabolic groups, and the study of new ecosystems, suggest that there is much that will be learned about the microbiology of sedimentary environments in the coming years.

Bacteria distinct from those that live in ocean sediments help nourish the vestimentifera worms. Instead of a gut, these worms have a specialized organ, the trophosome, which is made up of chambers that contain sulfide-oxidizing bacteria. The animal, in turn, can digest the bacteria and derive nutrition. *Riftia* has a specialized hemoglobin, which binds to sulfide and to oxygen. The sulfide is transported to the trophosome, where it can be used by the symbiotic bacteria. Some vent animals, such as crabs, can "graze" on the bacteria fields, much as a cow grazes in a pasture, but the immobile tube worms were found to contain colonies of the bacteria in their gut, which, in a purely symbiotic relationship, process the chemicals that provide nourishment for the worms. The proper scientific terminology for this phenomenon is "major sessile animal species [with] sulfur-oxidizing chemoautotrophic bacteria as endosymbionts." Where both partners benefit from a symbiotic relationship, it is known as mutualistic. (When it is harmful to one of the partners it is parasitic.) But if the trophosome that occupies most of the worm's body cavity has no channel through which particulate food might enter, how does it feed? Through the branchials (the plumes), the worm absorbs the raw materials needed to fuel its metabolism (carbon dioxide, oxygen, and hydrogen sulfide), which are transported to the trophosome by the host's circulatory system. In most animals, hydrogen sulfide inhibits respiration by blocking the oxygen's binding sites on the hemoglobin molecule, but the tube worms are able to resist the toxic effects by binding the oxygen molecules and the sulfide molecules simultaneously and separately, thus preventing the sulfide from combining with oxygen, which is ordinarily a poisonous combination.

This means of earning a living, known as chemosynthesis, is used by the tube worms, and certain clams, mussels, and crabs. The uniqueness of their adaptations is summed up by George Somero:

These animals have one of the most stressful habitats imaginable: high pressures, no light, therefore no photosynthetic productivity; and waters laden with toxic substances. Through evolutionary changes, the vent animals have met these challenges, and can tolerate and even thrive in their unusual environment.

As Cindy Van Dover wrote, "The implications of these findings are stunning: they suggest that hydrothermal vents support life in the absence of sunlight—without the photosynthesizing bacteria that provide most sea creatures with food."

The bivalve mollusks *Bathymodiolus thermophilus* and *Calyptogena magnifica* have sulfur-oxidizing bacteria as symbionts in the gills. The sulfur source is not unique to the deep-sea vent animals. Shallow-water animals in sulfide-rich sediments also appear to be festooned with sulfide-oxidizing bacteria, and also derive nutrition from them. There is some evidence that all the bacteria in both deep-sea and shallow-water bivalves belong to the same group of purple bacteria. The rift clam (*Calyptogena magnifica*) is clam-shaped, with a hinged pair of shells, but there the resemblance to other bivalves ceases. The shell of *Calyptogena* is white, and the animal inside is a deep, rich red, making the opened clam look not unlike a large piece of beef liver on a small plate. The largest rift clam measures almost a foot in length. Because of the hydrogen sulfide in its tissues, the vent clam gives off an overwhelming smell of rotten eggs, much to the consternation of the oceanographers who brought up the first samples. *Calyptogena* has a large foot that is usually inserted into a crevice, but the clam can also use the foot to change locations. The giant white clams clustered around the active vents have been responsible for some of the more fanciful names employed to identify an individual oasis in the Galápagos Rift, including Clambake I and II and Garden of Eden.

Clambake II suffered a shocking climate change, a cooling rather than a warming. Most benthic fauna is sparsely distributed, but the rift clams and mussels form dense aggregations that are most uncharacteristic of deep-sea animals. Clambake II differed from other oases in that all the clams were dead. They probably died when the hot water vents shut down, cutting off the supply of life-supporting hydrogen sulfide. Because rift clam shells dissolve in about fifteen years, the presence of such shells indicates that the hydrothermal circulation ceased within that period of time. The instability of the vents themselves means that the vent communities are relatively short-lived, perhaps lasting no more than a few decades. Isolation and mobility, adaptability versus intolerance of change, evolution of new species and extinction of the old ones must all be propelling the rise and fall of vent communities.

The mussel *Bathymodiolus thermophilus*, not quite as large as the rift clam, was first described from specimens collected by *Alvin* on dives at the Galápagos Rift in 1977. At the Galápagos sites, the mussels are always found nestled in among the tube worms, attached to each other and to the tubes. Like the tube worms and vent clams, *Bathymodiolus* has symbiotic intercellular bacteria, but because the mussel also has a functional mouth and gut (which the worms and clams do not), the role of these bacteria in the nutritional process is unclear. It may be that the mussels are able to process nutrients chemosynthetically and can also acquire nutrients not produced by the vents. *Bathymodiolus* has not been found far from the vent areas, and if they are removed, they starve, suggesting that they depend on the vent effluvia. Although a polychaete scale worm (*Branchipolynoe symmytilida*) appears to be involved in a commensal, or mutually beneficial, relationship with the host mussel, and 60 to 80 percent of the mussels near the Galápagos vent sites were found to be accompanied by the polychaete worms, the nature of the commensality is not understood.

Although the worms, clams, and mussels near the vents usually remain in one place, feeding on suspended bacteria in the water and processing them chemosynthetically, several species of crabs can and do move around. Except for the waving motion of the tube worms, the predominant movement around the vents is the scuttling of crabs. The crabs are white, and when seen in a submersible's lights or on film, they add an eerie note to an already supernatural tableau. (Where there are crabs, there are likely to be octopuses, and the vents are no exception. There are photographs of an unknown species of octopod hunting crabs in the vicinity of Clambake I.) The brachyuran (true crab) genera *Bythograea* and *Cyanograea* are usually seen in the vicinity of the tube worms and bivalves, scurrying over the fissures and crevices. *Cyanograea praedator*, as its name implies, is a predatory species, feeding on the annelid worm *Alvinella* (a new genus, named for the submersible), which has been found living close to the vents in superheated water of 285 degrees Celsius. The abundant galatheid crab (*Munidopsis subsquamosa*) is found in abundance around the vents, but it is not unique to the vent systems and is found in other deep-sea habitats.

If sulfur-digesting worms and foot-long clams characterize the Galápagos (and other) Pacific vent fauna, a most unusual shrimp dominates the fauna of the North Atlantic vents. *Rimicaris exoculata* was discovered by Peter Rona in 1985 at the 3,600-meter-deep TAG vent site, swarming in dense schools at springs spewing forth water that may reach 350 degrees Celsius. *Rimicaris* means "rift shrimp," and *exoculata* means "without eyes." In the first photographs, these swarming two-inch-long shrimp each showed a bright, reflective spot on its back. When examined by Cindy Van Dover and her colleagues, these spots turned out to be "paired lobes of very large and unusual organs just beneath

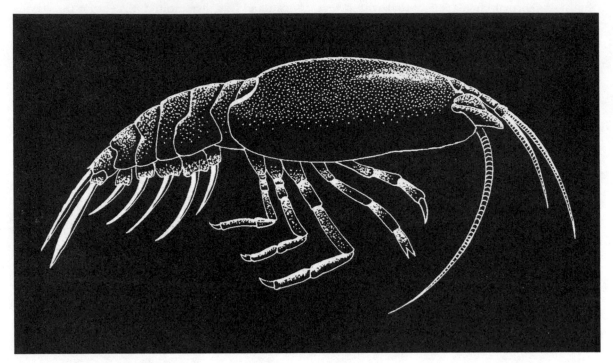

Rift shrimp (*Rimicaris exoculata*)

the thin, transparent carapace." The organs contained no image-forming devices, meaning that the shrimp could only distinguish light and dark, but they did contain a light-sensitive visual pigment. Since it is permanently pitch-black at the depth the shrimp inhabited, what was the purpose of these photoreceptors?

Van Dover guessed that *Rimicaris* was detecting low-level gradients of light emitted by the thermal vents themselves. Such a conjecture presupposed a light source certainly invisible to human eyes and barely photographable even with the most sophisticated equipment. Using cameras developed by Marine Imaging Systems to detect light from distant galaxies, pictures were taken of a black smoker and the results were surprising. Cindy Van Dover: "I expected to see some am-

biguous hint of a fuzz which, if one was willing to stretch the imagination, might be called a glow; I doubt I was alone in that expectation. Instead, what came up on the screen was a dramatic, unequivocal glow with a sharply-defined edge at the interface between the sulfide chimney and the vent water." The Atlantic rift shrimp may be able to locate thermal vents by sight. In 1994, however, experiments—some of which were conducted by Van Dover—seemed to disprove the idea that the light coming from the geysers' heat was strong enough to provide the glow.

The stomachs of rift shrimps are packed with sulfides, but they also contain the symbiotic bacteria that characterize the tube worms and bivalves of the Pacific. *Rimicaris* feeds by scraping the sides of the chimneys with specially adapted claws and drawing the minerals directly into its mouth. In the spirit of scientific inquiry, Van Dover and J. R. Cann boiled one of the shrimp over a Bunsen burner and ate it: "It did not turn an appetizing pink. If anything, it turned a still more unappealing shade of gray. As we might have expected, given the sulfide environment of the shrimp, the flesh tasted of rotten egg, and if that were not enough, the texture of the beast was as I imagine a rubber band might be. Perhaps it was overcooked. We concluded from our experiment that there will be no market for these shrimp among the gourmandizing public."

After the discovery of the chemosynthetic bacteria, tube worms, eyeless shrimp, and giant crabs and clams, it seemed that no more other-worldly life-forms could be found, but in the complex biology of the hydrothermal vents, there continue to be surprises. In 1994 Van Dover and others noted the importance of light in biochemical reactions such as photosynthesis, and suggested "the provocative possibility of geothermally driven photosynthesis in deep-sea hydrothermal vents." In *Alvin*, Van Dover and others descended to the "Hole-to-Hell" and "Snake-Pit" sites on the East Pacific Rise and the Mid-Atlantic Ridge in 2003 and collected samples to see what would grow in the lab. Then with Thomas Beatty, Robert Blankenship, and others, Van Dover published a description of "an obligately photosynthetic bacterial anaerobe," a green sulfur bacterium that must rely on light somehow generated by hydrothermal vents, as no sunlight ever reaches these depths.

What was not evident, however, is where the light came from. Suggestions included luminescence created when chemicals crystallize (crystalloluminescence); sonoluminescence, created by the sound of bubbles collapsing; triboluminescence, the result of rock crystals cracking; and luminescence caused by the radioactive decay of elements in the vent water. The light that causes these deep-sea bacteria to photosynthesize has not been identified, but, as Beatty et al. wrote in 2005, "This discovery expands the range of possible environments that could harbor life-forms which use light energy to drive endergonic biochemical reactions, and frees the thinking of the scientific community from the constraint that any form of life that depends on light energy is necessarily limited to solarly illuminated habitats." In other words, this discovery suggests that life can exist far from the sun, on Earth and on other worlds.

Because of the unique nature of the vent environment, many creatures have been discovered that are found only in the vicinity of the hydrothermal springs. This high degree of endemism is clearly demonstrated by the previously unknown clams, crabs, and shrimp, and of course, the completely unexpected giant tube worms, which are found nowhere else but around thermal vents and on "whale falls." In their 1983 summary of the fish fauna of the Galápagos Vent Region, Cohen and Haedrich list some twenty species that were found to live around the vents at depths of about seventy-eight hundred feet (2,400 meters). The samples consisted of pictures taken by deep-sea cameras that photographed fishes attracted to baited traps, fishes actually caught in the traps, and observations made by scientists aboard the submersible *Alvin*.

Of the twenty species of fish described by Cohen and Haedrich, the most frequently observed were an unknown species of pale halosaur, a narrow-tailed spiny eel; various unidentified species of rat-tails (Macrouridae), some of which were observed swimming head-down above the vents; and eelpouts (*Zoarcidae*), which are predators and are most commonly seen among the *Calyptogena* aggregations.[†] At least three species of fish—all previously unknown to science—have been observed around the vents, and nowhere else. A small, pink fish named *Bythites hollisi* (after Ralph Hollis, the pilot of the *Alvin*) is the most common in the eastern Pacific locations and is often seen hovering head-down above the vent, with its tail undulating to keep it in position. As many as eight have been seen together at a single vent, but they are usually seen one or two at a time. Many of the other rift species have no common names, and fish named *Bassozetus*, *Acanthonus*, and *Porogadus* would be recognizable only to ichthyologists. Skates have been seen gently gliding from light into darkness, and on one occasion, through the viewing ports of *Alvin*, the mysterious "tripod fish" (*Bathypterois*) was seen perched on the tips of its fins.

Until March 1984 the rift fauna—with the obvious exception of *Rimicaris*, the Atlantic rift shrimp—were known only from the various Pacific locations. On a geological dive to 3,266 meters at the "Florida Escarpment" in the Gulf of Mexico, *Alvin* encountered "the same types of organisms that characterize the Pacific vent communities—white bacterial mats; large dense beds of mussels; numerous small gastropods; the shells of live mussels; thick patches of 1-meter-long tube worms; red-fleshed vesicomyid clams; galatheid crabs; and eel-like zoarcid fish." But where the Pacific vent communities were always associated with hot springs, the Florida Escarpment communities exist in a completely different geological environment. At the base of the escarpment, a limestone cliff that rises some two thousand meters above the 3,280-meter-deep floor of the gulf, the Atlantic vent fauna proceeds chemosynthetically, but in the absence of hot springs, upwelling lava, or black smoking chimneys. The sulfide compounds to fuel this process seep out of the adjacent Florida platform as black sediments, and demonstrate that while heat dependence is not a necessary component of chemosynthesis in the depths, a steady source of inorganic compounds is. Vent communities are no longer believed to be isolated and rare phenomena located only at vent sites but have been found to be associated with virtually all deep-sea tectonic activity, including vents, subduction zones, fracture zones, and spreading centers in the deep trenches.

The clams, crabs, mussels, and tube worms of the "vent biota" are more widespread than scientists first believed. In August 1985, shortly after the discovery of the Florida Escarpment cold seep community, the NOAA vessel *Researcher* was cruising over the Mid-Atlantic Ridge at 26.13 degrees north latitude, a location approximately midway between Brazil and Cuba. Using a combination of sampling techniques, the staff identified black smokers, and, for the first time on the ridge, the now familiar—but still unexpected—vent animals. This site resembles the

---

[†] In 1986 Rosenblatt and Cohen described a new genus and two new species of eelpouts from the Galápagos Rift; one they named *Thermarces cerebrus*, from the Greek *thermos* meaning "heat" and *Cerebrus*, the three-headed dog that guarded the gates of Hell, and the second was christened *Thermarces andersoni*, after Eric Anderson, a student of the Zoarcidae.

early eastern Pacific sites but differs from those at the Florida Escarpment.

On November 18, 1929, decades before *Alvin* was launched, a huge earthquake performed a dated experiment for the submersible to explore later. A turbidity current stirred by the earthquake deposited a thick layer of sediment over a bottom formation known to geologists as the Laurentian Fan, south of Newfoundland. The successive rupture of cables as far as three hundred miles from the epicenter helped date the formation of the fan. The dating also dates the establishment and growth rate of the communities. Serendipitously, in 1987 the geologists in *Alvin*, while seeking only to explore the physical effects of the earthquake, encountered "four expansive occurrences of dense biological communities comprising vesicomyid and thyasirid clams, gastropods, pogonophoran tubes, galatheid crabs, and unidentified branched organisms" (Mayer et al. 1988). Not expecting to do any collecting on these dives, *Alvin* was unequipped to recover much of the biological material and therefore brought only a small amount to the surface for examination. From the submersible's viewing ports, however, dense fields of clams were seen, along with many empty shells. There were no mussels and no vestimentifaran worms.

The absence of mussels or worms and the redistribution of sediments by an underwater earthquake, however, do not give this site its special importance. As at the Florida Escarpment, these animals did not live near a hydrothermal vent. The geologists theorized that the original valley floor was scoured by gravel waves, exposing "previously buried horizons that are enriched in reduced compounds, or permeable enough to permit the migration of reduced compound-rich fluids." The full community of chemosynthetic organisms established itself on the floor of the deep Atlantic in the fifty-eight years from the earthquake to the discovery of the ventless vent fauna, indicating that whatever we thought we knew about the creatures of the hydrothermal vents is marginal at best, and that our knowledge of these phenomena is still in its infancy.

In 1988 a group of European scientists (Fricke, Giere, Stetter, et al., 1989) using the submersible *GEO*, discovered "a new type of Atlantic vent community in shallow water" off the island of Kolbeinsey, north of Iceland on the Jan-Mayen Ridge. At a depth of only ninety meters, they observed fissures, chimneys thirty meters high, and "large, crater-like dips, 1.5 to 2 m deep, with powerful outflows of hot water." While the ambient seawater temperature was 2.6 degrees Celsius, the temperature at the fissures was 89 degrees Celsius, and they also saw bubbles of boiling water issuing from the openings of craters. At this depth, the boiling point of seawater is 180 to 182 degrees Celsius. The living creatures at this site consisted mostly of bacteria, but there were also sponges and hydrozoans that appeared to be filtering the hydrothermal water. Crabs and a single sea bass were seen in the vicinity of the vents, but they were believed to be visitors. In a Southern California vent community in 1984, the abalone *Haliotis cracherodii* was seen foraging opportunistically on mats of sulfur-oxidizing bacteria, deriving nourishment from geothermal matter.

A question still unanswered by vent biologists is: How did the animals get to the sites in the first place? (In the Kolbeinsey communities, the bacteria were believed to have developed from surrounding cold-water fauna.) The vents, while more common than originally believed, are widely scattered, and spring up along the fissures, in (so far) unpredictable locations. It is even more difficult to predict the eruption of an underwater hot spring than it would be to predict an earthquake, and so far it has been almost impossible to predict a terrestrial disturbance. On land, various seismic devices have been employed, more or less unsatisfactorily, but the seafloor affords even fewer such opportunities.[‡] The seafloor vent appears and is somehow colonized by the rift animals. Of these creatures, however, only the crabs are mobile; the tube worms, clams, and mussels are what the biologists call "sessile," meaning they are more or less attached to the substrate. (The fishes are mobile, but very few species are considered endemic to the rift environments.) In any event, it is unlikely that a clam or a crab would leave one thermal vent in search of another, so it is up to the larvae to disperse themselves. Passive dispersal, where the larvae of many marine invertebrates become part of the plankton and drift about at the mercy of deep-ocean currents, is the strategy whereby most species colonize new areas. The larvae of vent animals might ride upward on the rising, heated plumes until they encounter horizontally moving currents, where they drift until they drop down to a new vent site. Some biologists subscribe to

the "founders" theory, which holds that the free-floating larvae of the various rift animals happen upon an erupting vent and colonize it. The species that arrives first and in the largest numbers becomes the dominant form at that location, explaining why some sites are dominated by tube worms, others by clams, and still others by mussels. In the Pacific, a vent community was found on the skeleton of a gray whale, suggesting to R. A. Wheatcroft and his colleagues (1989) that "whale skeletons may indeed provide persistent and abundant "stepping stones" for the dispersal of deep-sea chemosynthetic communities."

In June 1993 scientists Charles Langmuir of the Lamont-Doherty Earth Observatory and Gary Klinkhammer of Oregon State, investigating hot-water vents along the Mid-Atlantic Ridge in *Alvin*, discovered the largest hydrothermal vent in the Atlantic. It consisted of seven sites covering some fifteen acres, two hundred miles west of the Azores. As they described it in 1997, the "Lucky Strike" vent field contains numerous active and inactive hydrothermal vents, and twenty-one chimneys, some with spires 180 feet high, the largest ever found. Rather than being made of metallic minerals, they are made of carbonates (CO_3, typical of the rock limestone) and silica. The difference is in the type of the host rocks and the relatively low temperature of the vent water, only 160 degrees Fahrenheit (71 degrees Celsius). The chimneys are beautiful with multiple spires up to thirty feet wide at their tops and delicate, feathery minerals on their tops and flanks. "Lucky Strike" is inhabited by yellow mussels, a form of bivalve not seen at previous vent sites in the Atlantic or the Pacific, and by pink sea urchins. Hordes of *Rimicaris exoculata*, the eyeless rift

---

[‡] It has recently been revealed that the U.S. Navy has been seismically monitoring the seafloor with a sophisticated array of underwater hydrophones installed over the years to track the ships and submarines of potential enemies. In June 1993, geologists were able to monitor a deep-sea volcanic eruption as it was occurring along the Juan de Fuca Ridge, some four hundred kilometers off the coast of Oregon. Sites on the Juan de Fuca Ridge (part of the San Andreas Fault), such as the "Endeavor Segment," are known locations of hot springs.

shrimp, inhabit one chimney. Dense mats of bacteria cover the mussel beds, various snails creep about, and oceanographers amused themselves by naming an amphipod *Luckia striki*.

A natural experiment began in 1991 as researchers in *Alvin* off the west coast of Mexico witnessed a volcanic eruption that effectively killed all the vent animals at that site. Only a year later, brachyuran crabs had recolonized the site—dubbed "Tube Worm Barbecue" because of the charred remains of the worms—and less than two years later, the worms had grown to four feet in length, covering the site with their white tubes and feathery red gills. In April 1991, the fissure site dubbed "Hole to Hell" was devoid of life, but only twenty-one months later, a thicket of four-foot-long worms had appeared, making them possibly the fastest-growing of all marine invertebrates. In a 1994 *National Geographic* article, researchers Richard Lutz and Rachel Haymon commented on the unsuspected rapidity of the growth of the mineral chimneys and the speed with which the tube worms recolonized the site. *Alvin* accidentally knocked down one of the chimneys; it took only three months for it to grow another twenty feet. In a 1994 *New York Times* article, William Broad wrote, "Traditionally, the ocean abyss has been thought of as a slow-motion world where all development is frustrated by low temperatures, perpetual darkness and pressures so great as to defy comprehension." As a result of *Alvin*'s 1991–94 expeditions, we will have to rethink our ideas about life in the depths, especially at the mysterious vent sites.

In addition to the unsuspected animals and behavior associated with the hot springs, oceanographers also noticed yellow and orange stains on the basalts, which were shown to be a result of powerful seepages of hydrogen sulfide. The creatures of the vent systems make a living in a totally different way than any other creatures on earth, suggesting—at least to some imaginative researchers—that life may have begun in these deep-sea vents. Jack Corliss, in 1977 one of the discoverers of the Galápagos rift animals, was among the first to suggest the possibility of life having started in conditions similar to those found in the vents. Corliss, who was then at Oregon State University, became obsessed with the possibility of the vent systems as the source of life and left the university to devote himself full-time to working on the problem. By 1991 he had moved on to become chief scientist of *Biosphere 2*, the closed-system environment built in the Arizona desert.

Working with Corliss and John Baross, graduate student Sarah Hoffman formulated a theory that life had originated in the Archean period, about 4.2 billion years ago, on the seafloor, which was probably much more hydrothermically active than it is today. Corliss, Baross, and Hoffman suggested that the water issuing from the Archean vents was so hot—600 degrees Celsius—that it cracked the molecular bonds of the rocks and released carbon and carbon compounds (such as methane) into the solution. Then simple organic molecules form out of the newly formed chemical elements, and while some of them rise into the water column, some adhere to the rock faces and form a clay that provides a safe haven for these molecules, giving them the opportunity to form more complex organic molecules. Out of this jumble of molecules, argued Corliss and his colleagues, "biopolymers" can be formed, producing fragmentary nucleic and amino acids, which, in a system far from equilibrium, can organize themselves into new forms—primitive living cells. In 1985 Baross and Hoffman wrote that the hydrothermal activity "provided the multiple pathways for the abiotic synthesis of chemical compounds, origin, and evolution of 'precells' and 'precell communities,' and ultimately, the evolution of free-living organisms." One of the problems with this suggestion is that even if sulfur-based life did develop at the vents, it would have had to metamorphose into a photosynthetic form before it could give rise to the carbon-hydrogen-oxygen-nitrogen system currently in use.

When a whale dies—or is killed—at sea, unless the carcass washes ashore, the remains sink to the bottom. Until recently, that was the end of the story, but around 1990 investigators discovered that whale carcasses on the bottom—now known as "whale falls"—were rich havens for marine life. On a research cruise off California in 1987, Craig Smith, an oceanographer at the University of Hawaii, examined a video of a whale carcass and was surprised to see the same kind of vesicomyid clams that were usually seen around deep-sea vents, as well the usual suspects, hagfishes, worms, and bacteria. Smith found another whale fall in 1993 (again off California), but it was clear that his research could not depend on such serendipitous finds. He therefore put out the word that he wanted whale carcasses that had washed ashore. He then towed these carcasses out to sea, weighted them, and sank them where he could find them again for future examination. (All Smith's artificial "falls" have been in the eastern Pacific, but in 2002 another crew sank a whale

off Japan, and in 2004 a carcass was dropped off Sweden.) The first scavengers to a newly deposited carcass—artifical or natural—are usually hagfish, the eel-shaped, jawless fishes that earn a living feeding on carrion on the ocean floor. Other scavengers include a variety of polychaete worms, and in one instance, a gigantic Pacific sleeper shark (*Somniosus*) that came to bite chunks out of the rotting whale carcass. Bacterial mats form on the bones, which leads to the chemoautotrophic phase, where life on the whale falls begins to resemble that around a deep-sea vent. It is at this stage that the visicomyid clams appear, because they carry sulfide-metabolizing bacteria.

For a 1998 study, Feldman et al. returned to the site of a whale fall in the Santa Catalina Basin off Southern California, and at a depth of 4,067 feet (1,240 meters), they revisited a gray whale carcass that had been discovered in 1995. They found a "persistent community" of filamentous sulfur bacteria (*Beggiatoa* spp.), vesicomyid clams, limpets, snails, and a single vestimentifaran tube worm (*Escarpia spicata*), leading them to conclude that "The discovery of an adult vestimentifaran on the SCB whale fall suggests that such falls can support the recruitment and growth of at least one species of vestimentifaran. This finding, as well as the identification of seep and vent vesicomyids on whale falls, is consistent with the finding that whale caracasses may serve as stepping stones for seep and vent organisms."

Whale falls therefore represent a rich opportunity to examine the sequential colonization of a new food source on the ocean bottom, not only for known species, such as hagfish and crabs, but also for previously unsuspected species—with

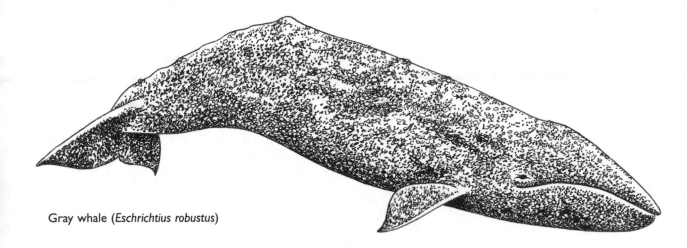

Gray whale (*Eschrichtius robustus*)

previously unsuspected habits. In a 2004 study of the fauna of whale falls, Thomas Dahlgren, Adrian Glover, Amy Baco, and Craig Smith identified a new species of polychaete worm that they named *Vigtorniella flokati* (*flokati* is Greek for a "shaggy, woolen rug"). The worms were found on two gray whale carcasses off San Diego and on a balaenopterid carcass off Oahu. As described by the authors, the worms exhibit a remarkable behavior, "clinging posteriorly to the whale bones or nearby sediments to form a writhing carpet at densities up to 8000 m^{-2} . . . suggesting that it is a whale fall specialist."

Generally speaking, the fauna that occupies whale remains is closer in character to the chemosynthetic vent fauna than it is to photosynthetic life-forms. "It is not surprising," wrote Craig Smith and colleagues in 1989, "that a whale carcass on the energy-poor deep-sea floor should produce a community with ecological and taxonomic similarities to other deep-sea reducing habitats. Microbial degradation of organic-rich whale remains appears certain to yield sulphide reduction and putrefaction. The consequent occurrence of sulphides with a nearby source of oxygen (in bottom water) should provide a habitat analogous to seeps and vents in its suitablity for sulphide-oxidizing bacteria and their metazoan hosts." The ability with which vent fauna move from vent to vent has always puzzled scientists, but whale falls (in the Pacific), which the authors of the study calculated might occur every couple of hundred miles, might serve as an intermediate step in the dispersal of deep-sea chemosynthetic communities.

Evidently, the similarities of whale-fall fauna to that of hydrothermal vents is even greater than was originally suspected. According to the 2004 report in *Science* by Greg Rouse, Shana Goffredi, and Robert Vrijenhoek, a new species of tube worm, which they named *Osedax*, digs into the whale carcass and remains there, feeding on the bones. Females of the bone-eating worms are about as long as your index finger and consist of an outer tube, an inner muscular trunk, an egg-carrying oviduct, and space for the miniature males. The egg sac is sheathed in bacteria-filled tissue that penetrates the bone like the roots of a plant. Like the giant vestimentaran tube worms (*Riftia*) to which they are related, *Osedax* worms are topped with red or white feathery structures that extract oxygen from the water for the worms and the bacteria living inside them.

When submersibles like *Alvin* lowered the barrier between the unknown and the known (and reminded us once again that some of the facts of life in the vents were probably unknowable), it involved much more than the discovery of new species. A whole new world of hotter temperatures, unknown sources of nutrition, strange shapes, and stranger lifestyles had been hiding from us in inner space. What else will the oceanographers find? And what will they do when they find it? ❧

The Novelty of Swimming Cucumbers

The name *Cucumis marinus*—"sea cucumber"—was bestowed upon them by Pliny the Elder, for what appeared to be obvious reasons, based on their familiar shape. Only recently, however, has the true nature of these curious animals begun to reveal itself. In a 1986 article, D. S. Billett wrote, "Sea cucumbers are supposed to be long and cylindrical and live at the bottom of the sea. Marine biologists are now finding that in the deep oceans these animals break all the rules and swim high above the ocean floor. . . ." As echinoderm specialist David Pawson has written, "knowledge of the deep-sea benthic fauna has increased tremendously in recent years, not only as a result of the fact that new collections of organisms have been described, and that several studies have been conducted on population structure and patterns of distribution, but also as a result of the increasing use of underwater cameras and manned submersibles to record the habits and interrelationships of living organisms *in situ*." By 1989, Pawson himself had "studied approximately 80,000 photographs of the deep-sea floor . . ." and "made probably 200 dives in manned submersibles, and always there are beautiful holothurians to be seen."

The class Holothuroidea includes some twelve hundred species, the commonest forms of which have the characteristic cucumber-like shape. At one end, modified tube feet (*podia*) form a circle of tentacles around the mouth, with the anal opening at the other end, used for discharging wastes and respiration. The bottom-dwellers plow along the sediments like vacuum cleaners, hoovering up muddy sediments that include bacteria, diatoms, and other microscopic organisms that make up their food supply. The mouth is typically at the front end of an elongated or flattened body, surrounded by a corona of oral tentacles, and the anus is at the other end. In order to extract nourishment from sand or mud, they have to process considerable amounts of inorganic matter; W. J. Crozier estimated that a single ten-inch-long *Stichopus* (a shallow-water species) ingests and egests two and a half pounds of bottom sediment every day. (He also estimated that in the 1.7 acres of Harrington Sound, Bermuda, the *Stichopus* population processes between five hundred and one thousand tons of bottom material per year.) Many holothurians breathe with a pair of "respiratory trees" in the body cavity that extend forward from the cloaca and keep the internal organs aerated and the body plump. Others lack trees, and respire through their body walls. They move by means of podia, which are usually disposed on the underside in rows down the mid-line, and on each edge of the outer margin, but there are many variations on this theme. As it "walks," the animal makes identifiable tracks in the sediment, some of which have been illustrated in the chapter "Footprints" in *The Face of the Deep.* (Heezen and Hollister wrote, "Holothurians feeding on the bottom sediments mix and till the surface muds on an enormous scale, producing features more widespread and more visibly evident than those produced by any other animals on earth.")

For the most part, sea cucumbers (holothurians) seem the most undramatic of the oceanic fauna, processing detritus while slowly puttering along the bottom. Some species are unusual in that they have strange protrusions covering the body, and one (*Psychropotes mirabilis*) has a narrow, upright "sail" that is longer than the body of the animal, and the function of which is a total mystery. There are some species, however, that do not conform to the sea-cucumber rules, and spend most—if not all—of their lives far from the bottom, swimming in the water column. Looking like an upside-down octopus (but without eyes and siphon) the holothurian *Pelagothuria* was first collected off the west coast of Central America in 1891 and subsequently from other locations in the tropical Pacific and Indian Oceans. Sea cucumbers that never seem to touch bottom appeared among the myriad unbelievable creatures pulled from the deep by *Galathea*'s trawls in the 1950s. In the China Sea, *Galathea* collected a new species, larger than the previous ones, which scientists of the *Galathea* Expedition named *Galatheathuria*. It was about six inches in diameter, dark violet, with a swimming fringe along either side.

Remarkable as this find was, it was not more so than the sighting from the submersible *Trieste* as it descended to the bottom of the Challenger Deep, the deepest point in the ocean, in 1960. Jacques Piccard and Don Walsh, *Trieste*'s pilots,

claimed to have seen a fish swim off the bottom at 35,800 feet, but shortly after *Trieste*'s record-shattering dive, Torben Wolff of the Zoological Museum of Copenhagen published a note in *Nature* in which he suggested that it was not a fish at all, but probably a holothurian, "perhaps related to the bathypelagic, cushion-shaped *Galatheathuria aspera*, which is almost a foot long and oval in outline." Years later in a *Newsweek* article on submersibles, writer Tony Emerson quoted ichthyologist Richard Rosenblatt of Scripps as saying, "Everyone agrees it was a sea cucumber."

Other startling behavior by cucumber acrobats joined the novelty acts of the deep when John Miller, David Pawson, and other scientists, in their research dives aboard the submersibles *Johnson Sea-Link* (off the Bahamas) and *Pisces* (off the Galápagos), observed four swimming species in 1989. These included *Hansenothuria benti*, a new species that they described and named for the Danish researcher Bent Hansen "in recognition of his superb contributions to our knowledge of deep-sea holothurians." (The late Dr. Hansen, an invertebrate specialist, wrote—among other things—the comprehensive "Systematics and Biology of the Deep-Sea Holothurians.") In their 1990 paper ("Swimming Sea Cucumbers . . . A Survey with Analysis of Swimming Behavior in Four Bathyal Species"), Miller and Pawson wrote, "the true natatorial acrobats among the class Holothuroidea are the deep-sea species of the orders Aspidochirotida and Elasipodida. Approximately 20 species . . . have been captured or observed near the bottom or at depths several hundred to several thousand meters above the seafloor. A few deep-sea species have even been found in surface waters."

Why sea cucumbers should be swimming is unknown, since most of the pelagic varieties appear adapted for feeding in the sediments. The swimmers may range upward to breed, or they may even have developed some method of filtering particles from the water, but not enough is known about the lives of most of the deep-water holothurians to determine exactly what they are doing off the bottom. Miller and Pawson identified possible reasons for swimming behavior, including "predator avoidance, escape from physical hazards, locomotion, seeking out suitable substrata for feeding, and dispersal of juveniles or adults." They identified *Pelagothuria natatrix* ("pelagic swimming holothurian") as the only known species to spend its entire life "swimming and drifting in the water column, feeding on re-suspended sediments or on the rain of detrital material from the shallower depths." *H. benti*, on the other hand, "has been found to swim only in response to a disturbance," flexing through a series of S-curves to propel itself away from the offender. *Paleopatides retifer*, a sweet-potato-shaped animal with a wide brim, flexes its body and pulsates the brim, like its relative *P. grisea*. *Pelagothuria natatrix*, they wrote, "is perhaps the most bizarre holothurian species in existence. Its shape is more reminiscent of a medusa, and it bears no obvious resemblance to most sea cucumbers." At the anterior end of the body is an enormous, umbrella-like web of feeding tentacles that may be as long as or longer than the slender, conical body, and that the animal pulsates to move through the water. When scientists attempted to capture a specimen of *Benthodytes* from the submersible *Archimede* off Madeira, "the movements of the grab made the holothurian expand very rapidly to three of four times its original volume. It thus became loaf-shaped instead of sausage-shaped, and its colour changing at the same time from dark brown to reddish violet . . . it escaped the grab" (Wolff 1971).

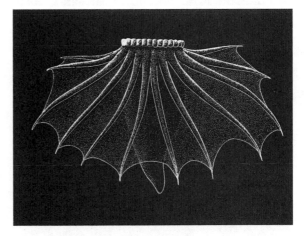

Swimming sea cucumber (*Pelagothuria natatrix*)

Diving (separately) off southern California in the submersibles *Sea Cliff* and *Turtle*, scientists (see Barnes, Quetin, Childress, and Pawson, 1976) were "surrounded by living hordes" of the swimming elasipod holothurian *Peniagone diaphana*, which they described as a small, flattened holothurian averaging about three inches in length, with a tentacled mouth at one end and a paddlelike postanal fan at the other. (This species is also known from the Atlantic at depths from 2,550 to 5,600 meters.) Originally, they were "never seen in contact with the substrate" (never resting or crawling on the bottom), but even more surprising, they were always swimming vertically. (There are very few marine animals other than sea horses and their relatives that maintain a constant vertical orientation.)

Later, *Peniagone diaphana* was also found living on the seafloor. It may feed on suspended detritus, but examination of captured specimens revealed "sponge spicules, holothurian spicules, diatom frustules, foraminiferan shells," indicating some seafloor feeding. (Not all *Peniagone* holothurians swim; nothing researchers in *Alvin* did could make one western Atlantic species leave the bottom, but other closely related forms were observed *only* off the bottom. In their 1989 paper, Foell and Pawson wrote that *P. leander* "may only spend about 25% of the time on the seafloor, presumably feeding on the sediments, while the remaining time is spent swimming or passively drifting at heights of up to at least 250 meters above the bottom.")

Some of these "natatorial acrobats" include glowing in the dark in their repertoire. In a 1974 study by Peter Herring on the bioluminescent qualities of various echinoderms, several North Atlantic holothurians were collected and presented a dazzling array of luminescent effects, but not for any obvious reason. (In 1961 J. A. C. Nicol suggested that sedentary animals might "flash or twinkle . . . when touched, and thus warn would-be settlers that the territory is already occupied.") The holothurian species *Kolga hyalina* "gave a bright blue light when handled," and the small orange species *Ellipinion* "emitted a brilliant blue light from a great many minute sparkling points all over the whole dorsal and lateral surface."

Not all sea cucumber populations are undisturbed. Galápagos National Park was established in 1959, and the islands were declared a World Heritage Site by UNESCO in 1978, and a Biosphere Reserve in 1985. The exploitation of sea cucumbers started in the islands in the early 1990s and concentrated on a single species, *Stichopus fuscus*. The fishery was introduced by Asian entrepreneurs who settled in mainland Ecuador around 1989. After depleting *Stichopus* populations along the coast of Ecuador, they moved their operations to the Galápagos. *Pepino* is "cucumber" in Spanish; the fishermen call themselves *pepineros*. The bottom-trawl fishery has had an enormous socioeconomic impact, increasing human migration to the Galápagos, illegal fishing, and violations of the National Park regulations. In 1992, by presidential decree, the government of Ecuador prohibited fishing for sea cucumbers in the Galápagos.

Two years later, an experimental two-month artisanal fishery was allowed. This harvest was closed a month after it started, due to the unwillingness of the pepineros to abide by the rules imposed by the National Park and Fisheries authorities. Although all sea cucumber fishing was banned in the Galápagos, clandestine fishing continued because the ban was unenforced. Meanwhile, population studies of *Stichopus* revealed a continuous decline, while the pepineros continued to petition the government to reopen the fishery. Their petition was accepted, and a two-month season was opened in April 1999. A total of 4,401,657 sea cucumbers were exported from the Galápagos during this harvest season, representing a total of over 122 metric tons of dry product, worth US$3.4 million. Virtually all of the "product" was exported to Asia, where sea cucumbers have historically been consumed as a delicacy. Known as *trepang* or *beche-de-mer* in the Indo-Pacific or along certain Oriental coasts, the animal is eviscerated, boiled, then dried or smoked. In recent times the demand has sky-rocketed, and markets in Japan, Hong Kong, Taiwan, and Singapore have turned to fisheries outside of Asian waters as their own stocks decline. Of the approximately 1,250 species of sea cucumbers worldwide, only a handful are commercially exploitable, and many of these are suffering from the pressures of commercial fishing.

In 2000, a new sea cucumber season was opened in the Galápagos, from May to July. A fixed quota and a zoning plan with "no take" areas were established, but just a few days before the season officially began, a group of pepineros took the National Park and Darwin Research Station offices on Isabela Island by force. They removed giant tortoises from the rearing center as ransom in an attempt to get the rights to collect cucumbers. Their threat was unsuccessful, but in May, 2005, the Ecuadorian government lifted the ban on sea cucumber fishing in the Galápagos anyway. The new authorization allowed fisherman to capture up to three million sea cucumbers in a sixty-day period that began on June 12. The decision ended a prohibition on fishing of sea cucumbers that was supposed to have been in effect until 2006.

Coming as it did over the protests of conservation groups, and even the Ecuadorian government, the decimation of the Galápagos *pepinos* was unexpected. Sea cucumbers have been collected and eaten since Pliny first likened the invertebrates to vegetables. There are some marine animals, however, whose "discovery" can be dated close to the end of the twentieth century. Instead of two thousand years, fishers on these newly discovered species had two decades, and during that period, they accomplished the same thing that the pepineros had in the Galápagos—they drove the object of their fisheries in the direction of extinction. ❧

Discovery Followed by Near-Destruction

The Patagonian toothfish exemplifies the discovery of a new resource followed by its exploitation, almost to extinction. Off the southern coast of Chile, on February 11, 1888, the research vessel *Albatross* hauled in a beam trawl that had been cast into six thousand feet of water. Among the creatures dumped on deck was a five-foot-long, large-mouthed fish, the likes of which no one had ever seen. Charles H. Townsend and Theodore Gill, ichthyologists aboard the *Albatross*, photographed it as it lay on the deck, then placed in a rough wooden box and salted it to preserve it for later study. Unfortunately, an overzealous bosun's mate pitched the box overboard, and all that remained of the fish was the photograph. Townsend and Gill then named it "*Macrias* with reference to its length as well as its bulk, and the specific name *amissus* is appropriate for it was an estray from its relatives as well as to indicate the loss of the type." *Macrias amissus* was by far the largest known of all deep-sea fishes, and in 1901, Gill and Townsend wrote a brief description of their lost specimen.

Thirty-five years later, Townsend wrote about it again in the *Bulletin* of the New York Zoological Society (he was the director of the society's aquarium, then located at the Battery in lower Manhattan). Because he came across the photograph while searching through old records of the *Albatross* voyage, he repeated his 1914 title, "The Largest Deep-Sea Fish," and included the subhead "A Long-Missing Photograph of the Monster Comes to Light After Nearly Half a Century." And there is *Macrias amissus*, on the deck of the *Albatross*. Townsend says:

> *Macrias amissus* never found its way into the published lists of fishes known to science. Perhaps the ichthyologists will relent when they see the photograph Dr. Gill and I regarded as that of a new fish from the depths and worthy of being described as something new to science, whether we had or had not, the type.

A couple of ichthyologists did relent, but not exactly as Townsend imagined they would. When Hugh DeWitt of Stanford University looked at the photograph, he "was immediately reminded of the illustration of *Dissostichus eleginoides* published by F. A. Smitt in 1898." Because of differences in Townsend's description (in *Science*) and Smitt's (in a Swedish journal), DeWitt decided that *Macrias amissus* was not exactly like *D. eleginoides* and therefore named it *Dissostichus amissus*.

DeWitt's article appeared in the ichthyological journal *Copeia* in 1962, but not many non-ichthyologists read it. Somehow, the "Albatross Fish" became one of the more popular subjects for those who would postulate large, unknown

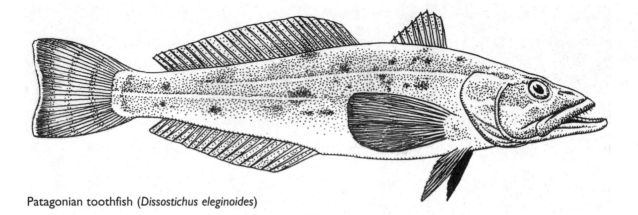

Patagonian toothfish (*Dissostichus eleginoides*)

fishes lurking at abyssal depths. For example, in Edward Ricciuti's 1973 *Killers of the Seas*, there is a section entitled "Survivors from Past Ages," and there, of all things, is the photograph of the fish from the *Albatross*. The caption reads:

> STRANGE FISH. This fish, about 5 feet long, was dredged from a depth of 6,000 feet by the research vessel *Albatross* in 1888. Shortly after this photo was taken on deck, a crewman tossed the fish overboard, to the dismay of scientists who had never seen anything like it before.

Soviet cetologists, however, had seen something like the *Albatross*'s fish; in fact, *Dissostichus* is a fairly common food item of Southern Ocean sperm whales. A. A. Berzin's 1972 monograph on sperm whales displayed a photograph of a fish with the caption: "Specimen of *Dissotichus* [sic] *mawsoni*, from the stomach of a sperm whale. . ." The stomachs of three sperm whales taken by Soviet whalers in 1963 contained about twenty fish per whale, from seventeen to fifty-three inches long, and weighing up to a hundred pounds. Although sperm whales are believed to hunt at great depths, how they are able to catch these presumably swift fishes in the dark is unknown. We may not know how sperm whales catch these fish, but we know how people do, and they do it so efficiently that the fish is on the fast track to extinction.

We are beginning to learn a little about *Dissostichus eleginoides*, a species that was virtually unknown until the early 1990s. Slow-growing and unbeautiful, this deep-water species can reach a length of six feet and a weight of two hundred pounds. Adult females are somewhat larger than males. Because they do not mature until about ten years of age, many of the fish are caught before achieving breeding potential, which is a population crash waiting to happen. Before the arrival of the longliners, *Dissostichus* was preyed on by deep-diving sperm whales and elephant seals; and also by large, predacious squid, such as the recently glamorized "colossal" squid, *Mesonychoteuthis*.

Now known as the Patagonian toothfish, *Dissostichus eleginoides* was first caught on longlines in the early 1990s by fishermen who were fishing the subantarctic waters north of 55 degrees south latitude around Patagonia, after the stocks of austral hake (*Merluccius australis*) and kingklip (*Genypterus blacodes*) had collapsed because of overfishing. In November 2000 a halibut fishing boat in the Davis Strait (between Greenland and Baffin Island) pulled in a Patagonian toothfish. "It is unlikely," wrote Møller et al. in *Nature*, "that an unknown population of toothfish exists off Greenland," so it is "more likely that this was a stray specimen from a South Atlantic population." Although hardly any information can be found on the growth rate of the fish or the size of the stocks, fishing boats flying the flags of Argentina, Chile, Uruguay, South Africa, France, and Great Britain are hauling in these fishes at an egregious rate. Consequently, CCAMLR (the Convention for the Conservation of Antarctic Marine Living Resources; pronounced *Camel-R*) has reported that fishers are taking more than ten times the ten-thousand-ton allotment. Islands like Crozet, Heard, Kerguelen, and South Georgia in Antarctic and subantarctic waters are mostly outside of any nation's exclusive economic zone (EEZ) and therefore outside the limits of islands owned by the various nations. The far greater problem is that there is hardly any way to monitor illegal fishing in the Southern Ocean.

Often unacknowledged, and therefore unlikely to find their way into fisheries statistics, are the catches of the so-called pirate fisheries. These fisheries—known by the acronym IUU for "illegal, unreported, and unregulated"—kill an almost incomprehensible number of the target species, plus countless sharks, seabirds, marine mammals, and other fishes. To avoid detection, IUU fisheries fish without a license, fish under a "flag of convenience," fish out of season, harvest prohibited species, use banned fishing gear—such as drift nets—and most insidious, do not report catches at all. On the high seas, unbound by regulations, IUU fishers will target the most valuable species, such as tuna and Patagonian toothfish, but they will take anything and everything. Although the Southern Ocean, mostly out of sight and out of the jurisdiction of any regulators, has been the hardest hit, the coastal waters of many developing states, particularly off the west coast of Africa, are also victimized. IUU fishers are stealing food from some of the poorest people in the world.

Mounting evidence of IUU fishing in the Southern Ocean has forced CCAMLR to propose actions that would halt the plunder of these seas. Since 1997, it is estimated that IUU fishing for *Dissostichus* species in the Southern Ocean has been about ninety thousand metric tons, more than twice the level of toothfish catches taken in CCAMLR-regulated fisheries. This unsustainable rate of extraction has led to a significant and alarming depletion of toothfish stocks in some areas. In 1998 the Australian government issued this statement: "If illegal and unregulated fishing continues at the current level, the population of Patagonian Toothfish will be so severely decimated that within the next two or three years the species will be commercially extinct."

The IUU pirates dwarf the legal fishery for toothfish, mostly in the South Atlantic and the southern Indian Ocean. Of the fifty-nine thousand metric tons of Patagonian toothfish caught in 1999/2000, the illegal and unreported portion could amount to as much as thirty-three thousand tons. In October 2002 the Australian government announced that it was sending armed patrol boats to the Southern Ocean to protect legitimate Australian fishers and arrest toothfish poachers. In *Black Market for White Gold*, the 2004 update of their 2001 report on Patagonian toothfish, the National Environmental Trust (NET), an advocacy organization in Washington, D.C., detailed the twenty-day chase through Antarctic seas and the capture of the Uruguayan-flagged longliner *Viarsa I* by the Australian customs ship *Southern Supporter*. With the help of British and South African ships that had joined the chase, *Viarsa I* was finally captured two thousand miles west of Cape Town with eighty-five tons of Patagonian toothfish in her freezers. At current prices, *Viasra*'s eighty-five tons of toothfish was worth more than a million dollars at the dock—certainly worth the risk of capture or seizure.

Restyled as "Chilean sea bass" to make the fish more palatable to American restaurant patrons, Patagonian toothfish was first served in a Los Angeles restaurant around 1982. Since then, its soft, snow-white flesh and mild flavor have made it one of the most popular menu items in America's finer restaurants. An Atlanta restaurateur said that he used to go through twelve hundred pounds a week. It is also known in English as black hake or black cod; the Chileans call it *bacalao de profundidad*, and the French know it as *légine austral*. The world champions at importing it, the Japanese call the highly prized white flesh *mero*. Japan imported fifteen thousand tons in 2001, followed by the United States and Canada. According to a recent TRAFFIC report (Lack and Sant 2001), "The Canadian, EU, Japanese and US markets imported nearly 30,000 tons of Patagonian toothfish products, with Japanese imports comprising over 55% of the total." The

leading exporters are Chile, Argentina, and Uruguay, which account for 47 percent of the legal total of ten thousand tons. The illegal catch, which obviously cannot be calculated, is hidden by mislabeling the species, falsifying permits, offloading at rogue ports where documentation is deficient, claiming catches were caught on the high seas when they were taken in CCAMLR-regulated waters, and transferring illegal catches at sea. "Even though there are legitimate fishermen getting their catch to the marketplace after complying with all the legal requirements," concludes the NET report, "their product is tainted by the illegal activities of those operators who use the Catch Documentation Scheme as a means to launder their ill-gotten gains. This in turn makes it impossible for wholesalers, retailers, and consumers to know if they are selling or buying an illegal product." (A barcode of life, discussed on pages 59–62, offers the means to identify such counterfeit products.)

The notoriety of the unfortunate depletion of the world's marine resources has made a crusade against overfishing popular in certain circles. One of the best ways to publicize illegal or overexploitive fisheries is to make those who buy the fish—in this case, the restaurants that serve it—aware of the problems. As was done with the dwindling North Atlantic swordfish populations, a campaign has been started to have chefs remove Chilean sea bass from their menus. "Take a Pass on Chilean Sea Bass," organized by the National Environmental Trust, an advocacy organization in Washington, D.C., claims to have signed on more than eight hundred restaurants in major cities across the United States. Perhaps the news that Patagonian toothfish, aka Chilean sea bass, contains high levels of mercury will dissuade diners from ordering it.

"The Southern Ocean and Anarctica are thought to be virtually free from direct anthropogenic sources of mercury," wrote McArthur, Butler, and Jackson in 2003, but their analysis showed that mercury was found in the tissues of the Patagonian toothfish, a top predator, and also the warty squid (*Moroteuthis ingens*), a "midtrophic species." Toothfish are opportunistic predators, consuming fish, cephalopods, and crustaceans, and the highest concentrations of mercury are usually found in predators at the top of the food chain. (Other animals found to have a high biomagnification of mercury are swordfish, tuna, pilot whales, and some dolphin species.) McArthur et al. went on to say that "the mercury levels in larger specimens of Macquarie Island toothfish are high enough to cause potential health concerns for sustained and regular human consumption." As has been shown with swordfish, however, people do not readily change their eating habits because of threats of mercury in fish that they like to eat. Despite a nationwide campaign to alert potential consumers to the dangers of mercury poisoning in swordfish, the catch—and therefore the consumption—of swordfish did not diminish significantly.

There is no campaign to prevent Antarctic killer whales from eating toothfish, however. In a study published in 2003, Robert Pitman and Paul Ensor reported on a population of killer whales, differing in some particulars from other populations, that feeds "mainly on Antarctic toothfish (*Dissostichus mawsoni*), a fish that grows to more than six feet long and more than 250 pounds." The Antarctic toothfish differs from its Patagonian cousin in that it is generally found under cover of heavy sea ice, south of the Antarctic Polar Front. As described by Joseph Eastman in his *Antarctic Fish Biology*, "Its blood is well fortified with antifreezes in the subzero habitat. Although commonly possessing a pattern of four dark vertical bands, fish are nearly pitch black when captured under the ice of McMurdo Sound." Fishing boats from New Zealand and elsewhere have recently begun to experiment with commercial fishing for *D. mawsoni* in the southern Ross Sea, and according to Pitman and Ensor, this species is the primary prey item of a form of killer whale that is characterized by smaller size, a "cape" pattern, and yellowish patches where those of other killer whale varieties are white. It is possible—but not yet shown by DNA analysis—that the population of killer whales that feeds on the Antarctic toothfish is a heretofore unrecognized species of *Orca*.

Southern Ocean killer whales, whatever the species, seem to favor toothfish, Patagonian or Antarctic. Observing from the Chilean longliner *B/F Friosur V* in the vicinity of the island of South Georgia, Ashford et al. (1996) noted that "most net fisheries using hooks and lines, particularly longlines, may actually attract marine mammals. They provide fish that are wounded and easy to take, and frequently of medium to large size." Killer whales (and maybe sperm whales) probably regard it as a boon that longliners pull in toothfish by the hundreds, saving the cetaceans the trouble of actually having to chase and catch them. (Sperm whales are also attracted to longliners, and as we've seen, they were among the first consumers of *Dissostichus* spp., but because sperm whales are so much larger than killer whales and feed at greater depths, the direct evidence of sperm whales feeding on hooked toothfish is sparse.) When the crew of the *Friosur* hauled in their long-lines, very few intact fish were brought on board, showing convincingly that killer whales were taking advantage of the buffet provided by the long-liners. In a study presented at a 2002 workshop in American Samoa on the interactions between cetaceans and longline fisheries (Donoghue, Reeves, and Stone, eds.), it was noted that "hooks with only the lips of teeth fish (no head or body) were recorded more often when sperm whales were in the vicinity of the vessel. Sperm whales were noted as being present in 84% of the observations when 'lips only' were found on hooks."

Sperm whales in the Gulf of Alaska are responsible for similar depredations on sablefish (*Anoplopoma fimbria*), also known as the Alaskan black cod. (Another "black cod" is Paranotothenia microlepidota, fished from New Zealand to the subantarctic waters of the Great Australian Bight, the Chilean coasts, and the Falkland Islands.) According to the study by Jan Straley et al. in the Samoa workshop, "sablefish depredation by sperm whales on longline gear was first reported in the eastern Gulf of Alaska in 1978." Unlike killer whales, which have a mouthful of powerful teeth, sperm whales are unique among the toothed whales in having teeth only in the lower jaw, so it is not immediately evident how they might remove fish—or parts of fish—from long-lines. They could, of course, swallow them whole, which would leave no trace of depredation. Longlining is an extremely efficient method of fishing and thus is bad for the target species and equally harmful to creatures not immediately targeted—the bycatch.* From an economic viewpoint—often the commercial fisherman's only viewpoint—longlining is a bonanza, replacing hand lines, nets, and trawls with the random, deadly efficiency of mile after mile of baited hooks. Longlining is good for fishermen but bad for fish, sharks, turtles, seabirds, and those cetaceans not clever enough to figure out how to use longlines for their benefit. ⚭

---

* "Bycatch" is the term used to refer to animals other than the targeted species caught in nets or on longlines. Longlines set for tuna or swordfish catch turtles, seabirds, sharks, whales, and other fishes; the "bycatch" in drift net fishing includes every living species that blunders into the nets. The worst offender is the shrimp fishery. "For every 10 pounds of Gulf of Mexico shrimp scraped from the seafloor," wrote Sylvia Earle in 1995, "80 to 90 pounds of 'trash fish'— rays, eels, flounder, butterfish, redfish, batfish, and more, including juveniles of many species—are mangled and discarded, in addition to tons of plants and animals not even considered worth reporting as 'bycatch,' i.e., starfish, sand dollars, urchins, crabs, turtle grass, seaweed, sponges, coral, sea hares, sea squirts, polychaete worms, horse conchs, and whatever else constitutes the seafloor communities that are in the path of the nets."

The Orange Roughy and the Convict

The orange roughy (*Hoplostethus atlanticus*) is a foot-long, big-headed, laterally compressed (like a vertical pancake) deepwater fish that inhabits deep, cold waters over steep continental slopes, ocean ridges, and seamounts. They have been recorded swimming as deep as six thousand feet in the North Atlantic Ocean. The specific name *atlanticus* was applied because the orange roughy was first described in 1889 from a specimen taken off the Azores. They are also found in the Indian Ocean and deep below the surface on the continental shelf slope between Port Stephens in New South Wales and Cape Naturaliste in Western Australia. The name is derived from the bright orange or red color of the body and fins, although there are silver tinges on the flanks, and they are fished commercially in South Africa, South Australia, and New Zealand. The New Zealand fishery was begun only in 1979; at depths that range from twenty-five hundred to five thousand feet, it is the deepest commercial fishery in the world.

Until the 1980s, when it was recruited as a replacement for declining flounder, the orange roughy was called the slimehead. It seemed abundant in deep water off New Zealand. Arriving in the markets of the Northern Hemisphere, it quickly became a seafood hit, valued for its mild white flesh. Big discount operators promoted it, and exports to the United States and Europe soared. By the time New Zealand adopted strict catch limits, 80 percent of the roughy population had been destroyed. Large factory trawlers now exploit another virgin roughy stock, in the southeast Atlantic Ocean. As a result, roughy is still abundant in the frozen food lockers—at least for the time being.

Orange roughys are among the longest-living of all vertebrates. They do not mature until they are over 30 years old, and there are documented records of individuals that reached 150, which means that there are probably orange roughys alive now that hatched before the American Civil War. With advances in deep-sea trawling, fishes that could not be caught before were hauled up in great quantities, and orange

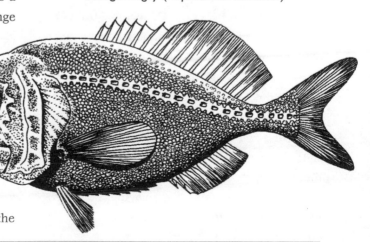

Orange roughy (*Hoplostethus atlanticus*)

roughys were extensively exported to the United States. When the fishery began, Australian and New Zealand fishers were completely ignorant of the population or breeding habits of the object of their fishery, and by the time they learned about this species, intense fishing pressure had already seriously reduced the populations. Because orange roughy school tightly, a five-minute tow can fill a trawl net with an astounding ten to fifty tons of fish. This schooling pattern plus the slow rate of growth and development make the orange roughy particularly susceptible to overfishing, and catches have fallen to a fraction of what they were earlier in the decade. Orange roughy was once a popular menu item in North American restaurants, but as it became to scarce to fish economically, it was replaced by another exotic Southern Hemisphere fish, the so-called "Chilean sea bass" (see previous chapter). Because of its extremely slow rate of reproduction, it will be a long time before the orange roughy can recover from the blitzkrieg fishing efforts that nearly drove it to extinction. In the meantime, we are learning a lot we didn't know about *Hoplostethus atlanticus*.

As reported by Franz Uiblein of MAR-ECO, an international research project conducted in conjunction with the Census of Marine Life, orange roughys found in the Bay of Biscay forty-five hundred feet (1,400 meters) down could be approached as close as one meter and made no effort to avoid the submersible. But even more startling was the color of many of the "orange" roughys: they were snow-white. Those fish that were not moving or were moving slowly remained white, but as they began to move more energetically, they began to turn red. Uiblein

asked, "Is the orange roughy really so 'clever' that it selects alternative deep-sea habitats which differ in hydrological conditions with good conditions for relaxation and [others for] making feeding excursions? And do they indeed 'switch off' their red color to save energy? For the moment, these observations clearly raise more questions then they can give answers." Obviously, any orange roughys hauled up in a net would be stressed and therefore orange in color, so without this type of observation, we would never have known about their ability to change color. The technology that allows observers to watch fishes' natural behavior 4,500 feet down represents a significant advance in marine biology and demonstrates how little we really know about the lives of fishes.

Consider the "convict goby," "convict blenny," or "engineer blenny." Properly known as *Pholidichthys leucotaenia*, it is neither a goby nor a blenny and was previously known primarily as a home aquarium fish. Recent DNA analysis shows that *Pholidichthys* is not related to any known family of fishes. Juveniles resemble the common eel catfish (*Plotosus lineatus*) in appearance and behavior: both are eel-shaped, blackish little fish with horizontal stripes and are found near rocky areas. As juveniles, *Pholidichthys leucotaenia* form vast swarms and appear as black, eel-like little things with glowing white stripes running from head to tail, but as they mature, the stripes change direction, and instead of running horizontally from head to tail, they run vertically from dorsal to ventral—from top to bottom. They inhabit Indo-Pacific waters, and a team led by Eugenie Clark (known as the "Shark Lady" for her previous work with various elasmobranchs) studied them in their natural habitat in Sulawesi. Genie Clark (who is eighty-three years old) was diving on the reefs when she spotted "clouds of young fish vanish[ing] into a hole in the coral reef." She also noticed poking through the opening a "serpentlike head," which turned out to be the adult. With a *National Geographic* film crew, she then traveled to the Solomon Islands, where they filmed clouds of the tiny fishes exploding from the reefs and openings in the seafloor, to venture as much as 165 feet from their burrows in pursuit of plankton. At the end of the day, the tiny fishes returned to their burrows—"a unique behavior for larval fish, which generally float among plankton and float for miles."

Clark and photographer Stephen Kogge rigged an endoscope to peer into the burrows, where they observed the larval fish hanging from the ceiling of the cave, their heads attached by almost invisible mucous threads. This was totally unexpected, but the biggest surprise was their observation that the adults never seemed to leave the burrows to feed. In captivity, when convict fish reach a length of about three and a half inches (nine centimeters) they burrow into the sand and never reappear. (Adults can reach a maximum length of twenty-two inches.) In the wild, however, every once in a while they were seen to take into their mouths a group of the juveniles and then spit them out. In a *National Geographic* article, Clark mused on what she had observed: "First I thought they were cannibals. Some damselfish eat dead or dying embryos to weed out the weaker links," but when she examined the stomachs of the adults, she found only an oozy green slime. Were the babies regurgitating digested plankton into their parent's mouths? "If so," said Clark, "it would be the first example of fish offspring feeding adults." At her lab at the Mote Marine Laboratory in Sarasota, Florida, Clark is raising convict fish in see-through burrows (wine bottles) to learn how the adults feed and whether they lay eggs or give birth to live young. *Pholidichtys leucotaenia* is a mystery fish. That *National Geographic* would devote a major article to this enigmatic creature (June 2005) is a clear indication of the universal fascination with the sea's mysterious denizens.

And none was more mysterious than a whale that was known only from two skulls that had been found on beaches thousands of miles apart. Aside from the fact that it was one of the "beaked whales"—cetaceans so poorly known that many of them have never been seen alive and are recorded only from stranded specimens—we knew nothing about *Indopacetus* except that it exists. ✐

Finding the Body to Fit the Skull

∞ Named for the elongated rostrum of the skull that to some resembles the beak of a bird, the beaked whales are the most poorly known of all cetaceans. Ranging in length from fifteen to forty feet, most species have been classified in the genus *Mesoplodon* ("middle tooth") for the two teeth in the middle of the lower jaw of the males. (Female beaked whales are mostly toothless.) The mesoplodonts are spindle-shaped, tapering noticeably at both ends. The blowhole is crescent-shaped, with the horns facing forward, and there are two throat grooves. The dorsal fin is usually small and located far back, and the tail lacks the median notch present in most other cetaceans. Many of the beaked whales are poorly known, but *Indopacetus pacificus* was the poorest known of all. Its existence was corroborated by two skulls, one of which was found on the beach in Queensland in 1882, the other in Somalia in 1955.

In 2002 in *Natural History*, Robert Pitman wrote: "It had to be out there somewhere. It wasn't just a set of car keys that had gone missing—somehow an entire species of whale had been lost for a century." It was not a wraith or a distant sighting at sea; it was a beaked whale whose existence was documented by two skulls that were obviously from the same species, but were different enough from the other beaked whales to warrant their own species designation. The Queensland skull is almost four feet in length, so it was assumed that this was one of the larger of the beaked whales. At first it was thought to be a rare member of the *Mesoplodon* genus, but in 1972, Joseph Moore assigned it to its own genus, *Indopacetus*, or "Indo-Pacific whale." Most of the other beaked whales are known from strandings around the world, but *Indopacetus* was known only from these two stranded skulls. Because we knew it existed, it seemed only a matter of time before another *Indopacetus* specimen showed up on a beach somewhere.

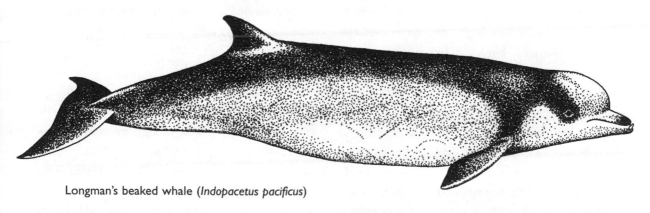

Longman's beaked whale (*Indopacetus pacificus*)

Instead, a little cetological detective work showed that *Indopacetus* has been visible for some time—we just didn't know what it was. For at least thirty years, an unidentified species of beaked whale has been reported in the tropical Indian and Pacific oceans. In his 1971 *Field Guide of Whales and Dolphins*, W. F. J. Mörzer Bruyns wrote (of *Indopacetus*) of "the possibility that the author observed these animals in the Gulf of Aden and the Sokotra area, being very large beaked whales and certainly not *Ziphius* [another genus of beaked whales]." Mörzer Bruyns also wrote that "Mr. K. C. Balcomb of Pacific Beach, Washington USA took a photo of a school of 25 beaked whales on the equator at 165° West [in the vicinity of the Gilbert Islands], which were almost certainly this species." In Balcomb's and other photographs, the animals looked more like bottlenose whales (*Hyperoodon*) than beaked whales, but the two species of bottlenose whales (*H. ampullatus* and *H. planifrons*) are from high northern and southern latitudes respectively, and had no business being in tropical waters. Both species have bulging foreheads, and although they are born dark gray or brown, they become lighter with age, especially around the head. Males differ so markedly from females (they are considerably larger and have a much more pronounced forehead bulge, commonly known as the "melon"), that early cetologists classified them as two different species. Maximum length for a male is thirty feet, and for a female, twenty-three feet. *Indopacetus pacificus*—the only species in the genus—was about to surface.

In 1999 Pitman et al. published an article in *Marine Mammal Science* with the intriguing title, "Sightings and possible identity of a bottlenose whale in the tropical Indopacific: *Indopacetus pacificus*?" The article incorporated a collection of photographs (one of which was Balcomb's 1966 picture), and when the photographs and eyewitness descriptions were compared, it was clear that the whale was a bottlenose whale, and it was neither the northern nor the southern version. The photographs clearly show a bottlenose whale whose body color "has been variously described as tan, light brown, acorn brown, gray-brown or just gray." When an adult female beaked whale stranded in late 1999 in the Maldives in the northern Indian Ocean, it was identified as *Indopacetus*, and comparison with the museum specimens showed once and for all that *Indopacetus* was actually the tropical bottlenose whale. In his 2002 article, Pitman wrote:

For a hundred years, cetologists had nothing to work with but two skulls on the shelf. We now have specimen material from six individuals (including five skulls and one complete skeleton) records of more than two dozen sightings, numerous photographs of large animals in the field, recordings of their vocalizations, and (welcome to the twenty-first century) eight minutes of digital video footage.

And then, in July 2003, a complete description of *Indopacetus pacificus* appeared in *Marine Mammal Science*. It was written by nine authors from New Zealand, Australia, the Maldives, South Africa, Kenya, and California (Robert Pitman was the California contributor). They examined the two original skulls from Queensland and Somalia and added four new specimens to the list: A skull that was found in the National Museum of Kenya; several ribs and vertebrae that had been found on a Natal beach in 1976; a skull, mandible, teeth, ribs, and ear bones of a specimen (mistakenly identified as *H. planifrons*) in the Port Elizabeth (South Africa) Museum; and the adult female that was collected in the Maldives in January 2000. DNA sequencing showed that all these specimens belonged to the same species, *Indopacetus pacificus*, now known as Longman's beaked whale. The range of this species is now known to incorporate "the western reaches of the tropical Pacific Ocean . . . and the western, northern, and southern latitudes of the tropical Indian Ocean." The authors concluded:

> The discovery of these four new specimens has extended the known range of Longman's beaked whale and led to the description of its external appearance for the first time. As this species is now known from six specimens, the title of the world's rarest whale must pass to the spade-toothed whale [another beaked whale] *Mesoplodon traversii* (= *M. bahamondi*) which to date is known from only three specimens.

In late 2003 an even bigger cetological surprise was sprung: Japanese scientists announced that they had found a completely new species of baleen whale. The baleen whales have been hunted for centuries by whalers, and if nothing else, we thought we knew how many species there were. In the journal *Nature* (November 20, 2003), Wada, Oishi, and Yamada described a "newly discovered species of living baleen whale," which they named *Baleonoptera omurai*, after the late Hideo Omura, one of Japan's foremost cetologists. In the 1970s, according to their report, eight specimens of unknown identity were collected in the South China Sea as part of Japan's research whaling program, and in 1998 another specimen, also of unknown identity, washed ashore onto an island in the Sea of Japan. In coloration and proportions, these nine specimens resembled fin whales (*Balaenoptera physalus*), but they were much smaller—thirty feet maximum length to the fin whale's seventy-five. After analyzing the DNA, skull, baleen plates, and the liver and muscle enzymes, the Japanese cetologists could affiliate their specimens with no known baleen whale species, and announced the new species. At the same time, and using the same techniques, they concluded that Bryde's whale (*B. edeni*) was actually two different species, *B. edeni* and *B. brydei*, bringing the total number of balaenopterid species to eight. The previous six were the blue whale (*B. musculus*), the fin whale (*B. physalus*) the sei whale (*B. borealis*), Bryde's whale (*B. edeni*), and two types of minke whale, the northern species (*B. acutorostrata*), and the Antarctic, (*B. bonaerensis*).

The Japanese have a history of finding new whale species. Around 1960, during the heyday of modern Japanese pelagic whaling, the nation's scientists also announced another subspecies of blue whale, which they called *Balaenoptera musculus brevicauda*, and because it was considerably smaller than the "ordinary" blue whale—which is, in fact, the largest animal that has ever lived on Earth—the new subspecies was nicknamed the "pygmy blue whale." The "pygmy" grows to be fully sixty feet long, so it is small only by blue whale standards. Finding a "new" species at that time meant—at least to the Japanese—that the quotas for blue whales did not apply to the pygmies, so they slaughtered them in large numbers. This is not to say that the discovery of *Balaenoptera omurai* is a sub-

Snubfin dolphin (*Orcaella heinsohni*)

terfuge to allow Japanese whalers to hunt a species not covered by International Whaling Commission regulations, but some researchers have suggested that the new discovery conveniently validates Japanese research whaling, which has been under attack for years, largely because the remaining tons of meat end up in the supermarket after the "research" on the whale carcasses has been done. If *B. omurai* is a new species of baleen whale, it is a cause for celebration, but the fact that it was unknown until 2003—in waters heavily fished by the Japanese for centuries—suggests that there are not very many of them. The jury is still out on *B. omurai*; most cetologists do not regard it as a valid species, regardless of how it fits into the Japanese whaling scenario.

About a new species of another marine mammal, however, no question remains. *Orcaella heinsohni* is an authentic, completely new species of dolphin. People around rivers and shallow coastal waters in southeastern Asia and Indonesia were familiar with the Irrawaddy River dolphin, scientifically known as *Orcaella brevirostris*. It was—and still is—a six-foot-long, gray, blunt-snouted dolphin with a small dorsal fin and large flippers, found in Thailand, Cambodia, Laos, the Philippines, Indonesia, and Northern Australia. In their

2002 *Guide to the Marine Mammals of the World*, Reeves, Stewart, Clapham, and Powell wrote, "The animals of Australia and Papua New Guinea differ morphologically from those in Southeast Asia, and the differences may prove great enough to warrant recognition of two separate species." And that's exactly what happened. Like Reeves et al., others had noticed that the dolphins of Australia differed from those of Southeast Asia, and in 2005, Isabel Beasley, Kelly Robertson, and Peter Arnold published "Description of a New Dolphin, the Australian Snubfin Dolphin *Orcaella heinsohni* sp. n. ["species novum"]." The new dolphin differed from *O. brevirostris* ("short beak") in the height of the dorsal fin and in the absence of a dorsal groove in the new species. A meticulous examination of the skulls of the two types showed significant differences, as did a molecular analysis. Also, where the Irrawaddy dolphins tended toward a "two-tone" color scheme, darker above fading to lighter below, the Australian snubfin has a tripartite arrangement with a "cape" on the dorsal surface, a lighter band below that, and a light-colored belly. Both species of *Orcaella* are in trouble throughout their range. Like many inshore and river dolphin species, they swim slowly and are frequently entangled in fishing nets and drowned. Furthermore, fishermen in the Mekong, Makaham, and Irrawaddy Rivers use gill nets and explosives that contribute to the mortality of the little dolphins.

Cetologists can delineate new species, even from a species that is one of the oceanarium's most popular performers. Although not often hunted by whalers, the killer whale is one of the best-known of all cetacean species, found around the world from tropical to polar seas but also in many oceanariums, where *Orcinus orca* performs tricks for cheering crowds. Everybody knows "Shamu," "Namu," and all the other strikingly black-and-white killer whales, sometimes performing, sometimes congregating in the waters of Puget Sound and British Columbia, sometimes charging into the shallows to grab hapless sea lion pups. Would it surprise you to learn that there might be three distinct species? When Soviet whalers "opportunistically" took more than nine hundred killer whales in Antarctic waters in the 1970s, they noticed that the whales differed from the more northerly species, but because the whales were all rendered for their "products," no type specimen was retained. Cetologists then began to recognize a different, smaller species, where the usual white patches were a yellowish ochre, and like some of the smaller dolphin species (killer whales are the largest of the Delphinidae, which means they are dolphins), these had a distinct "cape" pattern on the back. And finally, there was a third type with an eye patch (the white slash over the eye) that was much larger than that of the other Antarctic types. All three types were seen congregating only with similar whales, and the different types did not appear to mingle. The typical black-and-white killer whales were spotted only in open water; the ones with yellowish patches in open water and in loose sea ice; and the smallest ones, those with a distinct cape, small, angled eye patches,

Killer whale (*Orcinus orca*)

and yellowish markings, were found farther south, deeper into the pack ice. (It was these killer whales that were feeding almost exclusively on the Antarctic toothfish and were caught by Soviet trawlers.) In the conclusion of their paper, Pitman and Ensor wrote:

> A recent investigation of killer whale genetics found relatively little diversity among killer whales worldwide, but the only Antarctica sample available for that study . . . found that there are three morphologically distinct types of killer whales in Antarctica that do not appear to mingle in schools or hybridise, although they have overlapping geographic ranges. This suggests that isolating mechanisms are already in effect and . . . they may each warrant separate species status. Evidence from molecular genetic analyses and additional morphological studies will be important in verifying this interpretation. Killer whales are common top predators in Antarctica; in order to understand their role in the Antarctic ecosystem it will be necessary to clarify the taxonomic relationships, further identify the ecological traits, and determine the relative abundance of the three forms described here.

While new species are being discovered, hunting is driving other species of whales and dolphins to the brink of extinction. First armed with spears, then with harpoon cannons, whalers scoured the oceans for a thousand years in search of whales to kill. Humanity's failure to eliminate an entire species is certainly not for want of trying. The insertion of Longman's beaked whale into the catalog of living whale species does not offset the massive depredations of the past, but it is somehow fitting that among the unexpected "antidotes" to extinction would be a large cetacean whose existence was unknown thirty years ago, two new kinds of killer whale, a new little dolphin, and (maybe) a previously unsuspected species of baleen whale. It was not the whalemen who found *Indopacetus*; rather, in another example of technology enlarging the knowledge base of marine science, it was a sharp-eyed researcher comparing photo collections and recalling elongated skulls from two distant beaches that added *Indopacetus* to our list of known cetaceans. ✍

Why Carry a Sword?

On April 15, 2003, Mark Ferrari was swimming in water 250 feet deep in the AuAu Channel between the Hawaiian islands of Maui and Lanai. A whale researcher and filmmaker, Ferrari had been working for years in these waters with his wife and fellow researcher, Debbie Glockner-Ferrari. Their primary interest was the behavior of humpback whales, but on this day, Mark was following a school of false killer whales (*Pseudorca crassidens*), rarely photographed toothed whales that are akin to pilot whales and killer whales. (Killer whales, pilot whales, and false killer whales are actually large dolphins.) There were fifty or sixty of the coal-black whales, including many mothers and calves. Mark had his underwater video camera, but he was without scuba gear because he believed that the bubbles disturbed the whales, and besides, most of the whale action took place close to the surface, where he and the whales could get a breath of air when they needed it. The false killers, some of which were more than twenty feet long, swam rapidly in and out of his view, sometimes coming disarmingly close and "smiling"—baring their teeth—before swooping away with powerful beats of their horizontal tail flukes. In the clear blue water, off to his right about thirty feet away, he spotted a shadow, not as large as the false killers, but of a completely different configuration. From its protruding snout and vertical tail fin, he recognized it as a billfish, about fifteen feet long. Because female billfish are larger than males, and because this was a *very* large specimen, Mark assumed it was a female. Was it a

swordfish? A marlin? He shot a couple of frames of the fish, which seemed to be hovering in the water about twenty feet away, and when he lost sight of the false killers and the fish, he thought the encounter was over and climbed back in the boat.

At the surface, the black false killers with their curiously humped pectoral fins were leaping excitedly, and Mark decided to re-enter the water to see what was going on. Big mistake. The *Pseudorcas* had formed a sort of net beneath the fish, and every time she tried to escape by diving, one of them rushed in and bit a chunk from her flank. Mark was now ten feet from the wounded fish, and for a reason that will never be known, she charged directly at him. Was it mindless panic? A defensive maneuver aimed at whatever she could hit? He was struck high on his right chest, just at the base of the neck; his clavicle was broken and his scapula shattered. The sword, some of which had broken off in Mark's body, had missed his carotid artery by less than half an inch; a little lower and it would have punctured his lung. The sword did not pass through him, and with a toss of her head, the fish disengaged and swam off. Bleeding badly, Mark surfaced and called for Debbie, who was in the boat not far away. Once ashore they loaded him into an ambulance, held wet towels over the gaping wound, and drove him across the island to Maui Memorial Hospital in Wailuku. In addition to the broken bones, there was extensive nerve and muscle damage. He had lost so much blood that the surgeons thought he might not make it.

In his 1998 book about the North Atlantic swordfishery, Charles Dana Gibson (grandson of the artist of the same name) wrote, "The question of whether an unprovoked swordfish would attack a free-swimming man has often been debated. To date, there has not been one reported case, but this is far from conclusive when one considers how rare it would be for one to be swimming in waters frequented by swordfish. . . ." It might be argued that the fish that attacked Mark was "provoked," but it was certainly not by him, and therefore, Gibson's statement is no longer true. Mark Ferrari lived to tell his story (he told it to me in December 2004); but in 1886, Captain F. D. Lansford, a commercial fisherman, was killed fighting a hooked swordfish. The swordfish charged Lansford's dory, causing the line to go slack and the captain to fall backward into the boat; the fish then rammed the boat, stabbing through both boat and man. The dory with the swordfish attached was hauled aboard the schooner, the sword cut off and the fish killed. Lansford died three days later (Wilcox 1887). Undoubtedly because of its size and armament, the swordfish has always been regarded as a dangerous creature, and probably always will be. Here for example, is the description of "*Xyphias* [sic] *gladius communis*," from William Dewhurst's 1835 *Natural History of the Order Cetacea and the Oceanic Inhabitants of the Arctic Regions*. "The common sword-fish is a native of the Mediter-

ranean and Sicilian Seas; it grows to a very large size, sometimes measuring twenty feet in length; it is active and predacious, feeding on all kinds of fishes, and it likely a formidable enemy to the whale, which it destroys by piercing it with its sword-shaped snout." Never mind about mercury, which is higher in swordfish than any other food fish—this is a fish that can kill you.

The larger predatory sharks are usually considered the most dangerous fish in the sea because of their jaws, teeth, and their occasional predisposition to bite people. But the billfishes—swordfish, marlins, sailfishes—are the only fishes that are equipped with what truly qualifies as a *weapon*. In the marlins and sailfish—technically the Istiophoridae—the weapon is relatively short, sharply pointed, and round in cross section, but in *Xiphias gladius*, it is long, and flattened like a broadsword. Found worldwide in temperate and tropical waters, the broadbill swordfish gets its common name from its smooth, flattened bill, much longer and wider than that of any other billfish.

The weapon itself has prompted wild tales about the ferocity of the swordfish, and the early literature is filled with stories about swordfish attacking everything from boats to whales. Why have a weapon like that if you're not going to use it? In *Sea and Land*, an 1887 compilation of "The Wonderful and Curious Things of Nature Existing Before and Since the Deluge," J. W. Buel wrote:

Next to the shark in ferocity and voraciousness is the Swordfish, a habitant of nearly all the seas, but most populous in the Mediterranean. It grows to a length of twenty feet,

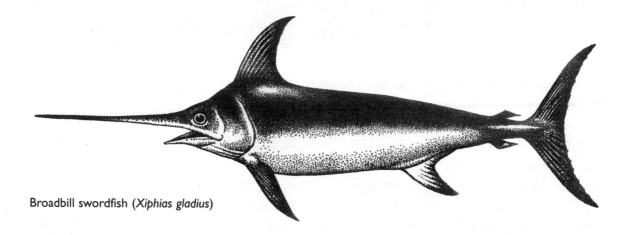

Broadbill swordfish (*Xiphias gladius*)

but the powerful, keen, and heavily denti-lated blade is one-third of its entire length. Like the shark, nature has equipped the swordfish with so dreadful a weapon, that its province seems to be war, though strange enough, it is comparatively innocent and extremely timid before man, confining its ravages to its fellow-denizens of the deep.

Humans can easily regard the bills as swords and believe that the swordfish defends itself and uses the bill to slash and debilitate its prey, which consists of squid, mackerel, bluefish, and many other mid- and deepwater species. Even today, however, we are not sure how a swordfish actually uses its bill. It is horizontally flattened and sharp on the edges, so it has been assumed that the swordfish enters a school of fishes, and slashes wildly, cutting, stunning, or otherwise incapacitating its prey, which it then eats at leisure. Nevertheless, since few people have ever actually witnessed the slashing, the use of the sword must remain conjectural. In a 1968 study of "The Food and Feeding Habits of the Swordfish," Scott and Tibbo wrote, "The swordfish differs

from the spearfishes (marlins and sailfishes) in that the sword is long and it is dorso-ventrally compressed (hence the name broadbill) whereas the spearfishes have a shorter spear and it is slightly compressed laterally. Thus, the sword-fish appears to be more highly specialized for lateral slashing. Such a specialization would seem to be pointless unless directed to a vertically oriented prey, or unless the swordfish slashes while vertically oriented, as when ascending or descending." But Ralph Bandini, a renowned fisher-man and one of the founding members of the Tuna Club of Catalina, saw a broadbill "cut a bar-racuda in half, *in the water*, as cleanly as it could be done with a butcher's cleaver on the block." Bandini does not mention the angle of attack, but the broadbill's sharp-edged sword can clearly be used with terrible effectiveness.

In contrast to almost every other suggestion about swordfish feeding techniques, Charles O. Mather (1976) wrote, "Essentially a bottom feeder, a broadbill is believed to use his bill as a tool to obtain crustaceans from their cracks or attach-ments and to enjoy crabs and crayfish." Because the swordfish is not a bottom-feeder; it does not use its bill as a pry bar, and it does not eat—let alone *enjoy*—crabs and crayfish, Mather's suggestion is preposterous. *Blue Planet*, the book that accompanied the 2001 BBC TV series of the same name, was written by Andrew Byatt, Alastair Fothergill, and Martha Holmes. Alongside a lovely shot of a free-swimming swordfish, we find this caption: "The swordfish is an extremely powerful deep-water predator that probably uses its bill to dig out prey from the sea floor." Ridiculous! A proud gladiator with powerful muscles that are warmed by countercurrent heat exchangers; eyes designed to pick out fast-moving prey items; and a slashing, sharp-edged broadsword, *Xiphias gladius* does not grub for worms in the seafloor.

In 1840, in his *Narrative of a Whaling Voyage Around the Globe*, Frederick Debell Bennett wrote that "the sword-fish . . . subsists by making rapid darts amongst a shoal of small fish, and after transfixing as many as possible on the beak or sword . . . shakes them off by a retrograde movement or by moving the sword violently from side to side and devouring them. . . . I have seen a sword-fish thus strike and devour three bonita in a very dexterous and rapid manner." In *Living Fishes of the World*, ichthyologist Earl Herald wrote that the sword may be used to impale fishes during feeding, which seems highly unlikely because the sword of *Xiphias* is not as sharply pointed as that of a marlin or spearfish; and even if such a process could be made to work, the swordfish would be unable to get at the dead fishes stuck on the end of its nose unless it shook them off.

Among the documented "victims" of swordfish attacks (never mind the attacks on boats, sub-marines, or floating bales of rubber) are sea turtles, mako sharks, tuna, and whales. In the hands of a man, a sword might be used to chop things up, but on the end of a fish's nose, chopping doesn't seem like a reasonable option, so we have to look elsewhere for the "reason" a swordfish might stab a whale or a turtle. In a discussion of sea turtles stabbed by swordfish, Harry Fierstine, a paleoichthyologist who has made a career of studying swordfish, past and present, wrote:

An extended debate has centered on the reason why billfish stab large objects which they cannot eat. Since billfish swallow their prey whole, it is difficult to understand how even the largest and hungriest of these fish could attempt to eat an adult-size marine turtle, especially when viewing the chelonian from perpendicular to the plastron or carapace. There is no evidence of turtle of any size occurring in the diet of any billfishes.

Although there is a comparable lack of evidence for whales occurring in the billfish's diet, in 1933 Australian marine biologist David Stead related the story of the crew of a fishing boat out of Auckland, New Zealand, who observed a great commotion on the surface, and as they approached it, they "discovered a cow whale [species unknown] defending her calf against the furious onslaught of a swordfish. After a long struggle the whale dealt a lucky blow when she gave the swordfish a tremendous stroke with one of her tailflukes, breaking the swordfish's large dorsal fin and apparently paralyzing it. The fishermen killed the disabled monster and brought it to Auckland, where it was found to measure 12 feet 6 inches in length." To a great extent, Stead relied for his natural history on fishermen's tales, so there is the outside possibility that the event didn't happen exactly as it was described to him. (Stead is also responsible for the story—reported in his *Sharks and Rays of Australian Seas*—of a ghostly white shark that was more than a hundred feet long, spotted by fishermen in the waters of New South Wales in 1918.)

In 1940, in the *Memoirs of the Royal Asiatic Society of Bengal*, Eugene W. Gudger wrote a paper entitled "The Alleged Pugnacity of the Swordfish and the Spearfishes as Shown by Their Attacks on Vessels." In this lengthy paper—at one hundred pages, almost a small book—Gudger reviewed every "attack" that he could find, and even worked out a formula for the force of the blow with relation to the known speed of the various billfishes. (Most of the attacks are attributed to swordfishes, but there are also numerous records of marlin bills embedded in ship's timbers.) Gudger, who was not associated with the Royal Society of Bengal but was an associate in ichthyology at the American Museum of Natural History in New York, did not believe any of the stories of swordfish attacks on whales, citing the negative evidence of whaling historians Frederick Debell Bennett, Robert Cushman Murphy, and Roy Chapman Andrews, none of whom ever recorded a sword in whale blubber, although between them, they probably saw thousands of whales cut up. It would be up to a modern whaling historian to provide irrefutable evidence of swordfish attacks on whales.

In 1959 Norwegian cetologist Åge Jonsgård wrote of two blue whales that were being flensed aboard Antarctic factory ships and were found with swordfish swords embedded in the blubber. Jonsgård asked "whether our material can in any way throw light on the question of what happened when the swordfishes stabbed the blue whales?" Then in 1962 Jonsgård reported on three fin whales, also taken aboard Antarctic factory ships for flensing, with a broken-off sword in each one. With these five records, more or less from randomly examined whales, Jonsgård suggests that "It seems possible that whales are stabbed by swordfish to a far greater extent than we have hitherto reckoned. This possibility is supported by the accounts contained in literature of the fights between swordfish and whales, which state that the whales are stabbed by the swordfish from the underside. No whales have so far been found which were stabbed from below, but this does not in any way signify that this is unusual. It must be supposed that a whale which is stabbed in the belly has very small chances of surviving."

Jonsgård does not address the most important question: Why would a fish-eating swordfish stab a whale in the first place? The evidence from the whale carcasses indicates that the sword was broken off in the whale's flesh or blubber, which would mean that the fish—even if it survived the wrenching off of its sword—would be unable in the future to use the sword, whatever its use might be. Stabbing whales, turtles, boats, bales of rubber, and submarines suggests something almost unheard of in the animal kingdom—random aggression that results in injury and even death to the aggressor. (Bee stings sometimes result in the death of the bee because the stinger is pulled out, but it is believed that the bee is acting defensively.) British Museum of Natural History ichthyologist Alfred Günther did not doubt that swordfishes attacked whales, although he said "the cause that excites them to such attacks is unknown." He noted that "they follow this instinct so blindly that they not rarely attack boats or large vessels in a similar manner, evidently mistaking them for Cetaceans." Maybe the swordfish isn't the aggressor; maybe it feels threatened by the rubber, whale, turtle, or submarine, and defends itself. There is also the possibility—also unique—that swordfishes sometimes do crazy, inexplicable things that could be inspired by raging hormones, a temporary mental breakdown, or phases of the moon. (The "intensity of swordfish feeding activity increases around the full moons, particularly where the thermocline is deep," said Ward and Elscot in 2000.)

One of the more inelegant of swordfish impalements is the one recorded—evidently from first-hand observation—by David Starr Jordan and Barton W. Evermann in their early twentieth-century discussion of the fishes of North America. They wrote:

Swordfish fight gamely on the surface or below when harpooned. Storer wrote long ago that they sometimes sound with such speed and force as to drive the sword into the bottom, which fishermen say is by no means uncommon; and we saw this off Halifax in August 1914, when a fish more than 10 feet long, which we had harpooned from the *Grampus*, plunged with such force that it buried itself in the mud beyond its eyes in 56 fathoms of water. When finally hauled up alongside it brought up enough mud plastered to its head to yield a good sample of the bottom.

Hard to imagine the mud not being washed off as the fish was hauled up through fifty-six fathoms (336 feet) of water, but maybe the mud off Halifax is especially sticky. Gudger finds similar accounts of *Xiphias* driving its sword into the bottom, including this one from Conrad Gesner, whose *Historia Animalium* was published in 1558: "When *Xiphias* sees a whale, he is filled with so much terror that he drives his sword into the earth, or a stone, or anything else that he finds at the bottom of the shallow water. Thus fixed by his head, he holds himself still. The whale indeed takes him for a log of wood or something like thereto, and ignoring him, passes by."

In *Twenty Thousand Leagues Under the Sea*, first published in 1888, Jules Verne predicted the swordfish-submarine conflict: "I saw there," says Captain Arronax, "some swordfish ten feet long, those prophetic heralds of the hurricane whose formidable sword would now and then strike the glass of the saloon." Underwater reality sometimes follows underwater fantasy, for in July 1967, at a depth of two thousand feet off Savannah, Georgia, an eight-foot swordfish charged the submersible *Alvin* and impaled itself in a joint between the upper and lower parts of the external hull. As the sub was brought to the surface, the fish was thrashing desperately, and as soon as they got a rope around its tail, the sword broke off. It took two hours to extract the sword, after which the fish was cooked and eaten. (The *New York Times* headline for January 14, 1968, was "Swordfish Duels Two-Man Research Submarine.")

Two years later, another swordfish attacked another submersible. On July 16, 1969 (the same day as the launching of *Apollo 11*, which put Neil Armstrong and Buzz Aldrin on the moon four days later), the mesoscaph (*meso* = middle; *scaphe* = boat) *Ben Franklin* was launched on a historic voyage, thirty days underwater, following the Gulf Stream from Palm Beach, Florida, to a point south of Nova Scotia. Designed by Jacques Piccard (the pilot of the *Trieste* in 1960 on her record dive to 35,800 feet in the Marianas Trench), *Ben Franklin* was forty-eight feet long, with twenty-nine viewing ports to permit maximum visibility for the crew of six. Somewhere off the coast of Florida, at a depth of 826 feet, three members of the crew watched as a six-foot-long broadbill swordfish attacked the submersible they were in. In *The Sun Beneath the Sea,* Piccard described the action: "It appears to parade up and down in front of the window, dashing to and fro, not knowing how to interpret our presence, swimming a few meters and then returning, as though fascinated by our great Plexiglas eye. Suddenly it attacks, dashing straight forward and striking the hull of the mesoscaph with the point of the sword, aiming perhaps at the porthole, but hitting only the steel of the hull." Piccard asks: "Why do these swordfish attack submarines? Are they fascinated, hypnotized by the portholes? If they mistake submarines for monsters, which perhaps they actually are, what courage these fishes show in attempting to impale an adversary so much bigger than themselves."

Were the swordfish mindlessly aggressive or were there extenuating circumstances? Sometimes swordfish charge the boats from which they have been harpooned or hooked, but in other cases, such as attacks on whales, bales of rubber, or submarines, the attack comes unmotivated out of the blue. Even sharks, long considered mindless man-eaters, do not attack people randomly or accidentally. Something moves them to bite: it may be fear, hunger, territoriality, electrical stimulation, or confusion about what is edible and what is not, but *Jaws* notwithstanding, most people do not consider sharks malicious or evil, but simply—as if this actually needed saying—animals that differ profoundly from us. They live in a world that author Henry Beston described as "older and more complex than ours," and they are "gifted with extensions of the senses we have lost or never attained, living by voices we shall never hear." Most animal behavior studies do not involve attacks on people; but when tigers eat people, sharks kill surfers, or swordfish attack divers, we are forced to reconsider our attitude toward very big, very heavily armed animals.

Xiphias the gladiator has no scales, no teeth, and no lateral line. It does have a brain-warmer, an eye-warmer, a bayonet, and a reputation for pugnacity unmatched in any other fish. This reputation, in fact, may be unmatched in any other animal. Some sharks occasionally "attack" some people, and less frequently, eat them, but while this behavior may be characterized in many ways—hunger, territoriality, mistaken identity—it is probably not aggression for aggression's sake. So too with lions, tigers, or crocodiles, often described as "man-eaters," but trying to catch and eat something is not aggression, no matter how violent and bloody. There are many animals whose bite, sting, or spines are venomous, and while people can die from the bites of snakes or spiders, these creatures are usually acting in self-defense, or possibly in defense of their offspring or nest. No other animal seems willing to go out of its way—and often to endanger its own life—to attack. As

we have seen, swordfish have been known to attack whales, sharks, fishing boats, submarines,
and people—not to mention the variety of fish
and squid species that they "attack" in order to
eat them, or to eat the pieces.

Nevertheless, a careful look at the subjects
of swordfish attacks—with the possible exception
of those on whales—will reveal a pattern, or perhaps more than one. First of all, let us note that
there are few records of *unprovoked* swordfish attacks on boats, few cases where cod fishermen or
recreational sailors looked down to find that
their hull had been pierced by a passing swordfish. Although a harpooned or hooked swordfish
may not understand that the boat or the people
in it are causing its pain, still, an injured, armed
fish might retaliate against the nearest foreign
intruder. Does not the swordfish leap and dive
and gyrate like crazy when it is hooked? Because
the swordfish regularly uses its sword, and because a charging swordfish arrives *sword first*, attacks on fishing boats should not surprise us that
much. As there would be no benefit to the fish in
spearing the ocean floor, it is reasonable to conclude that the harpooned fish that drove its
sword into the mud had been driven mad by the
pain, and in a panic, was diving to escape.

Attacks by swordfish that are not hooked or
harpooned are a little more difficult to explain,
but as Jordan and Evermann wrote, "driving
their swords through planking [may be] 'temporary insanity,' or more likely [accidents] while
pursuing dolphins or other fish." I must admit
that I can come up with no explanation that
would explain a swordfish attacking an eighty-
foot-long whale or a bale of rubber, but the attacks on the submersibles *Alvin* and *Ben Franklin*

might be understood if we recognize that swordfish at depth are stimulated by lights; swordfish
hunt bioluminescent lantern fish at depth, slashing at the blue lights in an effort to maim or in-
capacitate as many of the little fishes as possible.
Is it too much of a stretch to hypothesize that the
lighted portholes of the submersibles would flip
a switch in the swordfish's (overheated) brain
and provoke the "attack" response?

The average weight of swordfish caught since
the 1980s has dropped from 115 pounds to 60.
Today many restaurants are refusing to put swordfish on their menus in an attempt to discourage
fishermen from bringing in the smaller fishes. (At
Manhattan's Fulton Fish Market, swordfish that
are between 50 and 100 pounds are called "dogs";
from 25 to 50, "pups"; and under 25 pounds,
"rats.") In "Song for the Swordfish," a 1998 article
in *Audubon*, Carl Safina wrote, "These days, most
fishers know swordfish chiefly by their absence,
by old-timers' stories and black-and-white photos
on the walls of long-established harborside bars.
The swordfish, also known as the broadbill, may
be the fastest-declining creature in the Atlantic
Ocean. . . . U.S. longliners claim that Atlantic
swordfish can't recover unless all the countries
catching them agree to coordinated measures. But
in the 1970s, when concern over mercury levels
in swordfish forced U.S. and Canadian longliners
to stop fishing, the broadbills recovered within a
decade. They were depleted to current lows after
longlining resumed."

Most animals slated for extinction go qui-
etly. As she sat in a cage at the Cincinnati Zoo in
1914, the passenger pigeon named Martha didn't
cry out, "Wait, wait—I'm the last of my kind!" If
fish read the *New York Times*, the remaining

broadbills might be happy to learn that their story is "one of the few bright lights in the otherwise dismal story of overfishing," but alas, they are still being extensively longlined in the Mediterranean and the Pacific, and the *pez espada* is still one of the world's favorite food fishes. Perhaps the swordfish's pugnacity is a function of its dwindling numbers. Maybe all those peculiarities—the sword, the brain-warmer, the gigantic blue eyes—have granted this great and enigmatic fish an understanding of its circumstances that has been denied all other fish, and most other mammals, including us. Maybe the swordfish isn't crazy at all; it may be the only animal that is unwilling to go into the dark night of extinction without putting up a fight. §

Most Marine Life Is Too Small to See

Because of its density, distance, and depth, the ocean hides its occupants well. Fishermen, ichthyologists, teuthologists, cetologists, whalers, and marine biologists have been capturing their subjects for millennia, so we are beginning to learn about the habits and habitats of various components of the macrofauna but the oceans'

smaller inhabitants—the microorganisms—have not been that easy to capture. They have avoided analysis by being able to pass through all but the smallest-mesh nets; some by being so small that they could pass through the tightest filters; and some by being all but invisible until the development of electron microscopy.

"Not many years have elapsed," wrote John Murray and Johan Hjort in 1912, "since the scientific world became aware that the sea contains plants in abundance floating on and beneath its surface, and that they build up the organic substances upon which marine animals depend." In 1895, Sir John Murray compiled the records of the *Challenger* expedition, which collected plankton samples from various depths along with the numerous bottom-dwelling creatures that surprised not only the scientists but the public as well. Victor Hensen's *Plankton Expedition* of 1889 described and illustrated many minuscule marine plants (phytoplankton) for the first time, and Hensen recognized the importance of phytoplankton by calling them "the blood of the sea." As Murray and Hjort wrote in their chapter on pelagic plant life:

Most of the ocean plants exist in countless myriads of minute individuals, though they are invisible to the naked eye. Still, small as they are, they are in a way highly organized, and their organization is in strict accordance with the particular conditions of their life. . . . Their diffusion is also their best defense against their enemies, for, while animals have no great difficulty in finding and consuming the larger plants, these creatures, scattered everywhere like dust amidst the immeasurable water masses are not so easily available. The majority of the floating plants pass their lives as single cells, though they are frequently far more highly organized than the single cells that go on to form a higher plant.

The phytoplankton is composed of various types of unicellular algae that range from a few to several hundred microns in size. Phytoplankton includes algae, and algae includes the diatoms that are the dominant type of phytoplankton in the temperate and high latitudes. Planktonic diatoms have no swimming structures and do not normally move independently. Because diatoms must remain in the surface waters to carry out photosynthetic processes, they have developed a variety of adaptations to prevent sinking. Some diatoms have needlelike or featherlike projections that greatly increase their surface areas with little increase in body weight. A small body with a high ratio of surface to mass has a high drag factor and sinks very slowly. Other common types of phytoplankton include the dinoflagellate algae; these organisms have two whiplike "flagella" for swimming. Another major group, the coccolithophores, lacks a flagellum but instead is characterised by an external shell composed of a number of platelike structures called "coccoliths." The smallest plankton in the sea are the bacteria and the related prokaryotes known as bacterioplankton. Little understood, they nevertheless are thought to play a significant role in the nutrient cycles of the other planktonic animals that eat them.

Nutrient availability is often the key factor controlling phytoplankton production. Major nutrients required include phosphates, nitrates, and in some cases, silicates for diatom shells. Where nutrients abound, populations of microscopic plant life multiply rapidly and produce the characteristic green, turbid waters which contrast so dramatically with the clear waters of less productive regions. Oceanic circulation and water movements bring nutrient-rich deep water to the surface layer or euphotic zone through a number of physical oceanographic processes. Off the coasts of Peru and Chile, Oregon, Arabia, and Mauritania and Namibia in Africa, wind-driven upwellings occur between the coast and the main boundary currents (coastal upwellings). In a broad band stretching along the equator from the Americas almost to the western side of the Pacific, divergent water masses are formed by the interactions between the trade winds and the Coriolis force (equatorial upwellings). This produces mid-ocean upwelling areas that are rich in nutrients and therefore regions of high primary productivity. In the high latitudes of both the northern and southern hemispheres, the intense mixing in polar upwellings caused by winter storms may bring deep water to the surface. The upwelling waters, combined with spring sunshine, causes "spring plankton blooms" in these regions. Local combinations of seabed topography and currents may also mix water masses vertically. Strong vertical circulations can occur in the wakes of offshore islands or headlands projecting into the paths of moving water. Working together, these processes determine the levels of nutrients for phytoplankton growth and production. Therefore the distribution of phytoplankton in the oceans of the world is largely determined by the nutrient availability.

Although people tend to think that "photosynthesis" applies to green plants on land, it should be borne in mind that at least 50 percent of global carbon dioxide is fixed into organic molecules by countless trillions of microscopic autotrophic organisms that form part of the plankton community found in the surface waters of the oceans. "Our view of the organic matter in seawater has changed dramatically," wrote Farooq Azam in 1998. He continued: "The traditional dichotomy of particulate organic matter versus dissolved organic matter is being replaced by the concept of an organic matter continuum." His study, entitled "Microbial Control of Oceanic Carbon Flux: The Plot Thickens," concludes:

Behavioral and metabolic responses of bacteria to the complex and heterogeneous structure of the organic matter field at the microscale influence ocean-basin-scale carbon fluxes in all major pathways: microbial loop, sinking, grazing food chain, carbon storage, and carbon fixation itself. . . . Powerful new approaches are enabling us to study microbial ecology, including consortial activities, in an ecosystem context. . . . These ideas and approaches should lead to a synthesis of bacterial adaptation, evolution, ecology, and biogeochemistry, and should form a basis for integrating the roles of bacteria in predictive biogeochemical models.

The carbon fixation reactions represent the entry of inorganic carbon (in the form of carbon dioxide) into the biological world. In the light reactions of photosynthesis, light energy is captured and transferred into the chemical bonds of ATP (adenosine triphosphate) and NADP (nicotinamide adenine dinucleotide phosphate). During the carbon fixation reactions, carbon dioxide is fixed and then reduced into carbohydrate, using the energy stored in the ATP, and NADP, two of the most important coenzymes in the photosynthesizing cell.

As Jef Huisman and Franz Weissing wrote in 1999, "Competition theory predicts that, at equilibrium, the number of coexisting species cannot exceed the number of limiting resources, [and] for phytoplankton, only a few resources are potentially limiting: nitrogen, phosphorus, silicon, light, iron, inorganic carbon, and sometimes a few trace metals or vitamins." In their study, Huisman and Weissing showed that resource competition models can generate oscillations and chaos when species compete for three or more resources, and

that "these oscillations and chaotic fluctuations in species abundances allow the coexistence of many species on a handful of resources."

Marine viruses answer a puzzle that has been confounding biologists for years. G. Evelyn Hutchinson (1903–1991), an English-born, Cambridge-trained, Yale University biologist who specialized in the ecology of lakes and rivers (the science known as limnology), was puzzled by his observation that so many different kinds of plankton can coexist on only a few potentially limiting resources, while competition theory predicts just one or a few competitive winners. This conundrum, known as "The Paradox of the Plankton," from Hutchinson's 1961 paper of the same name, can now be explained by the existence of marine viruses that infect the original species, reducing its numbers until a new species takes over. When the original species develops an immunity to the pathogen, the virus mutates to infect the new species, and the cycle begins again. In his 1999 discussion of marine viruses, Jed Fuhrman of UCLA wrote, "Although several possible explanations may contribute to the answer, viral activity probably assists because the competitive dominants become particularly susceptible to infection, whereas rare species are relatively protected."

In the abstract of a paper entitled "Viruses in Aquatic Ecosystems," Eric Wommack and Rita Colwell noted that the "discovery that viruses may be the most abundant organisms in natural waters, surpassing the number of bacteria by an order of magnitude, has inspired a resurgence of interest in viruses in the aquatic environment. Surprisingly little was known of the interaction of viruses and their hosts in nature." Curtis Suttle, a microbiologist at the University of British Columbia, explored that interaction in a 1999 article that he called, "Do Viruses Control the Ocean?" He wrote:

Marine viruses, of course, infect more than just plankton. Cultivated stocks of crabs, oysters, mussels, clams, shrimp, salmon, and catfish, [virtually everything that is farmed in the ocean] for example, are all susceptible to viruses, and such infections have caused enormous losses in the aquaculture industry. The mere existence of infective viral species in cultured populations argues that viruses play a role in controlling natural populations too. . . . The collapse of a herring stock in Alaska in 1993 was known to have been caused by a virus. An epidemic of a previously unknown distemper virus in 1988 resulted in the death of more than 18,000 harbor seals in Northern Europe. A few years later, infected seals were discovered along New York's Long Island. Related viruses have also been found in dolphins and porpoises.

"But it would be a mistake," Suttle continued, "to look at sea viruses as mere pathogens that destroy other life. They are, rather, essential to the running of the marine ecosystem's engine. This was dramatically shown in an experiment in which we selectively removed viruses from seawater and measured the growth rates of the remaining planktonic organisms. We expected to see growth rates increase dramatically as the organisms were freed from viral infection. Much to our surprise, the plankton stopped growing

completely. What we had not realized was that the living organisms in the water depended on the nutrients released as other organisms were killed off. Without the death of phytoplankton at the hands of viruses, there was no fuel to keep the engine running." In 2005, Suttle wrote, "Our understanding of the effect of viruses on global systems and processes continues to unfold, overthrowing the idea that viruses and virus-mediated processes are sidebars to global processes."

Some of the mysteries of marine viruses are being solved, but for the most part, viruses do not give up their secrets willingly, and not all of these secrets are harmful. In a 2001 article on the role of marine microbes, Mitchell Leslie wrote, "Dip a bucket into the ocean anywhere and you can scoop up one of the great mysteries of science. Within that modest-looking pail of water swim millions of bacteria and billions of viruses. . . . Yet marine ecologists haven't a clue what most of the microbes in the bucket do for a living." Recently, however, Ed DeLong and his colleagues from the Monterey Bay Aquarium Research Institute (MBARI), using new gene-sequencing techniques, discovered that some oceanic bacteria convert light to energy; in other words, they are photosynthesizers. DeLong's findings were paralleled by those of Paul Falkowski of Rutgers, who found a type of bacterial chlorophyll in the bacteria he studied, although his approach was biophysical, rather than molecular. Falkowski was searching for organisms that might somehow use the dim light emitted from deep-sea vents, and while they didn't find any photosynthesizing microbes in the depths, they did find plenty on the surface. In fact, they estimated that about 1 percent of the surface bacteria are aerobic phototrophes, that is, photosynthesizers. Falkowski's discovery, along with that of DeLong, go a long way toward resolving a long-standing conundrum: how can there be so many bacteria in the ocean with so little for them to eat? These discoveries demonstrate not only that mysterious microbes populate the oceans, but also that these microbes play an unexpectedly important role in the life of the sea.

The use of modern epifluorescence microscopy techniques has substantially changed our perception of the role of bacteria in aquatic ecosystems during the recent past. Bacterioplankton, having high division and turnover rates, produces far more than previously thought. Bacterioplankton is no longer regarded solely as a final decomposer of organic material. In the "microbial loop hypothesis," bacterioplankton are at the center of a food web, having a similar function to phytoplankton and protists. It has been shown that bacterioplankton plays a central role in the carbon flux in aquatic ecosystems by taking up dissolved organic carbon and remineralizing the carbon.

The protists (Kingdom Protista) are divided into four major groups: protozoans, slime molds, unicellular algae, and multicellular algae. Protozoans include all protists that ingest their food, and thus they live primarily in aquatic habitats, such as ponds, drops of water in soil, or the digestive tracts of animals, where a small number of protozoans function as parasites. The slime molds are unique in having both unicellular and multicellular stages. When sufficient bacteria (food) are present, cellular slime molds are single amoeboid cells; however, when food becomes scarce, they aggregate into sluglike colonies, which become large reproductive structures.

Although simple, cyanobacteria were ultimately responsible for one of the most important global changes that the earth has undergone. "Combined studies of comparative genetics of modern organisms and of the fossil record," wrote Stjepko Golubic (1994), "demonstrate that cyanobacteria as a group can be credited for the introduction of oxygenic photosynthesis early in the planet's history." As stromatolites became more common 2.5 billion years ago, they gradually changed the earth's atmosphere from a carbon dioxide-rich mixture to the present-day oxygen-rich atmosphere. This paved the way for the next evolutionary step, the appearance of cells with a distinct membrane-bound nucleus, the eukaryotes. The identification of bacteria and viruses as the predominant life-forms in the ocean has changed our fundamental view of marine biodiversity and has resolved Hutchinson's paradox of the plankton. "Photosynthetic bacteria *Prochlorocossus* and *Synechococcus* are the most abundant oceanic primary producers, and their sequenced genomes provide new ecological insights," wrote Farooq Azam and Alexandra Worden in 2004.

Differences between plants and animals (photosynthesizing versus nonphotosynthesizing) seem at first to mark a basic division of life on Earth. Scientists now recognize an even more fundamental division: prokaryotic cells with no membrane around the nucleus versus eukaryotic cells with a membrane-bound nucleus. Bacteria and cyanobacteria are primitive prokaryotic life-forms, while all other plants and animals are based on more complex eukaryotic cells. In a 1998 article, Carl Woese called the microbial world "the sleeping giant," and quoted his colleague

Mark Wheelis: "The earth is a microbial planet, on which macroorganisms are recent additions—highly interesting and extremely complex in ways that most microbes aren't, but in the final analysis, relatively unimportant in a global context."*

In his 2001 essay entitled "Exploring the Unknown: The Silent Revolution of Microbiology," the Swiss molecular biologist Eduard Kellenberger (1920–2004) wrote:

No month passes without some new microorganisms being discovered, many of them having new, hitherto unknown properties. An example is the discovery of a new form of phototrophy in two widespread aerobic bacteria in surface waters of oceans (Beja et al. 2000; Kolber et al. 2000). One of these recently-discovered organisms has a new variant of light collecting rhodopsin. These bacteria harvest substantial amounts of energy and are supposed to play a very important role as a starter of the food chain that begins with plankton.

New technologies have inspired humans to plumb the depths of the oceans in pursuit of animals and information. The earlier barriers that separated the unknowable and unknown from the known are being demolished as we bring light—figuratively and literally—to the previously pervasive darkness of the depths. Perhaps nothing is more remarkable than the discovery of unexpected photosynthetic microbes that now appear to be the oceans' predominant life-forms. In 1988 when scientists identified photosynthetic free-living cyanobacteria in the ocean's euphotic zone (waters well-illuminated by sunlight) they wrote that "the recent discovery of photosynthetic picoplankton [organisms ranging in size from 0.2 to 2.0 micrometers], has changed our understanding of marine food webs" (Chisholm et al. 1988).

Previously, it was believed that the tiny plants—the phytoplankton—were the basis of the oceanic food chain. Then Zbigniew Kolber (with Cindy Van Dover, Robert Neiderman, and Paul Falkowski), found that the photosynthetic bacteria were incredibly plentiful: they wrote that the aerobic anoxygenic photoheterotrophs (AAPs) "are abundant in the upper open ocean and comprise at least 11% of the total microbial community." Further investigation revealed that the AAPs were of two genera, *Synechococcus* of the top twenty meters, and *Prochlorococcus*, of the upper one hundred meters. *Prochlorococcus* is the smallest known photosynthetic organism and "presumably the most abundant photosynthetic organism on earth," wrote French and German microbiologists Frédéric Partensky, Wolfgang Hess, and Daniel Vaulot in their 1999 review of *Prochlorococcus*, which, in what is otherwise a highly technical paper, they called "fascinating." Why?

In the decade since its discovery, *Prochlorococcus* has revealed itself to be a truly fascinating

---

* Microbiologists are particularly protective of their claim that their subjects actually dominate the earth. Consider this statement by Norman Pace (1997) of Berkeley: "Microbes receive little attention in our general texts of biology. They are largely ignored by most professional biologists and are virtually unknown to the public except in cases of disease or rot. Yet, the workings of the biosphere depend absolutely on the workings of the microbial world. Our texts articulate biodiversity in terms of large organisms: insects usually top the count of species. Yet, if we squeeze out any one of these insects and examine its contents under the microscope, we find hundreds of thousands of distinct microbial species. A handful of soil contains billions of microbial organisms, so many different types that accurate numbers remain unknown."

organism. It is unambiguously one of the most important components of marine phytoplankton in terms of biomass, although its real importance in terms of global production is still only very approximately estimated. The analysis of its natural distribution provides many clues to interpret the physiological and genetic features it displays in the laboratory and vice versa. Its most spectacular traits include its extremely small size, its unique pigmentation, and its ability to proliferate in nutrient-depleted areas. From a phylogenetic viewpoint, it is unfortunately not the long-sought-after direct ancestor of the green chloroplast. Still, the evolution of *Prochlorococcus, Prochloron, and Prochlorothrix,* which have evolved independently from different cyanobacterial ancestors and converged to recruit the same protein to build a novel antenna to replace the more complex phycobilisomes, is a very exciting topic. . . . Because of its many intriguing features, but even more importantly because of its true significance from a global environmental perspective, *Prochlorococcus* could establish itself in the near future as a standard model in photosynthetic prokaryote research, warranting a concerted effort to sequence its genome.

The minuscule photosynthetic cyanobacteria are so proliferate that they affect all life on the planet. Like *Prochlorococcus* in importance—but larger in size if not in effect—are the sometimes-anomalous weather systems that can affect almost the entire planet. El Niño is not only a mystery for the ocean; it is a mystery for the world. This meteorological phenomenon gets its name from its frequent appearance around Christmas; *El Niño* means "the Christ child" in Spanish. It consists of a weakening of atmospheric circulation, particularly the southeast trade winds off the west coast of South America. (This is sometimes known as the "southern oscillation," so the El Niño–Southern Oscillation is abbreviated as ENSO.) The cold Peru Current, which usually flows eastward toward land, reverses and flows away from it. Sea surface temperatures can rise as much as 14 degrees Fahrenheit. A halt of the upwelling of cold water along the shore either kills or drives the anchovies of that region into deeper water. Sea birds and larger fishes, such as tuna that feed on anchovies, begin to starve and die. The escaping gas from dead and decaying fish is said to be strong enough to blacken the paint of passing ships. The anchovies, which supply a third of the world's supply of fish meal, contribute much to the economy of Peru.

Although El Niño increases rainfall on the west coast of South America, with flooding and massive soil erosion, it can also disrupt the weather around the world, causing droughts, and maybe even cyclones and tornadoes. Completely unpredictable, destructive El Niño conditions occurred in 1891, 1925, 1941, 1958, 1972, and 1983. A major El Niño event took place in 1997–98, causing—among other things—drought in Indonesia, which resulted in major forest fires. It caused flooding in southern Brazil and drought in the north; a drought in Hawaii; heavy rains in the Galápagos; flooding in Peru and Ecuador; major rainstorms and flooding, warmer waters, and unexpected fish and squid species off California and Oregon; dying sea lions and elephant seals in California; and unprecedented South Pacific storms, such as supertyphoon *Paka*, which produced winds of 236 miles per hour—the highest surface winds ever recorded.

Rita Colwell served as the eleventh director of the U.S. National Science Foundation from 1998 to 2004, and she was a professor of microbiology and president of the University of Maryland Biotechnology Institute. In a 1996 article, she wrote, "On a global scale, cholera epidemics can now be related to climate and climate events, such as El Niño, as well as the global distribution of the plankton host. Remote sensing, with the use of satellite imagery, offers the potential for predicting conditions conducive to cholera outbreaks." Cholera outbreaks tied to El Niño! It seems that the abundance of the microorganism (*Vibrio cholerae*) that causes cholera increases with the abundance of copepods in ocean environments. Copepod production occurs in bursts when phytoplankton blooms, and epidemics, such as those in Bangladesh, 1987–90, and South America in 1991, can be correlated directly with El Niño events in those years. By 2000 Mercedes Pascual and her colleagues (one of whom was Rita Colwell) were prepared to state that:

> Analysis of a monthly 18-year cholera time series from Bangladesh shows that the temporal variability of cholera exhibits an interannual component at the dominant frequency of El Niño-Southern Oscillation (ENSO). Results from nonlinear time series analysis support a role for both ENSO and previous disease levels in the dynamics of

cholera. Cholera patterns are linked to the previously described changes in the atmospheric circulation of south Asia and, consistent with these changes, to regional temperature anomalies.

The cholera bacterium has now been found in copepods in the ballast water of tankers and freighters, giving it another way to spread its deadly message. As Alan Burdick wrote in his 2005 book on bioinvasions, *Out of Eden:*

> In July, 1991, six months after a cholera epidemic struck Peru, and several neighboring nations—the first ever cholera epidemic in South America—an identical strain of *V. cholerae 01* turned up in oyster beds in Mobile Bay, Alabama. Researchers sampled the ballast, bilge, and sewage water of nineteen ships docked at Mississippi ports; they found the toxigenic *01* strain on five ships, all of which had last stopped at a port in South America or Puerto Rico. Some of the ballast water had not been exchanged in months; evidently, the bacterium can survive on ships for extended periods, in a wide range of temperatures and salinities.

Viruses are tiny, but genes are even smaller. Indeed, viruses actually have genes. If it is difficult to envision a census of bacteria or viruses, try to imagine a census of genes. We have already censused the genes in the DNA of the Norway rat, the house (laboratory) mouse, the anopheles mosquito, the puffer fish, and hundreds of bacteria.

A leader in the science of gene sequencing is J. Craig Venter. Born in 1951, he received his

Ph.D. in physiology and pharmacology from the University of California, San Diego, in 1975. He spent the next ten years as a professor of biochemistry at the State University of New York at Buffalo and was a cancer research scientist at Roswell Park Memorial Institute in Buffalo and the National Institute for Neurological Disorders and Stroke until 1992. He founded The Institute for Genomic Research in Rockville, Maryland, where he and his team decoded the genome of the first free-living organism, the bacterium *Haemophilus influenzae*, pioneering the new whole-genome shotgun technique. Venter then founded Celera Genomics, specifically to sequence the human genome by using new algorithms and a battery of new, automated DNA-sequencing machines. Celera's genome project was completed and announced at the White House on June 26, 2000. President Clinton declared that the race to sequence the human genome was a tie between Celera and the government's Human Genome Project, but it was obvious that Celera had actually beaten the taxpayer-funded project soundly. The human genome was officially published in the journal *Science* in February 2001. (To nobody's surprise, Venter revealed that the human whose genome was sequenced was himself.) In addition to the human genome, Venter and his team at Celera sequenced the fruit fly, mouse, and rat genomes.

After leaving Celera in 2002, Venter founded the J. Craig Venter Science Foundation, which funds his current projects. In 2003 he launched a global expedition to obtain and study microbes from environments ranging from the world's oceans to urban centers. In a 2004 article in *Wired*, James Shreeve compared Venter's mission to those of Joseph Banks (aboard Captain Cook's *Endeavour*) and Charles Darwin:

> Young Joseph Banks was content just to describe the new varieties of life he collected on his voyage. For him, this was a survey of God's creation. Aboard the *Beagle* a half century later, Darwin was already questioning how the species he collected came to be. His ultimate answer wrested the helm from God and put it in the hands of natural processes instead. Now we're sailing into a new evolutionary time, when we will at least have a finger on the tiller. Venter is hardly the only scientist leading us there, but he alone is taking the measure of life's true diversity and dreaming up new life-forms at the same time.

This mission, now in progress, is yielding insights into genes that make up the vast realm of microbial life. Here is Venter's description of the *Sorcerer II* project (named for his 92-foot yacht) as published in *New Scientist*:

> The mission I am now engaged in is called the Sorcerer II microbial global sampling expedition. It is modeled on two 19th-century voyages of discovery: Charles Darwin's epic voyage on HMS *Beagle* and the *Challenger* expedition 40 years later, which was the first oceanographic research expedition. Like the *Challenger* expedition, we are collecting biological samples every 300 kilometres on a voyage to circumnavigate the globe. But unlike that mission, which focused on visible organisms, we are trying to characterise the biomass of the unseen

world of bacteria, archaea and viruses. This biomass rivals or exceeds that of all the plants and animals in the visible world.

From some of our earliest microbial genome shotgun sequencing efforts, it became clear that the assembly algorithms could uniquely sort different genome and chromosomal elements into the correct structures. After the new algorithms were developed for the *Drosophila* and human genomes I knew that we could shotgun sequence perhaps thousands of species simultaneously. We tested the idea with random sequence fragments from more than 100 genomes mixed together and were able to accurately reconstruct each genome. I wanted to test the idea to shotgun sequence the oceans.

We started with the Sargasso Sea in the north Atlantic, an area that many consider an ocean desert, with low levels of nutrients and correspondingly low biological diversity. Our analysis of the shotgun sequence data showed tremendous biological diversity. We discovered more than 1.2 million genes from sequencing the DNA of an estimated 1800 to 47,000 species. Most significantly, we found more than 800 variations of the gene that produces the photoreceptor rhodopsin, a pigment protein sensitive to light. This suggests that some new type of light-driven biology may explain the Sargasso Sea's unexpectedly high diversity of species.

The Sorcerer II expedition to create a unique environmental gene database began sampling in Halifax, Nova Scotia, in the summer of 2003, before working its way southwards along the east coast of the US.

We continued through the Panama canal to Cocos Island, and then sampled extensively in the Galápagos Islands of Ecuador, Darwin's source of inspiration. During the past year, the Sorcerer II has wended its way across the Pacific. It is now in Australia, and at the end of cyclone season we will head across the Indian Ocean for Africa.

Without a clear understanding of the biological components in the environment, it is hard to assess the damage we are doing. It is easy to count oil-soaked birds and sea mammals, or even to count plants and animals for an assessment of dwindling "macro" biodiversity. But to assess human impact on the invisible microbial world on which much of our biosystem depends, we need to know about its genetic make-up to understand how it works. The emerging science of environmental genomics is now beginning to reveal the ocean's vast store of genetic diversity.

From the smallest forms of life to the largest, the sea has hidden some of its most spectacular secrets well. Consider *Architeuthis*, long considered the largest of all living invertebrates. *Architeuthis* can be translated as "first" or "early" squid, but since it was certainly not the first squid described, it was probably given this name to signify that it was the first in importance or size. For centuries, seafarers and scientists were offered only tantalizing glimpses of the giant squid, washed up on beaches, or as part of the "stomach contents" of sperm whales. How could sperm whales capture the cephalopod that had so effectively evaded all human attempts to see one alive in its native habitat? And what exactly was this native habitat? ❧

A Legend Authenticated: The Giant Squid

The giant squid, the kraken of Scandinavian sea lore, is one of the first legendary and mysterious animals that comes to mind, but except for where they strand, and some morphological details, little is known about the life of *Architeuthis*. In his 1966 *Scientific American* article, Clyde Roper wrote, "on other matters, such as its habitat and method of reproduction, one can offer only educated guesses based on what is known of related oceanic squids." It is the largest invertebrate in the world, reaching a known length of sixty feet, and a maximum known weight of about a ton. In the past fifty years, *Architeuthis* has slowly (and reluctantly) begun to answer some of our questions about its heretofore unfathomable existence.

The real kraken did not reveal itself to science until 1853, when Danish zoologist Japetus Steenstrup examined a six-inch beak. (Squid have beaks like parrots, but the upper mandible fits in the lower.) But it was not until twenty years later that a scientist would actually examine the animal. For reasons that will probably go forever unexplained, giant squid began appearing off the beaches of Newfoundland during the decade 1870–80. As many as sixty of these beasts were found on the beach or floating offshore. *Architeuthis*, therefore, is the quintessential deep Atlantic monster, since it made its debut in Newfoundland, and although it has been recorded from other locations, such as New Zealand (where a late nineteenth-century invasion occurred of a magnitude almost equal to that of Newfoundland's), it is best known from both sides of the North Atlantic.

The giant squid is also known from British and European shores but again, only from stranded specimens. The earliest record seems to be of a carcass that washed ashore at Thingøre Sand, in Iceland, in 1639. It was introduced to the world by Professor Steenstrup, a lecturer in geology, botany, and zoology at Copenhagen University. In a paper read in 1849, he quoted a 1639 description that appeared in *Annalar Björns á Skardsa* (in Danish), which was translated as follows:

In the autumn on Thingøresand in Hunevandsyssel a peculiar creature or sea monster was stranded with *length and thickness like those of a man; it had 7 tails and each of these measured approximately two ells*. These tails were densely covered with a type of button, and the buttons looked as if there was an eye ball in each button, and round the eye ball an eyelid; these eyelids looked as if they were gilded. On this sea monster there was in addition *a single tail* which had grown out above those 7 tails; *it was extremely long, 4–5 fms [7.50–9.40 m]; no bone or cartilage were found in its body* but the whole to the sight and to the touch was like the soft body of the

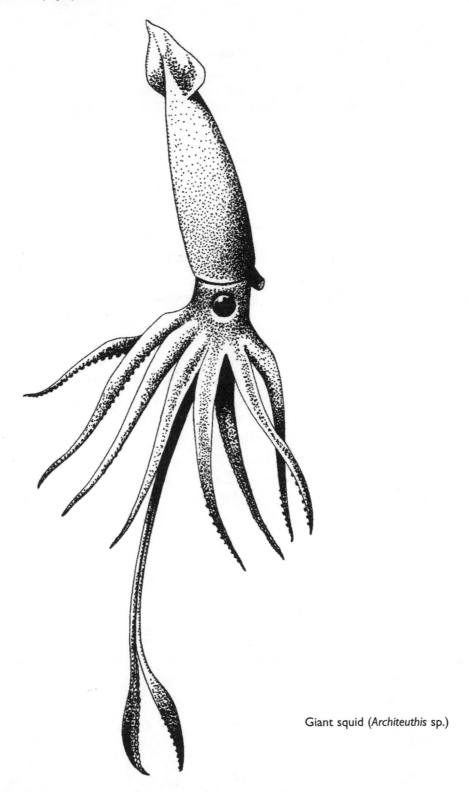

Giant squid (*Architeuthis* sp.)

female lumpfish (*Cyclopterus lumpus*). No trace was seen of the head, except the one aperture, or two, which were found behind the tails or at a short distance from them.*

Even though the annalist managed to read the animal upside down, confusing the head with the tail(s), the "monster" was obviously a giant squid that had lost one of its arms and one of its tentacles.

At irregular intervals, squid carcasses in various states of decomposition appeared on beaches around the world, and by 1735 Linnaeus was ready to include *Sepia microcosmos* in the first edition of his *Systema naturae*. (Perhaps because he doubted its existence, Linnaeus dropped *S. microcosmos* from subsequent editions, and it does not appear at all in the definitive tenth edition.) Steenstrup found another early record of a giant squid in Iceland; in the winter of 1790, a creature that the people called *Kolkrabbe* drifted ashore at Arnaraesvik. This one seems to have been considerably larger than its predecessor, with a total length of thirty-nine feet.

In December 1853 a gigantic cephalopod washed ashore at Raabjerg beach, on the Jutland peninsula of Denmark. It was cut up for fish bait, but the beak, which measured approximately three by four inches, was the basis for Steenstrup's designation of a new species, *Architeuthis monachus*. His description of the Raabjerg specimen, based on eyewitness accounts and the impressive beak, was published in 1857 and

marked the official transition of the giant squid from the realm of fable into the scientific literature. Three years later, Steenstrup described another new species of giant squid, *A. dux*, from the remains of another carcass that a Captain Hygom had brought from the Bahamas to Denmark. Another North Atlantic stranding took place in 1860, when a twenty-three-footer with a seven-foot-long head and mantle came ashore on the Scottish coast between Hillswick and Scalloway.

On November 30, 1861, off the island of Tenerife in the Canaries, the lookout of the French steam corvette *Alecton*, Lieutenant Bouyer commanding, spotted a monstrous animal floating on the surface, with a brick-red body that was sixteen to eighteen feet long (not counting the tentacles) and glimmering green eyes, which made the crew uneasy. As the corvette approached, the creature tried to move out of the way, but it did not dive below the surface. Lieutenant Bouyer determined to secure the animal, but he was reluctant to lower the boats for fear of the harm that might come to his men. When they began shooting at it, the animal dived, but it always reappeared. One shot hit a vital organ, for the animal vomited blood and froth, and at this time, it emitted a strong odor of musk. When they threw a loop around it to haul it aboard, the rope cut through the body, and the head and tentacles fell into the sea and sank. They brought the remaining tail section to Tenerife.

Following Lieutenant Bouyer's report, Sabine Berthelot, the French consul, presented the paper at the December meeting of the French Academy of Sciences. From the similarity of the details, it appears obvious that Verne saw the Bouyer report and adapted it for *Twenty*

---

* Translation (with italics) from a publication entitled *The Cephalopod Papers* of Japetus Steenstrup, by Agnete Volsøe, Jørgen Knudsen, and William Rees, published by the Danish Science Press in 1962.

Thousand Leagues Under the Sea, but made the *poulpe* far more aggressive that it actually was. In one instance, Bouyer wrote, "*Sa bouche, ou bec de perroquet, pouvait offrir près d'un demi-mètre*"—"its mouth, like the beak of a parakeet, could open nearly a half meter," and Verne's version, employing the same device, reads, *un bec de corne fait comme le bec d'un perroquet*, "a horny beak like the beak of a parakeet."

No one has ever seen a healthy adult giant squid—especially in its native habitat—but we assume they live at considerable depths. From examination of the carcasses, we can extrapolate something about their lives in the icy blackness. First there are the eyes: the giant squid's are among the largest in the animal kingdom, and can reach a diameter of ten inches—the size of a dinner plate. And they are highly developed eyes, as complex and capable as those of the higher vertebrates, but adapted for seeing in very low light levels—and of course, underwater, as well. Like all squids, *Architeuthis* has eight arms and two greatly elongated tentacles, which may grow to a length of thirty feet. The "clubs" on the two tentacles can grasp and hold prey items, whatever they might be. A series of "buttons" along the entire length of the tentacles can lock them together, freeing the club ends to function as pincers. The other eight arms have rows of suckers, each of which is individually movable and has a toothed ring around the perimeter, that digs into the flesh of its prey, holding on for eternity or death, whichever comes first. Unlike some other squid, *Architeuthis* has no hooks or "claws" on its tentacles. At the center of the corona of arms is the powerful beak, capable of ripping chunks of flesh from prey animals.

We do not know why giant squids wash ashore at irregular intervals at apparently unrelated locations around the world. To date, the greatest known concentration is the one reported in Newfoundland during the 1870s. Many specimens were recorded for science, but others were cut up for bait or dog food. Since that time, specimens have come ashore elsewhere, but they have also continued to appear—albeit less frequently—on the rocky shores of Newfoundland. Either giant squid have a Newfoundland suicide wish, or some other forces are at work that might explain this cycle. Frederick Aldrich, a teuthologist (squid specialist) who specialized in *Architeuthis*, suggested that fluctuations in the Labrador Current were responsible for the appearance of giant squid off Newfoundland every ninety years or so. When the cold portion of the current known as the Avalon Branch hits northeastern Newfoundland, the squid, following the cold mass of water, come close to shore, where for unknown reasons, they die. He predicted that the next period of *Architeuthis* strandings would occur around 1960, and he was proven correct when six giant squid stranded between 1964 and 1966.

Although the many fish species already caught, identified, and cataloged during a thousand years of fishing and two hundred years of scientific collecting give us a pretty good idea of what is living (or was living) in the ocean, an unknown number of species still lurk beyond our nets, our hooks, and our cameras. The giant squid, largest of all known invertebrates, was unknown to science until Steenstrup's description in 1853. Yet, despite hundreds of specimens that have been found washed ashore or trapped in fishing nets since then, *not a single, healthy adult giant squid has ever been seen alive*—not by scientists, not by submersible pilots or passengers, not by fishermen, not even by Jacques Cousteau, who wrote (in *Octopus and Squid: The Soft Intelligence*) that "even observers in diving bells have never sighted one." Nevertheless, later in the same book, he described "a very large cephalopod, only a few yards from the minisub, watching the vehicle as it moved slowly past. . . . It was there, nonetheless, enormous, alive, its huge eyes fixed on me." (He never comes out and says it was *Architeuthis*, but then he doesn't identify it as another species, either. By the way, how could a squid with eyes on either side of its head fix its *eyes* on Cousteau as it slowly moved past?)

In February 1997 an expedition was mounted to film *Architeuthis* in what was supposed to be its natural habitat. Led by Clyde Roper, the expedition consisted of Malcolm Clarke, Greg Stone of the New England Aquarium, *National Geographic* photographer Emory Kristof, Teddy Tucker of Bermuda, Adam Frankel of Cornell University's Bioacoustic Research Program, James Bellingham of MIT's Underwater Vehicles Laboratory, and various support teams, including programmers who were to send back daily dispatches to Smithsonian and *National Geographic* Web sites. Clyde Roper, a Smithsonian Institution teuthologist, was unquestionably the world's foremost authority on *Architeuthis*. He had assembled the expedition and raised the five million dollars that it was going to cost. He had published any number of papers on this species, and whenever anyone wanted an opinion about the giant squid—how big they got, where they lived, what they ate—they would go to him. And

in every one of these television, newspaper, or magazine interviews, he said that nobody has ever seen a living giant squid. "Then how do we know they exist?" was inevitably the interviewer's next question. "They have been washing up on beaches around the world for the last four hundred years," he would answer.

Roper and his colleagues were going to New Zealand: to Kaikoura on the northeastern coast of South Island, which was to be their jumping-off point, since it is on the edge of the deep Kaikoura Canyon. They selected Kaikoura Canyon because it was a favorite haunt of large sperm whales, creatures known to feed on squid, giant and otherwise. They planned to approach the problem from several angles. MIT's *Odyssey*, an autonomous underwater vehicle (AUV), would be deployed with a video camera in hopes of filming a squid swimming by. (The AUV could also measure water temperature and salinity to get an accurate picture of the type of habitat the squid prefers.) Emory Kristof planned to drop several baited cameras looking he said, "like a 4-1/2-foot box kite flying horizontally in the water" and containing six-gallon drums of smelly, liquefied tuna as bait for the squid. And finally, they were going to try to affix a video camera (the "crittercam") to a sperm whale, and as the whale descended in search of food it was going to film its prey. The camera was free-floating, attached harmlessly by a harpoon tag inserted into the whale's back by a short length of wire, and faced the same direction as its host. The camera had a link that dissolved in seawater after two hours and a radio beacon that enabled the researchers to collect it when it had come loose and floated to the surface. (Although this sounds like a mad scientist scheme, it was actually successfully employed with great white sharks in South African waters for the spectacular 1995 National Geographic film, *Great White Shark*.)

The presence of the huge, ivory-toothed whales in Kaikoura Canyon surely meant that *Architeuthis* was not far away. Roper and his team were buoyed by the fact that during the previous year, four giant squid had been trawled up by fishermen around New Zealand in locations less likely than Kaikoura Canyon to harbor *Architeuthis*. Now these squid hunters were heading to what they believed was an ideal place to spot a living example of this traditionally elusive and enigmatic creature. (The improbability that squid would attack an animal that might be fifty times heavier than itself renders descriptions of titanic battles between giant squid and sperm whales apocryphal. On the other hand, sperm whales are known to eat giant squid, so witnesses to the "battles" between these two giants were probably watching the desperate struggle of a squid trying not to be eaten.)

On an earlier expedition, during the 1980s, Frederick Aldrich, a Newfoundland scientist and Roper's predecessor as "world's foremost authority on the giant squid," had tried the same thing in a submersible with less sophisticated camera equipment. Of course, Aldrich and company wanted to get some pictures, but basically, they just wanted to *see* the damn thing. Roper and his team had much more ambitious plans. In its early stages, their expedition had also planned on a submersible, but they lacked the necessary time and money, so they decided to economize by sending unmanned, remote-controlled cameras into the depths of the canyon, with the hope

that a giant squid would pass in front of the lens. Six weeks of lowering cameras, watching monitors, and chasing sperm whales, produced not a single image of a giant squid.

For this and other similar "expeditions"—all made as television specials—they always brought in another expert: Steve O'Shea, a teuthologist whose responsibility at New Zealand's Institute of Water and Atmosphere was to examine and catalog the many specimens of *Architeuthis* that had been brought up from deep-sea trawls that were fishing a mile down for orange roughy (*Hoplostethus atlanticus*) and a New Zealand fish known as hoki (*Macruronus novaezelandiae*). O'Shea has studied more giant squid specimens than anyone else and now believes that he is beginning to gain some insight into the way these enigmatic creatures live. He has collected living *Architeuthis* larvae and tried to keep them alive in tanks, and although they did not survive, he has technically seen a living giant squid, meaning that it is no longer valid to say "no one has ever seen a living giant squid." (The half-inch-long larvae hardly qualified as "giant" squid, but they were unquestionably *Architeuthis*.) He also believes that *Architeuthis* hangs head-down, hovering at a forty-five-degree angle with its feeding tentacles extended and clamped together, with only the club ends—the parts with the suckers—opening and closing like pliers, as it fishes for prey that it brings to its mouth with its arms. But because no hoki and one (tentative) orange roughy remnant have been found in *Architeuthis* stomachs, O'Shea wrote in 2004, "it appears that *Architeuthis* probably preys on the same food items as hoki (small fish, prawns, and squid) instead of on the hoki itself."

If indeed *Architeuthis* hovers head-down over schools of fishes and then reaches down to snatch one or more of them, the giant squid would obviously need something to snatch them with, and a set of long pincers equipped with toothed, sticky suction cups is an almost perfect tool for this job. Also, if these arms are deployed at near full length, a connecting mechanism may be essential to keep the two tentacular clubs in close proximity and functional as there can be little leverage or control of the clubs at such great distance from the head, as well as a lack of visual feedback to guide such control. The huge eyes, of minimal value in visualizing prey in near total darkness, might be used to pick out the incidental bioluminescent flashes of light created by shoals of non-bioluminescent fishes like orange roughys and hoki. If correct, this hypothesis would mean that all the horizontal models of *Architeuthis* in various museums around the world are incorrectly oriented.

Steve O'Shea, along with the cameramen who filmed his efforts to keep *Architeuthis* alive, and the television viewers who saw the tiny creatures in a tank, can all claim to have seen a living giant squid—if seeing something on television counts. (It certainly doesn't for bird watchers.) Thanks to Jules Verne, Peter Benchley, Michael Crichton, and any number of science fantasists who promoted the giant squid as a terrifying sea monster, the image of *Architeuthis* as a man-eating, ship-sinking, anaconda-armed monster endures. Yes, it is true that squid—especially *giant* squid—are endowed with features—suction cups, beaks, a mucous coating, multiple appendages—that we do not encounter in the more familiar terrestrial creatures. Their

unfamiliar shape, with a cluster of arms at one end, huge eyes in the middle, and a tail at the other end, has only added to the impression that they are alien creatures from an unknown world—which is exactly what they are.

If O'Shea is correct—and we won't know until the moment that someone actually sees *Architeuthis* in action—it means that we are beginning to dispel the appellation of "unknown" that has characterized the giant squid for centuries. The unknown *Architeuthis* is (slowly) becoming known, and it is far from the "monster" people thought it was. It does not feed on or attack ships or people. It does not feed on or attack sperm whales. It does not even feed on or attack foot-long hoki or orange roughy. Rather, it hangs head-down, scanning the depths with its giant, lidless eyes, waiting to pluck small fishes and squid with its delicate, clipped-together feeding tentacles. At its great size, *Architeuthis* has the outward appearance of an awesome and terrifying predator, but recent studies have downgraded it to a harmless consumer of small fishes. Legends fall hard, however, and there are many who continue to believe that *Architeuthis* is the scourge of the depths, ready to wrap its snakelike arms around anything it can catch, and tear its luckless prey to pieces with its powerful beak.

Still a mystery, however, is how the sperm whale catches squid, giant or not, which are the staple of its diet. Like all odontocetes, sperm whales rely on echolocation to find their food. They send out sounds and process the returning echoes to determine the nature of nearby objects, including prey items. But that only explains part of the problem. The whale still has to catch its food. Contrary to legend, sperm whales do not feed exclusively on giant squid. They probably do not feed on *Architeuthis* very much at all. Rather, the stomachs of captured sperm whales have revealed much smaller squid, but in much larger numbers. For years, cetologists have wondered how the sperm whale, operating in total darkness, could gather enough of the swift cephalopods to sustain itself. The whale is a mammal and breathes air, so its deepest descents—which can last over an hour—are breath-hold dives. Squid have gills and breathe water, so they can remain below indefinitely—or at least up to the moment that they are captured by a whale—so the whale has to be able to capture enough squid per hunting dive to justify the energy expended to get there.

From examination of the stomach contents spilled on the decks of whaling ships, we know that sperm whales eat lots of squid, and based on the number of squid beaks found in the stomachs of captured sperm whales, we can get an idea of the quantity. Finds of five thousand to seven thousand beaks per whale are not uncommon, and Berzin mentions one Soviet scientist who found twenty-eight thousand beaks in the stomach of a single whale, uppers and lowers (squid beaks come in two parts), indicating a feeding frenzy in which some fourteen thousand squid were consumed. Such consumption would require a dense concentration of squid, and indeed, squid may be the most numerous large animals in the ocean.

From largely circumstantial (or nonexistent) evidence, Ivan Sanderson (in *Follow the Whale*) discusses the numbers of squid required to feed the world's population of sperm whales:

> Most people don't even know what a squid is, yet these animals probably make up a greater aggregate of pure animal matter on this earth than any other two kinds of living creatures put together. They exist in countless millions of apparently endless masses in every ocean and sea in the world, and almost three-quarters of this planet is covered by oceans and seas which are on the average nearly two and a half miles deep. Throughout this vast volume of liquid there are probably more squids than anything else.

In 1977 Malcolm Clarke, a British scientist who specializes in sperm whales and squid, commented on the complex interaction:

> Man's awareness of the existence of large squid came, not from what he caught in his nets, but from monsters floating dead or moribund at the sea surface and from the tales of whalers who had seen, with unbelieving eyes, whales vomit complete or dismembered kraken of immense proportions. Such doubtful tales hardened into drawings and recorded measurements over one century ago, and ever since, man has tried desperately to catch by net and line, these will-o'-the-wisps of the sea. Though our nets have become larger and larger and faster and faster, very little progress and most of that in the last decade, has been made towards catching any deep sea squids greater than half a meter or so in length. In a century, many tantalizing glimpses of the deep sea squids have come from strandings on the coast and from the stomachs of toothed whales, particularly the commercially exploited Sperm Whale.

In this study, Clarke estimated the amount of food required to feed the world population of sperm whales. Recognizing the difficulties of estimating whale populations, he wrote, "Estimates of the whale population are, unhappily, notoriously questionable, but a 1973 estimate placed this at 1-1/4 million." Using a mean weight of fifteen tons for males and five tons for females, Clarke arrived at a total weight of the world's sperm whales of ten million tons, which would require *a hundred million tons of squid per year*. This is larger than the biomass of the annual world catch of fish by fishermen "and probably approaches the total biomass of mankind." In other words, the weight of squid eaten every year by sperm whales is greater than the weight of the entire human race.

In a 1996 article by Richard Conniff in *Smithsonian* magazine, Clyde Roper said, "I've looked at the biology of the giant squid, and also of the sperm whale, the records of where strandings occur and the best concentrations of squid in stomach contents of sperm whales." He said he interviewed whalers in the Azores who used to harpoon sperm whales by hand from small boats. When they were harpooned, the whales vomited up *lula grande* (giant squid). Roper asked how often they ran into this, and they said that virtually every whale would have a giant squid in it. "You do the arithmetic—there are perhaps a million sperm whales in the world—and it follows that there have to be a lot of giant squid around."

The killing of sperm whales has stopped, but when they were being killed and hauled up onto the decks of factory ships, examination of their stomach contents was probably the best clue to what they ate. The contents reflected the numbers of squid consumed, as well as the nature of the squid themselves. Indeed, the whalers performed an important service for those who would study squid; no other way of collecting is nearly as productive. (Squid can often evade nets and trawls, but they seem to be less successful at avoiding the powerful, deep-diving whale that feeds on them. Unfortunately, specimens collected by whales are often partially digested by the time teuthologists get to look at them.)

One of the best books ever written about squid is Malcolm Clarke's massive *Cephalopoda in the Diet of Sperm Whales of the Southern Hemisphere and Their Bearing on Sperm Whale Biology*, published as a *Discovery Report* in 1980. As Clarke introduced this 324-page study, "Whale and squid biology are clearly closely linked, and consideration of both subjects in one paper is necessary to avoid duplication." Since beginning the study in 1962, Clarke and various colleagues have examined the stomach contents of 461 sperm whales collected at the whaling stations of Durban and Donkergat in South Africa; Cheynes Beach in Albany, Western Australia; the island of South Georgia; and the British pelagic factory ships *Southern Harvester* and *Southern Venturer*. In this study, Clarke noted that *Architeuthis* beaks are found in only 0.26 percent of Southern Ocean sperm whale stomachs.

By now we know that there are not a million and a quarter sperm whales; and that regardless of their numbers, they only rarely eat *Architeuthis*. The predominant squid eaten by sperm whales belong to the genus *Histioteuthis*, two-foot long deep-sea squid that are covered with lights and have one eye much larger than the other. Curiously, *Histioteuthis* is listed among

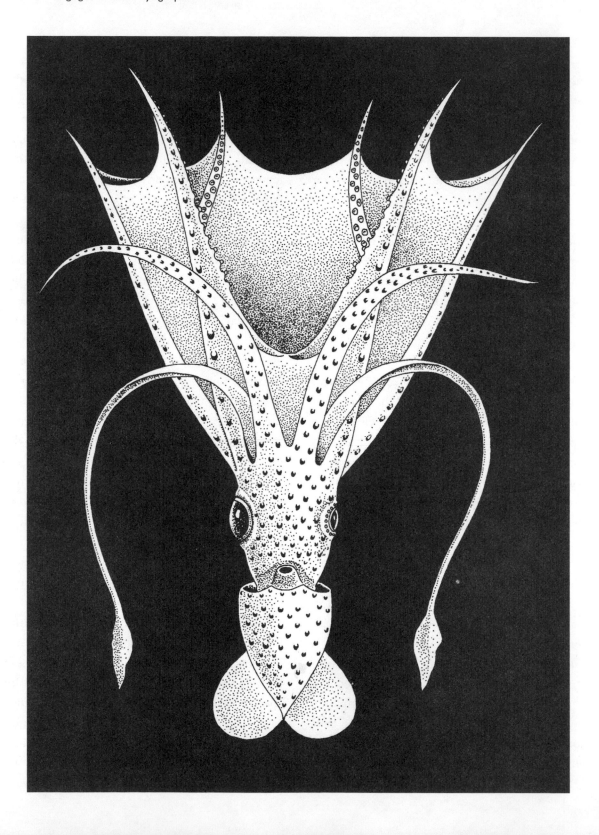

the ammoniacal genera, suggesting that ammonia is the seasoning of choice in the sperm whales' diet. Squid of different species and sizes also make up a large proportion of the diet of many other marine creatures, including fish, beaked whales, dolphins, pinnipeds, and albatrosses. Nevertheless, Clarke opined that sperm whales "are by far the most important predator of squid." Even if "only" three hundred thousand sperm whales remain, the relaxation of hunting pressure on them will (or should) enable them to increase their numbers, as they continue to eat large numbers of assorted squid species. Will the return of the squid's major predator affect squid populations, or are there simply so many cephalopods that the sperm whales cannot make a dent in their numbers?

The whale obviously cannot dash around snapping blindly at squid while holding its breath, so there has to be some way of slowing down or even stopping the prey. It has been speculated—but certainly not proven, since observations would require the diving capabilities of a sperm whale—that the whales stun their prey with focused bursts of sound, and then gobble them up at leisure (Norris and Møhl 1983.) In addition to these echolocating and sound-producing functions, the sperm whale also communicates with other whales by a series of clicks, bangs, and wheezes. While the questions about the teuthophagic whales endure; the eating habits of teuthids, large and small, are also more than a little mysterious.

Most of the examined specimens of giant squid had empty stomachs, so the question of

Umbrella squid (*Histioteuthis bonnelli*)

what they ate—never mind for the moment what ate them—has long been a mystery. When there was anything at all to be found in the squids' stomachs, it was often ground to an unrecognizable slurry. But when Bruce Deagle of the University of Tasmania and his colleagues (2005) analyzed the gut contents of a squid that had been caught by fishermen in 1999, they were more than a little surprised to find parts of three squid tentacles and twelve beaks. In the past, they would have had to rely on matching the beaks to Malcolm Clarke's extensive catalog for identification, but now they were able to take advantage of molecular analysis to identify the original owners of the tentacles and the beaks. Isolation of *Architeuthis* DNA from the tentacle fragments identified the prey species as *Architeuthis*, thereby raising the possibility of cannibalism. (Emma Young's *New Scientist* article on the subject is entitled "The Gruesome Eating Habits of the Giant Squid.") The previous year, Kat Bolstad and Steve O'Shea had described the gut contents of a giant squid from New Zealand waters, which contained fragments of an *Architeuthis* club, and they, too, suspected cannibalism. Did this squid, trapped in a net, bite off its own arms in its frenzy to escape? Bolstad and O'Shea conclude that "Whether intentional or not, ingestion of an entire *Architeuthis* tentacle club does constitute cannibalism."

Deep in the world's oceans, there are cephalopods whose existence almost defies description. Not exactly a squid and not exactly an octopus, *Vampyroteuthis infernalis* ("vampire squid from hell"), has eight tentacles and two wispy filaments instead of the grasping tentacles of the squids. It is a deepwater species that gets to be about a foot in length, and has the ability to wrap its arms over its head so that it effectively turns itself inside-out and resembles a spiky football. The reason for this behavior is a mystery. It is a warm sepia-brown in color, with startling, sky-blue eyes, which are proportionally the largest eyes of any animal in the world. It was previously known only from dead animals that had been captured in nets, but in recent years, the living animal has been photographed from a submersible. What else is "out there"? ⁞

Mysterious Squid and Octopuses Appear

We might go to Sulawesi to look for strange creatures. A new population of coelacanths was found off the northern coast of this Indonesian island in 1997, and one of the few megamouth sharks washed ashore there the following year. Now we have an octopus that can disguise itself as a snake.

The mimic octopus is one of the most fascinating new discoveries in all of marine zoology. It was filmed in 1998 by Australian underwater photographers Roger Steene and Rudie Kuiter, who showed their films to the Melbourne Museum's Mark Norman, an octopus expert and the author of *Cephalopods: A World Guide.* This long-armed octopus, which reaches a length of about two feet, is patterned with dark brown and white stripes crossways on the arms and can change its shape (and rearrange its stripes) so that it resembles any number of other, non-octopod creatures, such as a lionfish, a sea snake, a flatfish, or a stingray. It is not at all clear why the mimic octopus assumes these disguises, for many of them are predators, or poisonous, or both. Perhaps the appearance of a sea snake or a lionfish repels potential predators, but of course, we have no way of knowing the response of, say, a damselfish, to a sea snake. Most images and discussions of the mimic octopus have appeared on television or in popular magazines, but in 2001, with Julian Finn and Tom Tregenza, Mark Norman wrote "Dynamic Mimicry in an Indo-Malayan Octopus" in the *Proceedings of the Royal Society of London*, in which they wrote:

The mimic octopus may take on the appearance of a sea-snake simply because the same selective forces that make the black-and-white bands a useful signal for a sea-snake also apply to the octopus. However, it seems very unlikely that such a remarkable resemblance of animals with radically different morphologies and behaviours is not due to mimicry.

There are some seven hundred species of cephalopods—squid, octopuses, cuttlefishes, chambered nautilus—and within this broad classification, there are some forty genera of squid. Squid come in a dazzling array of sizes and shapes, equipped with claws, hooks, suckers, giant axons, eyes as complex as those of the "higher" vertebrates, beaks like parrots, or lights all over them. Some are tough and muscular, while others are as soft and gelatinous as a jellyfish. Some species can fly, others can descend to abyssal depths; some live in uncountable congregations, while others are solitary hunters, prowling the abyssal depths in search of food. They are the most numerous and varied of all the cephalopods, officially classified as mollusks, even though their shell (known as the *gladius* or "pen") is found inside the body. In the smaller species, the pen is less than a quarter of an inch long, while in *Architeuthis* it can be four feet in length. (The familiar chalky material used in bird cages is the pen of the cuttlefish.) The size range for the various squid is enormous, from the tiny *Pickfordiateuthis* (approximately the length of its name printed here) to *Architeuthis*, at a length of fifty-seven feet, among the largest of all (known) invertebrates.

Cephalopods have long been recognized as the intellectuals of the mollusk world. Cuttlefishes can cause waves of color to pass over their bodies; squids can change color in an instant and some can light up; some octopus species can change color and texture to match their surroundings, while others have been granted the problem-solving capabilities of a house cat. They can change color, festoon themselves with lumps, bumps, frills, and spikes, and when threatened, they can emit a cloud of ink—which doesn't blind the predator but rather assumes the shape of the octopus, which then turns white and dashes off. Some researchers believe that cephalopods communicate by changing color or shape. In their 1996 *Cephalopod Behaviour*, Roger Hanlon and John Messenger wrote, "There is compelling evidence that octopuses can learn quickly and retain stored information for a long time, at least in the laboratory. Yet it is surely unlikely that animals that are so good at learning in an aquarium would not put this ability to good use in the sea, and the inference must be that learning is extremely important to octopuses in their natural habitat." (Explorers would complain that giant squid have learned to avoid the prying eyes and snooping cameras of those who would observe them in their deep-ocean habitat.)

The mimic octopus—and a close relative known as "wonderpus," which does many of the same things—do not seem to change color much unless they change color so radically that observers don't even recognize them as mimics. One mimic was photographed with most of its arms buried in the sand and only its head protruding, and with spikes raised above its eyes, it looks not unlike a mantis shrimp, a predatory, aggressive and pugnacious crustacean.* If all the disguises of the mimic octopus are employed to imitate a venomous or otherwise dangerous animal (some flatfish are poisonous), that might explain their unusual behavior. Because few mimic octopuses have been observed in the wild—and none in the laboratory—no one knows if some mimics have the ability to put on only one disguise, or if every one has the same broad repertoire.

Despite intense, ongoing, and increasingly sophisticated studies of its structure, components, and inhabitants, the sea is very, very good at keeping secrets. Occasionally, people catch a fleeting glimpse of something utterly weird and wonderful. Discussing some remarkable new squid species filmed from submersibles, cephalopod

---

* "Mantis shrimp" are technically stomatopods—foot-long marine crustaceans that have a pair of arms that fold up underneath the head, like those of a praying mantis, which they use to strike and catch their prey. Where the strike of a praying mantis is about a hundred milliseconds, the strike of a mantis shrimp can be two milliseconds, about fifty times faster. The strike of a mantis shrimp, which can kill prey or break the glass in a home aquarium, is one of the fastest known animal movements. Mantis shrimp have the most sophisticated eyes in the animal kingdom, with four filters to tune the eight sensitive pigments in the eye, and the ability to see polarized light. This extraordinary visual system obviously helps the stomatopod to capture its prey, but it has been recently discovered that all species of mantis shrimp have fluorescent markings that they (probably) use for species identification and signaling.

biologist Michael Vecchione of the Smithsonian and his colleagues (2001) wrote, "The bathy-pelagic realm of the ocean encompasses more than 90% of the nonsubterranean biosphere, comprising the largest, yet least explored, ecosystem." In that "unexplored ecosystem," there are some very strange creatures, some completely unexpected. For many years, scientists have peered through the portholes of their submersibles, often filming what they saw, but not necessarily knowing what it was. Mike Vecchione had heard about a weird animal that had been videotaped by deep-ocean oil surveyors, and when he saw the video, he realized that it was a squid like nothing he—or anyone else—had ever seen. It had huge fins that made its body look like a double-bitted axe, and ten arms of equal length (most squid have eight arms and two longer tentacles) that were probably twelve feet long. Vecchione tracked down other videos of this "mystery squid," some of which were filmed in the Western Atlantic (at 4,735 meters), the Indian Ocean (2,340 meters), the Gulf of Mexico (2,195 meters), and the Central Pacific (3,380 meters), and saw something even more remarkable: all the arms bent at what can only be described as "elbows." As Vecchione, Richard Young, Angel Guerra, et al. described them in *Science*, "In most cases, the squids were first encountered within a few meters of the sea floor with their extremely large terminal fins undulating slowly and with arms and tentacles typically held in a unique position: spread outward from the body axis, then abruptly bent anteriorly." A twenty-foot-long deep-sea squid with elbows! Unnamed because the videos are the only evidence of its existence, and without a type specimen,

the creature cannot enter the scientific literature. "That such a substantial animal is common in the world's largest ecosystem," concluded Vecchione et al., "yet has not previously been captured or observed, is an indication of how little is known about life in the deep ocean."

Now another monster cephalopod competes with *Architeuthis* for the title of most gigantic. As described by Roper, Sweeney, and Nauen in 1984, *Mesonychoteuthis* is "a very large species" that figures prominently in the diet of Antarctic sperm whales. According to G. C. Robson's 1925 description of the type specimen (based on fragments of two specimens collected from the stomachs of sperm whales taken off the South Shetland Islands), the longest arm was 46.3 inches (118 centimeters) long, and its "hand" was equipped with a series of swivel-based hooks that could be rotated in any direction. The name can be translated as "middle-hooked squid" and refers to the location of the double row of hooks on the middle of each arm, between the basal and terminal ringed suckers. This is the only large squid with hooks on the tentacles as well as on the arms. The body of *Mesonychoteuthis* can be as large as or larger than that of *Architeuthis*, but its tentacles are much shorter. Nesis (1982) refers to it as a "giant," with a mantle length of 7 to 7.5 feet (200–225 centimeters) and a total length of 11.37 feet (350 centimeters) not including the tentacles, and one was caught in the Antarctic in 1981 that was nearly 17 feet long. *Mesonychoteuthis* is believed to have a circumpolar Antarctic distribution, and according to Nesis, it is "the leading member of the Antarctic teuthofauna by biomass."

Like *Architeuthis*, the adult *Mesonychoteuthis* has never been seen alive, and almost all of our

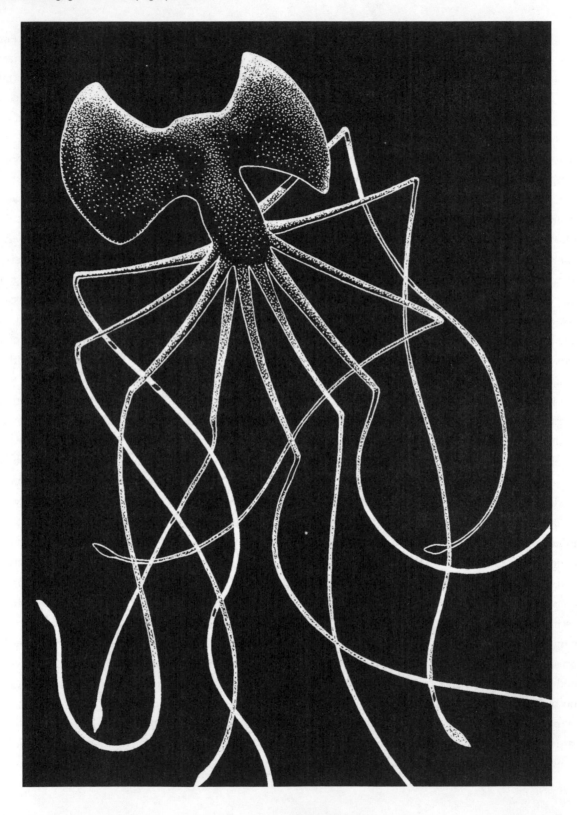

information comes from the examination of dead and often semidigested specimens. Its tentacles are comparatively short and thick, and its tail fins are broad, muscular, and heart-shaped, accounting for its name in Japanese, *daioo-hoozukai-ika.* As in *daiooika,* the name for *Architeuthis, daioo* is "great king," *ika* is "squid," and *hoozukai* is the bladder cherry plant, familiarly known as the "Chinese lantern," whose calyx is a fragile, bright orange bag pointed at the end away from the stem. *Mesonychoteuthis* is a cranchid squid, characterized by the fusion of the mantle to the head at one ventral and two dorsal points, and photophores on the ventral surface of the prominent, sometimes protruding, eyes.

In early 2003 a specimen of *Mesonychoteuthis hamiltoni* was retrieved virtually intact from the surface of the waters off Macquarie Island, about halfway between Tasmania and Antarctica. The carcass was examined by Steve O'Shea, now at New Zealand's Auckland University of Technology, who commented in a BBC report (Griggs 2003), "Now we know that it is moving right through the water column, right up to the very surface and it grows to a spectacular size. . . . we can say that it attains a size larger than the giant squid. We've got something that's even larger, and not just larger but an order of magnitude meaner." O'Shea opined that this species has one of the largest beaks of any squid and also has unique swiveling hooks on the clubs at the ends of its tentacles, which, he said, "allows it to attack fish as large as the Patagonian toothfish and probably to also attempt to maul sperm whales." The specimen

"Elbow" squid (Species unknown)

has a mantle length of 8.2 feet (2.5 meters), a larger mantle than any *Architeuthis* that O'Shea has ever seen, and he said that this specimen was immature: "It's only half to two-thirds grown, so it grows up to four metres in mantle length." The squid researchers are calling *Mesonychoteuthis hamiltoni* the "colossal squid." "This animal, armed as it is with hooks and beak, not only is colossal in size but is going to be a phenomenal predator and something you are not going to want to meet in the water," said Kat Bolstad, research associate at Auckland University of Technology.

Most authorities now believe, however, that the fearsome reputation of *Architeuthis* is undeserved. It is probably not a powerful, aggressive, ship-sinking monster, but more likely a weak-muscled fish eater that hangs tentacles-down waiting to pluck small fishes with its clipped-together feeding tentacles that Mark Norman has described as "very long chopsticks." The discovery of an almost complete specimen of *Mesonychoteuthis*, with its powerful muscles and claws, has given new life to the idea of large squids as dangerous sea monsters. In Emma Young's 2003 *New Scientist* discussion of the discovery of *Mesonychoteuthis*, we read, "The colossal squid is fascinating—and fearsome. In many ways, it is the mean machine *Architeuthis* was always thought to be. . . . When it comes to a fight, chances are that *Mesonychoteuthis* would give any sperm whale a run for its money." (That specimens—or parts—of *Mesonychoteuthis* have been found in the stomachs of sperm whales suggests that the whale wins at least some of the time.) Hyperbole aside—we have no way of knowing how "mean" a squid might be, or why a squid would attack a sperm whale—the discovery is a significant event in the ongoing investigation of little-known (or unknown) large animals of the ocean. You would probably not "meet one in the water"—unless you were planning to take a dip in the Ross Sea—but it is not the "sea monster" aspect of this creature that demands our attention: rather it is the realization that large animals still swim just outside our searchlights and submersibles, hidden, as they have always been, from the prying eyes of those who would solve the mysteries of the sea. ✍

Do Whales Sing in Inner Space?

Men have been hunting whales for thousands of years. Whales often obliged those who would study them by washing ashore—for reasons still not clearly understood—so they could be examined, dissected, and classified. Of course, living, as many whales do, in pelagic zones not often visited by scientists and spending large proportions of their lives underwater has not made the job of the cetacean taxonomist any easier, but examining various dead whales on beaches, flensing decks, or at whaling stations should have at least finalized the number of species there were. Imagine the surprise of the cetologists—and the rest of the world—when an entirely new species of beaked whale appeared in 1999.

Once upon a time, people thought the ocean was a "silent world"—as per the title of Jacques Cousteau's 1953 book—but for centuries names of fishes like grunts, drums, and croakers testify that people knew the sea was not so quiet. "Snapping shrimp" (*Alpheus heterochaelis*) have to stun their prey by snapping their oversize claw, which produces a cracking sound so loud that when colonies of the shrimp snap their claws simultaneously, the cacophony is intense enough that submarines can take advantage of it to hide from sonar. But no marine creatures make more noise underwater than the cetaceans, who rely on sound to communicate, and who virtually define the concept of marine bioacoustics.

At Marineland of Florida in 1953, America's first "oceanarium," curator Forrest G. Wood recorded the noises made by captive bottlenose dolphins and suggested that the noises might "possess the characteristics necessary for a pulse-modulated type of echo-ranging, and the behavior of *Tursiops* at the time it emits these sounds certainly suggests that they might be used for echo-locations or even what might be termed 'echo-investigation.'" By now we know that all dolphins echolocate (and echo-investigate) and that their repertoire of clicks, clacks, whistles, and bangs constitutes as sophisticated a communications system as exists in nature. Working off Bermuda in 1970, acoustician Roger Payne and his wife Katy recorded the sounds of humpback whales and came to the astonishing conclusion that the whales were singing—and not only singing, but changing their songs every year. The record made of these songs was the largest-selling animal record in history and brought the whales' mysterious vocalizations to the world's attention. As Peter Matthiessen said in 1971, "No word conveys the eeriness of the whale song, tuned by the ages to a purity beyond refining, a sound that man should hear each morning to remind him of the morning of the world." The sounds of humpbacks can be used to track their movements and in some areas, even to identify their migration routes.

Sperm whales, with the largest brain of any animal that has ever lived, can also generate a variety of clicks, bangs, clangs, and wheezes, probably used for interspecific communications, but also, according to some, to locate and then stun their prey (mostly squid) so they can gobble them during their long, deep, breath-hold dives. It now appears that all the mysticete (baleen) whales also make loud underwater noises, none apparently louder than the utterances of the blue whale (*Balaenoptera musculus*), not only the largest animal that ever lived but probably the loudest. The sounds of baleen whales are not thought to be echo-sounding noises but rather vocalizations designed to communicate with their fellows. Off the coast of Chile, Cummings and Thompson (1971) recorded the "low-frequency moans or pulses" of blue whales and described them as "the most powerful sustained utterances known from whales or any other living source." The very low-frequency sounds that a blue whale makes can travel thousands of miles in deep water, leading to speculation that the whales may be able to communicate across entire oceans.

Ever since Forrest Wood dropped his plastic-wrapped microphone into the dolphin tank at Marineland in 1946, researchers have recognized the usefulness of listening to whales and dolphins. Their singing and echolocating are acoustic functions, and hydrophone arrays facilitated most of the research on the numbers and movements of the hard-to-see bowheads of northern Alaskan waters. Chris Clark of Cornell University used hydrophones in at least three sites to locate the whales by triangulation from the sounds they made as they passed the listening stations, often invisible under the ice. In his 1991 article "Moving with the Heard," Clark wrote:

> During the many periods when the icescape appeared impenetrable and there seemed to be no place for whales to breathe, we consistently heard the whales calling. Later analysis showed that the whales were migrating and that the majority were over the horizon from our camps and array of hydrophones, out of eyeshot even if there had been open water. And when . . . the ice did break open to provide a clear lead of open water, many of the whales we heard, and knew to be close enough to be seen, were never spotted.

Since then, the deployment of sophisticated listening devices has enabled researchers to "look" more closely into the deep oceans, with rewarding results. For example, using a towed hydrophone array in the eastern tropical Pacific, Julie Oswald, Jay Barlow, and Thomas Norris (2003) reported the identification of the whistles of no fewer than nine species of dolphins: bottlenoses, spinners, spotters, pantropical spotters, striped dolphins, common dolphins, rough-toothed dolphins, false killer whales, and short-finned pilot whales. (False killer whales and pilot whales are actually dolphins.) Researchers are now assembling a database of dolphin whistles to identify and differentiate animals at sea, even if they cannot see them.

Singing or bellowing whales are extremely noisy, and not hard to locate with underwater listening devices, but submarines, especially those that are trying to infiltrate enemy waters, depend upon making as little noise as possible. By the 1950s, as Cold War tensions escalated, both the Americans and the Soviets deployed batteries of listening devices in their constant effort to pin-point enemy nuclear submarines. The United States deployed a network of listening posts throughout the world's oceans, which was known as SOSUS, the SOund SUrveillance System. As described by William Broad in the *New York Times* in 1994, SOSUS "was used during the cold war exclusively to track the ships and submarines of America's foes. Starting in the mid-1950s, it spans the globe with a network of more than 1,000 underwater microphones grouped in arrays and tied to Navy shore stations by some 30,000 miles of undersea cables. It can track undersea sounds over hundreds and sometimes thousands of miles of ocean."

At first SOSUS was so secret that the government refused to acknowledge its existence. The work product of all that listening remains, and they will probably never know what the Navy learned about Soviet subs, or what they knew about ours. With the dissolution of the Soviet Union in 1991, surveillance of their nuclear submarine fleet was no longer critical to American national defense, and the end of the SOSUS arrays at Bermuda, Adak (Aleutians), and Keflavik (Iceland) was announced. Those arrays that were left in place began continuous monitoring of North Pacific Ocean seismicity in August 1991. The hydroacoustic method allows detection of low-magnitude seismicity and volcanic activity with more accuracy than seismic networks on land. A system so finely tuned that it could detect a silent-running nuclear submarine hundreds of miles away would have no problem picking up the loud, low-frequency vocalizations of giant whales. The sounds of blue whales, fin whales, humpbacks, and minke whales have been identified, and other species such as sei whales, Bryde's whales, and sperm whales are on the list. In 1994 Chris Clark and David Mellinger of Cornell University's Bioacoustics Research Program, submitted this application to use the Navy's Integrated Undersea Surveillance System (IUSS):

The recent application of Navy Integrated Undersea Surveillance System (IUSS) data for detecting and tracking low-frequency sounds from whales has led to a renewed interest in the use of these arrays for marine mammal research. Previous work with sparse arrays has limited the detection and tracking to ranges of tens of kilometers, while the IUSS allows for orders of magnitude greater coverage. SOSUS data are processed via computer systems specifically developed for detecting and tracking whales, as well as through annotations, to determine individual, geographic, and seasonal variability in vocalizations for at least four species (blue, finback, humpback, and minke), and there are also numerous sounds from unidentified whales. Given that these animals use these deliberate patterns of intense low-frequency sounds for either communication, navigation, or food finding, verification of sound function will be deduced through careful examination of behavioral context and other environmental conditions such as local productivity, bathymetry, and oceanography.

Putting the system to use, Mellinger, Clark, and Carol Carson (2000) analyzed pulse trains detected by SOSUS arrays near Puerto Rico, and because visibility was poor, they had to rely on the sounds for identification. They identified the whales as minkes, and wrote, "Minke whales, like all mysticetes, are assumed to be dependent on sound for communication. We believe that research that includes a careful combination of multiple techniques, including tagging, genetics, visual observation and acoustic recording, will lead to a dramatic increase in our understanding of this often elusive species." Acoustic tracking can also tell us where the whales are and when. When Moore, Watkins, Daher, Davies, and Dahlheim (2002) recorded blue whale sounds in the Northwest Pacific between August and November, the data contradicted "the oft-repeated assumption that all blue whales migrate south in the fall to winter at temperate latitudes, and occupy North Pacific waters only in the late spring and summer."

If a ship strikes the shore, bad navigation is blamed. The first blue whale ever reported by humans washed ashore at the Firth of Forth in Scotland in 1692 and was described by Robert Sibbald. Whales and dolphins have been stranding at least as long as there were men to find them on the beach. We do not understand these self-destructive activities, but they have variously been attributed to illness, fear of predators, unusual tides or currents, failure of the navigational system, migraine headaches, suicide wishes, biotoxins, parasites, or oil spills. For the most part, whales and dolphns navigate by sound, as they broadcast sounds, often directionally, and read the returning echoes for a "sound picture" of the bottom, the beach, obstacles, or

other creatures. In those circumstances—as with the collection of data by arrays of listening devices—the sound originates with the cetacean. A threat has now appeared that is a function of sound, but sound *not* generated by the whale or dolphin.

The Allies introduced Sonar (an acronym for SOund NAvigation Ranging) during World War II to track German U-boats in the Atlantic. Sonar locates submerged objects and it can communicate by sound waves sent through the water. It reads the range, bearing, and the nature of the target by the returning echoes. Surface and submarine vessels use low-frequency active sonar (LFAS) as a navigational aid. Blasted from subsurface loudspeakers, rather like a powerful searchlight on land, sonar can scan the ocean waters. Some mid-frequency sonar (MFS) can put out more than 235 decibels, as loud as a Saturn V rocket at launch. Such blasts can affect the sensitive hearing apparatus of whales and dolphins in the vicinity, injuring them, causing them to beach themselves or otherwise behave strangely, and perhaps even killing them by cranial hemorrhaging.

On May 12, 1996, twelve Cuvier's beaked whales (*Ziphius cavirostris*) stranded along the shore of Kyparissiakos Gulf in Greece. Volunteers managed to push five of the whales back into the ocean, but seven died. Necropsies revealed no evident abnormalities or wounds, but it was learned that LFAS "sound-detecting system trials" had been performed by the NATO research vessel *Alliance* the previous day. From March 15 to March 20, 2000, fifteen beaked whales, a spotted dolphin (*Stenella frontalis*), and two minke whales (*Balaenoptera acutorostrata*) stranded or became trapped in the shallows of the Bahaman islands of

Abaco, North Eleuthera, and Grand Bahama. The two minke whales and eight of the beaked whales subsequently escaped or were escorted back into the sea, but five Cuvier's beaked whales, the spotted dolphin, and two other beaked whales died. During this period, U.S. Navy warships were conducting sonar tests and maneuvers in the area.

In July 2004 a group of two hundred melon-headed whales (*Peponocephala electra*) in Hanalei Bay off the Hawaiian island of Kauai swam in abnormally tight circles a hundred feet from shore. One beached itself and died. It was later discovered that a U.S–Japanese naval training exercise was being held in the vicinity. Other mass strandings that coincided with sonar exercises occurred in the U.S. Virgin Islands, the Canary Islands, and Madeira. In the summer of 2005, after a powerful typhoon had hit southern Taiwan, a number of cetaceans were found stranded along a 124-mile stretch of coastline. They included two dwarf sperm whales (*Kogia simus*), one of which died; two striped dolphins (*S. coeruleoalba*); and four beaked whales, two of which were identified as Longman's beaked whale (*Indopacetus pacificus*). Military excercises were reported in the region, but when John Wang, a cetacean researcher, attempted to examine the carcasses, he was denied access.*

The Navy will not accept responsibility for these stranding events, claiming instead on a U.S. Navy website (www.whalesandsonar.navy. mil/stranding_events.htm) that "sonar has been linked with only a very small fraction of marine-mammal strandings world-wide. One incident in which several whales stranded in the Bahamas, in March of 2000 following a chokepoint excercise, was the confluence of several factors acting together including a number of sonars, unusual bathymetry, limited egress routes, and specific species of marine mammal." Although they say that they "remain dedicated to the collective understanding of the effects of sonar on marine mammals," the Navy also emphasizes their "responsibility to defend the nation and insure the safety of our Sailors, Airmen and Marines."

The few necropsies of dead cetaceans showed no evidence of trauma or hemorrhage, but one cannot avoid the circumstantial connection between stranded beaked whales (most often Cuvier's) and nearby naval sonar testing. Since *Ziphius cavirostris* is a deep-diving species, sonar may cause them to change their normal diving pattern and come to the surface faster, which would cause "decompression sickness" (otherwise known as "the bends"), where gas bubbles form in the tissues and cause internal injury and possible death. In a plea for more research on the risk of acoustic impact on beaked whale populations, ten cetologists (Taylor et al. 2004) said:

> The worldwide increase in uses of high-intensity underwater sound raises serious conservation and management concerns for this suite of species. . . . Collaborative research between acousticians and biologists is needed to assess the magnitude of the problem. Such research should include mapping of current and planned high-intensity acoustic activities, mapping of beaked whale

---

* In a letter to me (July 30, 2005), he wrote, "The strandings have not yet stopped in Taiwan. There were three more *Kogia* strandings on July 29 and 30. . . . Although *Kogia* strandings are pretty common in Taiwan, such a large number of events over such a short period seems a bit unusual."

densities and identifying areas where no data are available, estimating beaked whale densities and population structures particularly in areas of high acoustic activity, investigating the mechanism of harm to beaked whales from high-intensity acoustics, developing improved beaked whale detection methods, and estimating the probability of detecting lethal effects on beaked whales.

As the twentieth century came to a close, marine biologists began to take advantage of exciting new technologies that will enable them to better understand the nature and future of life in the ocean. What might these technologies be? In the 1999 *Oceanography* issue, Jules Jaffe of Scripps identified some of them: "acoustics can be used to measure both the abundance and the species of fish. . . . The most modern sets of acoustical tools employ both multibeam echosounders and wide band sonars which . . . have the ability to count the numbers of individuals and to discriminate (to some degree) the type." With the obvious exception of sonar as a threat, acoustics is a very useful tool for future research on marine populations. In their 2002 report ("Future Directions for Acoustic Marine Mammal Surveys: Stock Assessment and Habitat Use"), Mellinger and Barlow wrote that "Acoustics holds eventual promise of gathering information about marine mammals at very low cost." Research is needed, they said, in several areas to realize this possibility: "Population structure; abundance and density, impacts of noise; relative density, seasonal distribution, and trends." ≫

Part Three
Putting Discovery to Work

Getting the Numbers Right

The disorder and religious encumbrances of the Middle Ages suspended or obscured any sort of biological investigations, and the only ichthyological studies that occurred probably answered how best to catch and preserve cod and herring. Science, which can be defined as observed facts systematically classified and brought

under general laws, lay more or less dormant until the sixteenth century, when the first generation of "naturalists" began to investigate and classify their fellow occupants of the natural world, which included air, sea, and land. Pierre Belon, John Ray, Francis Willughby, Peter Artedi, Comte de Lacépède, and George Cuvier all advanced the study of marine life. Edwin Forbes, who, while he did not believe that life could possibly exist at great depths, was a dedicated student of the shallower-water species he did recognize, and until his untimely death in 1854, did much to popularize the investigation of the marine environment. Charles Darwin's explorations (and publications) energized discussions of the origin of species, on land and in the sea, bringing natural history to the forefront of public awareness.

"By 1898," wrote Susan Schlee, "when it was suggested to King Oscar II of Sweden that he initiate an international program of marine investigations, it was generally accepted that the impersonal mysteries of nature, rather than the wrath of God, moved the herring and the cod." Voyages of biological and oceanographic investigation set sail from England, Denmark, Norway, Germany, and the United States to collect and examine marine life, and early in the twentieth century, as the whalers discovered the previously untapped stocks of baleen whales of the Southern Ocean, the world's attention was drawn to the unusual and abundant marine life of the Antarctic. And, of course, the celebrated expeditions of Amundsen, Scott, and Shackleton did more than a little to make the world aware of the

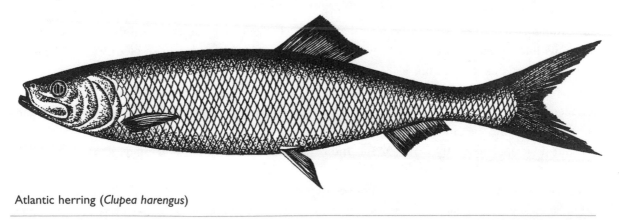

Atlantic herring (*Clupea harengus*)

North and South Poles. In Europe, Anton Dohrn opened the world's first marine biological station, complete with aquarium, at Naples in 1874. Louis Agassiz and his son Alexander (sequentially) inspired marine biological studies at the Museum of Comparative Zoology at Cambridge, Massachusetts, and the oceanographic institution at Woods Hole was founded in 1874. Other marine labs soon opened in Monaco, Washington, D.C., San Diego, and Plymouth, England.

But it was fishing that inspired the most concern for life in the oceans; speaking at the International Fisheries Exhibition in London in June 1883, Thomas Huxley discussed the state of the fisheries: "Those who have watched the fisheries off the Lofoden Islands on the coast of Norway say that the coming of the cod in January and February is one of the most wonderful sights in the world; that the cod form what is called a 'cod mountain' which may occupy a vertical height of from 20 to 30 fathoms—that is to say, 120 to 130 feet, in the sea, and that these shoals of enormous extent keep coming in great numbers from the westward and southward for a period of something like two months." On these and other grounds it seemed to Huxley that "this class of fisheries—cod, herring, pilchard, mackerel, &c.—might be regarded as inexhaustible." (He was disastrously wrong, of course; within a century of his address, the "inexhaustible" North Atlantic cod population was reduced to such low numbers that the New England and Maritime Canadian cod fisheries had to be shut down permanently.) In 1902 the International Council for the Exploration of the Sea was formed to give fisheries the benefit of scientific research.

Beneath the sea's shimmering surface, there is a world of life more intricately woven than that of any rain forest. The occupants range in size from the great whales, the largest animals ever to live on earth, to microscopic dinoflagellates and submicroscopic viruses. Humans have taken advantage of the ocean's bounty for virtually all of recorded history, probably starting when a prehistoric beachcomber found a freshly dead fish washed ashore. From that innocuous beginning, humans became whalers, sealers, aquaculturists, netters, trollers, purse seiners, longliners, bottom trawlers, rod and reelers, dynamiters, poisoners, and a myriad of other professions that remove living things from the ocean. Sometimes the animals were killed for oil, sometimes for baleen, and sometimes for their fur coats, but for the most part, they were eaten, and this seemed more than enough justification for the continuing slaughter of the oceans' wildlife. People had to eat, didn't they? Besides, the ocean was so big and so deep and so filled with edible items that there seemed no end to its productivity. If one population of whales (or seals, or fishes, or sharks) was depleted, the fishers simply moved to another area and attacked another population, or stayed put and changed their target. A number of fish species, previously regarded as so plentiful as to be unaffected by human enterprise, have instead shown themselves to be vulnerable to fishing to such a degree that they are now considered endangered. Deep-sea trawling, plankton nets, men (and women) in submersibles, and eventually ROVs expanded the database. Analysis of these historical records of fishing, whaling, and exploration will open new windows of understanding of what lived in the sea yesterday and what will live in the ocean tomorrow.

William Beebe in his bathysphere brought life in the benthos (some of it probably invented) to the attention of an eager (and gullible) public. The descent of the submersible *Trieste* to the bottom of the deepest canyon in the ocean, 35,800 feet down in the South Pacific, kindled the desire to investigate the life and circumstances in the abyss, and exploration began from the submersibles *Alvin*, *Deepstar*, *Aluminaut*, and others. Bob Ballard found the *Titanic*, and an *Alvin*-ful of oceanographers saw—for the first time ever—the astonishing sight of ten-foot-long tube worms, football-sized clams, and smoking towers belching forth superheated water five thousand feet down. We can now "see" into the ocean in ways heretofore unimagined: manned and unmanned cameras capture images of animals never suspected to exist, while sensitive recording devices reveal unsuspected animal signatures; sonar can now profile the shape of the bottom, the seamounts, and the mineral deposits of the vent areas. New techniques for population modeling may extend our understanding through the present, back to the past, and forward to the future of life in the sea.

In March 1997 twenty of the world's leading ichthyologists gathered at the Scripps Institute of Oceanography at La Jolla, California, to assess what is known, unknown, and unknowable about the diversity of marine fishes. They concluded that the known marine fish species numbered around fifteen thousand and that another five thousand remained to be discovered. As William Nierenberg (1999) said of that realization, "considering marine species alone, the age

of discovery is not over." Nierenberg went on to say that "A worldwide program to census fishes or marine life could clearly give a valuable boost to a field that has been rather neglected and can discover much." Following the 1997 meeting at La Jolla, the Alfred P. Sloan Foundation of New York initiated and funded the Census of Marine Life and convened a series of workshops about plankton, fishes, invertebrates, cephalopods, marine mammals, and marine reptiles. Then in 1998, the Sloan Foundation and the Office of Naval Research (ONR) sponsored a workshop at Monterey, California, which had three goals:

- To determine the biomass of marine biota, especially at the higher trophic levels

- To determine how this biomass is distributed spatially and by size and taxon

- To investigate how these distributions are maintained or changed

In other words, the goals were to find out how many fish, sharks, whales, seals, and assorted invertebrates live in the world's oceans; where the various vertebrates lived; and what is happening to the populations. Assembled at Monterey were "scientists representing benthic ecology, marine policy, acoustics, optics, fisheries and stock assessment, marine ecology, vertebrate and invertebrate biology, modeling, and biological oceanography" (Alldredge et al. 1999). By 1998, however, when the workshop was convened, it was clear that certain populations of marine animals were already in serious trouble. As Callum Roberts wrote in 1997:

The world's fisheries have been in the headlines again but the news gives little comfort: declining yields, stock collapse, crisis, conflict, and social dislocation. Almost every way you look at fisheries, the trends are in the wrong direction: decreasing catch per unit effort despite improved technology, reduced fish abundance, average size and reproductive output, loss of genetic variation, replacement of high-value species by "trash" fish, increased by catch mortality, recruitment failures, habitat degradation . . . the litany continues.

In a 2002 report, Villy Christensen and colleagues from the Fisheries Center of the University of British Columbia analyzed the abundance of various high-trophic-level fishes (those at the top of the food chain) in the North Atlantic, from 1950 to 1999. They concluded that the biomass of high-trophic-level fishes has declined by two thirds during that fifty year period. In the late 1960s, catches increased from 2.4 to 4.7 million tons annually, but by the 1990s, catches had dropped to below 2 million tons annually. The fishing intensity for high-trophic-level fishes tripled during the first half of the time period, and remained high during the last half, but as we have seen, fishing out the highest-trophic-level species is a recipe for disaster. They wrote, "Our results raise serious concern for the future of the North Atlantic as a diverse, healthy ecosystem; we may soon be left with only low-trophic-level species in the sea."

Beyond measuring how bad things are, the mission of the Census of Marine Life was to evaluate and select ways to sustain marine life, discarding the erroneous, avoiding the futile, and reinforcing the effective. An issue of the journal *Oceanography* in 1999 was dedicated to CoML and was introduced by Jesse Ausubel of the Sloan Foundation: "What did live in the ocean? What will live in the ocean? These questions, compelling for society and for science, motivate effort to mobilize the resources needed to conduct a worldwide Census of Marine Life." Ausubel described three tasks for the census:

History, like the 400-year record of fish catches assembled for Denmark, tells what lived in the ocean. *Exploration*, like the submarine discovery of sponge gardens nearly 4 km deep in a gap in the Mid-Atlantic Ridge, tells what lives in the ocean now. Only combining historical trends with what lives now can answer the core question of what will live in the ocean tomorrow. *Technology* and difficulty divide the oceans into realms for exploration. In the nearshore zone and on continental shelves and slopes, fish, shellfish, and lobster abound. In the light zone of the ocean's central water, drifting microbes photosynthesize food that miniature shrimp and swimming fish eat. In the dark of central water, jellyfishes swarm, and in the sediment snowed from above onto the abyssal plain, microbes and worms prosper. Around active seafloor vents, heat-resistant microbes survive. In polar oceans, algae photosynthesize on the underside of ice. The small, drifting organisms that photosynthesize all the primary food make up almost all the 145,000 million tons of marine biomass. Small animals like krill account for most of the animal mass, while prominent large animals, like fish and whales, constitute only a small but crucial percentage. In all oceanic realms, finding and naming species of animals show unflagging progress as well as unknowns yet to resolve. Estimating populations and biomass to distinguish between decline, fluctuation, and shift has only begun.

Men have been hunting bluefin tuna in the Atlantic and the Mediterranean for at least six thousand years; "the Phoenicians caught them with crude traps more than 4000 years ago and the Romans recorded catching thousands of tons with traps similar to those still in use" (Porch 2005). In the western North Atlantic, the purse seine and the longline changed the fishery so much that by 1964, the combined landings from these two fisheries had skyrocketed to twenty thousand tons, and it became apparent that some sort of conservation measures were necessary to protect the great fish from overfishing. The International Convention for the Conservation of Atlantic Tunas (ICCAT) was born in 1968, and for control purposes, they considered the Atlantic tuna as two stocks, separated by the 45 degrees west meridian in the North Atlantic, with a dogleg around the bulge of South America to 25 degrees west in the South Atlantic. Until the 1980s, most commercial tuna fishermen avoided taking the really big fish—bluefins can reach fifteen hundred pounds—because they were just too difficult to handle, but then the Japanese sushi market opened its insatiable maw, and the larger fish became the specific target of the fishery. In 2001 a single bluefin tuna weighing 444 pounds brought $173,600 on the Tokyo docks. At these prices, it was almost impossible to convince people not to fish for tuna, and soon the tuna of the world were under siege. In a 2005 article about the sustainability of the western Atlantic tuna fishery, Clay Porch wrote:

> Like other tunas, western bluefin have a broad geographic distribution, but they also have a tendency to concentrate in well known spawning and feeding grounds where they are very conspicuous and easy to catch. The bluefins' plight is exacerbated by its popularity as a game fish and the exorbitant prices paid by the Japanese sashimi market; spotter planes and other expensive services remain cost effective even at very low densities. Moreover, bluefin are often taken as a bycatch of the vast longline fleets spread across the Atlantic.

Beginning in 1996, Molly Lutcavage of the New England Aquarium, along with Paul Howey of Microwave Telemetry in Columbia, Maryland, developed microprocessor tags for Atlantic bluefin tunas to follow their migrations. Previous tags included only information about where and when it was inserted, so when the fish was caught, the most researchers could learn was how long the fish took to get from there to here. The new tags, however, log the fish's temperature hourly, then store the average. After sixty days, the tiny computer shuts down, an electric current is generated that corrodes the wires fastening it to the fish, and the tag floats to the surface, transmitting its data by satellite to waiting scientists.

Barbara Block of Stanford University launched thirty-seven of Howey's pop-off tags.

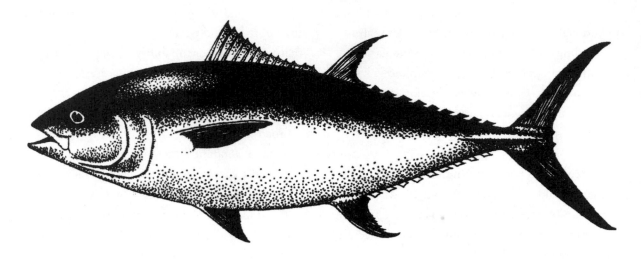

Bluefin tuna (*Thunnus thynnus*)

She also employed an "archival" tag lodged in the tuna's abdomen to measure not only water temperature but also light, depth, and internal body temperature encountered before the fish is caught and the tag is recovered. Surprisingly, the microprocessor tags revealed that tuna, long believed to travel and hunt near the surface, made regular dives to thirty-three hundred feet while feeding on squid, and could maintain a body temperature warmer than 80 degrees Fahrenheit in the ink-black, icy cold waters more than half a mile down. Most other fishes, commonly known as "cold-blooded," would have a body temperature of 39 degrees Fahrenheit in the 39-degree water at that depth. Because GPS tags do not work when the fish are on these deep dives, new devices had to be developed to track the tuna.

By 2000, a total of 377 fishes had been tagged along the east coast of North America with both types of microprocessor tags, "pop-offs" and "archival."* In 2001 in *Science*, Block and her colleagues showed that the migration of the bluefin was far more complex than anyone had imagined. Rather than segregating into eastern and western Atlantic populations, the tuna "mixed," which further complicated the already thorny issue of who has the right to catch which tuna. Moreover, they did not just mix near the midline boundary: some tuna traversed the entire

---

* On August 20, 2004, a juvenile great white shark was accidentally trapped in a fishermen's net in southern California waters, and kept in a pen off Malibu for three weeks before being brought to the Monterey Bay Aquarium. The five-foot-long female was exhibited in the million-gallon "Outer Bay" tank at the aquarium, where over a six-month period, she fed regularly, added a hundred pounds, and grew nearly a foot and a half in length. On March 31, 2005, the shark was outfitted with a pop-off satellite tag and released into the Pacific off Point Pinos in Monterey County. The tag recorded the travels of the shark over a thirty-day period, including her body temperature (great whites are "warm-blooded" like tuna), as well as the temperature and depth of the water she swam in, enabling scientists to learn more about the habits of *Caracharodon carcharias*, long a victim of undeserved and distorted calumny.

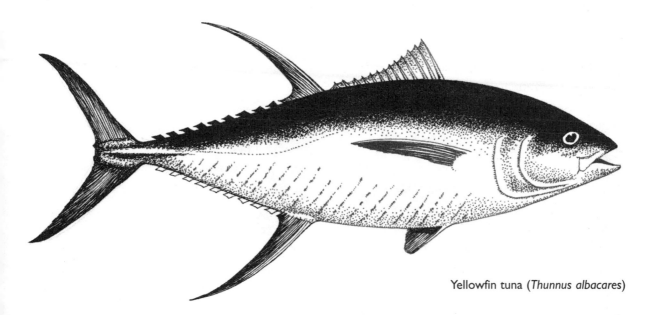

Yellowfin tuna (*Thunnus albacares*)

ocean—some 1,670 nautical miles—in less than ninety days. Before the era of tagging data, it was thought that perhaps 2 to 4 percent of the tuna might have crossed the forty-fifth meridian that separated the "American" tuna from the "European." ICCAT's quotas were based on the assumption that there were two distinct populations that did not mix. Instead, it now appears that the fish migrate across the Atlantic at will until they attain sexual maturity at eight to ten years, when they migrate to their particular spawning grounds, while there are two distinct spawning areas in either the Gulf of Mexico or the Mediterranean. Both eastern and western populations feed at western foraging spots, but they separate for breeding. Moreover, it wasn't 2 to 4 percent of the bluefins that crossed the ocean, it was closer to 30 percent.

Europeans catch tuna of the eastern zone, which is managed under a strict annual quota set by the European Union, while American fishermen catch tuna in the western Atlantic, which has been managed under strict catch quotas since 1995. Nevertheless, in both areas, the stocks of bluefin tuna have fallen dramatically: there has been an 80 percent decline in the eastern (European) stock over the past twenty years, and a 50 percent drop in the western Atlantic population. Over a nine-year period, Barbara Block and her colleagues tagged nearly eight hundred bluefins in the Atlantic, and confirmed the existence of two populations, one that spawns in the Mediterranean, and the other in the Gulf of Mexico. Fishermen for Gulf of Mexico yellowfin tuna (*Thunnus albacares*), working mostly along the Louisiana coast, were catching their target species, but they were also catching sexually immature bluefins, which would inhibit the breeding potential of an already depleted stock and lead to a further population crash.

None of this information—except perhaps the occasional catch of a juvenile bluefin in the Gulf of Mexico—would have been available before the development of electronic tags that transmit data to satellites. Summing up the technology that has enabled them to learn so much about the Atlantic bluefin stocks, Block and her colleagues (2005) concluded:

Collaborative studies that combine electronic tagging data, otolith microchemistry and genetics should provide a method for validating and quantifying the extent of mixing between the putative stocks. Significant questions remain, including the relationship of the two North Atlantic bluefin tuna stocks tagged in the western Atlantic to the recently identified genetically distinct stock in the eastern Mediterranean Sea. Quantifying the extent of spawning in one location relative to another, establishing whether individual adult bluefin tuna spawn every year and determining the influence of physical and biological oceanographic conditions on movements are essential to improved management strategies. If the electronic tagging results are used to develop and validate new models of population mixing in the context of the dynamic North Atlantic environment, ICCAT will have a better opportunity to prevent a further decline in the Atlantic Ocean's remaining bluefin tuna.

On May 3, 2005, Andrew Revkin wrote in the *New York Times*, "In just the past 35 years, exploding markets for sushi-grade tuna, combined with intensifying industrial scale hunts aided by satellites and spotters in airplanes, have devastated not only fish but also many fisheries." After discussing her tagging program, as detailed in *Nature* on April 28, 2005, Revkin quotes Barbara Block: "it's hard to believe that a fish of this size and beauty, an animal that has captured the hearts of fishermen and scientists alike for millennia, is slipping off the earth."

We can learn about the abundance (or lack thereof) of marine life from manned or unmanned undersea cameras, trawls, nets, and an analysis of fisheries statistics, but scientists today have techniques and technologies that their predecessors lacked. In his 2005 review of the bluefin tuna situation, Clay Porch of the NOAA Southeast Fisheries Science Center (Miami) lists the technological innovations that will enable us to understand—and maybe even resolve—the thorny problem of the Atlantic and Mediterranean tuna populations. He lists genetic analysis, analysis of the otoliths (earstones), and, of course, electronic tags, about which he writes, "Modern versions can store measurements of a tagged animal's movements, physiology (body temperature) and surrounding oceanographic conditions (depth, temperature) for several years. Some may be surgically implanted, in which case the fish must be recovered in order to obtain the data. . . . Electronic tags currently offer the best chance of determining the stock structure of Atlantic bluefin tuna (pending future developments in identifying natal origins via otolith microchemistry)." Porch concludes:

Regardless of one's management philosophy, it is clear that western Atlantic bluefin tuna do not fit the usual paradigms of tuna husbandry. They live long, mature slowly, and spawn during a brief window in space and time. Fundamentally, one would not expect them to be nearly so resilient to heavy fishing as their tropical counterparts. Yet, if anything, fishing pressure is greatest on this least resilient of tuna species. Bluefin have become so valuable that fishermen can afford to target them at very low densities. And even though they range widely across the Atlantic Ocean, they return predictably to specific feeding grounds where aggressive feeding habits make them easy to spot. Not only that, they are a significant bycatch of the vast longline fisheries distributed across the Atlantic Ocean. For these reasons ICCAT scientists warned from the beginning that fishing must be controlled in both management zones, yet fishing continues unabated in the east. If it turns out that the eastward excursions of western bluefin are as extensive as some suggest, then the stringent conservation measures enacted in the west may not be sufficient to rebuild the western stock. However, there are a growing number of advocates calling for greater protection of Atlantic bluefin tuna. Perhaps one day soon this grass roots movement will combine with irrefutable scientific evidence to change the political will. For the present, the future of western bluefin tuna does not seem as bleak as it once was for the Plains bison, but like its southern hemisphere counterpart, remains clouded nonetheless. ❧

Dolphins, Whales, and Whaling

A very special case of human predation grossly reducing the numbers of marine creatures involves the complex and poorly understood relationship between two species of dolphins and one species of tuna. For reasons still unknown, yellowfin tuna aggregate under schools of spotter and spinner dolphins, signaling their location to tuna fishermen. In 1966 biologists learned that tuna fishermen in the eastern tropical Pacific were trapping both dolphins and tuna in their nets, removing the dolphins, and dumping them overboard dead. (Even though the cetaceans being caught were commonly known as dolphins, the problem was referred to as "tuna-porpoise" because the fishermen called the animals porpoises.) When the fishermen converted from pole-and-line fishing to purse seining around 1960, between three million and five million dolphins were killed. The (U.S.) Marine Mammal Protection Act of 1972 outlawed harming any cetacean, but the tuna fishermen lobbied for an exemption and continued to kill dolphins in staggering numbers—more than three hundred thousand were killed in 1972 alone. The fishermen continued to set their nets "on dolphins" until they were sued in federal court by a consortium of conservation groups and forced to suspend their entire fishing operations. They were allowed to commence again only if they could abide by strict quotas imposed by the government and they agreed to kill no more than twenty thousand dolphins per year.

It was the tuna that were the object of the fishery, but millions of dolphns died too. Because estimating dolphin populations is an inexact science at best, we were never sure just how many dolphins there were, and therefore attempts to determine the effects of the tuna fishery on them were inconclusive. In a study

Spinner dolphin (*Stenella longirostris*)

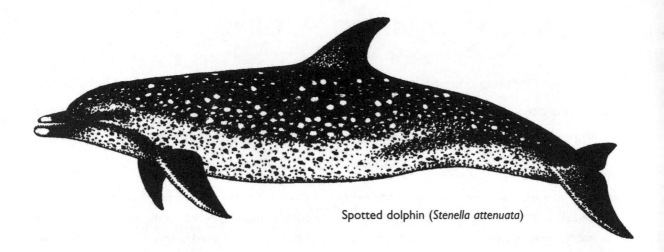

Spotted dolphin (*Stenella attenuata*)

conducted by U.S. government biologists, Frederick Archer and colleagues (2001) reported an insidious side effect of the tuna fishery, in which thousands of dolphin deaths went unreported. They wrote, "although the reported dolphin by-catch has drastically decreased, the populations are not recovering at expected rates." One factor might be the stress of the high-speed chase and encirclement, where calves would be unable to keep up with their mothers, and if the mothers were caught in the nets, the calves, having fallen behind, would have escaped, only to starve because their mothers were gone. Thus the counts, showing only the adults caught in the nets, did not account for thousands of calves, now calculated to represent an additional 10 to 15 percent spotted dolphin deaths, and 6 to 10 percent more spinners than were originally estimated.

According to an internal report from the U.S. Southwest Fisheries Science Center (SFSC) of the National Marine Fisheries Service in August 2002, "northeastern offshore spotted dolphins are at 20% and eastern spinner dolphins are at 35% of their pre-fishery levels; and neither population is

recovering at a rate consistent with these levels of depletion and the reported kills." The death of uncounted baby dolphins in the nets has contributed substantially to this decline, but the stress induced by the netting process has also resulted in drowning, decreased births, and impaired health. Tuna fishing in the eastern tropical Pacific is now being conducted mostly by boats out of Mexico, Colombia, Ecuador, Venezuela, and Peru, countries that are not required by law to avoid stressing dolphins. The SFSC report, which was released by the Earth Island Institute in December 2002, cites figures showing that tuna fishers set on dolphins about five thousand times a year, which means that some 6.8 million dolphins are pursued each year and two million are netted. Further broken down, these figures indicate that each offshore spotter is chased 10.6 times a year and captured in a net 3.2 times. Each eastern spinner dolphin is chased 5.6 times per year and captured 0.7 times. For the surviving dolphins, this is probably the functional definition of "stress."

So with all this information in hand—some of it generated by the National Marine Fisheries

Service—what did the U.S. government do? It concluded that circling dolphins in nets was harmless and threw open the door to allow Mexican fishers to sell tuna in the United States under a "dolphin safe" label. According to a January 6, 2003, report by the Environment News Service, an Internet watchdog of ecological issues, "On December 31, the National Marine Fisheries Service announced that after new research, it had concluded that the tuna purse-seine industry [practice] of encircling dolphins to catch tuna has 'no significant adverse impact on dolphin populations in the Eastern Tropical Pacific Ocean'" (Lazaroff 2003). Outraged environmentalists planned to contest the new ruling in court. David Phillips of the Earth Island Institute said, "The Bush administration's claim that chasing and netting of dolphins is 'safe' for dolphins is fraudulent and must be overturned."

The IATTC (International Tropical Tuna Commission)—which Carl Safina once ridiculed as the "International Conspiracy to Catch All Tuna"—has, under pressure from environmental groups and the U.S. government, finally come aboard the tuna-protection boat. At a 1992 meeting in La Jolla, a schedule of progressively decreasing annual limits on dolphin mortality was set, beginning with 19,500 in 1993, and scaling down to 5,000 in 1999. Dolphin deaths dropped substantially, but there was still the open question of "dolphin-safe" tuna. Some fishing nations complied with the stricture that only tuna caught under rules established at the La Jolla meeting could be marketed with a "dolphin-safe" label, but others, released by NAFTA (the North American Free Trade Agreement) from any such restrictions, could catch tuna

any way they wanted and sell it in the United States. In 2005, Jim Joseph of IATTC and Dale Squires of NOAA wrote:

> Considering the 99 percent reduction in dolphin mortality and the ecological costs in terms of increasing bycatches and growth overfishing resulting from a prohibition on fishing tuna in association with dolphins, and recognizing the possibility that the Latin American nations cooperating in the La Jolla Agreement might abandon it unless some relief from the embargoes placed on them by the United States was given, several environmental organizations began discussions with some of the Latin American governments to explore the possibility that an international agreement could be reached that would ensure the protection of dolphins, tunas and the ecosystem to which they belonged, would provide some relief from the embargoes, and would be binding on the participants. These discussions lead to the formulation of a binding agreement, the Agreement on the International Dolphin Conservation Program (AIDCP), which was adopted in 1998. The agreement was ratified and entered into force in 1999. All nations, and the European Union, that fish for tuna with purse-seine vessels in the EPO have now signed and ratified the agreement, or applied it provisionally pending ratification . . .

In 2005, Tim Gerrodette and Jaume Forcada reported on the nonrecovery of two spotted and spinner dolphin populations in the eastern tropical Pacific Ocean, noting that the dolphins were not recovering as expected, even though the by-catch has been substantially reduced. Visual surveys conducted from 1986 to 2000 over some twenty-six thousand miles (42,000 kilometers) yielded estimates that as of 2000, the population of spotters was about 640,000 animals, and of spinners, 450,000. This was considerably lower than earlier surveys and indicated that even with a lowering of the bycatch by two orders of magnitude, the stocks were not recovering. The reasons for this failure to recover are not evident, but Gerrodette and Forcada suggested several possibilities, including "underreporting of dolphin bycatch . . . effects of chase and encirclement on dolphin survival and reproduction; long-term changes in the ecosystem; and effects of other species on spotted and spinner dolphin population dynamics." It is probably no surprise to learn that the massive bycatch of spotters and spinners in the tuna purse-seine fishery has had deleterious effects on dolphin populations; it is only surprising that it took forty years to recognize that killing millions of animals in a population might permanently damage it.

Whales, like tuna, are large, smart, fast marine creatures that have been hunted for thousands of years, and some species are also slipping off the earth. The tuna were caught for food, but for the most part, the whales were caught for almost everything *but* food. The Faeroese, Icelanders, and Japanese have a history of whale meat consumption, but during the past millennium, the vast majority of whales were killed for their baleen plates—used to make corset stays, skirt hoops, and buggy whips—and their oil, which was used for everything from candles, lipstick,

shoe polish and soap to lighting, lubrication, nitroglycerine, fish meal, and margarine. On July 23, 1982, at their thirty-second annual meeting, the International Whaling Commission (IWC) decreed a moratorium on commercial whaling, putting an end—on paper, anyway—to the killing of whales for profit. The paragraph of the resolution, passed by a vote of 27 for, 7 against, with 5 abstentions, reads as follows:

> Notwithstanding the other provisions of paragraph 10 [which provide for otherwise allowable commercial whaling], catch limits for the killing for commercial purposes of whales from all stocks for the 1986 coastal season and for the 1985–86 pelagic seasons and thereafter shall be zero. This provision will be kept under review, based upon the best scientific advice, and by 1990 at the latest the Commission will undertake a comprehensive assessment of the effects of this decision on whale stocks and consider modification of this provision and the establishment of other catch limits.

Of course, it wasn't really that simple, and whale killing didn't exactly end. The bylaws of the IWC allow a country that takes exception to a resolution to file a protest, rendering that resolution nonbinding on that country, so as soon as the moratorium was passed, Norway took exception to it and continued whaling. Japan, Peru, and the Soviet Union also objected to the moratorium and could therefore have continued whaling, but Peru and the USSR intended to quit whaling anyway, and the Japanese withdrew their objection because they found a loophole in the form of "scientific whaling," which allows a county to issue itself a permit to catch whales for scientific research. That tons of whale meat end up in Japanese markets after the "research" has been completed points up the ineffectiveness of the moratorium, and the willingness of some countries to circumvent it.

Although many people believe that whaling is cruel and unnecessary, there can be no *legal* objection to Norway's continued whaling, as it takes place within IWC regulations. There are those, however, who object to Japan's "research whaling," claiming that the science—mostly consisting of finding out how old the whale was when it died—is spurious and that the main reason for the Japanese whale hunt is to get whale meat into the markets. The current Japanese research permit covers only North Pacific minke whales, but in a 2000 article in *Science*, Baker, Lento, et al. analyzed seven hundred "whale products" purchased in Japanese markets, and using molecular genetic methods, identifed the meat of baleen whales, sperm whales, beaked whales, killer whales, dolphins, porpoises, domestic sheep, and horses. They concluded:

Scientific hunting of an abundant population can also act as a cover for continued exploitation of a protected or endangered population of the same species. Using population-level molecular markers, we estimate that up to 43% of market products from the North Pacific minke whales do not originate from the reported scientific hunt in pelagic waters but, instead, from the illegal or unregulated exploitation of a protected population in the Sea of Japan. At this

rate of exploitation, the genetically unique Sea of Japan population is predicted to decline toward extinction over the next few decades.

Undeterred, the Japanese in 2000 awarded themselves a "scientific research permit" for minke whales, Bryde's whales, and sperm whales, and then went out and killed them. It's just a happy coincidence that the meat ends up in the fish markets, ostensibly to provide money for continued research projects, and those Japanese citizens who like whale meat can still find it in the markets. In early 2002 the Japanese decided to double their self-assigned quota for "research" whaling. In addition to the 440 minkes that Japanese whalers kill every year in the Antarctic, on February 22, 2002, they notified the IWC that they were going to take fifty minkes and fifty sei whales in the North Pacific.

The IWC has repeatedly passed resolutions critical of the research whaling program, but these are not binding. Critics point to the fact that meat from the "research" program is sold in restaurants and supermarkets as evidence that the program is commercial whaling under a different name. The Japanese government is lobbying for an end to the commercial whaling moratorium, claiming that whale population numbers are increasing rapidly and therefore threatening the recovery of fish stocks, a claim widely dismissed by most independent scientists. Japan proposed to expand its "research whaling" and take nine hundred minke whales in the Antarctic and sixteen hundred humpbacks and fin whales in the Southern Ocean. Despite the diplomatic protests of numerous countries (including Australia, in whose Antarctic waters the Japanese whaleships will be operating), the Japanese are taking a hard line, even going so far as to drop the "research" component and claim that they have to kill whales because their people have always eaten whale meat, and no country has the right to tell them what to eat.

At the fifty-seventh annual meeting of the IWC, held in Ulsan, South Korea, from June 20 to June 24, 2005, despite much backroom politicking (and threats to withdraw financial aid to countries that did not support its revised whaling plan), Japan's plan was soundly defeated. Arguing that Japan's "scientific" whaling provided little science and a lot of whale meat, opponents voted down the Japanese proposal and upheld the continuation of the nineteen-year-old moratorium. Not surprisingly, Japan threatened to quit the IWC altogether, automatically rendering any of its regulations moot and allowing the Japanese to kill as many whales as they wanted and to do whatever they wanted with the meat. It appears that Japan will continue its "scientific whaling program," and despite universal condemnation of their repudiation of the moratorium, they intend to kill protected humpbacks and fin whales anyway.

Estimates of whale populations depend largely on who is doing the estimating. Pro-whaling countries usually produced higher estimates to allow them to continue killing whales, while those who would reduce or eliminate whale killing for profit produce lower estimates, to show that the hunted whales were already in trouble. In the past, population estimates were based on the number of whales killed, the number of whales sighted in a given area, and other seat-of-the-pants methods, none of which really produced satisfactory results. Whale-counting is a difficult business at best, but to set the annual quotas, the IWC had to have some idea of the size of the stocks being fished. Sperm whales, hunted since the early eighteenth century by Yankee whalers, and later by almost every other whaling nation, are poorly understood, especially with regard to population size.

Of course, it was a lot easier to tally the number of sperm whales killed—especially in modern times. While Yankee whaling captains may have kept careful logbooks, many of these logbooks have been lost, so the totals for the eighteenth and nineteenth centuries are estimates at best. For his 1935 study, *The Distribution of Certain Whales as Shown by Logbook Records of American Whaleships,* Charles Haskins Townsend was able to find records of 36,909 sperm whales killed between 1753 and 1914. (For this 161-year period, that would average 229 whales per year for the entire whaling fleet, which at its peak around 1850, numbered over eight hundred ships. Townsend found some fifteen hundred logbooks; obviously, more than a few have gone missing.)

Townsend's paper (which is actually a small book) is accompanied by four charts that show the "plattings" of the whale catches listed in the book. There is one chart for humpbacks and bowheads, one for right whales, and two for sperm whales—the first for October to March and the second for April to September. For the most part, the records coincide with the old whaler's "grounds"—those areas where they could expect to find sperm whales with some regularity—but neither of the two sperm whale

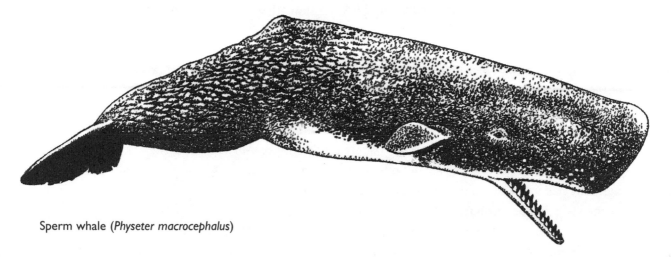

Sperm whale (*Physeter macrocephalus*)

charts shows any whale catches at all in the Pacific north of 40 north latitude. Sperm whales are thought to have first been taken by modern whaling in the North Pacific at the earliest by 1905, and by 1976, a grand total of 268,972 whales had been killed there by the whaling fleets of Japan and the USSR (Ohsumi 1980). By the twentieth century, hand-thrown harpoons had been replaced by cannons firing exploding grenades, and factory ships could process the carcasses at sea, factors that account for the great increase in numbers. In his 1974 history of the IWC, J. L. McHugh reported that 532,392 sperm whales had been killed by whalers from 1920 to 1971—a large proportion of them in the North Pacific.

Probably because the general public regards the sperm whale as the quintessential whale (Moby Dick was a sperm whale and therefore exemplified the Yankee whale fishery), there has always been a sort of subliminal awareness of the plight of the sperm whale. About a century after the New England fishery declined (about 1865), hunting for sperm whales resumed on a large scale. Shore-based fisheries existed in Albany,

Western Australia, and Durban, South Africa. After 1970–72, a shore fishery at Dildo, Newfoundland, killed a total of 105 sperm whales. They were all males, captured in water up to a thousand fathoms deep off the continental shelf (Mitchell 1975). In the Azores, the open-boat whalers continued their traditional fishery, initiated from shore observation posts. In the 1960s and 1970s, however, the major part of the sperm whale fishery was conducted by the Japanese and the Soviets using gigantic factory ships and flotillas of catcher boats in the North Pacific and the Southern Ocean. During 1972–73 and 1973–74, the IWC global quotas were twenty-three thousand sperm whales per year.

To establish these quotas, the whaling nations had to have some idea of the number of sperm whales and their reproduction rates so that the scientific committees of the IWC could determine how many could be killed without damaging the population's ability to regenerate. It had always been assumed that females were critical to the breeding populations, and, therefore, the numbers of females included in the yearly quotas were always less than the numbers of males. In 1977 E. D. Mitchell questioned this concept and suggested that within the complex social structure of the sperm whale, the removal of the single bull (the "harem master") servicing a group of females "could reduce the pregnancy rate in this school drastically." This was indeed a remarkable observation, for the early fishery emphasized the taking of the largest bulls (they naturally had more oil), and for years the decline of the fishery was attributed to economics, the Civil War, the discovery of petroleum, and other factors. Until Mitchell's suggestion, it seems no one believed that the whales might not have been able to reproduce enough to maintain the species. "It is possible," Mitchell continued, "that the techniques of the early American fishery, coupled with the complex social behavior of the sperm whale, might have resulted in reduction of the population over decades far out of proportion to reduction judged from the landed catch or oil yield alone."

If determining the relative importance of males and females to the population seems difficult, estimating the population itself turns out to be almost impossible. At best it is difficult to count whales, but when the species is migrating over two-thirds of the surface of the earth, the problem becomes almost insurmountable. In 1965 N. A. Mackintosh, an authority on whale populations, wrote, "It is hard to see any way at present of making even a wild estimate on the magnitude of world populations of sperm whales." Despite his warning, experts in population dynamics labored hard, and by using the marking of whales, the sighting of whales, and the application of various mathematical formulas, they tried to come up with some workable numbers. Estimates varied widely depending on who is doing the estimating and what methods are employed. (There is also the variable of whether the estimator is in the whaling business; Japanese estimates of sperm whale populations always appear higher than those of, say, British or Americans.) Best (1975) reviewed the various estimates of world sperm whale stocks, and reported:

> Division II. (East Atlantic). The least squares method gave estimates of 18,000 exploitable males (from Donkergat data) or 27,000 exploitable males (pelagic data) for the 1963 stock, and a rounded average of 22,000 was used to get an initial stock of 34,000 males. From this the original mature female stock was calculated to be 44,000 and the 1972 stock 42,000. An independent estimate of the mature female population size for the period 1957 to 1964 by Best (1970) gave values of 15,550 or 31,940, using fishing mortality rates and catches.

From this it would appear that Mackintosh was correct, and even the most sophisticated methods were not producing a particularly stong foundation for setting quotas. Since 1968 the Scientific Committee of the International Whaling Commission has been unable to devise an accurate method for estimating sperm whale stocks, and in addition to the annual meetings of the IWC, a number of special meetings were convened, at which the primary topic was the problem of sperm whale numbers. At one of these special meetings at La Jolla, California, in December 1976, in spite of the presentation of twenty-nine papers on sperm whale population biology, the scientists were forced to admit that they had very little real knowledge of the sheer numbers or the reproduction rate of the sperm whale. In short, the scientific committee was setting quotas for these whales with virtually no idea of how many there were or how to figure it out. In a report on the La Jolla meeting, Smith (1976) made the following comments: "We must assume that the harvesting of sperm whales is having an impact, even though we cannot determine the magnitude of that impact with certainty . . . the one thing we do know is that harvesting of large whales can cause rapid and extensive reductions in abundance." Not a great revelation, to be sure, but for the first time, the scientific community publicly conceded the possible adverse effects of "harvesting" whales without knowing their population figures.

In spite of their admitted ignorance, the Scientific Committee—under pressure from the sperm-whaling nations—recommended raising the 1977/78 quota to 13,037, as compared with 12,676 for the previous season. At another special meeting convened at Cronulla, Australia, in June 1977, the IWC Scientific Committee recommended a quota of 763 sperm whales for the North Pacific (the area where the Japanese and the Soviets concentrated their efforts, and where, only four years previously, the quota had been 10,000 animals), but in a move that shocked the world and the whaling community as well, the IWC general meeting set the quota at *6,444* sperm whales, nearly ten times the number recommended by their own scientists. Reaction to this maneuver was a worldwide outcry, and directly and indirectly applied presssure on the

IWC. At the 1978 meeting in London, no quota at all was set for sperm whales; confusion and indecision seemed to be the order of the day. It took still another special meeting in Tokyo in December 1978 to establish the North Pacific quota of 3,800 animals, a reduction of almost 40 percent from the previous year's calamitous 6,444. It was now apparent that the IWC could no longer continue to function as a "gentlemen's club" for the whaling nations of the world, and attention had to be given to the pressures being administered from without, especially from the numerous conservation and environmental groups that had mounted such massive "save the whale" campaigns.

In 1980 the IWC published a compilation of studies of the North Pacific populations called *"Sperm Whales: Special Issue."* The book, which was the report of a special meeting held in Australia in November 1977, contained forty-two papers by cetologists and population biologists from Australia, Japan, Great Britain, and the United States, and although Soviet scientists attended the meeting, they did not contribute to the report. With titles like "Catches of Sperm Whales by Modern Whaling in the North Pacific" (Ohsumi), "Size Distribution of Male Sperm Whales in Pelagic Catches" (Allen), "Biases in a Time Budget Model for Modern Whaling" (Rørvik), and even "Two Concerns About the Sperm Whale Model" (Holt), you might assume that the assembled body would have come up with an idea of how many sperm whales might be swimming around the North Pacific, if only to be able to determine the maximum sustainable yield (MSY), but they didn't. Despite the abundant equations, no population estimate appears in this report, and by the next IWC meeting (in

1978), the quotas for sperm whales in all oceans were set at 3,796 males and 898 females.

The estimates for the total number of sperm whales still vary widely. In a 1976 article in *National Geographic*, Victor Scheffer gave the following estimates for sperm whales: 212,000 males, 429,000 females, or 69 percent of the estimated pre-exploitation population of 922,000. As a further example of the difficulties inherent in estimating populations, M. R. Clarke (1977) offered the figure of 1.25 million sperm whales, a number considerably higher than Scheffer's estimate of the pre-exploitation population. In *Sea Guide to Whales of the World*, published in 1981, Lyall Watson wrote, "The best estimates suggest that there may be 350,000 in the southern hemisphere and another 175,000 in the north. These figures are based on approximations which may be hopelessly optimistic." In what is probably the most accurate assessment for its time, Dale Rice (1989) wrote, "Prior to extensive exploitation by modern-style whaling, the world population of the sperm whale was probably close to three million. It has since been reduced by about 31% to less than two million."

Townsend's figure of 36,909 sperm whales killed during the 161 years of Yankee whaling was seriously flawed, and probably too low by at least an order of magnitude. McHugh's half million sperm whales killed between 1920 and 1971 is an accurate compilation of what the whalers reported—but they were lying. After Soviet whaling had ceased—and in fact, after the Soviet Union itself had ceased—Russian cetologist Alexey Yablokov revealed in an article in *Nature* that the Soviet whalers had greatly underreported the number they killed. "It was also known in the 1960s," he wrote, "that a Soviet factory ship illegally operated for a couple of weeks in the Okhotsk Sea, and caught several hundred right whales. It was also well known in the Soviet Union that blue whales continued to be killed after they were protected by the IWC." Citing Yablokov, Phil Clapham and Scott Baker (2002) noted that "former soviet biologists revealed that the USSR had conducted a massive campaign of illegal whaling beginning shortly after World War II. Soviet factory fleets had killed virtually all the whales they encountered, irrespective of size, age, or protected status." In the Southern Hemisphere, while reporting a total catch of 2,710 humpbacks, the Soviets had actually taken more than 48,000. They exported all the meat from the illegally killed whales to Japan.

Further evidence of underreporting in Japanese coastal whaling operations shows that the problem was not limited to pelagic whaling operations and occurred despite the presence of onboard inspectors and observers. Isao Kondo, a former executive of Nihon Hogei (Japan Whaling Company) and director of whaling stations at Ayukawa, Taiji, and Wakkanai, published *Rise and Fall of the Japanese Coast Whaling* in 2001, in which he detailed the methods by which Japanese whalers "mis-reported" the whales they killed:

> Cheating on the taking of sperm whales began in 1950. And the degree became more terrible after 1955. According to a record of some company, the catch number made public was 326 while the true number of captured whales was 464 (the company concealed 138 whales), which was still more conscientious compared with concealment.

Then, the cover up of captured whales escalated. It was said that according to the data of one whaling company, the captured number made public was 30.3% of the actual number—in other words, they captured three times the number made public.

We do not have the numbers of "misreported" whales from Japan, but the numbers for the Soviet sperm whales—74,834 reported; 89,493 actually killed—are probably closer to reality. The deviation of the actual numbers killed from the reported numbers renders estimating the actual number of whales remaining increasingly difficult.

Even if they killed ten times the number that Townsend found in the logbooks, the Yankee whalers would not have made that much of a dent in the world population of sperm whales. As far as we knew, Townsend's estimate of seven hundred thousand remaining would reproduce and multiply as New England whaling declined. (The *Wanderer*, the last of the square-rigged whalers, set sail from New Bedford on August 27, 1924, and was wrecked the next day on Cuttyhunk Island.) In the 1960s the IWC set quotas for the North Pacific—where the Soviet and Japanese catcher boats and factory ships operated—that were merciless, but as long as the estimated world population of sperm whales was believed to number a million or more, even the most severe critics of sperm whaling were not really worried about the disappearance of *Physeter macrocephalus*.

But in 2002, after twenty years of studying sperm whales, Hal Whitehead of Dalhousie University wrote a report entitled, "Estimates of the current global population size and historical trajectory for sperm whales," and set the whale-counters back on their heels. In the introduction, he wrote, "Despite great commercial and scientific interest in the species, there has been no valid population estimate, globally or for any ocean basin." Using a population model based on that used by the IWC's Scientific Committee, he estimated that "pre-whaling numbers were about 1,110,000 animals . . . that the population was about 71% of its original level in 1880 . . . and about 32% of its original level in 1999." In his 2003 book *Sperm Whales*, Whitehead stated that approximately 360,000 sperm whales were alive in 2002. Thirty-two percent of an earlier population is a severely depleted species. The Yankee whalers and the early industrial whalers were wrong in their estimates; by the time the Soviets and Japanese were wreaking their havoc on the sperm whales of the North Pacific, they were killing representatives of a potentially endangered species.

Unlike whales, seals and sea lions spend some part of their lives on land, and are usually not that difficult to count. (Of course, this terrestrial propensity made them easier to kill, but that's another story.) But fishes spend their natural lives submerged, often at great depths; and whales and dolphins, even though they have to surface regularly to breathe, are underwater most of the time and are therefore maddeningly difficult to count. ("Is that whale surfacing over there the same one we saw ten minutes ago or is it a different one?") Better systems for estimating whale populations—and populations of other marine creatures as well—are critical to understanding and preserving marine biodiversity. In the introduction to their 2004 paper entitled "Modelling the past and future of whales and whaling," Scott Baker and Phillip Clapham wrote:

> Historical reconstruction of the population dynamics of whales before, during and after exploitation is crucial to marine ecological restoration and for the consideration of future commercial whaling. . . . At present, demographic and genetic estimates of pre-exploitation abundance differ by an order of magnitude, and, consequently, suggest vastly different baselines for judging recovery.

They continued: "Estimating the former abundance of whale populations and 'stocks' and reconstructing the historical trajectory of their decline are essential to make an accurate assessment of the true impact of whaling on the marine ecosystem, and to establish a baseline for judging the recovery of whale stocks." Modeling—the subject of their study—is the major tool for untangling and then predicting population dynamics. Modeling depends on the assignment of mathematical values to such factors as hunting pressure, birth and death rates, and environmental fluctuations, to estimate the population size during a given period. When the IWC was setting quotas on various species, models were employed by members of the Scientific Committee to determine the maximum sustainable yield for whales. High-speed computers now enable modelers to insert various different values into the model, to anticipate results of best-case or worst-case scenarios, and any variations in between. &

The "Right" Whales

Sperm whales have teeth; right whales do not. They became known as the "right" whales to hunt because they produced plentiful oil and whalebone (baleen), were slow swimmers and easy to kill, and they floated when dead. They are thickset, heavy animals with no dorsal fin, and can be sixty feet in length and weigh as many tons. They have extremely long baleen plates up to ten feet long, and feed by "skimming" through shoals of small crustaceans, allowing the water to enter through the opening between the two "sides" of baleen plates, and pass out through the plates while the food items are trapped in the inner fringes. Right whales are born with "callosities" on their heads, the patterns of which remain constant throughout their lives, making individual identification of the whales possible.

In the eleventh century—perhaps even earlier—the Basques who lived on the shores of the Bay of Biscay spotted right whales from stone towers called *vigias*, and launched their boats to pursue the hulking, black behemoths. Harpooning whales was a Basque innovation. (The Basque word *arpón* has come down to us as "harpoon.") When the whales became scarce, the Basques headed west, and around 1560, established the first whaling settlement in North America, at a place now known as Red Bay, Labrador. Because of their inshore breeding habits, right whales were often the first hunted when settlers arrived in a new area. Almost as soon as they were discovered, they were almost eliminated from the waters of Cape Cod, Alaska, South Africa, Japan, Australia, and New Zealand; only the lack of

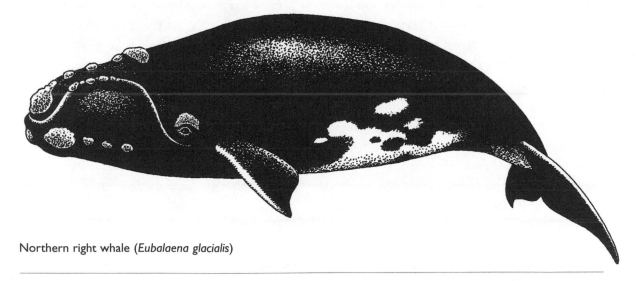

Northern right whale (*Eubalaena glacialis*)

arable land and settlers in Patagonia saved the right whale population there.

Although right whales have been protected worldwide since 1935, their numbers in the North Atlantic have precipitously declined in recent years, to the point where they are threatened with extinction. In 1999 Caswell, Fujiwara, and Brault wrote:

> The North Atlantic northern right whale (*Eubalaena glacialis*) is considered the most endangered large whale species. Its population has recovered only slowly since the cessation of commercial whaling and numbers about 300 individuals. . . . Population growth rate declined from about 1.053 in 1980 to about 0.976 in 1994. Under current conditions the population is doomed to extinction; an upper bound on the expected time to extinction is 191 years. The most effective way to improve the prospects of the population is to reduce [human-caused] mortality.

Researchers have recorded sightings annually since 1980 in calving areas off Florida and Georgia and in waters off New England and into the Bay of Fundy in Nova Scotia. Until this study, no one suspected that the survival probability for northern right whales was going down, or that the population was actually declining. As the report notes, the most effective way to improve the prospects for population persistence is to reduce mortality; among human causes, pollution and collisions with ships are particularly dangerous. In 1997 the National Oceanic and Atmospheric Administration introduced a five-hundred-yard protection zone to reduce the chances of human activity disturbing or altering the behavior of northern right whales. Since July 1995 at least fourteen right whales have died and nine have been killed or injured by entanglements in fishing gear, ship strikes, or other human-induced activities. This rate is about five times greater than in previous years, when one or two right whales died annually from human interaction.

Two years later, at the Northeast Fisheries Science Center at Woods Hole, Massachusetts, the IWC convened a workshop to discuss the "Status and Trends of Western North Atlantic Right Whales." The participants observed that while some other whale populations (Southern Hemisphere right whales and humpbacks, California gray whales) have recovered from very low observed abundance, the North Atlantic right whales have not, which may be a result of the "Allee Effect," where the population growth rate declines because of low numbers. As Levitan and McGovern (2005) wrote, "if a population dips below some threshold population density, population growth will decrease, making it more likely that the population will continue to dwindle. This effect, at its extreme, can result in a negative growth rate, leading to local or global extinction." A total of 263 right whales were counted in this intensively searched area (roughly from the Bay of Fundy to northeastern Florida); "the population," they concluded, "appears to be decreasing at present as a result of (i) a decreased rate of survival in the 1990s versus the 1980s; (ii) an increase in effective calving interval in the 1990s, and (iii) known direct anthropogenic removals (ship strikes and entanglements in fishing gear) that have been increasing in recent years."

Right whales are particularly susceptible to "ship strikes," a euphemism for a ship running into a whale and often killing it. Since 1976 ships have fatally struck at least ten right whales in the northwest Atlantic from Maine to Florida, seven of which were juveniles. In their 2001 discussion of ship collisions with whales, David Laist and colleagues noted that "young animals may be more vulnerable to being hit by ships. This could be caused by the relatively large amount of time that calves and juveniles spend at the surface . . . it may also indicate that whales learn to avoid vessels as they mature." A team from Woods Hole Oceanographic Institution attached noninvasive recording devices to North Atlantic right whales to analyze their swimming, diving, and acoustic behavior. Right whales were found to be positively buoyant and float near the surface where other marine mammal species were negatively buoyant and have to use their fins or flukes to stay near the surface. Though right whales glide when they ascend from their dives, they maintain an ascent rate similar to or greater than that of other species, which could only be achieved by some buoyant force. The faster ascents may provide insight into how the natural behavior of this whale species may increase its risk of being struck by ships. Even if a right whale correctly perceives a ship as a threat, its ability to maneuver may be compromised by its buoyancy, leaving it vulnerable to ship strikes. It is the whales' misfortune that the waters of their traditional breeding and feeding grounds are filled with tankers, freighters, cruise ships, and pleasure boats of all descriptions. The region inhabited by these whales includes major ports such as Boston, New York, and Miami, and is one of the busiest in the world. Just as it was when ships hunted whales, in the match of ships versus whales, the whales come out the losers.

In the 2002 *Encyclopedia of Marine Mammals*, Robert Kenney described the feeding behavior of right whales thus:

> Right whales are "skimmers." They feed by swimming forward with the mouth agape. Water flows into the opening at the front and out through the baleen, straining their prey from the water. Feeding can occur at or just below the surface, where it can be observed easily, or depth. At times, right whales feed very close to the bottom, because they are observed at the surface at the end of an extended dive with mud on the head. Typical feeding dives last for 10–20 minutes.

To gain some insight into the foraging of the highly endangered right whales, Mark Baumgartner and Bruce Mate (2005) of Oregon State University affixed time-depth recorders by suction cups to right whales in the Lower Bay of Fundy on the southwestern Scotian Shelf. During the summer of 2000, they tagged a total of twenty-eight whales and tracked sixty-three complete dives, of which fifty-nine were feeding dives. The whale's deep dives corresponded strongly with the known depth of concentrations of the copepod *Calanus finmarchicus*, but how the whales locate the copepods is unknown. They target the prey concentrations with uncanny accuracy. Because *C. finmarchicus* does not bioluminesce like some other copepods, it is unlikely that the whale can see a school of copepods near the bottom in water that is six hundred feet deep.

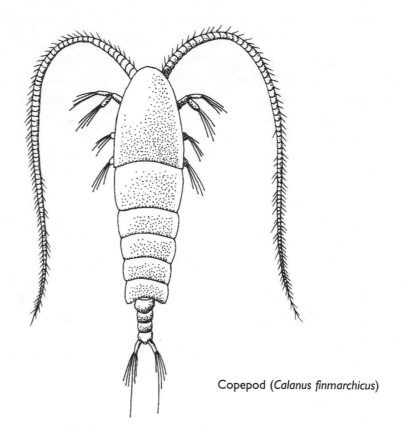

Copepod (*Calanus finmarchicus*)

Lacking a sense of smell, the whales may use taste or sensory hairs to detect movement in the water.

To locate the summer and fall feeding habitats of North Atlantic right whales, Baumgartner and Mate (2005) attached radio tags to thirty-five individuals in the Grand Manan Basin of the lower Bay of Fundy in 1989–1990 and again in 2000. Somehow, the whales knew where the copepods would be. The researchers learned to their surprise that the whales did not visit the deeper basins where there were large concentrations of the copepod *Calanus finmarchicus*, but visited areas characterized by low bottom water temperatures with high surface salinity, which seemed not propitious to gatherings of *C. finmarchicus*. In addition to clues about the whales' feeding preferences, radio tags provide information on the whales' movements that traditional ship-based or aerial surveys would not reveal. Science might redeem its inability to count whale populations with radio technology to alert a helmsman to where a whale might be headed before a ship strike. ⌇⌇

Squid "Fishing"

Even squid are seafood. Since the earliest days, much of what we know about the inhabitants of the oceans we linked to the term "seafood," meaning food that we get from the sea. We have learned about the inshore, pelagic, and midwater fishes by catching them, often in such vast numbers that we threatened the existence of the species. The same can be said of the great whales, and while there are some dolphins and porpoise species that have not been hunted or killed incidentally, many of the smaller cetaceans are now listed as threatened. The word "fishing," that is, taking edible things out of the sea for human consumption, is a term that extends to aquatic creatures from whales to shrimp. There used to be a whale fishery, and there is now a shrimp fishery. But "fishing" does not legitimately apply to some of the organisms taken from the sea, because, like whales and shrimp, they are not exactly fish. They are shellfish—typical mollusks such as clams, oysters, abalone, and mussels; and those most atypical of mollusks, octopuses, squid, and cuttlefishes.

During the 1970s, as worldwide fish stocks declined, Japanese exploratory fishers reported large aggregations of squid from various locations. The squid populations might have increased because the fishes that were their competitors for food declined, or the "top-down" effects of the removal of the squids' predators, such as dolphins and tuna, may have encouraged higher squid populations. Whatever the reason, wherever squid are fished commercially, landings have increased significantly while finfish landings have remained stable or declined. "At present," wrote Piatkowski et al. in 2001, "worldwide traditional finfish stocks are decreasing due to overfishing and environmental changes. In response, cephalopods have gained increasing attention as an alternative to the traditional marine harvest and will gain a much larger importance in the future to supply mankind with living marine resources. In fact, total cephalopod landings have steadily increased since the 1950s, peaking in 1997 at more than 3.3. million tons"

Will squid replace fish in global fisheries? Probably not, say Caddy and Rodhouse (1998). Many "groundfish" (flounder, halibut, soles, cod, hake, haddock, redfish, bass, jacks, mullets, sharks, and rays) eat squid, and so do many cetaceans, such as dolphins, porpoises, and pilot whales. But the sperm whale is the teuthophage *par exellence* (see "A Legend Authenticated: The Giant Squid" above). Regardless of how many squid are eaten by fishes and whales, that cannot give us an estimate of how many squid are left in the ocean, only how many are not. In *Out of Eden*, his book about bioinvasions, Alan Burdick quotes a biologist on population change: "By and large, nobody is monitoring it. For most species in most places, nobody has a clue. For deer, elk,

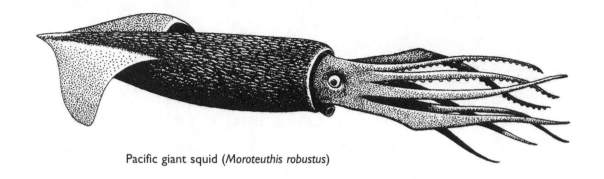

Pacific giant squid (*Moroteuthis robustus*)

a few economically important species, yeah. But vast numbers of species, including important ones of economic value, nobody knows. And the one reason that people don't know what's going on with population trends is because it's hard to make the measurements."

If it's hard to measure numbers of deer and elk, imagine how hard it is to measure the populations of animals that live underwater. When the northwest African "Saharan Bank" fishery for various species collapsed in the 1960s, a "spectacular increase" in catches of cephalopods was observed shortly thereafter (Balguerias et al. 2000), and many fishing fleets adapted their strategies and gear to catching squid, cuttlefishes, and octopuses. But is was not just that the cephalopods increased because the finfish decreased; there was a concurrent increase in the demand for cephalopods, and the discarding of dead material from conventional fisheries encouraged an increase in benthic octopus populations. In their 2001 study of the impact of cephalopods on the food chain and fisheries, Uwe Piatkowski, Graham Pierce, and Manuela Morais da Cunha noted that "Data from fifteen FAO key areas reveal that, with the exception of

the north-east Atlantic, cephalopod landings have increased significantly over the last 25 years. . . . Species replacement has been suggested as an underlying factor in changing fishery patterns in the Saharan Bank fishery, with cephalopods replacing sparids [porgies] as the main target species."

Squid are probably not the answer to declining fish harvests, partially because some larger squid are inedible to humans. The tissues of *Architeuthis* (the giant squid), *Mesonychoteuthis* (the colossal squid), and *Moroteuthis*, a large species found in the Southern Ocean, are suffused with ammonia. (A little ammonia doesn't seem to bother the sperm whales, who regularly dine on these large squid and many smaller ones.) Standard measurements for squid species rely upon mantle length, which is the length of the squid's body from the "neck" to the tail tip. Measurements of the arms or tentacles are variable and imprecise. *Architeuthis* has a known maximum mantle length of 6.65 feet (2.25 meters), but when forty-foot-long tentacles are added to the mantle length, the giant squid approaches monster proportions. An immature specimen of *Mesonychoteuthis hamilton* recently found floating in Antarctic waters had a mantle length, according to Steve O'Shea (2003), of 8.2 feet (2.5 meters) This species has swiveling hooks on its tentacles, larger eyes and a larger beak than *Architeuthis*, and we don't know how big a mature specimen would be. *Moroteuthis robsoni*, another Southern Ocean species, has a known mantle length of four feet.

In her 1991 article about marine biodiversity, Sylvia Earle (then chief scientist at NOAA), wrote, "An indication of the magnitude of ignorance . . . is evidenced by efforts to get to know the squids of the world. Several hundred species occur in the world's oceans, including a few species that are numerous enough to attract the attention of commercial fishing operations. Millions of tons of several kinds of squid, about which little is known except their gastronomic value, are extracted from the seas annually, particularly by fishermen from Japan, Taiwan, and Korea." When they wrote a summary of the squid fisheries in 1991, Clyde Roper and Warren Rathjen calculated the worldwide catches at 1.84 million tons. "Annual catches can vary widely," they wrote, "depending on a variety of environmental, biological and fishery-induced factors, all poorly understood. . . . Cephalopods are captured by a variety of gears, primarily jigging machines, trawls and drift nets." Several species are the objects of directed fisheries, some quite substantial, such as the California market squid (*Loligo opalescens*), the Argentine shortfin squid (*Illex argentinus*), the Patagonian squid (*Loligo gahi*), the neon flying squid (*Ommastrephes bartrami*), the Wellington flying squid (*Nototodarus sloani*), the northern shortfin squid (*Illex illecebrosus*) in the northwest Atlantic, and the flying squid (*Todarodes pacificus*) in Japanese waters.

Statistics on the Japanese squid fishery have been kept since 1910, when the fishing grounds were centered around southern Hokkaido and northeastern Honshu. After World War II, as the size of the squid boats increased and jigging machines* replaced hand lines, the catch of *Todarodes pacificus,* with a mantle length of twenty inches, reached 668,000 tons in 1968 (Okutani 1983). The Japanese *Todarodes* fishery crashed in the 1980s, only to be revived in the years 1986–96. Shifts in water temperature seemed to have affected the spawning schedule and recruitment of this species, and the Japanese managed to reestablish the fishery, so that by 1996 the total squid catch for Japan was up to 671,200 tons, the largest catch of any nation at the time. In their 1998 review of the genus *Todarodes*, Dunning and Wormuth (1998) wrote that "more is known about this species than any other ommastrephid due to economic importance. *Todarodes pacificus pacificus* forms the basis of the largest single-species fishery in the world, although the catch has recently been declining." By 2005 the title of largest single-species fishery had been awarded to the South Atlantic shortfin squid (*Illex argentinus*).

Even older than the Japanese squid fishery is the Newfoundland fishery for the northern

---

* Until about 1950, hand lines were used to catch squid, but then the Japanese, the leaders in squid-fishing technology, developed automated jigging machines, which deploy numerous jigs concurrently. The jig itself is a spindle-shaped lure with two or three rows of barbless hooks in a ring around the end away from the eye with which it is fastened to the line. Either by hand or by machine, the lures are "jiggled" in the water to attract the squid, but lights—underwater and topside—are also used. Most of the technology was developed in traditional fisheries for the common Japanese squid, but the equipment has been modified for catching the much larger and more powerful Humboldt squid (*Dosidicus gigas*) in the Humboldt Current off Peru and Chile.

shortfin squid (*Illex illecebrosus*), originally used as bait in the codfishery, but when the cod population was fished almost out of existence, squid became a desirable commodity. The bait fishery for squid originated in U.S. waters during the late 1800s, and during 1928–67, squid landings (including longfin inshore squid, *Loligo pealeii*) ranged between 500 and 2,000 tons annually. International fleets began to target *Illex illecebrosus* in U.S. waters during 1968 and in Canadian waters during 1976. Landings from U.S. and Canadian waters peaked at 179,300 tons in 1979, but declined to 100 tons in 1986, and since then have exceeded 10,000 tons only twice, in 1990 and 1997. These figures are not necessarily related to the massive changes in finfish abundance on the Grand Banks over the same period, which indicates that the correlations between the fisheries for cephalopods and for finfish are not at all obvious. During 1997 landings from Canadian waters (14,500 tons) rose to their highest levels since 1982 and are slightly greater than the 1997 U.S. landings (13,600 tons).

The southwest Atlantic supports fisheries for two species of squid, the Argentine shortfin squid and the Patagonian squid (*Loligo gahi*). *Illex argentinus* is found around the Falkland Islands, while the foot-long *Loligo gahi* is an oceanic species that makes long-distance migrations in the Brazil/Falkland Islands western boundary current system. Each fishery is the largest of its kind in the world: the *Loligo gahi* fishery is currently the largest oceanic squid fishery, while *Illex argentinus* is the largest neritic (inshore) squid fishery, with an average catch per annum in the 1990s approaching 700,000 tons (Agnew et al. 2005). The tremendous fluctuations in cephalopod fisheries may be connected with fishing pressure, but not enough is known about other factors to isolate any particular one. Because most squid species have a limited, specific range, often in one country's exclusive economic zone, there is a certain amount of teutho-piracy on the high seas. By May 2005, the Argentine navy had captured four South Korean vessels in Argentine waters, their ice-filled holds packed with *Illex argentinus*, one of the species that makes up the bulk of the international calamari market.

As of a 1998 study, the fishery for the California market squid (*Loligo opalescens*) was "the state's largest fishery in both tons landed and market value" (Vojkovich 1998). In the southwest Atlantic, vessels from several South American and Asian countries participate in the large Argentine squid fishery, which caught more than 1.1 million metric tons of the species in 2002. Dozens of countries are now exporting squid to the United States. The biggest supplier is Asia, where squid from all over the world are reprocessed into a variety of products, including cleaned tubes, tentacles, and steaks. China, the single largest supplier of squid, accounts for about one-quarter of all U.S. squid imports, followed by Taiwan, India, South Korea, and Thailand. The U.N. Food and Agriculture Organization records for total cephalopod catches for 2001 (the most recent year published), show a world total of 3,354,004 tons. That's a lot of calamari, but it doesn't approach the total catch for finfish, which, for the same period totaled 70,003,678 tons. For comparison, China alone harvested 10,981,866 tons of marine finfish, more than three times the world total for cephalopods.

Between 1990 and 1999, the global annual catch of cephalopods increased from 2.4 to 3.4 million tons per year. But, as Peter Boyle and Paul Rodhouse pointed out in 2005, in many locations, no one is really sure which squid species are being caught. They noted that "in 1999, less than 60% of the world cephalopod catch was identified as to species . . . this is especially the case in subsistence or artisinal fisheries where the resources needed to monitor the catch are not available or justifiable by national governments with other priorities." Cephalopod catch statistics include only one species of cuttlefish (*Sepia officinalis*) and one octopus (*Octopus vulgaris*); the bulk consists of squid. And within that category, four species contribute more than 50,000 tons apiece: *Todarodes pacificus* from the western Pacific; *Illex argentinus* and *Loligo gahi* from the South Atlantic, and *Dosidicus gigas* from the Eastern Pacific. With a 1999 total of 1,091,299 tons, *Illex argentinus* makes up almost one-third of the world catch; running second is *Todarodes pacificus*, with 497,877 tons, followed by *Dosidicus gigas* with 134,733 tons. *Loligo gahi* comes in at 42,505, not quite 50,000, but in 1995 the total for *L. gahi* was 85,186 tons.

Of the large squid species that are caught commercially, by far the largest is the Humboldt squid, with a mantle length of four feet (1.2 meters) and a total length, with tentacles, of ten feet. In the Humboldt Current, Peruvians and Chileans fish for the squid they call *jibia gigante*; and in the Gulf of California, between mainland Mexico and the Baja peninsula, there is another fishery for this species. Known in Baja as *calamar gigante*, *Dosidicus* is a top predator, preyed on only by sperm whales, which cannot catch these fast-moving cephalopods, but probably debilitate them with focused blasts of sound. *Dosidicus* is occasionally cannibalistic, but it usually attacks other *Dosidicus* when they are hooked and therefore defenseless. The Humboldt squid is probably the only squid species for which a sport fishery has developed. In 1940 an expedition from the American Museum of Natural History went to Peru in pursuit of swordfish and marlins, but they also caught *Dosidicus*, often to their displeasure because the squid came up squirting ink at them (Duncan 1940). Occasional "big-game" fishermen venture to offshore Peruvian and Ecuadorian waters in search of this big, powerful squid, and on those occasions when an oceanic weather anomaly such as El Niño drives these squid as far north as California and Oregon, fishermen try their luck against them there, too.

According to Ehrhardt et al. (1983), the Japanese started a Humboldt squid fishery in the Gulf of California in 1974 and by 1980 had taken twenty-two thousand tons of jumbo squid. Later their catch level dropped, and Japanese squid fishers abandoned the Gulf of California. There were virtually no catches from 1982 to 1988, but by 1989 the species reappeared, and by 1996, the *Dosidicus* harvest in the Gulf of California had reached a hundred thousand tons. Mexican fishers had replaced the Japanese, but they were fishing with hand lines from small boats known as *pangas*. In 1998 the entire Mexican population of *Dosidicus* relocated to the Pacific Ocean west of Baja and upper California, but in 1999 they were back in the gulf in substantial numbers. This unusual shift may have been related to the El Niño of 1997–98, but the correlations between the movement of squid populations and weather anomalies are not clearly understood. It is more likely that offshore movements by oceanic squid such as *Dosidicus* are

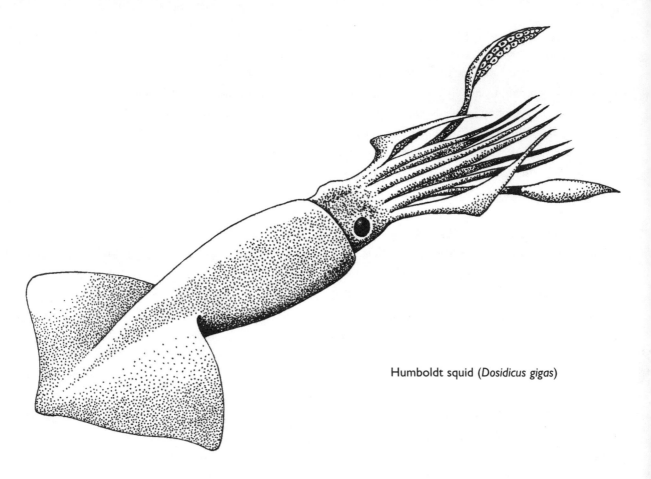

Humboldt squid (*Dosidicus gigas*)

seasonal feeding excursions rather than mass migrations. Some species, such as *Loligo*, aggregate in huge numbers for breeding, and in these cases the total number present could be used to indicate the total population. Ignorance about what percentage of adult *Dosidicus* gather for breeding in any one location leaves their mass movements an enigma.

Early in *Dosidicus* fishing, most of the catch was used for bait, but in recent years, the production of frozen *Dosidicus* products, known commercially as *daruma,* has increased greatly. The squid are harvested in Chilean, Peruvian, and Mexican waters, and sold primarily in China and Japan.[†] All the squid processing factories in Baja

are owned by Koreans, and the dried or frozen squid is shipped back to East Asia for distribution in China, Japan, and, of course, South Korea. There was no fishery in Chilean waters for *jibia gigante* from 1971 to 1991, but the increased demand for squid filets has now resurrected the fishery, and

[†] In February 2002, a New York City seafood restaurant called Esca claimed to have "giant squid" on the menu. Notes on the menu claimed that this was the fabled *Architeuthis*, the submarine attacker from *Twenty Thousand Leagues Under the Sea*; the sixty-foot-long monster with eyes as big as automobile hubcaps, etc. I went to the restaurant and ordered a "giant squid" appetizer, a small grilled piece with a drizzle of extra-virgin olive oil. The lack of ammonia convinced me that it was not *Architeuthis*, and when I asked the chef where it had originally come from, he admitted that it had come from Mexico. It was, of course, a filet of *daruma*.

by 1994 landings had reached 190,000 tons, and produced eighteen million dollars for the Chileans. The Gulf of California *Dosidicus* fishery is now conducted by three fishing fleets that move around the Gulf in pursuit of the migrating squid. It has been estimated (Hernández-Herrera et al. 1998) that the total population of *Dosidicus* in the Gulf of California is around 171,000 tons, but because squid like *Dosidicus* reproduce quickly, a depleted population can replenish itself quickly and effectively. Like most squid species, *Dosidicus* grows fast and dies young. In a 2004 study of age, growth, and maturation of the jumbo squid, Markaida et al. noted that *Dosidicus* shows the fastest growth rate of any squid species, but they don't live very long—the larger specimens may get to be two years old, but most complete their life cycle in less than a year.

In October 2001 Unai Markaida, Joshua Rosenthal, and William Gilly tagged 996 Humboldt squid in the Gulf of California in the vicinity of Santa Rosalia, and another 997 the following April, off Guaymas. Gilly's efforts are part of the project known as TOPP (Tagging of Pacific Pelagics), the Census of Marine Life's attempt to learn about the diversity and distribution of marine creatures by tagging large Pacific fauna such as tuna, whales, elephant seals, sea turtles, and now squid. These squid were caught on hand lines by commercial fishermen, and tagged as soon as they were brought on deck, often in less than thirty seconds. A reward of fifty dollars was offered for each tag collected by fishermen, and 160 tags were returned to the biologists, usually within a week or two of tagging. Based on the tag recoveries, Markaida, Rosenthal, and Gilly were able to learn a little about the jumbo squid's migration, its growth rate, and

its distribution in the Gulf, but there is still a lot we don't know about the squid known as *jibia*.

When Gilly, an electrophysiologist/teuthologist at Stanford University's Hopkins Marine Lab, tagged a half-dozen Humboldt squid in the Gulf of California with pop-off satellite tags, he learned that the squid spent a great deal of time in the depths at low oxygen levels, leading Gilly to question how they could get enough oxygen to function as high-speed predators. In a 2004 interview in the *Los Angeles Times*, Gilly described *Dosidicus* as "the most powerful of the squids with the armament for dealing with big prey: thousands of rings and sucker cups. Yet to see them feeding on little fish in the wild is really interesting. They reach out so delicately and grab them as though they're eating snacks at a cocktail party." Gilly has dived with *Dosidicus*, and has witnessed their stroboscopic color changes: in a split second they can go from bone white to neon red and back again.

An article in the *Monterey County Weekly* (Masters 2005) quoted Gilly as saying that "there is an astounding number of Humboldt squid in the ocean . . . 10 million living in one particularly dense area off the coast of Santa Rosalia alone." Ten million five-foot-long squid in one area? That's either a scuba diver's nightmare or a squid fisherman's wildest dream.[‡] If *Dosidicus* releases the

---

‡ When I asked Gilly about this "astounding number," he replied, "We came up with a figure of four or five million squid in an area about twenty-five square miles. It was based on the return of the tags we deployed over a five-day period and the number of squid landed commercially during the same days—and the assumption that our tagged squid were caught with the same probability as untagged squid." Because five million squid is still a hell of a lot of calamari, it is worth noting, as Gilly continued, that all the *Dosidicus* in this area were not all mature adults, but also paralarvae and juveniles, which "form a vital component of pelagic food webs and serve as essential prey for many (maybe nearly all) pelagic fish at some point in their lives."

typical number of eggs for an oceanic ommas-trephid—ranging from half a million to a million—then including the paralarvae and juveniles in the number undermines the whole estimate. Many fish species can also produce a million offspring each, but most of the eggs and larvae are consumed long before they reach adult size, so the idea of five or ten million *Dosidicus* is meaningless. Before we decide that *Dosidicus gigas* will provide relief for fishers and consumers from declining fish stocks, Gilly said that we "really need to know more about the entire life histories of all the species involved—and how they interact at various times—before we begin to get at causes."

Dosidicus's size, strength, and sporadic abundance may make it a worthwhile subject for consideration when discussing the estimation of marine populations: how many are there, how many will there be in the future, and what—if any—are the ramifications of these estimates for humans? Most of the variables influencing the population are still unknown, however, and by present techniques, probably unknowable. *Dosidicus* populations appear to be on the rise, and while removing those predators that feed on paralarvae or juveniles might contribute to this increase, the nature of *Dosidicus* itself also needs to be studied more carefully. As Gilly opined in 2005:

A pelagic predator that can tolerate a wide variety of prey types, temperatures, and oxygen-levels is likely to be one that can expand into new niches as things change, regardless of the cause of the change. True enough, if overfishing reduces the number of fish competitors in a given region, a supremely adaptable species like *Dosidicus* might expand into that niche, all other things being equal. Perhaps reducing the predation level on squid paralarvae, say from 90% to 80%, might give squid an advantage that could compound over time and lead to population increases and range expansions. But the same expansions could occur due to any other environmental perturbation that favored juvenile survival—changes in temperature, oxygen-levels, etc., that alter phytoplankton and zooplankton composition, etc. Of course these things change all the time due to natural as well as anthropogenic causes. *Dosidicus*, as a species, seems to me to be amoeboid—constantly sending out exploratory pseudopods into new areas in the periphery of its range, probing, testing, tasting for food (areas of high productivity). It would seem that adaptability to changing environmental conditions, which translates into the ability to take advantage of opportunities as they open up, may be the real secret to expansion and success of *Dosidicus*, and other species as well.

From October of 2004 to March of 2005, thousands of Humboldt squid washed ashore on beaches from California to Washington. More than fifteen hundred appeared on the Southern California beaches of San Onofre, Laguna Beach, and Newport Beach alone. There was no noticable weather anomaly during that time period, so these strandings cannot be attributed to El Niño or temporary climate change; some sort of marine toxin may have caused the squid to behave in a self-destructive fashion. Gilly could find no known toxins in the tissues of the beached Southern California specimens. The squid did not always wash up dead on the shore, but sometimes swam listlessly in shallow water until waves carried them onto the beach. In a *National Geographic News* interview in February 2005, Stefan Lovgren interviewed Gilly, who said, "We know so little about them because they spend 95 percent of their lives at depths well beyond those safely observed with scuba. We don't know where they spawn, and their eggs have never been found in the wild." About the strandings, Gilly said, "If whatever's killing them started killing them significantly more, we'd be up to our necks in squid on these beaches." Many squid die after mating once, so if future examinations show that the stranded squid were sexually mature, the cause of death might have been endogenous, that is, originating within the animal, and not attributable to any external or environmental factor.

Somehow connected to the thousands of jumbos that washed ashore and died in Southern California were the records of these spectacular cephalopods in places they had never been seen before. Before 1977 the northernmost record of *Dosidicus* was Oregon, but then they began to appear farther and farther north. A couple were dip netted off Sitka, Alaska, in October 2004, and the carcasses shipped to Erich Hochberg at the Santa Barbara Natural History Museum, who found nothing to suggest toxic poisoning. The water temperature off Alaska at that time was warmer than usual, but "global warming" doesn't seem a particularly helpful explanation. Because *Dosidicus* spends a lot of time in deep water, and entire populations have shifted from one location to another, it is too early to tell if the northward

movement of the jumbo squid is part of a trend or just a case of communal teuthological wanderlust.

There is one area where squid are the predominant predators—because there are no predatory fish there. When Paul Rodhouse and Martin White (1995) examined the data from research cruises in the Antarctic Polar Frontal Zone, they found that "the upper trophic levels are exceptional in that they contain no fish species." There "fishes are replaced by cephalopods," especially *Martialia hyadesi*, an ommastrephid squid that reaches a mantle (body) length of about a foot. The common name of *Martialia* is "sevenstar flying squid," which refers to the seven folds in the funnel that radiate out from the base. The 1984 FAO *Cephalopods of the World*, which was an annotated catalog of "species of interest to fisheries," says this about *Martialia hyadesi*: "So far, no fisheries have developed for this species, but it is believed to have some potential." And so, in June 1996, a scientific expedition headed for the waters of South Georgia to investigate the "potential" of a *Martialia* fishery. Aboard the Korean squid jigger *Ihn Sung #101*, fishing was conducted for eight days and the catch analyzed in labs on the Falkland Islands. The eight-day catch amounted to 65.63 tons, suggesting that the potential for a fishery for the sevenstar flying squid is significant—and it already has a wonderful menu name. But because we know almost nothing else about the biology or biogeography of *Martialia*, McArthur et al. warn "that any new fishery must be managed with caution."

How do the various squid species fit into the marine food chains? All squid are predators, but different sizes, morphologies, and inclinations put some at the top of the food chain, while others flit

California market squid (*Loligo opalescens*)

around the middle, preyed upon by a vast number of predatory marine animals, from fishes and dolphins to other squid species. Will any of the cephalopods replace the diminished cod or tuna stocks as a major food source for people? Annual landings of the Japanese flying squid (*Todarodes pacificus*) average about half a million tons per year, but some other species, such as the California market squid (*Loligo opalasecens*) fluctuate widely, from 3,000 tons in 1998 to 120,000 tons two years later. As we've seen, catches of *Dosidicus* can vary from year to year, affected by unpredictable variables such as predation, weather, change of address, or squid suicides. Around the world, the taste for barbecued, smoked, dried, fried, or raw squid is growing, and even without knowing the population of various species, squid fishing will increase, especially as landings of finfish decline. As finfish are depleted, do squid increase to fill their vacated niches? Does the removal of some squid predators, such as large finfish and cetaceans, increase squid populations? Or are both happening simultaneously? Only by studying the biological interaction between fish and squid populations, obtaining dependable distribution data and details of their physiology and life history, can humanity avoid disasters like those created by overfishing codfish. ✑

Overfishing Fishes, Too

Back in 1969, when fisheries biologist Sidney Holt wrote about the food resources of the ocean, they were mostly fish. He noted that "the present ocean harvest is about fifty-five million metric tons per year. More than 90 percent of that is finfish; the rest consists of whales, crustaceans, mollusks and some other invertebrates." At that time, the catches of individual fish species were led by the Peruvian *anchoveta* (10.5 million tons), Atlantic herring (3.8 million tons), Atlantic cod (3.1 million tons), Alaska walleye pollack (1.7 million tons), and the South African pilchard (1.1 million tons). Squid catches totaled three-quarters of a million tons, and shrimps, prawns, clams, and cockles together accounted for another million tons. The *anchovetas* from the Peru Current existed in such vast numbers that they headed the list of largest commercial catches: more than 11 million metric tons were caught in 1967. But this fishery completely collapsed in 1973 (due not just to overfishing but also to the El Niño of that year, and the *anchoveta*, once considered the most numerous fish in the world, is now classified as an endangered species).

By 2002 (*FAO Report on World Fisheries and Aquaculture*), the world fish catch is around ninety million tons, and the number appears to be stable. That is, until we run out of fish to catch. Of the present state of world fish populations, Thomas Hayden wrote in *U.S. News and World Report* in June 2003:

In a series of recent reports, scientists warn that fish stocks are dangerously overexploited and that many of the methods that provide the fish, crustaceans, and mollusks we so enjoy are destroying the very habitats and ecosystems needed to rebuild the stocks. . . . Even fish farming, which was supposed to take the pressure off wild stocks, turns out to pose so many environmental concerns that a major report this week will call for a moratorium on new farms until the problems can be resolved.

It was always assumed—at least by fishermen—that as a particular fish species grew scarce, they would simply find another place to fish. Or if a particular species declined, they would find another species. There are, after all, a lot of fish in the sea. But this rosy attitude has proven to be disastrously flawed. If you take most of the fish of a given species out of the ocean, there may not be enough left to regenerate the species. Gone are the days when codfishermen on the Grand Banks—once the world's richest neighborhood for *Gadus morhua*—could lower a basket on a rope and bring it up filled with wriggling cod. The codfisheries of New England and Maritime Canada can no longer sustain any level of commercial fishing. In May 2003

Ransom Myers and Boris Worm published a study in *Nature* in which they came to the startling conclusion that "the large predatory fish biomass today is only about 10% of pre-industrial levels"; that is, 90 percent of the world's predatory fish species (cod, tuna, billfishes, swordfish, flatfishes, sharks, skates, and rays—fish that people like to eat), have been fished out, and commercial fishers are now working on the remaining 10 percent.

Fisheries biologist Daniel Pauly is the author of the phrase "fishing down the food chain." In the phrase he captured the concept of taking out the apex predators first (large species like cod, tuna, and swordfish) because they are the most desirable species, and after they are gone, going down a trophic level and taking out their prey species (plankton-eaters such as anchovies) and then taking what's left. (From the Greek *trophe* meaning "food" or "nourishment," a "trophic level" refers to the ranking of prey species eaten by a particular group of fishes.) Fishing down the food chain means trading a limousine for a bicycle. This downward shift has occurred as overfishing has decimated predatory fish and fishers have been forced to harvest what is left, the predators' prey. To gauge the extent of this shift, researchers have assigned numbers to each trophic level, although the distinctions aren't as clear as one would like them to be because many creatures feed from multiple levels. The predators at the very top of the chain—humans—are level 5.0; piscene [fish] apex hunters like tuna and swordfish are level 4.0; then 3.0 is given to the prey of these predators—squid, anchovies, and the like. Level 2.0 is reserved for the zooplankton, such as copepods, on which creatures

at level 3.0 feed; and at the bottom, 1.0, the phytoplankton that supports the whole structure. "We firmly believe," wrote Pauly and his colleagues in a 2000 *American Scientist* article, "that the trophic level . . . is truly declining."

It takes very little to convince oneself that this situation is alarming—for seafood lovers as well as for environmentalists. After all, the average trophic level of the global catch has already slipped from 3.4 to 3.1 in just a few decades, and there are not many more appetizing species to be found below this level. Recall that 2.0 corresponds to copepods and other tiny zooplankton, creatures that are unlikely ever to be filling one's dinner plate. So if the trend continues, more and more regions are likely to experience complete collapse of their fisheries.

Because the top predators are usually sought first, "it stands to reason that prey populations and their effects on marine communities will increase after release from predator control. Accordingly, fishing alters the organization and structure of entire marine communities via 'cascading' trophic chain reactions" (Steneck 1998). Because the top predators are the least numerous, as one moves down a food web, biomass increases, but nowadays fish catches have stagnated as fishers have moved from top predators to species at lower trophic levels. Once a top predator has been depleted or exterminated by fishing, alternative predators of no commercial value thrive in the absence of competition and thus deplete the biomass of prey species at lower trophic levels. In 2005 Pauly and Maria-Lourdes Palomares suggested that fishing down the food web was "far more pervasive than previously thought, and in fact occurs in areas where initial

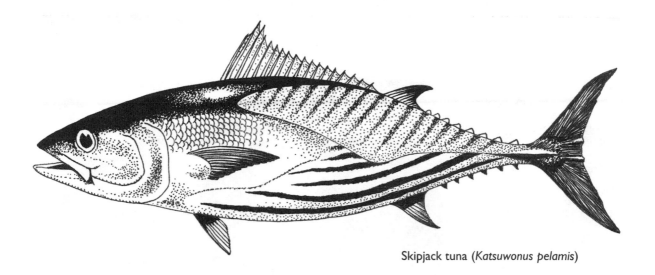

Skipjack tuna (*Katsuwonus pelamis*)

analyses failed to detect it. This confirms the common verdict of absent sustainability for most fisheries of the world."

Analyzing the data from Japanese longliners over the past fifty years and combining that with U.S. and Australian scientific observer data for the same period, Boris Worm and Ransom Myers of Dalhousie University, along with Marcel Sandow, Andreas Oschlies, and Heike Lotze of Germany's Leibniz Institute for Marine Science, found that the variety of species has dropped by as much as 50 percent in the past half century. To no one's surprise, overfishing was found to be the major cause of the decline, but temperature anomalies such as El Niño also contributed, as did habitat destruction and climate change. Their data, published in *Science* in July 2005, showed that pelagic longliners were catching half the number of fish—and half the number of species—that they were able to catch in the 1950s. The reduction in species diversity—primarily the removal of the large predators such as tuna, swordfish, and cod—leaves an ocean

ecosystem vulnerable to environmental changes like global warming. Interviewed by Cornelia Dean of the *New York Times* on July 29, 2005, Worm observed that the world's tuna fishery today is largely yellowfin and skipjack, because bluefin and albacore rarely appear on fishermen's lines. Said Worm, "If the ocean changes in a way that doesn't favor these two species [yellowfin and skipjack] any more, we have very little to fall back on. If you have a rich diversity of species, it's like a diverse stock portfolio."

In their 2005 study of the food web, Jordi Bascompte, Carlos Melián, and Enric Sala mapped the predator-prey interactions between 250 species of birds, fish, and invertebrates in a Caribbean marine reserve, where fishing was prohibited. They then modeled what would happen if specific members of the community were culled—by fishing, for example. The most damage was done to the web by the selective removal of the sharks (the top predators), which caused *their* prey to flourish, leading to excessive predation on the trophic level below the sharks' prey. The

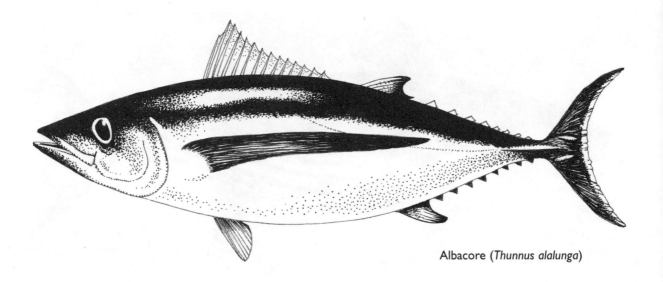

Albacore (*Thunnus alalunga*)

model and the reasoning incorporated in it suggested that the removal of the top predators greatly increases the likelihood of "trophic cascades." In an interview in *Science News* (Raloff 2005), Bascompte said, "Changes propagated throughout the entire food chain can cause a complete change in the architecture of the community."

When Ransom Myers and Boris Worm looked into the worldwide historical fisheries records, they found that over the past half century, populations of the large predatory fishes—cod, tuna, marlins, swordfish, sharks, and rays—had plummeted by 90 percent. In other words, only 10 percent of these popular food fishes have survived what Carl Safina has called "scorched earth fishing." Moreover, populations of marine creatures that are not foodfishes have also been shown to be in steep decline: sea turtles, whales, dolphins, seals, sea lions, and sea otters have been hunted, fished, clubbed, or shot so that in many cases, their populations are now regarded as endangered. Raking the bottom in

pursuit of groundfish like cod, haddock, pollock, redfish, and grenadiers, trawlers have been mowing down the fragile corals like bulldozers. In her 1999 testimony before Congress on the subject of endangered oceans, Sylvia Earle likened this method of fishing to dragging nets through marshes to capture ducks and geese, bulldozing forests to take songbirds, or dynamiting trees to catch squirrels. In a 2000 letter to the *New York Times*, Elliot Norse made clear just how huge the damaged area was: "on an annual basis trawlers scour an area equivalent to twice the size of the lower 48 states. . . . An activity that each year disturbs an area of seabed as large as Brazil, the Congo, and India combined must affect the structure, species composition, and biogeochemistry on both local and global scales."

Analyses of historical records of fishing, whaling, and exploration are useful in our attempt to learn what lived in the sea in the past and what will live in the ocean tomorrow. Deep-sea trawling, plankton nets, sonar, and population modeling have enabled us to get an idea of the current populations of marine animals. Unfortunately, these techniques, often effective, have provided mostly bad news. In a 2000 article in *American Scientist*, fisheries biologist Daniel Pauly (with Villy Christensen, Rainer Froese, and Maria Lourdes Palomares) said, "If one could don magic spectacles—with lenses that make the murky depths of the oceans become more transparent—and look back several centuries to an age before widespread abuse of the oceans began, even the most casual observer would quickly discover that fish were commonly much more abundant." Pauly published a series of papers and then a book (*In a Perfect Ocean*), in which he showed that the food web of the North Atlantic has been dramatically altered. He introduced the concept of "fishing down the food web," in which he demonstrated that the removal of top predators from the food chain affects every lower level, and results in a permanent distortion of marine relationships. The paradigm for this disaster was the wholesale removal of the codfish, one of the North Atlantic's top predators, which has been reduced to such low levels that the American and Canadian cod fisheries have been shut down.

When Kenneth Frank, Brian Petrie, Jae Choi, and William Leggett (2005) looked at the data from the last forty years of fishing on the Scotian Shelf in the western North Atlantic, they found that the systematic removal of the top predators—not only cod, but also haddock, hake, pollack, cusk, redfish, plaice, yellowtail flounder, skates, and rays—led to a trophic cascade that "involved the entire community, rather than only a subset of the species that occupy each of the trophic levels." Earlier (and simpler) ideas about the marine food chain—smallest animals eaten by larger ones until you get to the "apex predators" at the top of the chain—have been upended by the work of these scientists, who demonstrate that at least some ocean systems work from the top down, not from the bottom up. (In 2005, however, Daniel Ware and Richard Thomson published a study of a "bottom-up" ecosystem, wherein the continental margin ecosystem off Washington and southern British Columbia showed trophic linkages between phytoplankton, zooplankton, and resident fish. Where warmer upper-ocean temperatures caused a decline in plankton concentrations, fish yield also declined.)

Jonathan Swift (1667–1745) wrote of an analog where bigger fleas had lesser fleas to bite them, and so on ad infinitum. Just as the removal of wolves from some areas in North America had a "top-down" ripple effect on the entire ecosystem, so too did the removal of the top predators in the North Atlantic affect every trophic level. Plankton, of course, still forms the basis of the food chain, but when the cod and other predators were removed, the species they fed on experienced a population explosion. Crabs and shrimp, once the primary prey items of the large fish species, have replaced their former predators as the dominant species of the Scotian Shelf, marking a significant modification of the ecosystem. Removal of the top predators starts the cascade, and it rumbles down the food chain through the smaller fish that they feed on, the crabs and shrimp, all the way down to the plankton and algae, which are also being depleted because more small fish, crabs, and shrimp are feeding on them. This major shift on the Scotian Shelf means, among other things, that the cod stocks may never recover. As Frank and his colleagues concluded:

> The changes in top-predator abundance and the cascading effects on lower trophic levels . . . reflect a major perturbance of the eastern Scotia Shelf ecosystem. . . . One must acknowledge the ecological risks inherent in "fishing down the food web," as is currently occurring on the Scotian Shelf, or the ramifications associated with indirect effects reverberating across levels throughout the food web, such as altered primary production and nutrient cycling.

"Fishing down the food chain," of course, is not restricted to human fishers, but the concept helps in understanding the ripple effects of overfishing by humans. In Monterey Bay, California, first the sea otters were hunted to near extinction, which meant that the sea urchins on which they fed could proliferate unchecked. The urchins in turn gnawed on the holdfasts that anchored the giant kelp, which was thereby cut loose to float on the surface, thus eliminating the entire habitat of the fishes that called these great kelp forests home. Writing of worldwide fish populations, Daniel Pauly and Reg Watson (2003) wrote, "Overfishing has slashed stocks—especially of large predator species—to an all-time low worldwide, according to new data. If we don't manage this resource, we will be left with a diet of jellyfish sandwiches and plankton stew." The rampant destruction of fish populations has resulted in an ecological crisis of unprecedented proportions.

Because our lives are so tied to the sea, our very future depends on how we resolve this crisis.

Aristotle and his contemporaries had no way of estimating the population size of fishes that they were describing, but it is not unreasonable to assume that they thought the numbers were infinite. In 1961 Hawthorne Daniel and Francis Minot published *The Inexhaustible Sea*, a book described on the jacket as "The exciting story of the sea and its endless resources." Daniel and Minot hadn't been reading the newspapers carefully, because as they were writing their book, journalists were reporting that the anchovy population off the coast of Peru was crashing. Anchovies (genus *Engraulis*) and sardines (genera *Sardina* and *Sardinops*) are among the most important of all commercially fished species. The California sardine fishery, celebrated by John Steinbeck in his 1945 novel *Cannery Row*, had its peak of 1.5 billion pounds in 1936 but had ceased to exist by 1962. The *anchovetas* from the Peru Current existed in such vast numbers that they once headed the list of largest commercial catches: more than 11 million metric tons were caught in 1967. But this fishery completely collapsed in 1973 (due not just to overfishing but also to the El Niño of that year), and the *anchoveta*, once considered one of the most numerous fish in the world, is now classified as an endangered species. And the codfish, responsible for the discovery and early industrial success of New England, is essentially gone, its "inexhaustible" fishery closed indefinitely.

These declines in fish stocks can be attributed to twentieth-century overfishing, but can we know the state of the oceans before fishing? In a 2000 article in *Fisheries Research*, John Steele and Mary Schumacher wrote that "data from early fisheries in the Northwest Atlantic and elsewhere suggest that catch rates of demersal species were very high despite primitive fishing methods." But, they say, "circumstantial evidence suggests that earlier stocks may have been an order of magnitude greater than stocks in the last half century." In other words, early fishers caught a lot of fish, but there were a lot more fish to catch.

During the past millennia, we have learned much about the ocean and its inhabitants. To the ancient Romans, the Mediterranean, which they knew as *Mare Nostrum* ("our ocean"), was inhabited by an assortment of fishes and shellfish that constituted the known extent of marine life. From bacteria to whales, we now recognize some 210,000 species of living things in the ocean, and the number is on the increase. Much of the information we have gathered is new—that is, it was unknown a generation ago. Then we did not know that hot vents bubbled from the ocean floor, that sea cucumbers swam far from the bottom, or that coelacanths had set up shop in Indonesian waters. Through the window of population modeling, we can now see the Caribbean as Columbus did, teeming with thirty million green turtles rather than the million left today.

Because it encompasses what we know and, to a certain extent, what we recognize that we don't know, we tend to think of scientific investigation as a process that has brought us to the present state of knowledge. But combining the known and the unknown leads inexorably to the unknowable; we cannot predict what devices or methods will be invented that will enable us to better understand the nature of life in the marine environment. Steadily evolving scientific

methodology has revealed some disturbing realities: marine fish species, whales, and shellfish populations are down around the world, often beyond levels of possible recovery. Will new technologies enable us to find new poplulations or new species to fish on? Probably not; there is only so much that technology can do. In a 2002 article in *New Scientist*, Kurt Kleiner quoted fisheries biologist Daniel Pauly: "Jellyfish is already being exported. In the Gulf of Maine people were catching cod a few decades ago. Now they're catching sea cucumbers."

Contrary to widespread popular belief, fishing is a far greater threat to marine life than "pollution." It stands to reason, after all, that killing large numbers of fish is going to have more of an effect on the population of a given species than dumping garbage or even oil. But, argue Daniel Pauly, Reg Watson, and Jackie Adler (2005), people didn't seem to understand this simple equation, and they say that the reason "has to do with notions from another age, when fishing was indeed a matter of wrestling one's sustenance from a foreign, hostile sea, and from tiny boats, close to one's village, using equipment barely capable of making a dent in the huge populations of fish known to inhabit the ocean's unfathomable depths." That image, they suspect, is still prevalent, even though the commercial fisheries industry is now a giant enterprise that "is having so severe an impact on its own resources base that, if present trends continue, it will collapse in the next decades, and drag down with it, into oblivion, many of the fishes it exploits, together with their supporting ecosystems."

One of the critical questions addressed by the Census of Marine Life was not how many fish *are* in the sea, but rather, how many fish (or squid or whales or dolphins) *were* in the sea. One of the first projects undertaken by the CoML, therefore, was the History of Marine Animal Populations, better known—as are most CoML initiatives—by its acronym, H-MAP. By studying historical fishing statistics as well as port and customs archives over the past five hundred years, H-MAP will provide baseline numbers regarding the catches of past times, enabling us to identify exploitations (or over-exploitations) that have brought us to where we are today. The goals of H-MAP are to examine the ecological impacts of large-scale harvesting, long-term changes in stock abundance, and the role of marine resources in historical development. The concept was originally proposed by Poul Holm, Tim Smith, and David Starkey, who subsequently edited *The Exploited Seas (Research in Maritime History No. 21)*, published by CoML in Newfoundland in 2001.

Among the subjects covered in this collection are "The Newfoundland Fisheries, c. 1500–1900" (Starkey and Haines); "Historical Approaches to the Northern California Current Ecosystem" (Francis); "Potential for Historical-Ecological Studies of Latin American Fisheries (Reid); "The South African Fisheries: A Preliminary Survey of Historical Sources" (van Sittert); "The Potential for Historical Studies of Fisheries in Australia and New Zealand" (Tull and Polachek); and "Examining Cetacean Ecology Using Historical Fishery Data" (Smith). The subtitle of the book is *New Directions for Marine Environmental History*, and in their introduction, the authors wrote: "In combining the approaches of maritime history and ecological science it contributes to the field of environmental history, which has emerged in recent years as a distinctive branch of historical enquiry. The key to this new area of study is the integrated analysis of ecosystems and human societies, in particular the place of mankind in the historical development of ecosystems."

Because water conducts sound much more effectively than it does light, it was soon realized that sound could be an extremely important tool in the study of marine life; some thought it could be used even for remote species identification (RSID). In the introduction to a 1998 report on RSID, John Horne wrote, "Noninvasive species identification remains a long term goal of fishers and researchers using sound to locate, map, and count aquatic organisms. Since the first application of underwater acoustics to biological research, commercial fishing, and resource management, four approaches have been used to discriminate and classify fish and zooplankton species: prior knowledge and direct sampling, passive sonar, echo statistics from high frequency measures, and matching models to low frequency measures."

Other RSID components are optical sensing, which James Bohnsack and Edie Widder (1998) described as "ideal for species identification and quantitative marine resource assessment," and far superior to acoustical technology because "much of our scientific knowledge and understanding of marine systems has occurred because of direct human observations or photography by divers or observers using submersibles or other underwater platforms." In the future, optical assessment methods will incorporate remotely-operated vehicles equipped with sophisticated camera systems that can transmit their sightings (monocular or stereo) to shipboard or land-based computer networks. Bioluminescence, the rule rather than the exception in deep oceans, can be used as an index of abundance of various marine organisms, ranging from fishes to copepods and cephalopods, often too fragile for net sampling. "Perhaps the most novel new approach," wrote the authors of the workshop report, "is the use of trained animals to provide an entirely new perspective for marine assessment. Some marine mammals routinely dive four hundred to five hundred times per day and to depths of at least three hundred to four hundred meters. Cameras carried by trained dolphins, for example, have been used to determine the sex of whales."

The latest in fish-finding technology is OARS (ocean acoustic remote sensing), developed by Nicholas Makris of MIT's Ocean Engineering Department. In previous experiments off the New Jersey Continental Shelf, Makris and his colleagues found that their long-range acoustic sensing system made it possible to "continuously observe the spatial and temporal variability of environmental returns over wide areas"—in other words, they could spot fish schools at a distance, as compared with the downward-directed beam of fish-finding sonar that typically provides a swath only thirty feet wide directly below the ship (Symonds, Ratilal, Nero, and Makris 2003). Long-range acoustic waveguide sensing, which tracks scattering from the fishes' swim bladders, could locate fish schools over areas spanning hundreds of square miles. OARS is "a new lower frequency acoustic method for instantaneously detecting, imaging, and spatially charting fish populations over continental shelf scales, and

then continuously monitoring the areal densities and behavior of these fish populations over time." Mackris's idea is that fish populations can be monitored from a distance to determine the health and migratory movements of the stocks, an opportunity heretofore unavailable. (Previously, the status of fish populations was determined by fishing until too few appeared in the nets, trawls, or longlines, and then concluding that the stock had been overfished.) If and when the OARS technology is used by commercial fishermen, however, it will open to them a new window into the sea that might not be so beneficial to fish stocks.

And then there's OBIS—the Ocean Biographic Information System—the information component of CoML, which consists of a network of researchers in forty-five countries engaged in a ten-year initiative to assess and explain the diversity, distribution, and abundance of life in the oceans—past, present, and future. When you log onto the OBIS Web site (http://www.iobis.org)—try it!—you can type in the name (common or scientific) of any sea creature, click on it, and it opens Google Scholar, which gives you access to any number of recent scientific publications. According to its Web site, OBIS has been designed to allow professionals access to "a dynamic, global facility in four dimensions (the three dimensions of space plus time), [to] reveal new spatial/temporal patterns; to generate new hypotheses about the global marine ecosystem; and to guide future field expeditions." It is obviously a wonderful new tool for oceanographers, ichthyologists, cetologists, and anyone else who studies life in the oceans, but because it is one of the few programs available to the layperson by the click of a mouse, it also provides a remarkable insight into how modern science works.

We always believed that what Rachel Carson called "the circling sea," would nurture us and save us—if and when we needed saving. But now, it is not us that needs saving, it is the very sea that we thought would protect us. In a sense, we have overwhelmed the seas with our carelessness, but there is still the opportunity to rescue them. The technology that allowed us to plunder the oceans might enable us to save them. As oceanographer Sylvia Earle put it:

Traditionally, the sea has been regarded as the common heritage for all mankind; now its care must be acknowledged as a common responsibility. To ensure a decent quality of life for the rest of our lives, as well as for all those who follow, we must develop global policies that recognize the interdependence of life and the need for nations to agree on mutually beneficial measures to protect and maintain the basic elements of life support, on a planetary scale. . . . Through computer imaging and sophisticated number crunching, it is possible to gain better insight than ever before possible concerning future realities. Scientists can generate predictions, convincing visualizations, and alternative simulations. The consequences to the planet of a slight warming trend are seen to be profound: The polar ice caps melt, sea level rises, seaside cities are inundated, climate and weather change . . . people die. The consequences of too many people vying for too few fish can be anticipated, as can the consequences of dumping toxic pollutants into places near and far. Perhaps with knowing will come caring, and with caring, an impetus toward the needed sea change of attitude, one that combines the wisdom of science and the sensitivity of art to create an enduring ethic.

Part Four
Conclusion

Where Do We Go From Here?

While we have never been able to move faster than the speed of science, in recent years we have experienced a remarkable acceleration that has enabled us to move forward into the new world of high-tech oceanographic exploration. Of underwater archaeology, for example, Robert Ballard (2004) wrote:

Until recent years, marine archaeologists have been limited to a depth of 200 feet, the safe limit for scuba divers, leaving 91 percent of the ocean unexplored. Technological advances have afforded underwater archaeologists tools that open up that underwater wilderness. In expeditions to the Black Sea and the Mediterranean in the summer of 2003, Internet2 and a high bandwidth satellite link made it possible for scientists to work on the ocean floor from the comfort of their university laboratory. This real-time networking capability coupled with two underwater vehicles outfitted with high definition video cameras and a two-way audio link to shore greatly increased the number of scientists able to participate in the research. In the future a survey team aboard ship would consist primarily of engineers and technicians operating the exploration technology with only a few scientists on the expedition.

And in virtually every other area of oceanographic investigation, from bottom profiling to population estimates, technology has cleared the way for an exponential increase in knowlege. With increased knowledge, of course, comes the possibility of better understanding, and with understanding, the possibility of intelligent management of resources heretofore treated as mysterious or unknowable quantities.

During the twentieth century, we witnessed any number of new and unexpected developments, as many other creatures swam or drifted from the realm of the unknown into that of the known. After William Beebe's historic descents in the bathysphere—some of which were actually broadcast on the radio—he published books and magazine articles revealing some of the heretofore unknown components of deep-sea life: bioluminescent squid and fishes, strange flashing jellyfish, and a host of creatures that neither he nor anyone else was able to identify. Even if some of his identifications are doubtful, his descents, publications, and promotions brought the wonder and weirdness of deep-sea creatures to the world's attention.

The lobe-finned coelacanth was thought to have become extinct at the same time as the terrestrial dinosaurs did, sixty-five million years ago. When one was caught in 1938 off Port Elizabeth, South Africa, zoologists tripped over each other to proclaim the unexpected appearance of *Latimeria chalumnae* "the zoological wonder of the century." In 1975, when a very large shark was captured in Hawaiian waters, nobody knew what it was. That was because nobody had ever seen one before, and "Megamouth" was designated a new family, genus, and species. The first coelacanth was caught by fishermen off Port Elizabeth, South Africa, in 1938, but the first megamouth was hauled in off Oahu because it had swallowed a cargo parachute that was used as a sea anchor by a U.S. Navy research vessel. A consortium of cetologists matched two beaked whale skeletons to a series of photographs of unknown beaked whales taken at various locations in the Southern Hemisphere, and *voila!* A brandnew species of whale. We would have missed the hydrothermal vents entirely, but for the submersible *Alvin*, whose occupants serendipitously spotted the first one in 1977 along the Galápagos Rift Zone. Subsequent technological innovations enabled us to better estimate populations of whales, squid, and fishes, and the development of databases like OBIS gave scientists new tools with which to process what has become an information avalanche. Robot cameras, now the workhorses of undersea exploration, are revealing surprises every day, such as the blue-eyed *Vampyroteuthis*, the squid with elbows, and the octopus that can make itself look like a flounder.

Consider the siphonophore *Erenna*, a relative of the jellyfishes, recently observed and filmed at depths between five thousand feet (1,600 meters) and seventy-five hundred feet (2,300 meters) by Stephen Haddock and his fellow aquanauts from the ROV *Tiburon*, off the California coast.* "Unlike most siphophores," wrote Haddock et al., "*Erenna* does not feed on crustaceans but preys instead upon fish, remains of

which were found inside two of the specimens." The bioluminscent tentacles of *Erenna* appear to serve as lures to attract prey species, much like the lures of certain deep-sea anglerfishes. But where most fishes bioluminesce in wavelengths of blue or green because these colors travel long distances in water, *Erenna*'s lures glow red. The authors wrote that "the assertion that red light acts as an attractant is at odds with the prevailing view that deep-living creatures cannot detect long wavelengths; however, our knowledge of deep-sea visual abilities is limited." But even if science cannot—for the moment anyway—explain the red lights at the ends of the tentacles of *Erenna*, they do exist, and they probably function as lures. The "supporting online material" for the article by Haddock et al. in *Science* (July 8, 2005) consists of a little movie of *Erenna* that was shot more than a mile down, so almost anyone with Internet access can see this remarkable animal for themselves, demonstrating how easily modern technology can bring new discoveries to the public.

We can now "see" into the ocean in ways heretofore unimagined: manned and unmanned cameras capture images of animals never suspected

---

* The ROV *Tiburon* was designed and built by the Monterey Bay Aquarium Research Institute specifically for scientific exploration of the deep sea. From its launching in 1997 to the present, the *Tiburon* has made over four hundred dives. With a maximum operating depth of four thousand meters, the *Tiburon* is capable of diving in all areas of the Monterey Submarine Canyon, and can access undersea volcanoes and hydrothermal vents in the eastern Pacific. The *Tiburon* is controlled from a special control room on board its tender vessel, the R/V *Western Flyer*, from which it receives power and control signals through a tether that contains both electrical wires and fiber-optic strands. Data from sensors and video signals from the ROV's cameras travel back up the tether to the control room, where they are displayed on a series of monitors.

to exist, while sensitive recording devices reveal unsuspected animal signatures; sophisticated sonar can now profile the shape of the bottom, the seamounts, the presence of mineral deposits; and the shipboard device known as a "fishfinder" can locate schools of fish far below the surface. A complex piece of electronic gadgetry, the fishfinder works exactly like the echolocation system of dolphins. A pulse of energy is sent out (downward from a fishing boat), and when it hits a solid or semisolid object, like the bottom or a school of fish, a return signal bounces off and returns to the sender. The fishfinder displays the returning echo on a computer monitor, while the dolphin (we believe) reads and interprets the image instantaneously.

Global positioning systems, drift nets, longlines, fishfinders, factory ships, and other innovations in modern fishing technology, perceived as a boon to fishermen, have instead brought many marine populations to the brink of annihilation. But while some innovations in biological technology have potentially negative applications, most can be used in a purely scientific manner to increase our knowledge base. Satellite tags or remote sensing might inform fishermen of where their prey is, but our ability to understand the population dynamics, migration patterns, and behavior of fishes (or whales or squid) far outweighs the invitation to fishermen to abuse the technology.

Early whalers and sailors often heard the sounds of whales—some so powerful that they reverberated through the ship's timbers—but the seamen had no idea where the booming sounds were coming from. Much of the underwater behavior of whales—including their diving, feeding,

courting, and vocal activities—was unknown before the deployment of hydrophones, so the idea that we could learn about whales by listening to them is one of the more remarkable innovations of the twentieth century. In 1949 William Schevill and his wife, Barbara Lawrence, made some of the earliest recordings of whale sounds, the warbling of belugas in the Saguenay River of Quebec. At Marineland of Florida in 1953, curator Forrest G. Wood recorded the noises made by captive bottlenose dolphins and made the novel (and correct) assumption that the sounds might be used for echolocation. Roger and Katy Payne recorded the first humpback whale "songs" off Bermuda in 1970, which led to the identification of humpback vocalizations as a sophisticated communications system. In 1983 Payne edited *Communication and Behavior of Whales*, a compilation of studies by various authors of how whale species (mostly humpbacks, but also gray and right whales), use sound to communicate. As Payne said in the introduction, "One of the main features common to all of the studies in this book is that they are all based on passive observation techniques. There is no result in this book that was derived from killing, capturing, confining, or even touching a whale."

With the first underwater recordings of humpback whale vocalizations, Roger Payne was a trailblazer in the acoustic studies of whales—and an unwavering opponent of whale killing for profit. Payne was also the first to study the behavior of Patagonian right whales, but in recent years he has changed his subject species—but not his level of concern—to the sperm whale. In 2000, having raised the necessary funds and the necessary research vessel, he and his twelve-person

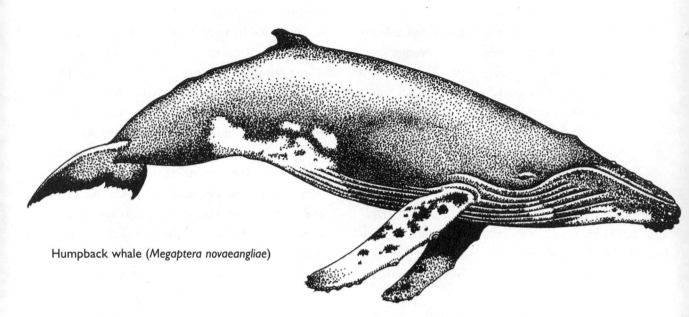

Humpback whale (*Megaptera novaeangliae*)

crew set off on what *Science* magazine (2004) characterized as a "Toxic Odyssey"—a five-year cruise of the world's oceans in an effort to learn the extent of persistent organic pollutants (POPs) in marine mammals. Using crossbows to fire arrows designed to harmlessly remove a tiny blubber sample, the crew analyzed the POP content aboard the twenty-eight-meter *Odyssey*, which is equipped with a molecular lab. The results are in, and according to a follow-up article in *Science* (Ferber, 2005), "they're not pretty." Samples from 424 sperm whales showed significant levels of pollutants, especially in those whales that lived in the Sea of Cortez (between Mexico and Baja California), where agricultural runoff might have been responsible. Whales sampled from the mid-Pacific also showed high POP levels, but not as high as those from the Sea of Cortez. To demonstrate the pernicious nature of these chemicals, wrote Ferber, "Payne's team is planning to circumnavigate the globe in 2007 to test for pollutants in people who live near especially contaminated areas."

Howard Gardner of Harvard once observed that Western classical music, as epitomized in the compositions of Bach, Beethoven, Brahms, and Mozart, has probably given more pleasure to more individuals, with less negative fallout, than any other human endeavor, but it is obvious that chronological innovations can be used as much for good as for evil. The technology that brought us the automobile also clouded our skies with pollution. Medical advances have saved countless lives but have encouraged population growth that threatens many nations with overcrowding and famine. Sometimes seen as a double-edged sword, antibiotics can be used to cure many ailments, but the application of the

theory of evolution (itself one of the most important scientific contributions ever conceived)
shows that certain pathogens can adapt to the
threat of antibiotics, rendering them less than
useful. Airplanes that can carry people and
equipment around the world can also carry
atomic bombs. It is almost as easy to list the negative or harmful possibilities of computers, plastics, the Internet, television, microchips, lasers,
sonar, submarines, jet aircraft, and helicopters,
as it is to identify the good these inventions have
done. We can identify the benign or beneficial
applications of atomic energy, but its military applications so far outweigh its commercial potential that it tops the list of threats to the existence
of the human race—if not the planet Earth. Alfred Nobel (1833–1896), a Swedish chemist and
inventor, established a fund that gives awards for
work in physics, chemistry, medicine, literature,
and peace (economics was added in 1969) in an
attempt to counteract the wartime uses of dynamite, which he invented in 1866. (Dynamite is
also used in an ethically questionable "fishing"
technique, wherein underwater explosions are
used to kill or stun fish that are later collected as
they float on the surface.)

In their 2005 discussion of the importance of
marine conservation biology, Elliot Norse and
Larry Crowder wrote that "hunters cannot
legally use nonselective methods such as poison
gas, explosives, or bulldozers to kill wildlife. In
the sea, however, technologies to transport fishermen to find and catch fish have improved continuously, while selectivity has decreased. Steel
hulls have replaced wood, diesel engines have
replaced sail, freezers have replaced salt curing
and crushed ice, nylon has replaced hemp,

global positioning systems have replaced sex-
tants, and satellite oceanography feeds, preci-
sion depth finders, and fish finders have
replaced guessing where fish are. Larger and
more powerful oceangoing vessels are deploying
gear such as sixty-mile pelagic longlines armed
with thousands of hooks and rockhopper and
roller trawls that can fish even on mile-deep
boulder and reef bottoms."

For the most part, life on land is visible, but
marine life is mostly underwater, and has been
invisible for most of human history. And there is
a lot of room for marine life under the surface.
As Norse and Crowder wrote:

> The marine realm is much, much larger
> than the terrestrial realm; the area of the Pa-
> cific ocean alone would be great enough to
> accommodate all of the continents even if
> there were two Australias. Moreover, the sea
> averages more than 3,700 meters deep,
> while multicellular life on land and in fresh-
> waters permanently lives in a thin film that
> averages a few tens of meters in thickness.
> Hence the sea comprises more than 99 per-
> cent of the known biosphere.

On one of the 1934 dives off Bermuda, as
the bathysphere reached a record depth of
three thousand feet, William Beebe recorded his
impressions:

> Before we began to ascend, I had to stop
> making notes of my own, so numb were my
> fingers from the cold steel of the window
> sill, and to change from my cushion to the
> metal floor, was like shifting to a cake of ice.

Of the blackness of the water I have already written too much. . . . Whenever I sink below the last rays of light, similes pour in upon me. . . . The only place comparable to these marvelous nether regions, must surely be naked space itself, out far beyond atmosphere, between the stars, where sunlight has no grip upon the dust and rubbish of planetary air, where the blackness of space, the shining planets, comets, suns, and stars, must really be closely akin to the world of life as it appears to the eyes of an awed human being, in the open ocean, one half mile down.

First we sent people like Beebe down in little bathyspheres to look into the blackness of the abyss, but after we realized that such a practice was labor-intensive, expensive, and possibly life threatening, we switched over to robots. The parallel between the exploration of *outer* space and the exploration of *inner* space is unavoidable: the first space explorers landed in the Moon in 1969; after several more manned spaceflights (some of which ended in horrendous human disasters), the emphasis shifted to vehicles that required humans only to design and launch them, not to accompany them into the dark and dangerous airlessness of space. We have now mapped the moon and landed unmanned spacecraft on Mars. The twin *Voyager* spacecraft, launched in the summer of 1977, and now heading out of the solar system, have come close enough to Jupiter, Saturn, Uranus, and Neptune, to give us a startling look at these outer planets, and, incidentally, to learn that Europa, one of Jupiter's moons, is covered with ice, a situation that indicates the

presence of water, a fundamental necessity for life as we know it.[†] The *Voyager* space probes provide us with images of unfamiliar worlds, but so far, no signs of life. In contrast, the oceanic probes have revealed an abundance of life-forms and lifestyles heretofore unexpected in the depths and vastness of the sea. What was once *mare incognita*—the unknown ocean—is beginning to surrender some of its closely guarded submarine secrets. Through the applications of curiosity, necessity, science, and technology, the unknowns of the marine realm are becoming known.

At least for the moment, there are aspects of the natural world that we do not understand. As closely as they are studied and analyzed, the gigantic weather anomalies known as El Niño and La Niña are beyond our predictive powers. No system of classification can predict that a new, unexpected species will appear; indeed, the very size and depth of the ocean mitigates against such a prediction. And no one foresaw the tsunami of December 26, 2004, that killed upwards of 250,000 people in Indonesia and adjacent islands. The earthquake that generated the tsunami that was among the most powerful in modern history, with a magnitude ranging from 9.0 to 9.3. It was the second-largest earthquake ever recorded on a seismograph. The earthquake

---

† When James Cameron, director of the blockbuster epic *Titanic* (1997) made an Imax film called *Aliens of the Deep* in 2005, he showed scientists (and himself) marveling at the wonders of life around the hydrothermal vents, but then, awed by the connection between inner and outer space, he took his film on a fantastic voyage to Europa, where they crashed though the ice and found a world of marine life even more fantastic than the living wonders of the deep sea. Where Cameron's "Europan" life-forms were silly cartoon monsters, the creatures he saw and filmed first—ghostly octopuses, clouds of eyeless shrimp, blood-red tube worms—were just as unbelievable, but they were real.

itself lasted nearly ten minutes when most major earthquakes last no more than a few seconds; it caused the entire planet to vibrate. The earthquake originated in the Indian Ocean just north of Simeulue Island, off the western coast of northern Sumatra, Indonesia. The resulting tsunami devastated the shores of Indonesia, Sri Lanka, South India, Thailand, and other countries with waves up to a hundred feet high. It also triggered earthquakes elsewhere, as far away as Alaska. We are not much better at predicting earthquakes now than we were when the ancient Chinese relied upon the movements of goldfish.

New sharks, new fishes, and even a new way of earning a living underwater have been recently revealed, but these discoveries, while fascinating, have little bearing on the lives of anyone but scientists. Population studies of fishes, squid, and whales, can affect the lives of hundreds of thousands of consumers and fishermen, and therefore, the increase in applied technology can improve the quality of life for millions. Despite what might be called setbacks in the pursuit of knowledge—almost eliminating species we would study, for example—we have entered a new era of marine biological investigation. Enhanced by developments that were unthinkable a decade ago, marine biology has become a thrilling scientific adventure, visiting heretofore unexpected worlds, encountering new, almost unbelievable creatures, and probably most exciting, finding new ways to learn about what's under the water. Discoveries expand everyone's awareness of the wonders of life under the ocean, and delight and enrich us with this new knowledge. Standing on the shore and looking out to sea, the boy said, "There's a lot of water out there," and the wise old oceanographer responded, "And that's only the top of it." ⬧

Guide to Further Reading

The following books, all of which have been used in the preparation of this one, are recommended as general works that can be used to enhance one's knowledge of a particular subject.

BEEBE, W. 1934. *Half Mile Down*. Harcourt, Brace.

BROAD, W. J. 1997. *The Universe Below: Discovering the Secrets of the Deep Sea*. Simon & Schuster.

DEACON, M. B. 1971. *Scientists and the Sea, 1650-1900: A Study of Marine Science*. Academic Press.

ELLIS, R. 1991. *Men and Whales*. Knopf.

——. 1994. *Monsters of the Sea*. Knopf.

——. 1996. *Deep Atlantic: Life, Death, and Exploration in the Abyss*. Knopf.

——. 1998. *The Search for the Giant Squid*. Lyons Press.

——. 2003. *The Empty Ocean*. Island Press.

HANLON, R. T. and J. B. MESSENGER. 1997. *Cephalopod Behaviour*. Cambridge University Press.

HARDY, A. 1956. *The Open Sea: Its Natural History. Part I: The World of Plankton*. Houghton Mifflin.

——. 1958. *The Open Sea: Its Natural History. Part II: Fish and Fisheries*. Houghton Mifflin.

——. 1967. *Great Waters*. Harper & Row.

HEEZEN, B. C. and C. D. HOLLISTER. 1971. *The Face of the Deep*. Oxford University Press.

MATSEN, B. 2005. *Descent: The Heroic Discovery of the Abyss*. Pantheon.

MILLS, E. L. 1989. *Biological Oceanography: An Early History, 1870–1960*. Cornell University Press.

MOYLE, P. B. and J. J. CECH. 2004. *Fishes: A History of Ichthyology*. Prentice-Hall.

MURRAY, J. and J. HJORT. 1912. *The Depths of the Ocean*. Macmillan. London. (1965 reprint, Weldon & Wesley, Ltd., Stechert-Hafner, Inc.)

NORMAN, M. V. 2000. *Cephalopods: A World Guide*. Conch Books.

NORSE, E. and L. B. CROWDER (eds.). 2005. *Marine Conservation Biology*. Island Press.

PAULY, D. and J. MACLEAN. 2002. *In a Perfect Ocean: The State of Fisheries and Ecosystems in the North Atlantic Ocean*. Island Press.

PAYNE, R. (ed.). 1983. *Communication and Behavior of Whales*. American Association for the Advancement of Science.

SAFINA, C. 1997. *Song for the Blue Ocean*. Henry Holt.

SCHLEE, S. 1973. *The Edge of an Unfamiliar World: A History of Oceanography*. E. P. Dutton.

THOMSON, K. S. 1991. *Living Fossil: The Story of the Coelacanth*. Norton.

VAN DOVER, C. L. 2000. *The Ecology of Deep-Sea Hydrothermal Vents*. Princeton University Press.

WHITEHEAD, H. 2003. *Sperm Whales: Social Evolution in the Ocean*. University of Chicago Press.

References

ADAMS, A. B. 1969. *Eternal Quest: The Story of the Great Naturalists*. Putnam.

AELIAN, n.d. *Aelian on the Characteristics of Animals*. Loeb Classical Library, Harvard University.

AGNEW, D. J., S. L. HILL, J. R. BEDDINGTON, V. V. PURCHASE, and R. C. WAKEFORD. 2005. Sustainability and management of southwest Atlantic squid fisheries. *Bulletin of Marine Science* 76 (2): 579–593.

ALDRICH, F. A. 1991. The history and evolution of the Newfoundland squid jigger and jigging. *Journal of Cephalopod Biology* 2 (1): 23–30.

ALLDREDGE, A. L., D. L. BRADLEY, D. BUTTERWORTH, and J. H. STEELE. 1999. Assessing the global distribution and abundance of marine life. *Oceanography* 12 (3): 41–46.

ANON. 1991. Megamouth reveals a phantom shark's realm. *National Geographic* 179 (3): 136.

ARCHER, F., T. GERRODETTE, A. DIZON, K. ABELLA, and S. SOUTHERN. 2001. Unobserved kill of nursing dolphin calves in a tuna purse-seine fishery. *Marine Mammal Science* 17 (3): 540–54.

ARGÜELLES, J., P. G. RODHOUSE, P. VILLEGAS, and G. CASTILLO. 2001. Age, growth and population structure of the jumbo flying squid *Dosidicus gigas* in Peruvian waters. *Fisheries Research* 54: 51–61.

ARISTOTLE. n.d. *Historia animalium*. Loeb Classical Library. Harvard University Press.

ARRIAN. n.d. *History of Alexander and Indica*. Loeb Classical Library. Harvard University Press.

ASHFORD, J. R., P. S. RUBILAR, and A. R. MARTIN. 1996. Interactions between cetaceans and longline fishery operations around South Georgia. *Marine Mammal Science* 12 (3): 452–457.

AUSUBEL, J. H. 1999. Toward a census of marine life. *Oceanography* 12 (3): 4–5.

AZAM, F. 1998. Microbial control of oceanic carbon flux: the plot thickens. *Science* 280: 694–696.

AZAM, F. and A. Z. WORDEN. 2004. Microbes, molecules and marine ecosystems. *Science* 303: 1622–1624.

BACO, A. R. and C. R. SMITH. 2003. High species richness in deep-sea chemo-autotrophic whale skeleton communities. *Marine Ecology Progress Series* 260: 109–114.

BAILEY, H. S. 1953. The voyage of the *Challenger*. *Scientific American* 188 (5): 88–94.

BAKER, C. S. and P. J. CLAPHAM. 2004. Modelling the past and future of whales and whaling. *Trends in Ecology and Evolution* 19 (7): 365–371.

BAKER, C. S., G. M. LENTO, F. CIPRIANO, M. L. DALEBOUT, and S. R. PALUMBI. 2000. Scientific whaling: source of illegal products for market? *Science* 290: 1695–1696.

BALCOMB, K. C. and D. E. CLARIDGE. 2001. A mass stranding of cetaceans caused by naval sonar in the Bahamas. *Bahamas Journal of Science* 2: 2–12.

BALGUERIAS, E., M. E. QUINTERO, and C. L. HERNÁNDEZ-GONZÁLEZ. 2000. The origin of the Saharan Bank cephalopod fishery. *Journal of Marine Science* 57: 15–23.

BALLANCE, L. T., R. C. ANDERSON, R. L. PITMAN, K. STAFFORD, A. SHAAN, Z. WAHEED, and R. L. BROWNELL. 2001. Cetacean sightings around the Republic of the Maldives, April 1998. *Journal of Cetacean Research and Management* 3 (2): 213–218.

BALLARD, R. D. 1975a. Project FAMOUS II: Dive into the Great Rift. *National Geographic* 147 (5): 604–15.

——. 1975b. Photography from a submersible during Project FAMOUS. *Oceanus* 18: 31–39.

——. 1976. The Cayman Trough: window on Earth's interior. *National Geographic* 150 (2): 228–49.

——. 1977. Notes on a major oceanographic find. *Oceanus* 20 (3): 35–44.

——. 1983. Argo-Jason. *Oceans* 16 (2): 18–19.

——. 1984. The Exploits of *Alvin* and ANGUS: Exploring the East Pacific Rise. *Oceanus* 27 (3): 7–14.

——. 1985. How we found *Titanic*. *National Geographic* 168 (6): 696–719.

——. 1994a. Deep-sea exploration: The challenge continues. *Woods Hole Currents* 3 (1): 4–5.

——. 1995. *Explorations: My Quest for Adventure and Discovery Under the Sea.* Hyperion.

BALLARD, R. D. and T. EUGENE. 2004. *Mystery of the Ancient Seafarers: Early Maritime Civilization.* National Geographic.

BARKHAM, S. H. 1984. The Basque whaling establishment in Labrador 1536–1632—a summary. *Arctic* 37: 515–19.

BARNES, A. T., L. B. QUETIN, J. J. CHILDRESS, and D. L. PAWSON. 1976. Deep-sea macroplanktonic sea cucumbers: suspended sediment feeders captured from deep submergence vehicle. *Science* 194: 1083–85.

BAROSS, J. A. and S. E. HOFFMAN. 1985. Submarine hydrothermal vents and associated gradient environments as sites for the origin and evolution of life. *Orig. Life* 15 (4): 327–45.

BARTON, O. 1930. The bathysphere. *Bulletin of the New York Zoological Society* 33 (6): 232–34.

——. 1953. *The World Beneath the Sea.* Crowell.

BASCOM, W. 1969. Technology and the ocean. *Scientific American* 221 (3): 198–217.

——. 1988. *The Crest of the Wave: Adventures in Oceanography.* Harper & Row.

BASCOMPTE, J., C. J. MELIÁN, and E. SALA. 2005. Interaction strength combinations and the overfishing of a marine food web. *Proceedings of the National Academy of Sciences* 102 (15): 5443–5447.

BAUMGARTNER, M. F. and B. R. MATE. 2005. Summer and fall habitat of North Atlantic right whales (*Eubalaena glacialis*) inferred from satellite telemetry. *Canadian Journal of Fisheries and Aquatic Sciences* 62: 527–543.

BEASLEY, I., K. M. ROBERTSON, and P. ARNOLD. 2005. Description of a new dolphin, the Australian snubfin dolphin *Orcaella hein-sohni* sp. n (Cetacea, Delphinidae). *Marine Mammal Science* 21 (3): 365–410.

BEATTY, J. T., J. OVERMANN, M. T. LINCE, A. K. MANSKE, S. S. LANG, R. E. BLANKENSHIP, C. L. VAN DOVER, T. A. MARTINSON, and F. G PLUMLEY. 2005. An obligately photosynthetic bacterial anaerobe from a deep-sea hydrothermal vent. *Proceedings of the National Academy of Sciences* 102 (26): 9306–9310.

BEEBE, W. 1926. *The Arcturus Adventure*. Putnam.

——. 1931. A round trip to Davy Jones's Locker. *National Geographic* 59 (6): 653–78.

——. 1932a. The depths of the sea. *National Geographic* 61 (1): 5–68.

——. 1932b. *Nonsuch: Land of Water*. Harcourt, Brace.

——. 1932c. A new deep-sea fish. *Bulletin of the New York Zoological Society* 35 (5): 175–77.

——. 1934a. A half mile down. *National Geographic* 66 (6): 661–704.

——. 1934b. *Half Mile Down*. Harcourt, Brace.

——. 1934c. Three new deep-sea fish seen from the bathysphere. *Bulletin of the New York Zoological Society* 37 (6): 190–93.

BEJA, O., L. ARAVIND, E. V. KOONIN, M. T. SUZUKI, A. HADD, L. P. NGUYEN, S. B. JOVANOVICH, C. M. GATES, R. A. FELDMAN, J. L. SPUDICH, E. N., SPUDICH, and E. F. DELONG. 2000. Bacterial rhodopsin: evidence for a new type of phototrophy in the sea. *Science* 289: 1902–1906.

BERRA, T. M. 1977. *William Beebe: An Annotated Bibliography*. Archon Books.

——. 1997. Some twentieth-century fish discoveries. *Environmental Biology of Fishes* 50: 1–12.

BERTIN, L. 1934. Les poissons apodes appartenant au sous-ordre des Lyomeres. *Dana Report* 3: 3–55.

——. 1937. Les poissons abyssaux du genre *Cyema* Günther. *Dana Report* 10: 4–30.

——. 1938. Formes nouvelles et formes larvaires de poissons apodes appartenant au sous-orde des Lyoméres. *Dana Report* 15: 1–25.

——. 1954. Les larves leptocephaliennes géantes et le probleme du "serpent de mer." *La Nature* 3232: 312–13.

——. 1956. *Eels: A Biological Study*. Cleaver-Hume.

BERZIN, A. A. 1972. *The Sperm Whale*. Izdatgel'stvo "Pischevaya Promyshlennost" Moskva 1971. Translated from the Russian by Israel Program for Scientific Translation, Jerusalem.

BEST, P. B. 1975. Review of world sperm whale stocks. *FAO Marine Mammals Symposium*. ACMRR/MM/EC/8.

BILLET, D. S. 1986. The rise and rise of the sea cucumber. *New Scientist* 109 (1500): 48–51.

BLOCK, B. A., H. DEWAR, C. FARWELL, and E. D. PRINCE. 1998. A new satellite technology for tracking the movements of Atlantic bluefin tuna. *Proceedings of the National Academy of Sciences* 95 (16): 9384–89.

BLOCK, B. A., H. DEWAR, S. B. BLACKWELL, T. D. WILLIAMS, E D. PRINCE, C. J. FARWELL, A. BOUSTANY, S. L. H. TEO, A. SEITZ, A. WALLI, and D. FUDGE. 2001. Migratory movements, depth preferences, and thermal biology of Atlantic bluefin tuna. *Science* 293: 1310–14.

BLOCK, B. A., S. L. H. TEO, A. WALLI, A. BOUSTANY, M. J. W. STOKESBURY, C. J. FARWELL, K. C. WENG, H. DEWAR, and T. D. WILLIAMS. 2005. Electronic tagging and population structure of Atlantic bluefin tuna. *Nature* 434: 1121–1127.

BOCK, P. G. 1966. *A Study in International Regulation: The Case of Whaling*. New York University Ph.D. dissertation. University Microfilms.

BOHANNON, J. 2004. A toxic odyssey. *Science* 304: 1584–1586.

BOHNSACK, J. A. and E. WIDDER. 1998. The potential of optical technology for advancing marine resources technology. Pp. 60–86. in J. K. Parrish, (ed.) *Remote Species Identification Workshop Report October 1998, Monterey Bay Aquarium Research Institute*.

BOLSTAD, K. S. and S. O'SHEA. 2004. Gut contents of a giant squid (Cephalopoda: Oegopsida) from New Zealand waters. *New Zealand Journal of Zoology* 31: 15–21.

BOYLE, P. and P. RODHOUSE. 2005. *Cephalopods: Ecology and Fisheries*. Blackwell.

BRADLEY, A., D. R. YOERGER, and B. B. WALDEN. 1995. An AB(L)E bodied vehicle. *Oceanus* 38 (1): 18–20.

BRADLEY, D. L. 1999. Assessing the global distribution and abundance of marine organisms. *Oceanography* 12 (3): 19–23.

BROAD, W. J. 1994a. Scientists fight Navy plan to shut far-flung undersea spy system. *New York Times* June 12: A1, A4.

——. 1994b. Squid emerge as smart, elusive hunters of mid-sea. *New York Times* August 30: C1, C8.

——. 1997. *The Universe Below: Discovering the Secrets of the Deep Sea*. Simon & Schuster.

——. 2005. Newly found cousin of the jellyfish spurs fresh theories on seeing red. *New York Times* July 12: F3.

BROWNLEE, C. 2004. DNA barcodes: Life under the scanner. *Science News* 166 (23): 340–341.

BRUUN, A. F. 1937. Contribution to the life histories of the deep sea eels: Synaphobranchidae. *Dana Report* 9: 1–31.

——. 1943. The biology of *Spirula spirula* (L.). *Dana Report* 24: 1–44.

——. 1951. The Philippine Trench and its bottom *Fauna*. 168: 692.

——. 1956a. The abyssal fauna: its ecology, distribution and origin. *Nature* 177 (4520): 1105–08.

——. 1956b. Animal life of the deep-sea bottom. Pp. 149–95 in A. F. Bruun, S. Greve, H. Mielche, and R. Sparck, eds. *The Galathea Deep Sea Expedition 1950–1952*. Allen and Unwin.

——. 1957. Deep sea and abyssal depths. *Memoirs of the Geological Society of America* 67 (1): 641–72.

BUCHANAN, J. Y. 1896. The sperm whale and its food. *Nature* 1367 (53): 223–225.

BURDICK, A. 2005. *Out of Eden*. Farrar, Straus and Giroux.

BURTON, M. 1957. *Animal Legends*. Coward-McCann.

BUTMAN, C. A., J. T. CARLTON, and S. R. PALUMBI. 1994. Whaling effects on deep-sea biodiversity. *Conservation Biology* 9 (2): 462–464.

CADDY, J. F. and F. CAROCCI. 1999. On cruise tracks for a global Census of Marine Life. *Oceanography* 12 (3): 47–52.

CADDY, J. F. and P. D. RODHOUSE. 1998. Cephalopod and groundfish landings: Evidence of ecological change in global fisheries? *Reviews in Fish Biology and Fisheries* 8: 431–444.

CADIGAN, S. T. and J. A. HUTCHINGS. 2001. Nineteenth-century expansion of the Newfoundland fishery for Atlantic cod: An exploration of underlying causes. Pp. 31–65 in P. Holm, T. D. Smith, and D. J. Starkey (eds.) 2001. *Research in Maritime History No. 21*. International Maritime History Association/Census of Marine Life.

CARSON, R. L. 1941. *Under the Sea Wind*. Oxford University Press.

——. 1943. Food from the sea: fish and shellfish of New England. *U.S. Department of the Interior Fish and Wildlife Service Bulletin* 33: 1–73.

——. 1951. *The Sea Around Us*. Oxford University Press.

——. 1955. *The Edge of the Sea*. Houghton Mifflin.

CASTLE, P. J. H. 1959. A large leptocephalid (Teleostei, Apodes) from off South Westland, New Zealand. *Transactions of the Royal Society of New Zealand* 87 (1&2): 179–84.

——. 1964a. Deep-sea eels: family Synaphobranchidae. *Galathea Report* 7: 29–42.

——. 1964b. Eels and eel-larvae of the *Tui* oceanographic cruise 1962 to the South Fiji Basin. *Transactions of the Royal Society of New Zealand* 5 (7): 71–84.

——. 1967. Two remarkable eel-larvae from off southern Africa. *Special Publications Department of Ichthyology Rhodes University South Africa* 1: 1–12.

——. 1973. A giant notanthiform leptocephalus from the Chatham Islands, New Zealand. *Records of the Dominion Museum* 8 (8): 121–124.

CASTLE, P. J. H. and N. S. RAJU. 1975. Some rare leptocephali from the Atlantic and Indo-Pacific Oceans. *Dana Report* 85: 1–25.

CASWELL, H., M. FUJIWARA, and S. BRAULT. 1999. Declining survival probability threatens the North Atlantic right whale. *Proceedings of the National Academy of Sciences* 96: 3308–13.

CHARIF, R. A., P. J. CLAPHAM, and C. W. CLARK. 2001. Acoustic detections of singing humpback whales in deep waters off the British Isles. *Marine Mammal Science* 17 (4): 751–768.

CHAVEZ, F. P., J. RYAN, S. E. LLUCH-COTA, and M. ÑIQUEN. 2003. From anchovies to sardines and back: multidecadal change in the Pacific Ocean. *Science* 299: 217–221.

CHILDRESS, J. J. 1988. Biology and chemistry of a hydrothermal vent of the Galápagos Rift; the Rose Garden in 1985. *Deep-Sea Research* 35 (10/11A): 1677–80.

CHILDRESS, J. J. and T. J. MICKEL. 1982. Oxygen and sulfide consumption rates of the vent clam *Calyptogena pacifica*. *Marine Biology Letters* 3: 3–79.

——. 1985. Metabolic rates of animals from the hydrothermal vents and other deep-sea habitats. *Bulletin of the Biological Society of Washington* 6: 249–60.

CHILDRESS, J. J., H. FELBECK, and G. N. SOMERO. 1987. Symbiosis in the deep sea. *Scientific American* 256 (5): 115–20.

CHILDRESS, J. J., C.R. FISHER, J. M. BROOKS, M. C. KENNICUT, R. R. BIDIGARE, and A. E. ANDERSON. 1986. A methanotrophic marine molluscan (Bivalvia: Mytilidae) symbiosis: mussels fueled by gas. *Science* 233: 1306–08.

CHISHOLM, S. W., R. J. OLSON, E. R. ZETTLER, R. GOERICKE, J. B. WATERBURY, and N. A. WELSCHMEYER. 1988. A novel free-living prochlorophyte abundant in the oceanic euphotic zone. *Nature* 334: 340–343.

CHRISTENSEN, V., S. GUÉNETTE, J. J. HEYMANS, C. J. WALTERS, R. WATSON, D. ZELLER, and D. PAULY. 2002. Estimating fish abundance of the North Atlantic, 1950 to 1999. In S. Guénette, V. Christensen, and D. Pauly, eds. *Fisheries Impacts on North Atlantic Ecosystems: Models and Analyses.* Fisheries Centre Research Reports 9 (4): 1–25.

CLAPHAM, P. 1996. Too much is never enough: can the whaling industry be trusted? *Whalewatcher* 30 (1): 4–7.

CLARK, C. W. 1991. Moving with the heard. *Natural History* 3/91: 38–42.

CLARK, C. W. and J. H. JOHNSON. 1984. The sounds of the bowhead whale, *Balaena mysticetus*, during the spring migrations of 1979 and 1980. *Canadian Journal of Zoology* 62: 1436–1441.

CLARK, C. W. and D. K. MELLINGER. 1994. Application of Navy IUSS for whale research. *Journal of the Acoustical Society of America* 96 (5): 3315.

CLARK, E. and J. CASTRO. 1995. 'Megamama' is a virgin: dissection of the first female specimen of *Megachasma pelagios*. *Environmental Biology of Fishes* 43: 329–32.

CLARKE, M. R. 1977. Beaks, nets, and numbers. *Symposium Zoological Society of London* 38: 89–126.

——. 1980. Cephalopoda in the diet of sperm whales of the Southern Hemisphere and their bearing on sperm whale biology. *Discovery Reports* 37: 1–324.

——. 1983. Cephalopod biomass—estimation from predation. *Memoirs of the National Museum of Victoria.* 44: 95–107

CLARKE, M. R. and G. E. MAUL. 1962. A description of the "scaled" squid *Lepidoteuthis grimaldi* Joubin 1895. *Proceedings of the Zoological Society of London* 139 (1): 97–118.

CLARKE, M. R., E. J. DENTON, and J. B. GILPIN-BROWN. 1979. On the use of ammonium for buoyancy in squids. *Journal of the Marine Biological Association U.K.* 59: 359–276.

COHEN, P. 2000. Sun, sea and surprises: Biologists find oceans awash with photo-synthetic bacteria. *New Scientist* 2257: 4.

COLEMAN, D. F., R. D. BALLARD, and T. GREGORY. 2003. Marine archaeological exploration of the Black Sea. *Oceans 2003 Conference Papers, Marine Technology Society, 2003.* http://iao.gso.uri.edu/publications/index.php

COLWELL, R. R. 1996. Global climate and infectious disease: The cholera paradigm. *Science* 274: 2025–2031.

COMPAGNO, L. J. V. 1981. Legend versus reality: The Jaws image and shark diversity. *Oceanus* 24 (4): 3–16.

——. 1984a. *Sharks of the World. FAO Species Catalog. Vol. 4. Part 1: Hexanchiformes to Lamniformes.* UN Development Programme. Rome.

——. 1984b. *Sharks of the World. FAO Species Catalog. Vol. 4. Part 2: Carcharhiniformes.* UN Development Programme. Rome.

COMPAGNO, L. J. V., M. DANDO, and S. FOWLER. 2005. *Sharks of the World.* Princeton University Press.

CONE, J. 1991. *Fire Under the Sea.* William Morrow.

CONNIFF, R. 1996. Clyde Roper can't wait to be attacked by a giant squid. *Smithsonian* 27 (2): 126–137.

COPLEY, J. 2004. All wired up. *Nature* 427: 10–12.

CORLISS, J. B. and R. D. BALLARD. 1977. Oases of life in the cold abyss. *National Geographic* 152 (4): 441–453.

COURCHAMP, F., T. CLUTTON-BROCK, and B. GRENFELL. 1999. Inverse density dependence and the Allee effect. *Trends in Ecology and Evolution* 14: 405–10.

COURT, W. G. 1980. Japan's squid fishing industry. *Marine Fisheries Review* 42 (7–8): 1–9.

COUSTEAU, J.-Y. and P. DIOLÉ. 1973. *Octopus and Squid: The Soft Intelligence.* Doubleday.

COWEN, R. C. 1960. *Frontiers of the Sea: The Story of Oceanic Exploration.* Doubleday.

CRONIN, T. W., N. J. MARSHALL, and R. L. CALDWELL. 2000. Spectral tuning and the visual ecology of mantis shrimps. *Philosophical Transactions of the Royal Society of London* 355: 1263–1267.

CROWDER, L. B. 2005. Back to the future in marine conservation. Pp. 19–29 in E. Norse and L. B. Crowder, eds. *Marine Conservation Biology.* Island Press.

CROWDER, L. B. and E. A. NORSE. 2005. Marine populations: the basics. Pp. 31–32 in E. Norse and L. B. Crowder, eds. *Marine Conservation Biology.* Island Press.

CROZIER, W. J. 1918. The amount of bottom material ingested by holothurians (*Stichopus*). *Journal of Experimental Zoology* 26: 379–89.

CUMMINGS, W. C. and P. O. THOMPSON. 1971. Underwater sounds from the blue whale, *Balaenoptera musculus. Journal of the Acoustical Society of America* 50 (4): 1193–1198.

CUSHING, D. H. 1988. *The Provident Sea.* Cambridge University Press.

DAHLGREN, T. G., A.G. GLOVER, A. BACO, and C. R. SMITH. 2004. Fauna of whale falls: systematics and ecology of a new polychaetid (Annedlida: Chrysopetalidae) from the deep Pacific Ocean. *Deep-Sea Research I* 51: 1873–1887.

DALEBOUT, M. L., G. J. B. ROSS, C. S. BAKER, R. C. ANDERSON, P.B. BEST, V. G. COCKCROFT, H. L. HINSZ, V. PEDDEMORS, and R. L. PITMAN. 2003. Appearance, distribution, and genetic distinctiveness of Longman's beaked whale, *Indopacetus pacificus*. *Marine Mammal Science* 19(3): 421–61.

DALTON, R. 2005. Satellite tags give fresh angle on tuna quota. *Nature* 434: 1056–1057.

DARWIN, C. 1839. *The Voyage of the Beagle.* Henry Colburn. (Doubleday Anchor edition, 1962.)

——. 1859. *The Origin of Species by Means of Natural Selection.* John Murray.

DEACON, M. B. 1971. *Scientists and the Sea, 1650–1900: A Study of Marine Science.* Academic Press.

——. (ed.) 1978. *Oceanography Concepts and History.* Dowden, Hutchinson & Ross.

DEAGLE, B. E., S. N. JARMAN, D. PEMBERTON, and N. J. GALES. 2005. Genetic screening for prey in the gut contents of the giant squid (*Architeuthis* sp.). *Journal of Heredity* 96 (4): 417–423.

DEAN, C. 2005. Scientists warn fewer kinds of fish are swimming in the oceans. *New York Times* July 29: A6.

DEMING, J. W., A.-L. REYSENBACH, S. A. MACKO, and C. R. SMITH. 1997. Evidence for the microbial basis of a chemoautotrophic invertebrate community at a whale fall on the deep seafloor: Bone-colonizing bacteria and invertebrate endosymbionts. *Microscopy Research and Technique* 37 (2): 162–170.

DES MARAIS, D. J. 2000. When did photosynthesis emerge on Earth? *Science* 289: 1703–05.

DEWHURST, W. H. 1835. *The Natural History of the Order Cetacea and the Oceanic Inhabitants of the Arctic Regions.* London.

DOBBS, D. 2005. *Reef Madness: Charles Darwin, Alexander Agassiz, and the Meaning of Coral.* Pantheon.

DONOGHUE, M., R. R. REEVES, and G. S. STONE, (eds.). 2003. *Report of the Workshop on Interaction Between Cetaceans and Longline Fisheries.* New England Aquarium Press.

DUNCAN, D. 1941. Fighting giants of the Humboldt. *National Geographic* 79 (3): 373–400.

DUNNING, M. C. and J. H. WORMUTH. 1998. The ommastrephid squid genus *Todarodes*: A review of systematics, distribution, and biology (Cephalopoda: Teuthoidea). Pp. 385–391 in N. A. Voss, M. Vecchione, R. B. Toll, and M. J. Sweeney, eds. *Systematics and Biogeography of Cephalopods.* Smithsonian Institution Press.

DUVAL, M. A. and D. N. RADCER. 1999. Environmental and advocacy implications of a proposed "Census of the Fishes." *Oceanography* 12 (3): 35–38.

EARLE, S. A. 1991. Sharks, squids, and horseshoe crabs—the significance of marine biodiversity. *BioScience* 41 (7): 506–509.

——. 1995. *Sea Change: A Message of the Oceans.* Fawcett Columbine.

EASTMAN, J. T. 1993. *Antarctic Fish Biology: Evolution in a Unique Environment.* Academic Press.

EHRHARDT, N. M., P. S. JAQUEMIN, F. GARCIA, G. GONZALES D. J. M. LOPEZ, J. ORTIZ C., and A. SOLIS. 1983. Summary of the fishery and biology of the jumbo squid (*Dosidicus gigas*) in the Gulf of California, Mexico. *Memoirs of the National Museum of Victoria* 44: 305–311.

ELLIS, R. 1980. *The Book of Whales*. Knopf.

——. 1991. *Men and Whales*. Knopf.

——. 1996. *Deep Atlantic: Life, Death, and Exploration in the Abyss*. Knopf.

——. 1998. *The Search for the Giant Squid*. Lyons Press.

——. 2003. *The Empty Ocean*. Island Press.

ELLIS, S. L. 1988. Allyn Collins Vine: Man of vision. *Oceanus* 31 (4): 61–66.

EMERSON, T. and H. TAKAYAMA. 1993. Down to the bottom. *Newsweek* 72 (1): 60–64.

ERDMANN, M. V. 1998. Sulawesi coelacanths. *Ocean Realm*. Winter 1998–99: 26–28.

ERDMANN, M. V. and R. L. CALDWELL. 2000. How new technology put a coelacanth among the heirs of Piltdown Man. *Nature* 406: 343.

ERDMANN, M. V., R. L. CALDWELL, and M. KASIM MOOSA. 1998. Indonesian "king of the sea" discovered. *Nature* 395: 335.

ERDMANN, M. V., R. L. CALDWELL, S. L. JEWETT, and A. TJAKRAWIDJAJA. 1999. The second recorded living coelacanth from north Sulawesi. *Environmental Biology of Fishes* 54: 445–451.

ESCHMEYER, W. N. 1990. *Catalog of Genera of Recent Fishes*. California Academy of Sciences.

ETTER, R. J. and J. F. GRASSLE. 1992. Patterns of species diversity in the deep sea as a function of sediment particle size diversity. *Nature* 360: 576–578.

FELDMAN, R.A., T. M. SHANK, M. B. BLACK, A. R. BACO, C. R. SMITH, and R. C. VRIJENHOEK. 1998. Vestimentaran on a whale fall. *Biological Bulletin* 194: 116–119.

FERBER, D. 2005. Sperm whales bear testimony to worldwide pollution. *Science* 309: 1166.

FERNÁNDEZ, F. and J. A. VÁSQUEZ. 1995. La jibia gigante *Dosidicus gigas* (Orbigny 1835) en Chile: Analisis de una pesquería efimera. *Estudios Oceanologicos* 14: 17–21.

FIELD, J. G., G. HEMPEL, and C. P. SUMMERHAYES. 2002. *Oceans 2020: Science, Trends, and the Challenge of Sustainability*. Island Press.

FITCH, J. E. and R. J. LAVENBERG. 1968. *Deepwater Fishes of California*. University of California Press.

FOELL, E. J. and D. L. PAWSON. 1989. Assessment of abyssal benthic megafauna on a ferromanganese nodule deposit using videotaped television survey data. *Paper Presented at the 21st Offshore Technology Conference, Houston, Texas, May 1–4, 1989*: 313–20.

FORBES, E. 1844. On the Light thrown on Geology by Submarine Researches; being the Substance of a Communication made to the Royal Society of Great Britain, Friday Evening, the 23rd February, 1844. *Edinburgh New Philosophy Journal* 36: 318–327.

FRANCIS, C. R. I. C and M. R. CLARKE. 2005. Sustainability issues for orange roughy fisheries. *Bulletin of Marine Science* 76 (2): 337–352.

FRANK, K. T., B. PETRIE, J. S. CHOI, and W. C. LEGGETT. 2005. Trophic cascades in a formerly cod-dominated ecosystem. *Science* 308: 1621–1623.

FRANTZIS, A. 1998. Does acoustic testing strand whales? *Nature* 392: 29.

FREDERICKSON, J. K. and T. C. ONSTOTT. 1996. Microbes deep inside the earth. *Scientific American* 275 (4): 68–73.

FRICKE, H., K. HISSMANN, J. SCHAUER, M. ERDMANN, M. K. MOOSA, and R. PLANTE. 2000. Biogeography of Indonesian coelacanths. *Nature* 403: 38–39.

FRICKE, H., O. GIERE, K. STETTER, G. A. ALFREDSSON, J. K. KRISTJANSSON, P. STOFFERS, and J. SVAVARSSON. 1989. Hydrothermal vent communities in the shallow subpolar Mid-Atlantic Ridge. *Marine Biology* 102: 425–429.

FROMENTIN, J.-M. and C. RAVIER. 2005. The East Atlantic and Mediterranean bluefin tuna stock: Looking for sustainability in a context of large uncertainties and strong political pressures. *Bulletin of Marine Science* 76 (2): 353–361.

FUHRMAN, J. A. 1999. Marine viruses and their biogeochemical and ecological effects. *Nature* 399: 541–48.

FUHRMAN J. A. and R. T. NOBLE. 1995. Viruses and protists cause similar bacterial mortality in coastal seawater. *Limnology and Oceanography* 40: 1236–1242.

FUHRMAN, J. A. and C. A. SUTTLE. 1993. Viruses in marine planktonic systems. *Oceanography* 6: 50–62.

FUSON, R. H. (trans.) 1987. *The Log of Christopher Columbus.* International Marine.

GAGE, J. D. and P. E. TYLER. 1991. *Deep-Sea Biology: A Natural History of Organisms at the Deep-Sea Floor.* Cambridge University Press.

GALES, N. J., T. KASUYA, P. J. CLAPHAM, and R. L. BROWNELL. 2005. Japan's whaling plan under scrutiny. *Nature* 435: 883–884.

GARCIA, S. M. and R. J. R. GRAINGER. 2005. Gloom and doom? The future of marine capture fisheries. *Philosophical Transactions of the Royal Society B.* 360: 21–46.

GARDNER, T. A., I. M. CÔTÉ, J. A. GILL, A. GRANT, and A. R. WATKINSON. 2003. Long-term region-wide declines in Caribbean corals. *Science* 301 958–960.

GEORGE, A. S. 1999. *William Dampier in New Holland: Australia's First Natural Historian.* Bloomings.

GERRODETTE, T. 2002. Tuna-dolphin issue. Pp. 1269–73 in W. F. Perrin, B. Würsig, and J. G. M. Thewissen, eds. *Encyclopedia of Marine Mammals.* Academic Press.

GERRODETTE, T. and J. FORCADA. 2005. Non-recovery of two spotted and spinner dolphin populations in the eastern tropical Pacific Ocean. *Marine Ecology Progress Series* 291: 1–21.

GIBSON, C. D. 1981. A history of the swordfishery in the Northwestern Atlantic. *American Neptune* 41 (1): 36–65.

——. 1998. *The Broadbill Swordfishery in the North Atlantic.* Ensign.

GOLD, T. 1992. The deep, hot biosphere. *Proceedings of the National Academy of Sciences* 89: 6045–6049.

——. 1999. *The Deep Hot Biosphere.* Copernicus.

GOLUBIC, S. 1994. The continuing importance of cyanobacteria. Pp. 334–40. *in* S. Bengston, ed. *Early Life on Earth. Nobel Symposium No. 84.* Columbia University Press.

GONZÁLEZ, A. F. and P. G. RODHOUSE. 1998. Fishery biology of the seven star flying squid *Martalia hyadesi* at South Georgia during winter. *Polar Biology* 19: 231–236.

GRANT, A. 2000. Deep-sea diversity: Overlooked messages from shallow-water sediments. *Marine Ecology* 21 (2): 97–112.

GRASSLE, J. F. 1978. Diversity and population-dynamics of benthic organisms. *Oceanus* 21 (1): 42–49.

——. 1984. Animals in the soft sediments near the hydrothermal vents. *Oceanus* 27 (3): 63–66.

——. 1985. Hydrothermal vent animals: distribution and biology. *Science* 229 (4715): 713–17.

——. 1986. The ecology of deep-sea hydrothermal vent communities. *Advanced Marine Biology* 23: 301–62.

——. 1988. A plethora of unexpected life. *Oceanus* 31 (4): 41–46.

——. 1989. Species diversity in deep-sea communities. *Trends in Ecology and Evolution* 4: 12–15.

——. 1991. Deep-sea benthic biodiversity. *BioScience* 41 (7): 464–469.

GRASSLE, J. F. and N. J. MACIOLEK. 1992. Deep-sea species richness: Regional and local diversity estimated from quantitative bottom samples. *American Naturalist* 139 (2): 313–341.

GRASSLE, J. F. and K. I. STOCKS. 1999. A global ocean biogeographic information system (OBIS) for the Census of Marine Life. *Oceanography* 12 (3): 12–14.

GRASSLE, J. F., H. L. SANDERS, R. R. HEISLER, G. T. ROWE, and T. MCLELLAN. 1975. Pattern and zonation: a study of the bathyal megafauna using the research submersible *Alvin. Deep-Sea Research* 22: 457–81.

GRIGGS, K. 2003. Super squid surfaces in Antarctic. *BBC News* http://news.bbc.co.uk /1/hi/sci/tech/2910849.stm

GÜNTHER, A. C. L. G. 1859–1870. *Catalogue of the Fishes of the British Museum.* British Museum (Natural History.)

——. 1880. *An Introduction to the Study of Fishes.* Adam and Charles Black.

——. 1887. Report on the deep-sea fishes collected by H.M.S. *Challenger* during the Years 1873–76. *Report on the Scientific Results of the Voyage of H.M.S. "Challenger" Zoology* 22.

HADDOCK, S. H. D., C. W. DUNN, P. R. PUGH, and C. E. SCHNITZLER. 2005. Bioluminescent and red-fluorescent lures in a deep-sea siphonophore. *Science* 309: 263.

HALL-SPENCER, J., V. ALLAIN, and J. H. FOSSA. 2002. Trawling damage to Northeast Atlantic ancient coral reefs. *Proceedings of the Royal Society (Biological Sciences)* 269 (1490): 507–11.

HAMABE, M., C. HAMURO, and M. OGURA. 1982. *Squid Jigging from Small Boats.* FAO/Fishing News Books.

HANLON, R. T. and J. B. MESSENGER. 1997. *Cephalopod Behaviour.* Cambridge University Press.

HANSEN, B. 1956. Holothurioidea from depth exceeding 6000 meters. *Galathea Report* 2: 33–54.

——. 1967. The taxonomy and zoogeography of the deep-sea holothurians in their evolutionary aspects. *Studies in Tropical Oceanography* 5: 480–501.

——. 1972. Photographic evidence of a unique type of walking in deep-sea holothurians. *Deep-Sea Research* 19: 461–62.

——. 1975. Systematics and biology of the deep-sea holothurians. *Galathea Report* 13: 1–262.

HARDER, B. 2003. Whale meat in Japan is loaded with mercury. *Science News* 163 (23): 365.

HARDY, A. 1956. *The Open Sea: Its Natural History. Part I: The World of Plankton.* Houghton Mifflin.

——. 1958. *The Open Sea: Its Natural History. Part II: Fish and Fisheries.* Houghton Mifflin.

——. 1960a. Was man more aquatic in the past? *New Scientist* 7 (174): 642–45.

——. 1960b. Will man be more aquatic in the future? *New Scientist* 7 (175): 730–33.

——. 1967. *Great Waters.* Harper & Row.

HARRISSON, C. M. H. 1967. On methods of sampling mesopelagic fishes. *Symposium of the Zoological Society of London* 19: 71–126.

HASTINGS, J. W. 1998. Bioluminescence. Pp. 984–1000. in N. Sperelakis, ed. *Cell Physiology Source Book, Second Edition.* Academic Press.

HATFIELD, E. M. C. and P. G. RODHOUSE. 1998. Biology and fishery of the Patagonian squid, *Loligo gahi* (D'Orbigny, 1835): A review of current knowledge. *Journal of Cephalopod Biology* 2 (1): 23–30.

HAYDEN, T. 2003. Empty oceans: why the world's seafood supply is disappearing. *U.S. News and World Report* 134 (20): 38–45.

HEBERT, P. D. N., A. CYWINSKA, S. L. BALL, and J. R. DEWAARD. 2003. Biological identifications through DNA barcodes. *Proceedings of the Royal Society of London B.* 270: 313–321.

HEBERT, P. D. N., E. H. PENTON, J. M. BURNS, D. H. JANZEN, and W. HALLWACHS. 2004. Ten species in one: DNA barcoding reveals cryptic species in the neotropical skipper butterfly *Astraptes fulgerator. Proceedings of the National Academy of Sciences* 101 (41): 14812–14817.

HEEZEN, B. C. and C. D. HOLLISTER. 1971. *The Face of the Deep.* Oxford University Press.

HEEZEN, B. C. and A. S. LAUGHTON. 1963. Abyssal plains. Pp. 281–311 in MM. N. Hill, ed. *The Sea, Vol. 3: The Earth Beneath the Sea.* Wiley Interscience.

HENISCH, B. A. 1976. *Fast and Feast: Food in Medieval Society.* Pennsylvania State University Press.

HEREU, B., M. ZABALA, C. LINARES, and E. SALA. 2005. The effects of predator abundance and habitat structural complexity on survival of juvenile sea urchins. *Marine Biology* 146 (2): 293–299.

HERNÁNDEZ-HERRERA, A., E. MORALES-BORÓRQUEZ, M. A. CISNEROS-MATA, M. O. NEVÁREZ-MARTÍNEZ, and G. I. RIVERA-PARRA. 1998. Management strategy for the giant squid (*Dosidicus gigas*) fishery in the Gulf of California, Mexico. *CalCOFI Report* 39: 212–218.

HERRING, P. J. 1974. New observations on the bioluminescence of echinoderms. *Journal of Zoology London* 172: 401–18.

HESSLER, R. R. and H. L. SANDERS. 1967. Faunal Diversity in the Deep-Sea. *Deep-Sea Research* 14: 65–78.

HEUVELMANS, B. 1968. *In the Wake of Sea Serpents*. Hill and Wang.

HOLDER, M. T., M. V. ERDMANN, T. P. WILCOX, R. L. CALDWELL, and D. M. HILLIS. 1999. Two living species of coelacanths? *Proceedings of the National Academy of Sciences* 96 (22): 12616–12620.

HOLM, P. and M. BAGER. 2001. The Danish fisheries, c. 1450–1800: Medieval and early modern sources and their potential for marine environmental history. Pp. 97–122 in P. Holm, T. D. Smith, and D. J. Starkey (eds.) 2001. *Research in Maritime History No. 21*. International Maritime History Association/Census of Marine Life.

HOLM, P., T. D. SMITH, and D. J. STARKEY (eds.) 2001. *Research in Maritime History No. 21*. International Maritime History Association/Census of Marine Life.

HOLME, N. A. and A. D MCINTYRE. 1971. *Methods for the Study of the Marine Benthos*. International Biological Programme/Blackwell Scientific.

HOLT, S. 1969 The food resources of the ocean. *Scientific American* 221 (2): 178–194.

HOLT, S. J. 2004. Counting whales in the North Atlantic. *Science* 303: 39.

HORNE, J. K. 1998. Acoustic approaches to remote species identification. Pp. 31–58. in J. K. Parrish, (ed.) *Remote Species Identification Workshop Report October 1998, Monterey Bay Aquarium Research Institute.*

HOYT, E. 2001. *Creatures of the Deep.* Firefly.

HUBBS, C. L. 1935. Review of *Half Mile Down*, by William Beebe. *Copeia* 2: 105.

HUGHES, T. P., A. H. BAIRD, D. R. BELLWOOD, M. CARD, S. R. CONNOLY, C. FOLKE, R. GROSBERG, O. HOEGH-GULDBERG, J. B. C. JACKSON, J. KLERYPAS, J. H. LOUGH, P. MARSHALL, M. NUSTROM, S. R. PALUMBI, J. M. PANDOLFI, B. ROSEN, and J. ROUGHGARDEN. 2003. Climate change, human impacts, and the resilience of coral reefs. *Science* 301: 929–955.

HUISMAN, J. and F. J. WEISSING. 1999. Biodiversity of plankton by species oscillations and chaos. *Nature* 402: 407–410.

HUTCHINS, B. 1992. Megamouth: gentle giant of the deep. *Australian Natural History* 23 (12): 910–17.

HUTCHINSON, G. E. 1961. The paradox of the plankton. *American Naturalist* 95: 137–45.

IRIGOIEN, X., J. HUISMAN, and R. P. HARRIS. 2004. Global biodiversity patterns of marine phytoplankton and zooplankton. *Nature* 424: 863–869.

ISAACS, J. P. and R. A. SCHWARTZLOSE. 1975. Active animals of the deep-sea floor. *Scientific American* 233 (4): 85–91.

JACKSON, G. D. and S. O'SHEA. 2003. Unique hooks in the male scaled squid *Lepidoteuthis grimaldi*. *Journal of the Marine Biological Association U.K.* 83: 1099–1100.

JACKSON, G. D., A. G. P. SHAW, and C. LALAS. 2000. Distribution and biomass of two squid species off southern New Zealand: *Nototodarus sloanii* and *Moroteuthis ingens*. *Polar Biology* 23: 699–705.

JACKSON, J. B. C. 1991. Adaptation and diversity of reef corals. *BioScience* 41 (7): 475–82.

——. 1997. Reefs since Columbus. *Coral Reefs* 16 (5): S23–S32.

JACKSON, J. B. C. and K. G. JOHNSON. 2001. Measuring past biodiversity. *Science* 293: 2401–03.

JACKSON, J. B. C., M. X. KIRBY, W. H. BERGER, K. A. BJORNDAL, L. W. BOTSFORD, B. J. BOURQUE, R. H. BRADBURY, R. COOKE, J. ERLANDSON, J. A. ESTES, T. P. HUGHES, S. KIDWELL, C. B. LANGE, H. S. LENIHAN, J. M. PANDOLFI, C. H. PETERSON, R. S. STENECK, M. J. TEGNER, and R. R. WARNER. 2001. Historical overfishing and the recent collapse of coastal ecosystems. *Science* 293: 629–38.

JAFFE, J. S. 1999. Technology workshop for a census of marine life. *Oceanography* 12 (3): 8–11.

JENG, M.-S., N. K. NG, and P. K. L. NG. 2004. Hydrothermal vent crabs feed on sea 'snow.' *Nature* 432: 969.

JENSEN, A. and R. FREDERIKSEN. 1992. The fauna associated with the bank-forming deepwater coral *Lophelia pertusa* (Scleractinia) on the Faroe Shelf. *Sarsia* 77: 53–69.

JORDAN, D. S. and B. W. EVERMANN. 1896. The fishes of North and Middle America: a descriptive catalogue of the species of fish-like vertebrates found in the waters of North America, north of the Isthmus of Panama. Part I. *Bulletin of the United States National Museum* 1–1240.

KAEPPLER, A. L. 1978. *Artificial Curiosities: An Exposition of Native Manufactures, Collected on the Three Pacific Voyages of Captain James Cook, R. N.* Bishop Museum Press.

KAHARL, V. A. 1988. A famously successful expedition to the boundary of creation. *Oceanus* 31 (4): 34–40.

——. 1990. *Water Baby: The Story of* Alvin. Oxford University Press.

KAUFMANN, C. 2005. Clues from a convict. *National Geographic* 207 (6): 84–89.

KELLEY, D. S., J. A. KARSON, D. K. BLACKMAN, G. L. FRÜH-GREEN, D. A. BUTTERFIELD, M. D. LILLEY, E. J. OLSON, M. O. SCHRENK, K. K. ROE, G. T. LEBON, P. RIVIZZIGNO, and the AT3-60 SHIPBOARD PARTY. 2001. An off-axis hydrothermal vent field near the Mid-Atlantic Ridge at 30° N. *Nature* 412: 145–149.

KELLEY, D. S., J. A. KARSON, G. L. FRÜH-GREEN, D. R. YOERGER, T. M. SHANK, D. A. BUTTERFIELD, J. M. HAYES, M. O. SCHRENK, E. J. OLSON, G. PROSKUROWSKI, M. JABULA, A. BRADLEY, B. LARSON, K. LUDWIG, D. GLICKSON, K. L. BUCKMAN, A. S. BRADLEY, W. J. BRAZELTON, K. ROE, M. J. ELEND, A. DELACOUR, S. M. BERNASCONI, M. D. LILLEY, J. A. BAROSS, R. E. SUMMONS, and S. P. SYLVA. 2005. A serpentine-hosted ecosystem: the Lost City hydrothermal field. *Science* 307: 1428–1434.

KENNEY, R. 2002. North Atlantic, North Pacific, and southern right whales. Pp. 806–813. in W. F. Perrin, B. Würsig, and J. G. M. Thewissen, eds. *Encyclopedia of Marine Mammals.* Academic Press.

KIYOFUJI, H. and S. SAITOH. 2004. Use of nighttime visible images to detect Japanese common squid *Todarodes pacificus* fishing areas and potential migration routes in the Sea of Japan. *Marine Ecology Progress Series* 276: 173–186.

KNUDTSON, P. M. 1977. The case of the missing monk seal. *Natural History* 86 (8): 78–83.

KOLBER, Z. S., C. L. VAN DOVER, R. A. NIEDERMAN, and P. G. FALKOWSKI. 2000. Bacterial photosynthesis in surface waters of the open ocean. *Nature* 407: 177–79.

KOLBER, Z. S., F. G. PLUMLEY, A. S. LANG, J. T. BEATTY, R. E. BLANKENSHIP, C. L. VAN DOVER, C. VETRIANI, M. KOBLIZEK, C. RATHGEBER, and P.G. FALKOWSKI. 2001. Contribution of aerobic photoeterotrophic bacteria to the carbon cycle in the ocean. *Science* 292: 2492–2495.

KONDO, I. 2001. *Rise and Fall of the Japanese Coast Whaling.* Sanyosha.

KRAMP, P. L. 1956. Pelagic fauna. Pp. 65–86. in A. F. Bruun, S. Greve, H. Mielche, and R. Sparck, eds. *The Galathea Deep Sea Expedition 1950–1952.* Allen and Unwin.

KUBODERA, T. and K. MORI. 2005. First-ever observations of a live giant squid in the wild. *Proceedings of the Royal Society B* doi: 10.1098/rspb.2005.3158.

LACK, M. and G. SANT. 2001. *Patagonian Toothfish: Are Conservation and Trade Measures Working?* TRAFFIC International.

LAGLER, K. F., J. E. BARDACH, and R. R. MILLER. 1962. *Ichthyology.* John Wiley & Sons.

LAIST, D. W., A. R. KNOWLTON, J. G. MEAD, A. S. COLLETT, and M. PODESTA. 2001. Collisions between ships and whales. *Marine Mammal Science* 17 (1): 35–75.

LANGMUIR, C., S. HUMPHRIS, D. FORNARI, C. VAN DOVER, K. VON DAMM, M. K. TIVER, D. COLODNER, J.-L. CHALOU, D. DESONIE, C. WILSON, Y. FOUQUET, G. KLINKHAMMER, and H. BOUGAULT. 1997. Hydrothermal vents near a mantle hot spot: the Lucky Strike vent field at 37°N on the Mid-Atlantic Ridge. *Earth and Planetary Science Letters* 148 (1–2): 69–91.

LASSEN, T. J. 1999. Census of Marine Life: Fishing industry perspectives. *Oceanography* 12 (3): 39–46.

LEVI, C., G. STONE, and J. R. SCHUBEL. 1999. Censusing non-fish nekton. *Oceanography* 12 (3): 15–16.

LEVITAN, D. R. and T. M. MCGOVERN. 2005. The Allee Effect in the sea. Pp. 47–57 in E. Norse and L. B. Crowder, eds. *Marine Conservation Biology.* Island Press

LIPINSKI, M. and K. TUROBOYSKI. 1983. The ammonium content in the tissues of selected species of squid (Cepahalopoda: Teuthoidea). *Journal of Experimental Marine Biology and Ecology* 69: 145–150.

LOVGREN, S. 2005. Jumbo squid mass "suicide" stumps California scientists. *National Geographic News* http://news.national geographic.com/news/2005/02/0223 _050223_gia.

Lutz, R. A., T. M. Shank, and R. Evans. 2001. Life after death in the deep sea. *American Scientist* 89 (5): 422–431.

Maas, P. A. Y., G. D. O'Mullan, R. A. Lutz, and R. C. Vrijenhoek. 1999. Genetic and morphometric characterization of mussels (Bivalvia: Mytilidae) from Mid-Atlantic hydrothermal vents. *Biological Bulletin* 196: 265–272.

Makris, N., P. Ratilal, D. T. Symonds, and R. W. Nero. 2004. Continuous wide area monitoring of fish shoaling behavior with acoustic waveguide sensing and bioclutter implications. *Journal of the Acoustical Society of America* 115 (5): 2619.

Makris, N., Y. Lai, I. Bertsatos, D. T. Symonds, S. Lee, and P. Ratilal. 2004. Expected Doppler shift and spread in long range scattering from fish schools on the continental shelf. *Journal of the Acoustical Society of America* 116 (4): 2488.

Makris, N., P. Ratilal, Y. Lai, D. T. Symonds, L. A. Ruhlmann, and E. K. Scheer. 2002. The Geoclutter Experiment 2001: Remote acoustic imaging of sub-bottom and seafloor geomorphology in continental shelf waters. *Journal of the Acoustical Society of America* 112 (5): 2280.

Mann, N. H., A. Cook, A. Millard, S. Bailey, and M. Clokie. 2003. Bacterial photosynthesis genes in a virus. *Nature* 424: 741.

Marinatos, N. 1985. *Art and Religion in Thera: Reconstructing a Bronze Age Society.* Andromedas.

Markaida, U., J. J.C. Rosenthal, and W. F. Gilly. 2005. Tagging studies on the jumbo squid (*Dosidicus gigas*) in the Gulf of California, Mexico. *Fisheries Bulletin* 103: 219–226.

Markaida, U., C. Quiñones-Velásquez, and O. Sosa-Nishizaki. 2004. Age, growth and maturation of jumbo squid *Dosidicus gigas* (Cephalopoda: Ommastrephidae) from the Gulf of California, Mexico. *Fisheries Research* 66: 31–47.

Marshall, N. 1999. *In the Wake of a Great Yankee Oceanographer.* Anchorage.

Masters, R. 2005. Real sea monsters. *Monterey County Weekly.* March 10.

Matsen, B. 2005. *Descent: The Heroic Discovery of the Abyss.* Pantheon.

Mayer, L. A., A. N. Shor, J. H. Clarke, and D. J. Piper. 1988. Dense biological communities at 3,850m on the Laurentian Fan and their relationship to the deposits of the 1929 Grand Banks Earthquake. *Deep-Sea Research* 35 (8A): 1235–46.

McArthur, T., E. C. V. Butler, and G. D. Jackson. 2003. Mercury in the marine food chain of the Southern Ocean at Macquarie Island: An analysis of a top predator, Patagonian toothfish (*Dissostichus eleginoides*) and a mid-trophic species, the warty squid (*Moroteuthis ingens*). *Polar Biology* 27: 1–5.

McCabe, H. and J. Wright. 2000. Tangled tale of a lost, stolen, and disputed coelacanth. *Nature* 406: 114.

McGowan, J. A. 1999. A biological World Ocean Circulation Experiment (WOCE). *Oceanography* 12 (3): 4–5.

McHugh, J. L. 1974. Role and history of the IWC. Pp. 305–335 in W. E. Schevill, ed. *The Whale Problem.* Harvard University Press.

McSweeny, E. S. 1970. Description of the juvenile form of the Antarctic squid *Mesonychoteuthis hamiltoni* Robson. *Malacologia* 10: 323–332.

MELLINGER, D. and J. BARLOW. 2002. *Future Directions for Acoustic Marine Mammal Surveys: Stock Assessment and Habitat Use.* Report of a workshop held in La Jolla, CA, 20–22 November 2002. NOAA OAR Special Report, NOAA/PMEL Contribution No. 2557. 37 pp.

MELLINGER, D. K., C. CARSON, and C. W. CLARK. 2000. Characteristics of minke whale (*Balaenoptera acutorostrata*) pulse trains recorded near Puerto Rico. *Marine Mammal Science* 16: 739–756.

MELLINGER, D. K., K. M. STAFFORD, and C. G. FOX. 2004. Seasonal occurrence of sperm whales (*Physeter macrocephalus*) sounds in the Gulf of Alaska. *Marine Mammal Science* 20 (1): 48–62.

MELLINGER, D. K., K. M. STAFFORD, S. E. MOORE, L. MUNGER, and C. G. FOX. 2004. Detection of North Pacific right whale (*Eubalaena japonica*) calls in the Gulf of Alaska. *Marine Mammal Science* 20 (4): 872–879.

MELVILLE, H. 1851. *Moby-Dick.* Harper and Brothers.

M'GONIGLE, R. M. 1980. The "economizing" of ecology: why big, rare whales still die. *Ecology Law Quarterly* 9 (119): 121–237.

MILIUS, S. 2001a. It's a snake! No, a fish. An octopus? *Science News* 160 (9): 132.

——. 2001b. Unknown squids—with elbows—tease science. *Science News* 160 (12): 390.

——. 2005. Decades of dinner: Underwater community begins with the remains of a whale. *Science News* 167: 298–300.

MILLER, J. E. and D. L. PAWSON. 1989. *Hansenothuria benti*, new genus, species (Echinodermata: Holothuroidea) from the Tropical Western Atlantic: a bathyal, epibenthic holothurian with swimming abilities. *Proceedings of the Biological Society of Washington* 102 (4): 977–86.

——. 1990. Swimming sea cucumbers (Echinodermata: Holothuroidea): a survey, with analysis of swimming behavior in four bathyal species. *Smithsonian Contributions to the Marine Sciences* 35: 1–18.

MILLS, E. L. 1989. *Biological Oceanography: An Early History,1870–1960.* Cornell University Press.

MITCHELL, E. D. 1975. Preliminary report on Nova Scotia fishery for sperm whales. *Report of the International Whaling Commission* 25: 226–235.

——. 1977. Sperm whale maximum length limit: proposed protection of "harem masters." *Report of the International Whaling Commission.* 27: 224–227.

MØLLER, P. R., J. G. NIELSEN, and I. FOSSEN. 2003. Patagonian toothfish found off Greenland. *Nature* 421: 599.

MOORE, L. R., G. ROCAP, and E. W. CHISHOLM. 1998. Physiology and molecular phylogeny of coexisting *Prochlorococcus* ecotypes. *Nature* 393: 464–467.

MOORE, S. E., W. A. WATKINS, M. A. DAHER, J. R. DAVIES, and M. E. DAHLHEIM. 2002. Blue whale habitat associations in the Northwest Pacific: Analysis of remotely-sensed data using a Geographic Information System. *Oceanography* 15 (3): 20–25.

MORALES-BOJÓRQUEZ, E., S. MARTÍNEZ-AGUILAR, F. ARREGUÍN-SÁNCHEZ, M. O. NEVÁREZ-MARTÍNEZ, and G. I. RIVERA-PARRA. 2001. Estimations and catchability-at-length for the jumbo squid (*Dosidicus gigas*) fishery in the Gulf of California, Mexico. *CalCOFI Report* 42: 167–171.

MORROW, J. E. and R. H. GIBBS. 1964. Melanostomiatidae. Pp. 351–511 in H.B. Bigelow, D. M. Cohen, M. W. Dick, R. H. Gibbs, M. Grey, J. E. Morrow, L. P. Schultz, and V. Waters, eds. *Part IV, Fishes of the Western North Atlantic*. Memoirs of the Sears Foundation for Marine Research. New Haven: Yale University.

MÖRZER BRUYNS, W. J. F. 1971. *Field Guide of Whales and Dolphins*. Amsterdam.

MOYLE, P.B. and J. J. CECH. 2004. *Fishes: A History of Ichthyology*. Prentice-Hall.

MURRAY, J. 1876. Preliminary reports to Professor Wyville Thomson, F.R.S., director of the civilian scientific staff, on work done on board the *Challenger*. *Proceedings of the Royal Society* 27: 471–531.

——. 1895. A summary of the scientific results obtained at the sounding, dredging and trawling stations of H.M.S. *Challenger*. *Report on the Scientific Results of the Voyage of H.M.S. Challenger During the Years 1873–76*. Summary of Results. 2: 1–1608.

MURRAY, J. and J. HJORT. 1912. *The Depths of the Ocean*. Macmillan. London. (1965 reprint, Weldon & Wesley, Ltd., Stechert-Hafner, Inc.)

MYERS, R. A. and C. A. OTTENSMEYER. 2005. Extinction risk in marine species. Pp. 58–79 in E. Norse and L. B. Crowder, eds., *Marine Conservation Biology*. Island Press

MYERS, R. A. and B. WORM. 2003. Rapid worldwide depletion of predatory fish communities. *Nature* 423: 280–283.

NAKAYA, K., K. YANO, K. TAKADA, and H. HIRUDA. 1997. Morphology of the first female megamouth shark, *Megachasma pelagios* (Elasmobranchii: Megachasmidae), landed at Fukuoka, Japan. Pp. 51–62 in K. Yano, J. F. Morrisey, Y. Yabumoto, and K. Nakaya (eds.). *Biology of the Megamouth Shark*. Tokai University Press.

NATIONAL ENVIRONMENTAL TRUST. 2001. *Destined for Extinction: The Fate of the Chilean Sea Bass*. NET.

——. 2004. *Black Market for White Gold: The Illegal Trade in Chilean Sea Bass*. NET.

NEALSON, K. H. 1997. Sediment bacteria: Who's there, what are they doing, and what's new? *Annual Review of Earth and Planetary Sciences* 25: 403–34.

NESIS, K. N. 1982. *Cephalopods of the World*. T. F. H. Publishing.

——. 1983. *Dosidicus gigas*. Pp. 215–231 in P. R. Boyle, ed. *Cephalopod Life Cycles, Vol. I: Species Accounts*. Academic Press.

NICOL, J. A. C. 1958. Observations on luminescence in pelagic animals. *Journal of the Marine Biological Association U.K.* 37: 705–22.

——. 1961. Luminescence in marine organisms. *Smithsonian Reports* 1960: 447–56.

——. 1967. The luminescence of fishes. *Symposium of the Zoological Society London* 19: 27–56.

NIELSEN, J. G. 1964. Fishes from depths exceeding 6000 meters. *Galathea Report* 7: 113–24.

NIELSEN, J. G. and V. LARSEN. 1970. Remarks on the identity of the giant *Dana* eel larva. *Vidensk. Medd. fra Dansk Naturh. Foren.* 133: 149–57.

NIERENBERG, W. A. 1999. The diversity of fishes: The known and the unknown. *Oceanography* 12 (3): 6–7.

NOLAN, R. S. and R. H. ROSENBLATT. 1975. A review of the deep-sea anglerfish genus *Lasiognathus* (Pisces: Thaumatichthyidae). *Copeia* 1975: 60–66.

NORMAN, M. V. 2000. *Cephalopods: A World Guide.* Conch Books.

NORMAN, M. V., J. FINN, and T. TREGENZA. 2001. Dynamic mimicry in an Indo-Malayan octopus. *Proceedings of the Royal Society London* 268: 1755–1758.

NORMILE, D. 2000. Japan's whaling program carries heavy baggage. *Science* 289: 2264–2265.

NORRIS, K. S. and B. MØHL. 1983. Can odontocetes debilitate prey with sound? *American Naturalist* 122 (1): 85–104.

NORSE, E. 2000. Protecting coral. *New York Times.* September 26: D3.

NORSE, E. and L. B. CROWDER. 2005. Why *marine* conservation biology? Pp. 1–18 in E. Norse and L. B. Crowder, eds. *Marine Conservation Biology.* Island Press.

NYBAKKEN, J. W. and S. K. WEBSTER. 1998. Life in the ocean. *Scientific American* 273 (5): 74–87.

O'DOR, R. K. 1983. *Illex illecebrosus.* Pp.175–199 in P. R. Boyle, ed. *Cephalopod Life Cycles, Vol. I: Species Accounts.* Academic Press.

——. 2003. *The Unknown Ocean: The Baseline Report of the Census of Marine Life Research Program.* Consortium for Oceanographic Research and Education.

OHSUMI, S. 1980. Catches of sperm whales by modern whaling in the North Pacific. *Report of the International Whaling Commission* (Special Issue 2: Sperm Whales): 11–19.

OKUTANI, T. 1983. *Todarodes pacificus.* Pp.201–214 in P. R. Boyle, ed. *Cephalopod Life Cycles, Vol. I: Species Accounts.* Academic Press.

OSWALD, J. N., J. BARLOW, and T. F. NORRIS. 2003. Acoustic identification of nine delphinid species in the eastern tropical Pacific Ocean. *Marine Mammal Science* 19 (1): 20–37.

PACE, N. 1997. A molecular view of microbial diversity and the biosphere. *Science* 276: 734–40.

PALENIK, B., B. BRAHAMSHA, F. W. LARIMER, M. LAND, L. HAUSER, P. CHAIN, J. LAMERDIN, W. REGALA, E. E. ALLEN, J. MCCARREN, I. PAULSEN, A. DUFRESNE, F. PARTENSKY, E. A. WEBB, and J. WATERBURY. 2003. The genome of a motile marine *Synechococcus. Nature* 424: 1037–1042.

PALUMBI, S. R. and D. HEDGECOCK. 2005. Implications of marine population biology to conservation policy. Pp. 33–46 in E. Norse and L. B. Crowder, eds. *Marine Conservation Biology.* Island Press.

PALUMBI, S. R. and J. ROMAN. 2004. Counting whales in the North Atlantic—response. *Science* 303: 40.

PANDOLFI, J. M., J. B. C. JACKSON, N. BARON, R. H. BRADBURY, H. M. GUZMAN, T. P. HUGHES, C. V. KAPPEL, F. MICHELI, J. C. OGDEN, H. P. POSSINGHAM, and E. SALA. 2005. Are U.S. coral reefs on the slippery slope to slime? *Science* 307: 1725–1726.

PANDOLFI, J. M., R. H. BRADBURY, E. SALA, T. P. HUGHES, K. A. BJORNDAL, R. G. COOKE, D. MCARDLE, L. MCCLENACHAN, M. J. H. NEWMAN, G. PAREDES, R. R. WARNER, and J.B.C. JACKSON. 2003. Global trajectories of the long-term decline of coral reef ecosystems. *Science* 301: 955–958.

PARFIT, M. 1995. Diminishing returns: exploiting the ocean's bounty. *National Geographic* 188 (5): 2–37.

PARRISH, J. K. 1999. Toward remote species identification. *Oceanography* 12 (3): 30–32.

PARTENSKY, F., W. R. HESS, and D. VAULOT. 1999. *Prochlorococcus*, a marine photosynthetic prokaryote of global significance. *Microbiology and Molecular Biology Reviews* 63 (1): 106–127.

PASCUAL, M., X. RODÓ, S. P. ELLNER, R. COLWELL, and M. J. BOUMA. 2000. Cholera dynamics and El Niño–Southern Oscillation. *Science* 289: 1766–1769.

PATEK, S. N., W. L. KORFF, and R. L. CALDWELL. 2004. Deadly strike mechanism of a mantis shrimp. *Nature* 428: 819–820.

PAULY, D. 1995. Anecdotes and the shifting baseline syndrome of fisheries. *Trends in Ecology and Evolution* 10 (10): 430.

PAULY, D. and J. MACLEAN. 2002. *In a Perfect Ocean: The State of Fisheries and Ecosystems in the North Atlantic Ocean.* Island Press.

PAULY, D. and M.-L. PALOMARES. 2005. Fishing down marine food web: It is far more pervasive than we thought. *Bulletin of Marine Science* 76 (2): 197–212.

PAULY, D. and R. WATSON. 2003. Counting the last fish. *Scientific American* 289 (1): 42–47.

PAULY, D., V. CHRISTENSEN, R. FROESE, and M.-L. PALOMARES. 2000. Fishing down aquatic food webs. *American Scientist* 88 (1): 46–51.

PAULY, D., V. CHRISTENSEN, J. DALSGAARD, R. FROESE, and F. TORRES. 1998. Fishing down marine food webs. *Science* 279: 860–63.

PAULY, D., J. ALDER, E. BENNETT, V. CHRISTENSEN, P. TYEDMERS, and R. WATSON. 2003. The future for fisheries. *Science* 302: 1359–1361.

PAWSON, D. L. 1976. Some aspects of the biology of deep-sea echinoderms. *Thalassia Jugoslavica* 12: 287–93.

——. 1982. Deep-sea echinoderms in the Tongue of the Ocean, Bahama Islands: A survey using the research submersible *Alvin*. *Australian Museum Memoir* 16: 129–45.

——. 1985. *Psychropotes hyalinus*, a new species, a swimming elasipod sea cucumber (Echinodermata: Holothuroidea) from the North Central Pacific Ocean. *Proceedings of the Biological Society of Washington* 98 (1): 523–25.

PAYNE, R. 1970. *Songs of the Humpback Whale.* Capitol Records. ST-620.

PAYNE, R. (ed.). 1983. *Communication and Behavior of Whales*. American Association for the Advancement of Science.

PAYNE, R. and S. MCVAY. Songs of humpback whales. *Science* 173: 585–597.

PERRIN, W.F. and J. R. GERACI. 2002. Stranding. Pp. 1192–1197 in W.F. Perrin, B. Würsig, and J. G. M. Thewissen, eds. *Encyclopedia of Marine Mammals*. Academic Press.

PIATKOWSKI, U., G. J. PIERCE, and M. MORAIS DA CUNHA. 2001. Impact of cephalopods on the food chain and their interaction with the environment and fisheries: An overview. *Fisheries Research* 52: 5–10.

PICCARD, J. 1960. Man's deepest dive. *National Geographic* 118 (2): 225–39.

——. 1971. *The Sun Beneath the Sea*. Scribner's.

PICCARD, J. and R. S. DIETZ. 1957. Oceanographic observations by the bathyscaph *Trieste* (1953–1956). *Deep-Sea Research* 4: 221–29.

——. 1961. *Seven Miles Down: The Story of the Bathyscaph* TRIESTE. Putnam.

PITCHER, T. J. 2001. Fisheries managed to rebuild ecosystems? Reconstructing the past to salvage the future. *Ecological Applications* 11 (2): 601–617.

PITMAN, R. L. 2002. Alive and whale: a missing cetacean resurfaces in the tropics. *Natural History* 111 (7): 32–36.

——. 2004. Good whale hunting. *Natural History* XX: 24–28.

PITMAN, R. L. and P. ENSOR. 2003. Three forms of killer whales (*Orcinus orca*) in Antarctic waters. *Journal of Cetacean Research and Management* 5 (2): 131–139.

PITMAN, R. L., A. AGUAYO, and J. URBAN. 1987. Observations of an unidentified beaked whale (*Mesoplodon* sp.) in the Eastern Tropical Pacific. *Marine Mammal Science* 3 (4): 345–352.

PITMAN, R. L., D. M. PALACIOS, P. L. R. BRENNAN, B. J. BRENNAN, K. C. BALCOMB, and T. MIYASHITA. 1999. Sightings and possible identity of a bottlenose whale in the tropical Indopacific: *Indopacetus pacificus*? *Marine Mammal Science* 15 (2): 531–49.

PLINY. n.d. *Natural History*. 10 Vols. Loeb Classical Library. Harvard University Press.

POMEROY, L. R. and W. J. WIEBE. 1988. Energetics of microbial food webs. *Hydrobiologia* 159: 7–18.

PORCH, C. E. 2005. The sustainability of Western Atlantic bluefin tuna: A warm-blooded fish in a hot-blooded fishery. *Bulletin of Marine Science.* 76 (2): 363–384.

POUYAUD, L., S. WIRJOATMODJO, I. RACHMATIKA, A. TJAKRAWIDJAJA, R. HADIATY, and W. HADIE. 1999. Une nouvelle espèce de coelacanthe. Preuves génétiques et morphologiques. *Comptes Rendus Academie des Sciences Paris* 322: 261–67.

PREIKSHOT, D. and D. PAULY. 2005. Global fisheries and marine conservation: Is coexistence possible? Pp. 185–197 in E. Norse and L. B. Crowder, eds. *Marine Conservation Biology*. Island Press

RADCLIFFE, W. 1921. *Fishing from the Earliest Times*. John Murray. (1974 reprint, Ares Publishers, Chicago.)

RALOFF, J. 2005. Empty nets. *Science News* 167 (23): 360–362.

REID, C. 2001. Potential for historical-ecological studies of Latin American fisheries. Pp. 141–166 in P. Holm, T. D. Smith, and D. J. Starkey (eds.) 2001. *Research in Maritime History No. 21*. International Maritime History Association/Census of Marine Life.

REVKIN, A. C. 2005. Tracking the imperiled bluefin from ocean to sushi platter. *New York Times* May 3: F1–F4.

REX, M. A., C. T. STUART, and G. COYNE. 2000. Latitudinal gradients of species richness in deep-sea benthos of the North Atlantic. *Proceedings of the National Academy of Sciences* 97 (8): 4082–4085.

RICE, D.W. 1989. Sperm whale, *Physeter macrocephalus*. Pp. 177–233 in S.H. Ridgway and R. Harrison, eds., *Handbook of Marine Mammals, Vol. 4: River Dolphins and the Larger Toothed Whales*. Academic Press.

RICHERSON, P., R. ARMSTRONG, and C. R. GOLDMAN. 1970. Contemporaneous dis-equilibrium, a new hypothesis to explain the "Paradox of the Plankton." *Proceedings of the National Academy of Sciences*. 67 (4): 1710–1714.

RILEY, G. A. and D. F. BUMPUS. 1946. Phytoplankton-zooplankton relationships on Georges Bank. *Journal of Marine Research* 6: 33–47.

ROBERTS, C. M. 1997. Ecological advice for the global fisheries crisis. *Trends in Ecology and Evolution* 12 (1): 35–38.

ROBERTS, C. M. and J. P. HAWKINS. 1999. Extinction risk in the sea. *Trends in Ecology and Evolution* 14 (6): 241–46.

ROBISON, B. 1995. Light in the ocean's midwater. *Scientific American* 273 (1): 60–64.

ROCAP, G., F. W. LARIMER, J. LAMERDIN, S. MALFATTI, P. CHAIN, N. A. AHLGREN, A. ARELLANO, M. COLEMAN, L. HAUSER, W. R. HESS, Z.I. JOHNSON, M. LAND, D. LINDELL, A. F. POST, W. REGALA, M. SHAH, S. L. SHAW, C. STEGLICH, M. B. SULLIVAN, C. S. TING, A. TOLONEN, E.A. WEBB, E. R. ZINSER, and S. W. CHISHOLM. 2003. Genome divergence in two *Prochlorococcus* ecotypes reflects oceanic niche differentiation. *Nature* 1042–10.

RODHOUSE, P. G. 2001. Managing and forecasting squid fisheries in variable environments. *Fisheries Research* 54: 3–8.

RODHOUSE, P. G. and M. R. CLARKE. 1985. Growth and distribution of young *Mesonychoteuthis hamiltoni* Robson (Mollusca: Cephalopoda): an Antarctic squid. *Vie Milieu* 35 (3/4): 223–230.

RODHOUSE, P. G. and M. G. WHITE. 1995. Cephalopods occupy the ecological niche of epipelagic fish in the Antarctic Polar Frontal Zone. *Biological Bulletin* 189: 77–80.

ROFEN, R. R. 1966. Family Paralepididae. Pp. 205–462. *Part V. Fishes of the Western North Atlantic*. Memoirs of the Sears Foundation for Marine Research. Yale University.

ROMAN, J. and S. R. PALUMBI. 2003. Whales before whaling in the North Atlantic. *Science* 301: 508–510.

RONA, P. 2004. Secret survivor. *Natural History* 113 (7): 50–55.

ROPER, C. F. E. and W. RATHJEN. 1998. World-wide squid fisheries: A summary of landings and capture techniques. *Journal of Cephalopod Biology* 2 (1): 23–30.

ROPER, C. F. E., C. C. LU, and M. VECCHIONE. 1998. A revision of the systematics and distribution of *Illex* species (Cephalopoda: Ommastrephidae). Pp. 405–423 in N. A. Voss, M. Vecchione, R. B. Toll, and M. J. Sweeney, eds. *Systematics and Biogeography of Cephalopods*. Smithsonian Institution Press.

ROPER, C. F. E., M. J. SWEENEY, and C. E. NAUEN. 1984. *FAO Species Catalogue. Vol. 3. Cephalopods of the World. An Annotated Catalogue of Species of Interest to Fisheries*. Rome.

ROSS, J. 1819. *A Voyage of Discovery made under the Orders of the Admiralty, in HMS* Isabella *and* Alexander, *for the purpose of exploring Baffin's Bay, and inquiring into the probability of a North-West Passage*. John Murray.

ROUSE, G., W. S. K. GOFFREDI, and R. C. VRIJEN-HOEK. 2004. *Osedax*: Bone-eating marine worms with dwarf males. *Science* 305: 668–671.

ROZWADOWSKI, H. M. 2005. *Fathoming the Ocean: The Discovery and Exploration of the Deep Sea*. Harvard University Press.

SAFINA, C. 1995. The world's imperiled fish. *Scientific American* 273 (5): 46–53.

———. 1997. *Song for the Blue Ocean*. Henry Holt.

———. 1998a. Song for the swordfish. *Audubon* 100 (3): 58–69.

———. 1998b. Scorched-earth fishing. *Issues in Science and Technology* 14 (3): 33–36.

SAFINA, C., A. ROSENBERG, R. A. MYERS, T. J. QUINN, and J. S. COLLIE. 2005. U.S. ocean fish recovery: staying the course. *Science* 309: 707–708.

SAKURAI, Y., H. KIYOFUJI, S. SAITOH, T. GOTO, and Y. HIYAMA. 2000. Changes in inferred spawning areas of *Todarodes pacificus* (Cephalopoda Ommasrephidae) due to changing environmental conditions. *ICES Journal of Marine Sciences* 57: 24–30.

SANDERS, H. L. 1968. Marine benthic diversity: A comparative study. *American Naturalist* 102 (925): 243–282.

SANDERSON, I. 1956. *Follow the Whale*. Little, Brown.

SAVOURS, A. 2001. *The Voyages of the Discovery*. Chatham.

SCAMMON, C. M. 1874. *The Marine Mammals of the Northwestern Coast of North America; Together with an Account of the American Whale Fishery*. Carmany, and G. P. Putnam's.

SCHEFFER, M., S. RINALDI, J. HUISMAN, and F. J. WESSING. 2003. Why plankton communities have no equilibrium: solutions to the paradox. *Hydrobiologia* 491: 9–18.

SCHEFFER, V. B. 1976. Exploring the lives of whales. *National Geographic* 150 (6): 752–767.

SCHEVILL, W. E. and B. LAWRENCE. 1949. Underwater listening to the white porpoise (*Delphinaptrerus leucas*). *Science* 109: 143–144.

SCHLEE, S. 1970. Prince Albert's way of catching squid. *Natural History* 74 (2): 20–25.

——. 1973. *The Edge of an Unfamiliar World: A History of Oceanography*. E. P. Dutton.

Schmidt, J. 1922. Live specimens of *Spirula*. *Nature* 110: 788–90.

Scoresby, W. 1820. *An Account of the Arctic Regions with a History and Description of the Northern Whale Fishery*. 2 Vols. Archibald Constable. (David & Charles reprint, 1969.)

Shreeve, J. 2004. Craig Venter's epic voyage to redefine the origin of species. *Wired* 12 (8): 104–113.

Simmonds, M. P. and L. F. Lopez-Jurado. 1991. Whales and the military. *Nature* 351: 448.

Smith, C. R., H. Kukert, R. A. Wheatcroft, P. A. Jumars, and J. W. Deming. 1989. Vent fauna on whale remains. *Nature* 341: 27–28.

Smith, D. G. 1970. Notacanthiform leptocephali in the Western North Atlantic. *Copeia* 1970 (1): 1–9.

——. 1989a. Order Anguilliformes. Family Anguillidae (freshwater eels). Pp. 25–47 in Part 9, Vol. 1. *Fishes of the Western North Atlantic*. Memoirs of the Sears Foundation for Marine Research. Yale University.

——. 1989b. Suborder Cyematoidei. Family Cyematidae. Pp. 630–35 in Part 9, Vol. 1. *Fishes of the Western North Atlantic*. Memoirs of the Sears Foundation for Marine Research. Yale University.

——. 1989c. Introduction to Leptocephali. Pp. 657–68 in Part 9, Vol. 2. *Fishes of the Western North Atlantic*. Memoirs of the Sears Foundation for Marine Research. Yale University.

Smith, D. G. and J. G. Nielsen. 1989. Family Nemichthyidae (Snipe Eels.) Pp. 441–59 in Part 9, Vol. 1. *Fishes of the Western North Atlantic*. Memoirs of the Sears Foundation for Marine Research. Yale University.

Smith, J. L. B. 1956. *Old Fourlegs: The Story of the Coelacanth*. Longmans Green.

Smith, T. D. 2001. Examining cetacean ecology using historical fishery data. Pp. 207–214 in P. Holm, T. D. Smith, and D. J. Starkey (eds.) 2001. *Research in Maritime History No. 21*. International Maritime History Association/Census of Marine Life.

Spärck, R. 1956. The density of animals on the ocean floor. Pp. 196–201 in A. F. Bruun, S. Greve, H. Mielche, and R. Sparck, eds. *The Galathea Deep Sea Expedition 1950–1952*. Allen and Unwin.

Springer, V.G. 1999. Are the Indonesian and western Indian Ocean coelacanths conspecific: a prediction. *Environmental Biology of Fishes* 54: 453–456.

Spry, W. J. J. 1877. *The Cruise of Her Majesty's Ship "Challenger."* Harper & Brothers.

Stafford, K. M., C. G. Fox, and D. S. Clark. 1998. Long-range acoustic detection and localization of blue whale calls in the northeast Pacific Ocean. *Journal of the Acoustical Society of America* 104 (6): 3616–3625.

Steele, J. H. and M. Schumacher. 1999. On the history of marine fisheries: Report of the Woods Hole workshop. *Oceanography* 12 (3): 28–29.

——. 2000. Ecosystem structure before fishing. *Fisheries Research* 44: 201–205.

STEJNEGER, L. 1884. Contributions to the history of the Commander Islands. No. 2. investigations relating to the date of the extermination of Steller's sea-cow. *Proceedings of the United States National Museum* 8: 181–189.

———. 1887. How the great northern sea-cow (*Rytina*) became exterminated. *American Naturalist* 21: 1047–54.

———. 1936. *Georg Wilhelm Steller*. Harvard University Press.

STELLER, G. W. 1781. *Journal of a Voyage with Bering, 1741–1742*. (Translation by O.W. Frost. 1988 Edition, Stanford University Press.)

STEVENS, J. D., R. BONFIL, N. K. DULVY, and P. A. WALKER. 2000. The effects of fishing on sharks, rays, and chimeras (chondrichthyans), and the implications for marine ecosystems. *ICES Journal of Marine Sciences* 57: 476–494.

STOECKLE, M. 2003. Taxonomy, DNA, and the bar code of life. *BioScience* 53 (9): 2–3.

STOMP, M., J. HUISMAN, F. DE JONGH, A. J. VERAART, D. GERLA, M. RIJKEBOER, B. W. IBELINGS, U. I. A. WOLLENZEIN, and L. J. STAL. 2004. Adaptive divergence in pigment composition promoted plankton biodiversity. *Nature* 432: 104–107.

STONE, G., J. SCHUBEL, and H. TAUSIG. 1999. Electronic marine animal tagging: New frontier in ocean science. *Oceanography* 12 (3): 24–27.

SYMONDS, D. T., P. RATILAL, R. W. NERO, and N. MAKRIS. 2003. Fish schools are the dominant cause of long range active sonar clutter in the New Jersey Continental Shelf: Quantitative correlations. *Journal of the Acoustical Society of America* 114 (4): 2375.

SYMONDS, D. T., P. RATILAL, N. MAKRIS, and R. W. NERO. 2004. Inferring fish school distributions from long range acoustic images: main acoustic clutter experiment. *Journal of the Acoustical Society of America* 115 (5): 2618–2619.

TAYLOR, B., J. BARLOW, R. PITMAN, L. BALLANCE, T. KLINGER, D. DEMASTER, J. HILDEBRAND, J. URBAN, D. PLACIOS, and J. MEAD. 2004. A call for research to assess risk of acoustic impact on beaked whale populations. *Scientific Report of the International Whaling Commission* SC/56/E36.

TAYLOR, L. R. 1993. *Sharks of Hawaii: Their Biological and Cultural Significance.* University of Hawaii Press.

TAYLOR, L. R., L. J. V. COMPAGNO, and P. J. STRUHSAKER. 1983. Megamouth—a new species, genus, and family of lamnoid shark (*Megachasma pelagios*, family Megachasmidae) from the Hawaiian Islands. *Proceedings of the California Academy of Sciences* 43 (8): 87–110.

THISTLE, D. 1981. Natural physical disturbances and communities of marine soft bottoms. *Marine Ecological Progress Series* 6: 223–228.

THOMAS, P. 2004. Are squid vicious? *Los Angeles Times* February 10.

THOMSON, C. W. 1873. *The Depths of the Sea.* Macmillan.

——. 1878. *The Atlantic: A Preliminary Account of the General Results of the Exploring Voyage of H.M.S.* Challenger. Macmillan.

THOMSON, K. S. 1991. *Living Fossil: The Story of the Coelacanth.* Norton.

THORNDIKE, J. J. (ed.). 1980. *Mysteries of the Deep.* American Heritage.

TOWNSEND, C. H. 1935. The distribution of certain whales as shown by logbook records of American whaleships. *Zoologica* 29 (1): 1–50.

TRAVIS, J. 2003. Probing ocean depths: Photosynthetic bacteria bare their DNA. *Science News* 164 (7): 14.

TULL, M. and T. POLACHEK. 2001. The potential for historical studies of fisheries in Australia and New Zealand. Pp. 181–205 in P. Holm, T. D. Smith, and D. J. Starkey (eds.) 2001. *Research in Maritime History No. 21.* International Maritime History Association/Census of Marine Life.

UIBLEIN, F. 2005. White orange roughy. http://www.mar-eco.no/learning-one /backgrounders/deepsea_life_forms /white_orange_roughy

VAN DOVER, C. L. 1989. Do "eyeless" shrimp see the light of glowing deep-sea vents? *Oceanus* 31 (4): 47–52.

——. 1993. Depths of ignorance. *Discover* 14 (9): 37–39.

——. 1996. *The Octopus's Garden: Hydrothermal Vents and Other Mysteries of the Deep Sea.* Addison-Wesley.

——. 2000. *The Ecology of Deep-Sea Hydrothermal Vents.* Princeton University Press.

VAN DOVER, C. L., P. J. S. FRANKS, and R. D. BALLARD. 1987. Prediction of hydro-thermal vent locations from distribution of brachyuran crabs. *Limnology and Oceanography* 32: 1006–10.

VAN DOVER, C. L., G. T. REYNOLDS, A. D. CHAVE, and J. A. TYSON. 1996. Light at deep-sea hydrothermal vents. *Geophysical Research Letters* 23 (16): 2049–2052.

VAN DOVER, C. L., E. Z. SZUTS, B. C. CHAMBERLAIN, and J. R. CANN. 1989. A novel eye in "eyeless" shrimp from hydrothermal vents of the Mid-Atlantic Ridge. *Nature* 337: 458–60.

VAN DOVER, C. L., B. FRY, J. F. GRASSLE, S. HUMPHRIS, and P. A. RONA. 1988. Feeding biology of the shrimp *Rimicaris exoculata* at hydrothermal vents on the Mid-Atlantic Ridge. *Marine Biology* 98 (2): 1432–1793.

VAN DOVER, C. L., C. R. GERMAN, K. G. SPEER, L. M. PARSON, and R. C. VRIJEN-HOEK. 2002. Evolution and biogeography of deep-sea and seep invertebrates. *Science* 295: 1253–1257.

VAN DOVER, C. L., S. E. HUMPHRIS, D. FORNARI, C. M. CAVANAUGH, R. COLLIER, S. G. GOFFREDI, J. HASHIMOTO, M. D. LILLEY, A. L. REYSENBACH, T. M. SHANK, K. L. VON DAMM, A. BANTA, R. M. GALLANT, D. GÖTZ, D. GREEN, J. HALL, T. L. HARMER, L. A. HURTADO, P. JOHNSON, Z. P. MCKINESS, C. MEREDITH, E. OLSON, I. L. PAN, M. TURNIPSEED, Y. WON, C. R. YOUNG III, and R. C. VRIJENHOEK. 2001. Biogeography and ecological setting of Indian Ocean hydrothermal vents. *Science* 294: 818–823.

VECCHIONE, M., R. E. YOUNG, A. GUERRA, D. J. LINDSAY, D. A. CLAGUE, J. M. BERNHARD, W. W. SAGER, A. F. GONZALEZ, F. J. ROCHA, and M. SEGONZAC. 2001. Worldwide observations of remarkable deep-sea squids. *Science* 294: 2505.

VENTER, C. 2005. Sea of genes. *New Scientist* 186 (2499): 21.

VERNE, J. 1864. *Voyage to the Center of the Earth.* Paris.

———. 1870. *Twenty Thousand Leagues Under the Sea.* Paris.

VON BRANDT, A. 1972. *Revised and Enlarged Fish Catching Methods of the World.* Fishing News (Books).

VON DAMM, K. L. 2001. Lost city found. *Nature* 412: 127–128.

VOJKOVICH, M. 1998. The California fishery for market squid (*Loligo opalescens*). *CalCOFI Report* 39: 55–60.

VOSS, N. A. 1980. A generic revision of the Cranchiidae (Cephalopoda; Oegopsida). *Bulletin of Marine Science* 30: 365–412.

VOSS, N. A., K. N. NESIS, and P. G. RODHOUSE. 1998. The cephalopod family Histioteuthidae (Oegopsida): Systematics, Biology, and Biogeography. Pp. 293–372 in N. A. Voss, M. Vecchione, R. B. Toll, and M. J. Sweeney, eds. *Systematics and Biogeography of Cephalopods.* Smithsonian Institution Press.

WADE, N. 2004. A species in a second: Promise of DNA "bar codes." *New York Times.* December 14.

WALDMAN, P. 2005. Mercury and tuna: U.S. advice leaves lots of questions. *The Wall Street Journal* August 1: A1.

WARE, D. M. and R. E. THOMSON. 2005. Bottom-up ecosystem trophic dynamics determine fish production in the Northeast Pacific. *Science* 308: 1280–1284.

WATLING, L. and E. A. NORSE. 1998a. Effects of mobile fishing gear on marine benthos: introduction. *Conservation Biology* 12 (6): 1178–79.

———. 1998b. Disturbance of the seabed by mobile fishing gear: a comparison to forest clearcutting. *Conservation Biology* 12 (6): 1180–97.

WATSON, L. 1981. *Sea Guide to Whales of the World.* Hutchinson.

WELLS, H. G. 1905. "In the Abyss." Pp. 493–509 in *Twenty-Eight Science Fiction Stories by H. G. Wells.* Scribner's (Dover edition, 1952.)

WHEELWRIGHT, J. 2003. Squid sensitivity. *Discover* 24 (4): 42–49.

WHITE, T. H. 1954. *The Book of Beasts.* Jonathan Cape.

WHITEHEAD, H. 2002. Estimates of the current global population size and historical trajectory for sperm whales. *Marine Ecology Progress Series* 242: 249–304.

———. 2003. *Sperm Whales: Social Evolution in the Ocean.* University of Chicago Press.

WHITLEY, G. P. 1933. *Ompax spatuloides* Castelnau, a mythical Australian fish. *American Midland Naturalist* 67: 1–4.

———. 1940. *The Fishes of Australia. Part I. The Sharks, Rays, Devil-Fish, and Other Primitive Fishes of Australia and New Zealand.* Royal Zoological Society of New South Wales.

WILCOX, W. A. 1887. A man killed by a swordfish. *Bulletin of the U.S. Fisheries Commission* 6: 417.

WILSON, E. O. 2002. *The Future of Life.* Knopf.

WINSOR, M. P. 1991. *Reading the Shape of Nature: Comparative Zoology at the Agassiz Museum.* University of Chicago Press.

WOESE, C. R. 1998. Default taxonomy: Ernst Mayr's view of the microbial world. *Proceedings of the National Academy of Sciences* 95 (19): 11043–46.

WOLFF, T. 1960. The hadal community: an introduction. *Deep-Sea Research* 6: 5–124.

———. 1961a. Animal life from a single abyssal trawling. *Galathea Report* 5: 129–62.

———. 1961b. The deepest recorded fishes. *Nature* 190: 283.

———. 1970. The concept of the hadal or ultra-abyssal fauna. *Deep-Sea Research* 17: 983–1003.

———. 1971. *Archemide* dive 7 to 4160 metres at Madeira: observations and collecting results. *Vidensk. Meddr .Dansk naturh. Foren.* 134: 127–47.

———. 1977. Diversity and faunal composition of the deep-sea benthos. *Nature* 267 (5614): 780–85.

WOMMACK, K. E. and R. R. COLWELL. 2000. Virioplankton: Viruses in aquatic ecosystems. *Microbiology and Molecular Biology Reviews* 64 (1): 69–114.

WOOD, F. G. 1953. Underwater sound production and concurrent behavior of captive porpoises, *Tursiops truncatus* and *Stenella plagiodon. Bulletin of Marine Science of the Gulf and Caribbean.* 3: 120–133.

WORM, B., H. K. LOTZE, and R. A. MYERS. 2003. Predator diversity hotspots in the blue ocean. *Proceedings of the National Academy of Sciences USA* 100: 9884–9888.

WORM, B., M. SANDOW, A. OSCHLIES, H. K. LOTZE, and R. S. MYERS. 2005. Global patterns of predator diversity in the open ocean. *Science* 309: 1365–1369.

WRIGHT, P. 2005. Tag a giant. *Marlin* 24 (4): 66–71.

XIONG, J., W. M. FISHER, K. INOUE, M. NAKAHARA, and C. E. BAUER. 2000. Molecular evidence for the early evolution of photosynthesis. *Science* 289: 1724–30.

YABLOKOV, A.V. 1994. Validity of whaling data. *Nature* 367: 108.

YANO, K. and M. DAHLHEIM. 1996. Killer whale, *Orcinus orca,* depredation on longline catches of bottomfish in the southeastern Bering Sea and adjacent waters. *Fishery Bulletin* 93: 355–372.

YANO, K., J. F. MORRISEY, Y. YABUMOTO, and K. NAKAYA (eds.) 1997. *Biology of the Megamouth Shark.* Tokai University Press.

YOERGER, D. R. 1991. Robotic undersea technology. *Oceanus* 34 (1): 32–37.

YOUNG, E. 2003a. Giant squid emerges from the ocean's deep. *New Scientist* 178 (2390): 18.

——. 2003b. Monsters of the deep. *New Scientist* 178 (2406): 24–29.

——. 2005. The gruesome eating habits of the giant squid. *New Scientist* 187 (2510): 9.

ZEMSKY, V., Y. MIKHALIEV, and A. BERZIN. 1996. Supplementary information about Soviet whaling in the Southern Hemisphere. *Report of the International Whaling Commission* 46: 131–138.

Index of Subjects

ABE (Autonomous Benthic Explorer), 56

Academy of Natural Sciences of Philadelphia, 25

Account of the Arctic Regions (Scoresby), 18, 34

Aerobic anoxygenic photoheterotrophs
(AAPs), 136

Akrotiri, 3

Albatross, 26, 105

Alecton, 143

Alfred P. Sloan Foundation, 169

Aliens of the Deep, 220

"Allee effect," 190

Aluminaut, 48

Alvin, xii, 48–49, 51, 52–53, 81, 92, 93, 95, 126

Anchoveta, 203, 208

ANGUS (Acoustically Navigated Geophysical
Underwater Survey), 51, 52, 53

Animal Legends (Burton), 68

Antarctic Fish Biology (Eastman), 109

Antarctic toothfish (*Dissostichus mawsoni*), 109

Aqua-Lung, xii

Aquatic Ape Theory, 33

Arcturus Adventure, The (Beebe), 39

Argo/Jason, 53

Art and Religion in Thera (Marianatos), 3

Atlantic herring (*Clupea harengus*), 167

Atolls, 26, 29, 30

Autonomous underwater vehicle (AUV), 145

"Azoic" Theory, 20, 23–24, 26, 44

Bacillus infernus, 86

Bacterio-plankton, 132, 135

Baleen, xiii, 180, 189

Baleonoptera omurai, 117, 118

Barcode initiative, 60–61

Bathybius, 22

Bathymodiolus thermophilus (vent mussels),
88, 89

Bathysphere, xii, 38–39, 44

Beagle, HMS, 21

Ben Franklin, 127

Benthoscope, 44

Bering Island, 12

Bering Sea, 11

Bible, 5–6

"Biogenetic Law" (Haeckel), 21

"Biopolymers," 95–96

Biosphere 2, 95

Bismarck, 53

Black Sea, 56

"Black smokers," xi, 81, 82–84

Blue Planet (Byatt, Fothergill, Holmes), 124

Book of Beasts, The (White), 6

Botany Bay, 14

Bottlenose dolphin (*Tursiops truncatus*), 159

Bottlenose whales (*Hyperoodon* spp.), 116

Bycatch, 110

Bythites hollisi, 92

Calanus finmarchicus (copepod), 191–92

California Academy of Sciences, 35

Calyptogena magnifica (Rift clam), 88

Campeachy, Bay of, 9

Carlsberg Foundation, 33

CCAMLR (Convention for the Conservation of
Antarctic Marine Living Resources), 107

Celera, 139

Census of Marine Life (CoML), vii, xvi, 169, 170–71, 199, 209–10

Cephalopods. *See also* specific species, xiv–xv, 153–58, 193, 194

Challenger, HMS, ix, 22, 23–25, 131, 139

Challenger Deep, 47, 55, 100

Chemosynthesis, xii, 85, 88, 92

Chemosynthetic bacteria, 85, 86, 87

"Chilean Sea Bass," 108–9

Cholera, 138

"Clambake II" (hydrothermal vent site), 88–89

Cnidarians, 27

Coccolithophores, 132

Coccoliths, 132

Codfish (*Gadus morhua*), 6–8, 168, 207, 208

Coelacanth (*Latimeria chalumnae*), 62, 68, 69–74, 215–16

Comoro Islands, 69, 71, 72

Consortium for the Barcode of Life (CBoL), 60–61

"Convict blenny" (*Pholidichtys leucotaenia*), 112–13

Copepods, 138

Coral, xiv, 26–27

Coral reef, xiv, 29–30

Crabs, brachyuran, 54, 89, 95

Creatures of the Deep (Hoyt), 42, 44

Crittercam, 145–46

Cryptozoology, 43

Cuttlefish (*Sepia officinalis*), 154, 197

Cuvier's beaked whale (*Ziphius cavirostris*), 162, 163

Cyanobacteria, 135, 136

Cyclops, HMS, 22

Dana Expeditions, 66

Dana Reports, 33, 66

Daruma. See also Squid, Humboldt (*Dosidicus gigas*), 198

Deep Hot Biosphere, The (Gold), 86

Deep-scattering layer (DSL), 80

Deepwater crab (*Lithodes agassizii*), 51

Depth, average of ocean, x

Depths of the Ocean, The (Murray & Hjort), 34

Descent: The Heroic Discovery of the Abyss (Matsen), 39

Discovery, 33–34

Discovery Expeditions, 33

DNA. *See also* Barcode initiative, 60

Doctor Faustus (Mann), 39

Dolphin, Peale's (*Lagenorhynchus australis*), 15

Dolphin, spinner (*Stenella longirostris*), 160, 177–80

Dolphin, spotted (*Stenella frontalis*), 160, 162, 163, 177–80

Dolphin, striped (*Stenella coeruleoalba*), 160, 163

Driftnetting, 107, 110

Dwarf sperm whale (*Kogia sima*), 163

Dynamite, 219

Echolocation, 147, 159, 217

Eelpouts (*Zoarcidae*), 92

"Elbow squid," 156

Electric Boat Co., 48

El Niño, 137–38, 197, 205

El Niño-Southern Oscillation (ENSO), 137, 138

Empty Ocean, The (Ellis), xiv

Enewetak Island, 30

Environment New Service (ENS), 179

Erenna (siphonophore), 216

Esca (restaurant), 198

Europa, 220

Exploited Seas, The (Hom, Smith & Starkey), **210**

Explorations (Ballard), **57**

Exploring Expedition. *See* Great United States Exploring Expedition

Eyeless shrimp (*Rimicaris exoculata*), **xii, 89–91, 94–95**

Face of Deep, The (Heezen & Hollister), **45, 49, 99–100**

Fast and Feast (Henisch), **7**

Fast Days, **7**

Field Guide of Whales and Dolphins (Mörzer Bruyns), **116**

Fish, dolphin (*Coryphaena hippurus*), **3**

"Fishing down the food chain," **204–5, 207, 208**

Fishing From the Earliest Times (Radcliffe), **3**

"Five-lined constellation-fish" (*Bathysidus pentagrammus*), **40, 41, 43**

Flatfish, eyes of, **21**

Florida Escarpment, **92**

FNRS-2, **46**

Follow the Whale (Sanderson), **148**

Food chain. *See also* "Fishing down the food chain," **xv**

Friosur, **110**

Fulton Fish Market, **128**

Funafuti Atoll, **30**

Gadus morhua (codfish), **6–8**

Galápagos National Park, **102**

Galápagos Rift Zone, **xii, 62, 81**

Galathea, **45, 66, 74–75, 100**

"Gama Land," **11**

"Garden of Eden" (hydrothermal vent site), **51**

Genesis, **5–6**

Georges Bank, **33**

Giant Pacific squid (*Moroteuthis* spp.), **194**

Grand Banks, **7, 196, 203**

Great Barrier Reef, **xiv, 14, 29**

Great United States Exploring Expedition, **14–15**

Great white shark (*Caracharodon carcharias*), **xv, 79, 146, 172**

Gulf of Alaska, **110**

Gulf Stream, **15**

Half Mile Down (Beebe), **39, 41–42**

Halieutica (Oppian), **5**

Handbook of Deep-Sea Hydrothermal Vent Fauna (Desbruyères & Segonzac), **85**

Harpoon, grenade, **xiii, 183**

Hercules (ROV), **57**

Herring, **7, 167**

Hirondelle, **31**

Historia Animalium (Aristotle), **4**

Historia Animalium (Gesner), **126**

Historia Piscium (Ray & Willughby), **8**

Hoki (*Macruronus novaezelandiae*), **146**

"Hole to Hell" (vent site), **95**

Holothuroidea, **99**

Hopkins Marine Station, **34**

Hudson Gorge, **39**

Human Operated Vehicle (HOV), **56**

Humboldt Current, **197**

Hydrodamalis gigas (Steller's sea cow), **12–13**

Ichthyologica (Artedi), **17**

Indo-Pacific beaked whale (*Indopacetus pacificus*), **61, 115–17, 120, 163**

Inexhaustible Sea, The (Daniel & Minot), **208**

Institute for Exploration (Mystic Aquarium), **53**

Intergrated Undersea Surveillance System (IUSS), **161**

International Convention for the Conservation of Atlantic Tunas (ICCAT), **171**

International Council for the Exploration of the Sea (ICES), 168

International Whaling Commission (IWC), 118, 180–88

"In the Abyss" (Wells), 38

In the Wake of the Sea-Serpents (Heuvelmans), 66

Introduction to the Study of Fishes (Günther), 18

Irrawaddy River dolphin (*Orcaella brevirostris*), 118–19

IUU (Illegal, Unreported and Unregulated fishing), 107

Jan-Mayen Ridge, 93

Japanese Marine Science and Technology Center (JAMSTEC), 55

Jason Jr., 53–54

JASON Project, 57

Jaws (Benchley), 127

Jellyfishes, 209, 216

Jibia gigante, 197, 198–99

Jigging, squid, 195

Johnson Sea-Link, 100

Juan de Fuca Ridge, 94

Kaiko, 55

Kaikoura Canyon (New Zealand), 145

Kamchatka, 12

Kealakekua Bay (Hawaii), 14

Killer whale (*Orcinus orca*), xv, 109, 119–20

Knorr, 51

Kolbeinsey (Iceland), 93

Kraken, 141

Kwa-Zulu-Natal, 73

Kyparissiakos Gulf (Greece), 162

Latimeria menadoensis, 72, 73

Laurentian Fan, 93

Leptocephalus, 65–68

Living Fishes of the World (Herald), 124

Living Fossil: The Story of the Coelacanth (Thomson), 69

Loch Ness Monster, 65, 67

Lofoden Islands, 168

Longlining, 106–7, 109–10, 219

Longman's beaked whale (*Indopacetus pacificus*), 61, 115–17, 120, 163

"Lucky Strike" (hydrothermal vent field), 54, 94–95

Lumpfish (*Cyclopterus lumpus*), 143

Lusitania, 53, 54

Macrias amissus. See also Patagonian toothfish (*Dissostichus eleginoides*), 105

Madagascar, 69, 71

Magnificent Voyagers (Smithsonian), 15

Manado Tua, 71, 72, 78

Manatee, 9

Mantis shrimp, 154

Mare Nostrum. See also Mediterranean Sea, 209

Marianas Trench, 47, 55

Marine Biological Association (MBA), 32

Marine biology, xvi, 4

Marine Imaging Systems, 90

Marineland of Florida, 159, 217

Marine Mammal Protection Act of 1972, 177

Marine Mammals of the Northwestern Coast of North America, The (Scammon), 34

Mattanza (Maggio), 5

Mediterranean Sea, 3, 4, 5, 209

Megamouth (*Megachasma pelagios*), 62, 75, 77–80, 216

Melon-headed whales (*Peponocephala electra*), 163

Mercury poisoning, 109

Mesonychoteuthis hamiltoni, 106, 155, 157–58

Mesoplodon, 115

Mesoscaph, 127

Michael Sars, 34

Mid-Atlantic Ridge, 51, 54, 92–93

Mid-ocean ridge, 51, 81, 82

Mimic octopus, 153, 154

Minoan Civilization, 3–4

Moby-Dick (Melville), 20

Monera, 22

Monk seal, Caribbean (*Monachus tropicalis*), 9

Monoplacophora, 75

Monterey Bay Aquarium, 134, 172

Mozambique, 69, 71

Museum of Comparative Zoology (Harvard University), 15, 25, 168

Mystery of the Ancient Seafarers (Ballard), 56

Nantucket, xiii

Narwhal, 19

National Environmental Trust (NET), 108

National Marine Fisheries Service (NMFS), 178–79

National Oceanic and Atmospheric Administration (NOAA), 54, 174, 190

Nautile, 54

Nemo, 53

Neopolina galatheae, 74–75

New Bedford (MA), 34, 187

New Voyage Around the World (Dampier), 9, 10

New York Zoological Society, 35, 39

Nonsuch: Land of Water (Beebe), 39

Nonsuch Island (Bermuda), 39

Northern fur seal (*Callorhinus ursinus*), 13

Northwest Passage, 14, 15

Notocanth, 67–68

Ocean Acoustic Remote Sensing (OARS), 211

Ocean Biographic Information System (OBIS), vii, 211–12

Oceanographic Museum of Monaco, 31, 35

Octopus, common (*Octopus vulgaris*), 197

Octopus's Garden, The (Van Dover), 85

Office of Naval Research (ONR), 47, 169

Oil, whale, xiii, 180

Oilfish (*Ruvettus pretiosus*), 69

Ompax spatuloides, 43

Open Sea: The World of Plankton (Hardy), 33

Orange roughy (*Hoplostethus atlanticus*), 111–12

Orca. *See* Killer whale (*Orcinus orca*)

Origin of Species, The (Darwin), xii, 21

Osedax (bone-eating worm), 97–98

Outermost House, The (Beston), 127

Out of Eden (Burdick), 138, 193

Pacific Ocean, volume of, ix

Paleodictyon, 86

"Pallid sailfin" (*Bathyembryx istiophasma*), 40–41, 43

"Paradox of the Plankton," 32–33, 133

Passenger pigeon, 128

Patagonian toothfish (*Dissostichus eleginoides*), 105–10

Peabody Museum (Yale University), 36

Peale's dolphin (*Lagenorhynchus australis*), 15

Pelagothuria natatrix. *See also* Swimming sea cucumbers, 100, 101

Peniagone diaphana, 101–2

Penikese Island, 25

Peru Current, 208

Phoenicians, 4

Photosynthesis, ix, xii, 81, 85, 132–33, 134–35, 136

Physiologus, 6

Phytoplankton, 33, 131–32, 134, 137

Pickfordiateuthis, 154

Pisces, 100

Plankton Expedition (Hensen), 32, 131

Plate tectonics, xi, 51

Pogonophores, 84–85

Poisoning. *See* Mercury poisoning

Polychaete scale worms, **89**

Pop-up tags, 171, 172, 199

Princesse Alice II, 31

Procaryotes, **87**, 135

Prochlorococcus, **xi**, 135, 136–37

Project FAMOUS, 52

Protista, **22**, 135

"Rainbow gars," 41–42, 43

Rat-tails, 92

Reef. *See* Great Barrier Reef

Reef Madness (Dobbs), 30

Remote Species Identification (RSID), 210

"Research whaling," 118, 181–82

Rift clam (*Calyptogena magnifica*), **88**

Riftia pachyptila (tube worms), **xii**, 84, 85, 87–88, 91, 95

Rift Zone. See Galápagos Rift Zone

Rimicaris exoculata (eyeless shrimp), **xii**, 89–91, 94–95

ROV (Remotely Operated Vehicle), 49, 57, 74, 210–11

Sablefish (*Anoplopoma fimbria*), 110

"Saharan Bank," 194

Santorini (Thera), 3

Sardines, **208**

Sargasso Sea, **66**, 140

Scientific Committee. *See also* International Whaling Commission (IWC), 184–85

"Scientific whaling," 181–82

Scientists and the Sea, 1650–1900 (Deacon), 8

Scotian Shelf, 207–8

Scripps Institution of Oceanography (SIO), 31, 35, 169

Sea bass, Chilean, 108–9

Sea Cliff, 54

Sea cow, Steller's, 12–13

Sea cucumber (*Cucumis marinus*), **48**, **62**, 99–103

Sea-floor, spreading, 51, 81–82

Sea otter (*Enhydra lutris*), 13

Search for the Giant Squid, The (Ellis), **ii**, 223

Shark, basking (*Cetorhinus maximus*), 79

Shark, great white (*Carcharodon carcharias*), **xv**, 79, 146, 172

Shark, Greenland (*Somniosus microcephalus*), 43, 53, 79

Shark, Portuguese (*Centroscymnus coelolepis*), 53

Shark, sixgill (*Hexanchus griseus*), 43

Shark, whale (*Rincodon typus*), 79

Sharks of the World (Compagno), 79

Shinkai-6500, **54**, 55

"Ship strikes," 191

Silent World, The (Cousteau), 159

Skates, 92

Smithsonian Institution, 15

Smokers, black, **xi**, 81, 82–84

Snapping shrimp (*Alpheus heterochaelis*), 159

Snubfin dolphin (*Orcaella heinsohni*), 118

Sodwana Bay, 73, 74

SONAR, 162

Sorcerer II, 139–40

SOSUS (Sound Surveillance System), 161

South Georgia Island, 107, 201

Sperm whale, dwarf (*Kogia sima*), 163

Sperm whale (*Physeter macrocephalus*), **xiii**, 20, 109–10, 146–49, 151, 160

setting quotas, 182–88

Squid, Argentine shortfin (*Illex argentinus*), 195, 196, 197

Squid, California market (*Loligo opalescens*), 195, 196, 202

Squid, colossal (*Mesonychoteuthis hamiltoni*), 106, 155, 157–58, 194–95

Squid, giant (*Architeuthis*), **xvii**, 140, 141–49, 154, 157, 194

Squid, Humboldt (*Dosidicus gigas*), 197–98, 199–202

Squid, Japanese flying (*Todarodes pacificus*), 195, 197, 202

Squid, longfin inshore (*Loligo pealeii*), 196

Squid, neon flying (*Ommastrephes bartrami*), 195

Squid, Northern shortfin (*Illex illecebrosus*), 195–96

Squid, Pacific giant (*Moroteuthis robustus*), 194

Squid, Patagonian (*Loligo gahi*), 195, 196, 197

Squid, scaled (*Lepidoteuthis grimaldii*), 31

Squid, sevenstar flying (*Martialia hyadesi*), 201

Squid, umbrella (*Histioteuthis bonnelli*), 149–51

Squid, Wellington flying (*Nototodarus sloani*), 195

Stazione Zoologica (Naples), 32, 35, 168

Strandings, whale, 4, 162–64

Structure and Distribution of Coral Reefs, The (Darwin), 29

Sulawesi, 71, 72–73, 78, 113, 153

Supertyphoon *Paka*, 138

Surtsey (Iceland), 82

Swimming sea cucumbers, 99–103

Swordfish, broadbill (*Xiphias gladius*), 122–29

Synechococcus, 135, 136

Systema naturae (Linnaeus), 17

TAG (hydrothermal vent field), 54–55

Taxonomy, 59–60

Tenerife (Canary Islands), 143

"Three-starred angler-fish" (*Bathyceratias trilychnus*), 40, 41, 44

Tiburon (ROV), 216

Titanic, RMS, 52, 53, 54

Titanic (movie), 220

Toothfish, Patagonian (*Dissosthichus eleginoides*), 105–10

Tree of Life Initiative, 59

Trieste, 44, 46, 47–48, 100, 169

Tripod fish (*Bathypterois*), 92

Trophic levels, 170, 201, 204–5, 207–8

Tsunami, 220–21

Tube worms (*Riftia pachyptila*), xii, 84, 85, 87–88, 91, 95

Tuna, albacore (*Thunnus alalunga*), 206

Tuna, bluefin (*Thunnus thynnus*), 4–5, 171–75

Tuna, skipjack (*Katsuwonus pelamis*), 205

Tuna, yellowfin (*Thunnus albacares*), 173, 177

Twenty Thousand Leagues Under the Sea (Verne), vii, 36, 126, 143–44

"Untouchable bathysphere fish" (*Bathysphaera intacta*), 39–40, 43, 44

Urschleim, 22

U.S. National Museum, 15

U.S. Navy, 30, 94, 161, 163

U.S. Virgin Islands, 163

USS *Central America*, 53

Vampyroteuthis infernalis ("vampire squid from hell"), 151–52

Vents, hydrothermal, xi, xii–xiii, 51, 81, 82, 88, 91–98, 216

Vestimentifera, 84, 96

Viruses, 133–35

Volcanoes, underwater, xi, 81

Voyage of the Beagle, The (Darwin), 29

Voyager spacecraft, 220

Voyage to the Center of the Earth (Verne), 14

Wake of the Sea-Serpents, The (Heuvelmans), 66

Wanderer, 187

WaterBaby (Kaharl), 52

Whale, blue (*Balaenoptera musculus*), x, xiii, 19, 117, 160, 162

Whale, bowhead, xiii, 19, 20, 34

Whale, California gray, 34, 97

Whale, fin, xiii, 19, 117

Whale, Greenland, xiii

Whale, humpback (*Megaptera movaeangliae*), 19, 159, 186, 217, 218

Whale, Indo-Pacific beaked (*Indopacetus pacificus*), 61

Whale, killer, xv, 109, 119–20, 121

Whale, minke, 117, 162–63, 181

Whale, northern right (*Eubalaena glacialis*), xiii, 182, 187, 189–92

Whale, pygmy blue, 117–18

Whale, sperm, xiii, 20, 109–10, 146–49, 151, 160

  setting quotas, 182–88

"Whale falls," 91, 96–98

Whalers, 34

  Azorean, 31, 149, 183

  Nantucket, xiii

Whaling

  moratorium on, xiii–xiv, 180–81

  Yankee, xiii, 182, 187

"Wonderpus," 154

Woods Hole, 25

Woods Hole Oceanographic Institution (WHOI), 35, 48, 52, 56, 168, 191

World Beneath the Sea, The (Barton), 39, 43

Zooanxthellae, 29

Index of People

Adams, John Quincy, 14

Adler, Jackie, 209

Aelian, 3

Agassiz, Alexander, 25–26, 29–30, 168

Agassiz, Louis, 15, 21, 25, 30, 168

Agate, Alfred, 14

Albert, Prince of Monaco, 31

Aldrich, Frederick, 144, 146

Alexander the Great, 4, 37

Amundsen, Roald, 33, 167

Andrews, Roy Chapman, 125

Archer, Frederick, 178

Aristotle, xi, 3, 4, 208

Arrian, 4

Arronax, Pierre, 36

Artedi, Peter, 17, 167

Atwater, Tanya, 52

Ausubel, Jesse, viii, 170

Azam, Farooq, 132, 135

Baco, Amy, 97

Baker, Scott, 186, 188

Balcomb, Kenneth C., III, 116

Ballard, Robert, 53–54, 55–57, 81, 169, 215

Bandini, Ralph, 123

Banks, Joseph, 10, 13, 139

Barlow, Jay, 160, 164

Barnes, Lawrence, 101

Baross, John, 95, 96

Barton, Otis, viii, 38, 43, 44

Bascompte, Jordi, 205–6

Baumgartner, Mark, 191

Beebe, William, viii, xii, 38–44, 169, 219–20

Bellingham, James, 145

Belon, Pierre, 8, 167

Benchley, Peter, 147

Bennett, Frederick Debell, 124, 125

Bering, Vitus, xii, 11

Berthelot, Sabine, 143

Bertin, Léon, 66–67

Berzin, A. A., 106, 148

Best, Peter, 184

Beston, Henry, 127

Bigelow, Henry, 35

Billett, David S., 99

Bingham, Harry Payne, 35–36

Block, Barbara, 171–72, 173, 174

Bohnsack, James, 210

Bolstad, Kat, 151, 157

Bondi, Hermann, 86

Bostelmann, Else, 41

Bourne, William, 37

Boyle, Peter, viii, 197

Brackenridge, William, 14

Bradley, Albert, 56

Broad, William, 95, 161

Bruun, Anton, 74

Bryan, W. B., 82

Buchanan, J. Y., 22, 23, 31, 84

Bucklin, Ann, 84

Buel, J. W., 122

Buffon, Comte de, 17

Bumpus, Dean, 33

Burdick, Alan, 138, 193
Burton, Maurice, 68
Bushnell, David, xii

Cabot, John, 6, 15
Cabot, Sebastian, 15
Caddy, John F., 193
Caldwell, Roy, 72
Cameron, James, 220
Cann, J. R., 91
Carpenter, William, 22
Carson, Carol, 162
Carson, Rachel, x, 212
Castro, José, 78
"Charley Coffin," 20
Childress, James J., 101
Chirikov, Alexei, 11
Choi, Jae, 207
Christensen, Villy, 170
Clapham, Phillip, 118, 186, 188
Clark, Christopher, 160, 161–62
Clark, Eugenie, 78, 112–13
Clarke, Malcolm, 145, 148, 149,
    151, 186
Cohen, Daniel M., 91, 92
Columbus, Christopher, 8, 9
Colwell, Rita, 133, 138
Compagno, Leonard, 79, 80
Conniff, Richard, 149
Conseil, 36
Cook, James, vii, xii, 13–14
Corliss, John, 81, 95
Coste, J. J., 22
Courtney-Latimer, Margaret, 62, 69
Cousteau, Jacques-Yves, xii, 31, 145, 159
Couthouy, Joseph, 14
Crane, Jocelyn, 40
Crichton, Michael, 147
Crowder, Lawrence, 219

Crozier, W. J., 99
Cuvier, Georges, vii, 18, 167

Da Gama, Vasco, 8
Dahlgren, Thomas, 97
Dampier, William, 9–10
Dana, James Dwight, 14
Darwin, Charles, vii, xii, 21, 26, 29–30,
    139, 167
Da Vinci, Leonardo, 37
Deacon, Margaret, 8, 20
Deagle, Bruce, 151
De Bougainville, Louis-Antoine, 14
DeLong, Edward, 134
Desbruyères, Daniel, 85
Dewhurst, William, 122
DeWitt, Hugh, 105
Dias, Bartolomeu, 8
Dietz, Robert, 47
Dobbs, David, 30
Dohrn, Anton, 35, 168
Drayton, Joseph, 14
Duncan, David Douglas, 197
Dunning, Malcolm C., 195
D'Urville, Dumont, 14

Earle, Sylvia, 110, 195, 206, 212
Eastman, Joseph, 109
Edmund, John, 81
Ehrhardt, Nelson M., 197
Ensor, Paul, 109, 120
Erdmann, Mark, 71–72, 73
Evermann, Barton W., 34, 126, 128

Falkowski, Paul, 134
Feldman, Robert A., 96
Ferrari, Mark, 121–22

Fierstine, Harry, 124
FitzRoy, James, 14
Forbes, Edward, ix, 20, 44, 167
Forcada, Jaume, 179–80
Foyn, Svend, xiii
Frank, Kenneth, 207, 208
Frankel, Adam, 145
Frederickson, James, 87
Fricke, Hans, 70–71, 73
Fuhrman, Jed, 133
Fuson, Robert, 9

Gagnan, Emile, xii
Gardner, Howard, 218
Gerrodette, Tim, 179–80
Gervais, Paul, 22
Gesner, Conrad, 126
Gibson, Charles Dana, 122
Gill, Theodore, 66, 105
Gilly, William, viii, 199–201
Glover, Adrian, 97
Goffredi, Shana, 97
Gold, Thomas, 86
Golubic, Stjepko, 135
Gosnold, Bartholomew, 7
Grassle, J. Frederick, vii, 24, 48–49
Gudger, Eurgene W., 125
Guerra, Angel, 155
Günther, Albert G. L. C., 8, 18, 32, 125–26

Haddock, Stephen, 216
Haeckel, Ernst, 21, 22, 32
Haedrich, Richard L., 91
Hale, Horatio, 14
Hanlon, Roger, 154
Hansen, Bent, 100
Harding, Dennis, 73–74

Hardy, Alister, 33, 34
Hawkes, Graham, 55
Hayden, Thomas, 203
Haymon, Rachel, 95
Hebert, Paul, 60–61
Heezen, Bruce, 45, 49, 100
Heirtzler, J. R., 82
Henisch, Bridget, 7
Hensen, Victor, 32, 131
Herald, Earl, 124
Herring, Peter, 102
Hess, Wolfgang, 136
Hessler, Robert R., 23
Heuvelmans, Bernard, 66
Hjort, Johan, 34, 131
Hochberg, Erich, 201
Hoffman, Sarah, 95, 96
Hollis, Ralph, 92
Hollister, Charles, 45, 49, 100
Holm, Poul, 210
Holt, Sidney, 203
Homer, 4
Horne, John, 210
Howey, Paul, 171
Hoyle, Fred, 86
Hoyt, Erich, 42, 44
Hubble, Linda, 78
Hubbs, Carl, 40, 41
Huisman, Jef, 32, 133
Hutchinson, G. Evelyn, 32, 133
Huxley, Thomas Henry, 22, 168
Hyman, Libby, 84

Idyll, C. P., 84
Issacs, John, 43

Jackson, George, viii
Jackson, Jeremy, xiv

Jaffe, Jules, 164
James I, King, 37
Jonah, 8
Jones, Meredith, 84
Jonsgård, Åge, 125
Jordan, David Starr, 34, 126, 128

Kaeppler, Adrienne, 13–14
Kaharl, Victoria, 52
Kellenberger, Eduard, 136
Kenney, Robert, 191
Klinkhammer, Gary, 94
Knudtson, Peter, 9
Kogge, Stephen, 113
Kolber, Zbigniew, 136
Kondo, Isao, 186–87
Kristof, Emory, 145
Kubodera, Tsunemi, xvii
Kuiter, Rudie, 153

Lacépède, Comte de, 17–18, 167
Laist, David, 191
Land, Ned, 36
Langmuir, Charles, 94
Lankester, E. Ray, 32
La Perouse, Jean-François, 14
Larsen, Verner, 67
Lawrence, Barbara, 217
Leggett, William, 207
Lemche, Henning, 74
Leslie, Mitchell, 134
Lind, James, 11
Linnaeus, Carolus, 17, 59
Lotze, Heike, 205
Lovgren, Stefan, 201
Lutcavage, Molly, 171
Lutz, Richard, 95
Lyell, Charles, 17

Mackintosh, Neil A., 184
Magellan, Ferdinand, 8
Maggio, Teresa, 5
Makris, Nicholas, 211
Mann, Thomas, 39
Marinatos, Nanno, 3
Markaida, Unai, 199
Masters, Ryan, 199
Mate, Bruce, 191
Mather, Charles O., 123
Matsen, Brad, viii, 39
Matthiessen, Peter, 159
McHugh, J. L., 183, 186
Mehta, Arnaz, 71
Melián, Carlos, 205
Mellinger, David, 161, 162, 164
Melville, Herman, 20
Messenger, John, 154
Miller, John, 100, 101
Miller, Walter, 36
Mills, Eric, 32
Mitchell, Edward D., 184
Møhl, Bertel, 151
Moore, Joseph, 115
Morais da Cunha, Manuela, 194
Morgan, Elaine, 33
Mori, Kyoichi, xvii
Mörzer, Bruyns, W. F. J., 116
Moseley, H. N., 23
Murphy, Robert Cushman, 125
Murray, John, 23, 24, 25, 29, 34, 131
Myers, Ransom, 204, 205, 206

Nares, George, 23
Nealson, Kenneth, 87
Nelson, Don, 79
Nemo, Captain, vii, 36
Nicol, J. A. C., 102
Nielsen, Jorgen, 67

Nierenberg, William, 169
Nobel, Alfred, 219
Norman, Mark, 153, 157
Norris, Kenneth, 151
Norris, Thomas, 160
Norse, Elliot, 206, 219

O'Dor, Ron, vii, viii
Ohsumi, Seiji, 183
Omura, Hideo, 117
Onstott, Tullis, 87
Oppian, 3, 5
Oscar II (King of Sweden), 167
Oschlies, Andreas, 205
O'Shea, Steve, viii, 146, 147, 151,
    157, 195
Oswald, Julie, 160

Pace, Norman, 136
Palomares, Marie-Lourdes, 204
Parkinson, Sydney, 13
Parr, Alfred E., 32, 35
Partensky, Frédéric, 136
Pascual, Mercedes, 138
Pauly, Daniel, 204, 207, 208, 209
Pawson, David, 99, 100, 101, 102
Payne, Katy, 159, 217
Payne, Roger, 159, 217
Peale, Titian R., 14, 15
Peron, François, 20
Peter the Great, 11
Petrie, Brian, 207
Phillips, David, 179
Piatkowski, Uwe, viii, 193, 194
Piccard, Auguste, 45, 46
Piccard, Jacques, 46, 47, 100, 127
Pickering, Charles, 14
Pierce, Graham, 194

Pitman, Robert, viii, 109, 115, 116, 120
Pliny, 3, 99
Porch, Clay, 171, 174–75
Pouyaud, Laurent, 72

Radcliffe, William, 3
Rafinesque, Constantine S., 67
Rathjean, Warren, 195
Ray, John, 8, 167
Reeves, Randall R., 118
Revkin, Andrew, 174
Reynolds, J. Louis, 48
Reynolds, Jeremiah N., 14
Ricciuti, Edward, 106
Rice, Dale, 186
Rich, William, 14
Riley, Gordon, 32, 33
Rinaldi, Sergio, 32
Ritter, William E., 31
Roberts, Callum, 169–70
Robson, G. C., 155
Rodhouse, Paul, viii, 193, 197, 201
Rona, Peter, viii, 54, 85–86, 89
Rondelet, Guillaume, 8
Roper, Clyde F. E., viii, 141, 145,
    149, 195
Rosenblatt, Richard, viii, 92, 100
Rosenthal, Joshua, 199
Ross, James Clark, 20
Ross, Sir John, 20
Rouse, Greg, 97
Rozwadowski, Helen, 25
Ryan, William B. F., 52

Safina, Carl, 127, 179, 206
Saint-Hillaire, Geoffroy, 18
Sala, Enric, 205
Sanders, Howard L., 23, 24

Sanderson, Ivan, 148
Sandow, Marcel, 205
Scammon, Charles Melville, 34
Scheffer, Martin, 32
Scheffer, Victor B., 186
Schevill, William, 217
Schlee, Susan, 32, 167
Schmidt, Johannes, 33, 66
Schroeder, William C., 35
Schumacher, Mary, 209
Schwartzlose, Richard, 43
Scoresby, William, 18–20, 34
Scott, Robert Falcon, 33, 167
Segonzan, Michel, 85
Seilacher, Adolf, 86
Serre, George, 72
Shackleton, Ernest H., 167
Shreeve, James, 139
Sibbald, Robert, 162
Smith, Craig, 96, 97
Smith, David G., 67, 68
Smith, J. L. B., 69, 71
Smith, T. D., 185, 210
Solander, Daniel, 13
Somero, George, 88
Spärck, Ragnar, 45
Spöring, Heinrich, 13
Springer, Victor, 73
Spurling, Christian, 65
Staiger, Carl T., 43
Starkey, David, 210
Stead, David, 124–25
Steele, John, 208–9
Steene, Roger, 153
Steenstrup, Japetus, 141, 143
Steinbeck, John, 208
Stejneger, Leonhard, 13
Steller, Georg Wilhelm, 11–12
Steneck, Robert, 204
Stone, Greg, 145

Straley, Jan, 110
Suttle, Curtis, 133–34
Swift, Jonathan, 207
Symmes, John Cleves, 14

Taylor, R. Leighton, 77
Thompson, Geoff, 54
Thomson, Charles Wyville, 22, 23, 25, 44
Thomson, Keith, 69
Townsend, Charles H., 105, 182,
    186, 187
Tucker, Teddy, 145

Uiblein, Franz, 112

Valenciennes, Achille, 18
Van Andel, Tjeerd, 81
Van Beneden, Pierre-Joseph, 22
Van Dover, Cindy Lee, 85, 88, 89–90, 91
Van Drebbel, Cornelis, 37
Vaulot, Daniel, 136
Vecchione, Michael, 155
Venter, J. Craig, 138–40
Venter, Pieter, 73
Verne, Jules, 14, 36, 39, 126,
    143–44, 147
Vine, Allyn, 48
von Willemöes-Suhm, Rudolf, 23
Vrijenhoek, Robert, 97

Walsh, Don, 47, 100
Wang, John, 163
Ward, Rachel, 30–31
Watson, Lyall, 186
Watson, Reg, 208, 209
Waxell, Sven, 11

Weissing, Franz, **32, 113**

Wells, H. G., **38**

Wetherell, Marmaduke Arundel, **65**

Wheatcroft, R. A., **94**

Wheelis, Mark, **136**

White, Martin, **201**

White, T. H., **6**

Whitehead, Hal, **187**

Whitley, Gilbert, **43**

Widder, Edie, **210**

Wild, J. J., **23**

Wilkes, Lt. Charles, **14–15**

Willughby, Francis, **8, 167**

Wilson, Edward O., **xi**

Wilson, R. Kenneth, **65**

Woese, Carl, **135**

Wolff, Torben, **24, 47–48, 100**

Wommack, Eric, **133**

Wood, Forrest G., **159, 217**

Worden, Alexandra, **135**

Worm, Boris, **204, 205, 206**

Wormuth, John H., **195**

Yablokov, Alexey, **186**

Yoerger, Dana, **56**

Young, Emma, **151, 157**

Young, Richard, **155**